Thomas Webster

History of the Methodist Episcopal Church in Canada

Thomas Webster

History of the Methodist Episcopal Church in Canada

ISBN/EAN: 9783743331785

Manufactured in Europe, USA, Canada, Australia, Japa

Cover: Foto ©Lupo / pixelio.de

Manufactured and distributed by brebook publishing software
(www.brebook.com)

Thomas Webster

History of the Methodist Episcopal Church in Canada

PREFACE.

In this history I have labored to place the original Methodists in their true position before the Christian Church and the public generally; and although some readers may think the following pages are more controversial in their character than is usual in such a work, it must be remembered that the first history of a country or a church should embrace, as far as possible, the leading incidents connected with its career.

Though I have in some instances (perhaps sharply) refuted the attacks made by leading men of the Canada Conference on the Methodist Episcopal Church in this country, I have not done so through malice, nor from personal ill-will to the parties engaged in the controversy; but from a consciousness of duty to God, to the Church, and to Christian liberty.

I have been at very great pains to collect proper material for this publication; and one of my most difficult tasks has been to condense and arrange the matter in a way suitable for such a sized book.

I have made as few notes as possible, and have not given the names of all the authorities whom I have consulted, in the body of the work, as it would have very much enlarged the volume and added to its price. I have consulted and am indebted to the following authors, pamphlets, and papers for much valuable information on Methodism. I am also indebted to many parties who have given me much reliable information that I could not derive from books.

I am indebted to European works as follows:—

Whitehead's "Life of Wesley;" Moore's "Life of Wesley;" Watson's "Life of Wesley;" "The Life of Charles Wesley;" "Ireland and the Centenary of Methodism," by Rev. William Crook, with several other English and Irish publications.

American works consulted have been, "Young's History of Methodism;" Dr. Bang's "Vindication of Methodist Episcopacy;" Bang's "Original Church of Christ," and also his "History of the M. E. Church;" Dr. Stevens' "History of the Religious Movement of the Eighteenth Century;" Stevens' "History of the Methodist Episcopal Church," and his "Life and Times of Dr. Bangs;" "The Methodist Magazine;" "Methodist Quarterly Review;" Gorrie's "History of Methodism;" Emory's "Defence of Our Fathers;" Dr. Bond's "Appeal to the Methodists in Opposition to Changes Proposed in their Church Government;" "The American Minutes;" Asbury's "Journal;" "Journals of the General Conference," with other papers treating on the subject of Methodism.

Canadian publications referred to are, A. E. Meacham's "History of Methodism;" Playter's "History of Methodism;" "Works of Rev. John Carroll;" "Journal of Rev. Peter Jones;" Several volumes of "The Christian Guardian;" Numerous papers respecting the "Union" of 1833; Claims of Churchmen and Dissenters; Judges' opinions regarding the Church suits; Fowler's "Report of the Belleville Chapel Case;" "Dr. Alder's Evidence before the English House of Commons in 1828," and published in Canada in 1829; Pamphlet of W. & E. Ryerson, published in England; Pamphlet of Ritche & Stinson; Lindsay's "History of the Clergy Reserves;" "Report of a Select Committee of the Legislative Council of Upper Canada respecting the support of a Protestant Clergy, 1835;" "The Public Accounts respecting Religious Grants," with various other Parliamentary Reports and papers respecting Methodism in Canada.

I would here acknowledge my obligations to Bishops Smith and Richardson, and to Rev. David Culp and other brethren who have so kindly assisted in procuring information for this work.

THOMAS WEBSTER.

NEWBURY, 1869.

HISTORY

OF THE

METHODIST EPISCOPAL CHURCH

IN CANADA.

CHAPTER I.

THE ORIGIN OF METHODISM.

The Holy Club—Called Methodists—Their proceedings approved by the father of the Wesleys—The parents of the Wesleys—Careful religious training—Escape of John Wesley from death by fire—His mother's mind impressed thereby—Becomes his father's curate—Declines the living—The brothers sail for America—Disappointment and return—Continued disquietude of mind—Conversion of the brothers—They begin to preach a present salvation—Shut out of the churches—Field preaching—Multitudes flock to hear—First preaching-house—The foundry—Mr. Maxfield—John Nelson—Organization of classes—First Conference—Methodism spreads through England and Wales—Mr. Wesley visits Ireland—Mr. Williams—Mr. C. Wesley visits Dublin—Is mobbed—Well received elsewhere—John Wesley re-visits Ireland—Court Mattress—The Palatines.

THE commencement of the great religious movement which has produced the various Methodist bodies throughout the world, originated from the personal efforts of three students at the University of Oxford, in England. These young men being anxious to promote the glory of God, their own spiritual welfare, and the happiness of others, in the year 1729 formed themselves into a society for the purpose of reading the "Greek Testament, and in other respects assisting each other in a course of 'holy living' and useful study."

This little band at first consisted of Charles Wesley, Mr. Morgan and Mr. Kirkman, but in November of the same year Mr. John Wesley reached Oxford, and immediately identified himself with this small and despised community. The next year the number was increased by the addition of three or four pupils of the Wesleys who obtained permission to join the "Holy Club," a name applied by the irreligious to this company of sincere seekers after truth and righteousness. By common consent the direction of the society was committed to Mr. John Wesley, who before this had distinguished himself for method and zeal in all his religious and literary movements. Already the Wesleys were called Methodists; the term having been at first applied to Mr. Charles Wesley by a fellow-student. The name, however, did not originate with the Oxford student, as the same appellation had been given to a body of Anabaptists in the sixteenth century. These people, who appear to have had a strong preference for plain and pointed preaching, had been termed "plain pack staff Methodists." The name had also been applied to a class of physicians many generations before the birth of the founders of modern Methodism.

The Holy Club was very much strengthened in 1732 by the accession of the Messrs. Ingham, Broughton, Clayton and Hervey. The latter gentleman was afterwards known as the author of "Hervey's Meditations." To these was added, in 1735, Mr. George Whitefield, a man who shortly afterward, by his eloquence, moved the masses of Europe and America as the trees of the forest are moved by the winds of heaven. So truthful is it that—

"From small beginnings
Mighty fabrics rise."

Or, as Mr. Wesley expresses the same sentiment in one of his incomparable hymns:

"Saw ye not the cloud arise,
Little as a human hand;
Now it spreads along the skies,
Hangs o'er all the thirsty land."

Shortly after Mr. John Wesley began to give his attention to the importance of experimental religion, he adopted the erroneous idea that he could serve God better by a decided seclusion from the world than by public intercourse with it. This monkish sentiment, however, received no encouragement from his more enlightened parents; but he, being anxious to consult others upon the subject, went some distance in order to see a "serious man," and advise with him respecting those things which now so deeply engrossed his attention. Upon his arrival he made known his views to his friend, who replied most judiciously. "Sir," said he, "you wish to serve God and go to heaven; remember you cannot serve Him alone; you must therefore *find* companions or *make* them; the Bible knows nothing of solitary religion." These were words fitly spoken, and were, under God, the means of directing Wesley's steps in the path of duty.

Mr. Morgan, who was by birth an Irishman, not being so monastic in his sentiments as was Mr. Wesley at this period, commenced to visit the gaol, instruct the prisoners, and pray with the sick in the vicinity, reporting the result to the society. The Wesleys followed his example, and soon the "Holy Club" entered on a systematic plan for imparting religious instruction to the inmates of the prison, comforting the afflicted, and relieving the poor so far as they could consistently with the income and time at their disposal.

Some of the ministers of the Church of England viewed this new movement with distrust; and many in "high life" spoke of the conduct of these young men with contempt and ridicule, while the baser sort began to persecute them. Lest there might be some irregularity in the course they were pursuing,

Mr. John Wesley wrote to his father, soliciting his advice with regard to the conduct of himself and his associates. His father replied in the most affectionate manner, approving of their efforts to do good, and urging them to steadfastness in the ways of righteousness.

It might naturally have been imagined that those at least who professed to love God, or to desire the amelioration of the condition of mankind, would have countenanced these devoted young men by affording them, at the very least, their sympathy and approbation. Such, however, was not the case. To the lukewarm and ungodly masses by which they were surrounded, their practice of so frequently partaking of the Lord's Supper, and their repeated fastings and prayer, together with their continued efforts for the general good of the people, appeared as foolish and unnecessary self-denial, or as hypocritical cant. But none of these things moved them.

Mr. Morgan, who was earnestly devoted to the cause, was, in consequence of his very delicate constitution, compelled after a time to leave the field, and return to the green isle of his nativity, where he shortly afterwards "died in great peace." Thus early fell a prominent member of the first Methodist Society. A leading spirit had been removed from the little band, but God supplied his place, and the work progressed rapidly.

Nearly one hundred and forty years have transpired since Mr. Morgan first associated himself with what was then, out of derision, termed the "Holy Club." Could he now take part with the millions of Methodists at the present time engaged in the service of God upon earth, would he not unite with them in singing,

"See how great a flame aspires,
Kindled by a spark of grace;
Jesus' love the nations fires—
Sets the kingdoms in a blaze

"More and more it spreads and grows
Ever mighty to prevail:
Sin's strongholds it now o'erthrows,
Shakes the trembling gates of hell."

Mr. John Wesley "was born at Epworth, on the 17th of June, 1703, (old style)," and his brother Charles, Dec. 18th, 1708. Their father, the Rev. Samuel Wesley, was a man of very considerable talent, learning and piety. Mrs. Susannah Wesley, their mother, was also a person of superior intelligence, being admirably qualified to fulfil her duties as a mother.

The children were all brought up in strict conformity to the doctrines and usages of the Church of England, great care being taken to model the minds of the whole family in a strictly religious mould. This was especially the case with John and Charles. John having had a miraculous escape from death, at the time of the destruction of the Rectory by fire, having been rescued from the devouring element through a window just as the roof fell in, his mother was impressed with the idea that the Almighty had preserved him for some great purpose; and to this may be attributed her unceasing efforts in training him up for the service of his divine Master. In reference to this same circumstance Mr. Wesley himself remarks, "Is not this a brand plucked out of the burning."

He finished his theological studies and was ordained Deacon in 1725, and shortly afterwards became his father's curate at Epwotth. In 1728 he received Priest's orders, but declined to serve in his father's church when the living was offered to him, "preferring the world as his parish." But though Mr. Wesley could neither be induced by the entreaties of his parents, nor the sterner reasoning of his brother Samuel to accept the living of Epworth, as a means of doing good, and a support for the family, yet he appears to have cheerfully complied with the invitation of the Trustees of the new Colony of Georgia, to go out with General Oglethorpe to the wilds of America as a missionary to the colonists and the Indians.

His father died in April, 1735, the family were, consequently, soon scattered, and a new incumbent appointed to the Rectory. Mr. Wesley, accompanied by his brother Charles, and the Messrs. Ingham and Delamotte, left London on the 14th day of October, 1735, in order to sail with General Oglethorpe for America.

The minds of both the Wesleys had been for some considerable time much concerned for their own personal salvation, as well as for the salvation of others, for as yet they had neither of them received the assurance of their acceptance with God through justification by faith in the atonement made by Christ. With their two companions they were now leaving England in order to be instrumental in the conversion of the heathen, themselves still in darkness and in doubt. A merciful Providence was, however, about to lead them in a way they knew not, in order that they might be brought into the full enjoyment of the love of God, and rejoice in His pardoning grace.

Upon this voyage they found among the passengers a number of pious German Moravians, and from these devoted people they were to learn more fully the way of holiness; though it was not until after their return to England that, through the instructions and instrumentality of the Moravians, they obtained peace through believing in Jesus.

The Wesleys did not succeed in Georgia as well as they had hoped to do when they left Europe, but they learned much at that time which was very advantageous to them in after years, and this visit to the New World accomplished much in preparing them for the great work before them. Charles returned home in about a year, and John was again in his native land in February, 1738, the people of the colony not being willing to listen to the pointed preaching of these plain

"Methodists," though they were accredited clergymen of the Church of England.

Immediately after their return they sought frequent intercourse with the Moravians, and Charles Wesley dates his conversion on the 21st of May, 1738, and John upon the 24th of the same month. They could say with the apostle, "Therefore being justified by faith we have peace with God through our Lord Jesus Christ. By whom also we have access by faith into this grace wherein we stand and rejoice in hope of the glory of God." And again they could exclaim, in the language of the service of the Church of England, that religion is "a sure trust and confidence which a man hath in God, that through the merits of Christ his sins are forgiven, and he reconciled to the favor of God."

They became even more zealous than before in their pulpit duties, entering the parish churches where they could obtain permission to do so, and preaching a present salvation from sin to all who would repent and believe the Gospel; but their devoted perseverance in this course procured them many enemies as well as friends. The clergy shut their churches against them, and the majority of the laity denounced them as being righteous overmuch; but thousands of the "common people heard them gladly."

A new epoch among the Methodists was at hand. Whitefield had recently returned from America, where he too had gone as a missionary, after the Wesleys had returned to England, and where he, too, had been shut out of the pulpits because of his zeal for the Lord of Hosts. Upon his return Mr. Whitefield immediately commenced preaching in the fields, and by his eloquence attracted thousands to his meetings, and thus much good was accomplished. He advised the Wesleys to go and do likewise, but being tenacious observers of church order they were at first in doubt as to whether such a course would be for the glory of God, or the benefit of the people; but at length perceiving the Providential openings made for them by the Head of the Church, they yielded to Mr. Whitefield's judgment in the matter, John taking the "field" on the 2nd of May, 1739, and Charles on the 24th of June following.

It will be remembered that the pious Morgan had led the way by visiting the prisoners, praying with the sick, relieving the poor, and instructing the children in and about Oxford, the Wesleys following in his footsteps. Mr. Whitefield now inaugurates field preaching as a means of carrying on the work of God, he, with his associates of the "Holy Club," having been ejected from the national churches. The Wesleys were slow in adopting any new system, but once convinced that they invaded no man's right, and that the cause of God would be advanced by such a course of procedure, they adopted the measure and henceforward studied only the glory of God and the salvation of sinners. They were not so famous for originating new projects as they were for seizing upon and putting into practical application plans which were calculated to advance the interests of the human family by whosoever suggested. Being now fully committed to field-preaching they went out, literally, into the highways and lanes of the cities, proclaiming the unsearchable riches of Christ to the thousands who came to listen. Whitefield leading the way, they visited London, Bristol, and other towns, besides various other public places, such as Kingswood, Moorsfield, and Gloucester, collecting immense crowds and preaching to them wherever they went. By this means "the poor had the Gospel preached to them."

The societies of which Mr. John Wesley speaks so frequently in his journal, about this period in his career, were not classes such as we have now among Methodists, but small associations organized in London by two clergymen named Horneck and Smithies, in 1667, composed of a class of young men who "began to apply themselves in a very serious way to religious thoughts and purposes." These societies met weekly, made contributions for the use of the poor, and appointed stewards to distribute their freewill offerings, but do not appear to have held class-meetings as the Methodist societies of the present day do. The principal objects of these societies were the "suppression of vice," the encouragement of religious and secular education, and to assist the poor. Persons were appointed to travel among the people, teaching them to read the Scriptures, and catechizing the children. These itinerant instructors accomplished much good, but notwithstanding that they were countenanced by some of the most zealous of the English Bishops, their societies never became very numerous; they seem to have made but little progress after the reign of William and Mary. At the time of the commencement of Methodism but few of these societies were in vigorous operation. Eight or nine were still in existence in Ireland, and a limited number in London and Bristol. The Wesleys esteemed these societies very highly because of the piety and usefulness of their members, they therefore frequently met with them and shared in their "feasts of charity." They have, however, long since ceased to exist, having most probably been merged in Mr. Wesley's more perfect organization, viz., his societies called classes.

Another important step for the more complete development of Methodism was now about to be taken by Mr. Wesley and his friends, without, however, any design of forming a separate body from the Established Church. The first meeting-house was built in Bristol, the corner stone having been laid on the 12th day of May, 1739. The closing of the churches against Mr. Wesley and his adherents rendered the building of this house necessary. The large numbers who had been awakened to the importance of spiritual things by his preaching in the fields made places of worship, which should be under his own control, in which to accomodate those who thronged to hear him, indispensable.

This "preaching-house," or chapel, was not dedicated until after the Foundry at London had been opened for Divine service. This latter edifice was an old dilapidated building which had been used by the Government for the purpose of casting cannon. Mr. Wesley was invited to preach in it. He did so, and afterwards secured it for a place of worship, and it soon became the headquarters of Methodism in London. It was opened "on the 11th of November, 1739."

This year may be made the date of the commencement of Methodism properly organized. Up to this period, and for some months afterward, Mr. Wesley and his brother Charles, as well as Mr. Whitefield, had associated with the Moravians at Fetter Lane and other places. A necessity for a separation from the Moravian Brethren about this time arose, and like Abram and Lot they parted because their followers could not agree to dwell together in peace. Mr. Wesley ardently loved the Moravian preachers, they had been the means of great spiritual benefit to him, but the time had arrived for him and them to lead different departments in the Christian army.

With regard to the origin of the United Societies, Mr. Wesley says that "in the latter end of the year 1739 eight or ten persons came to me in London who appeared to be deeply convinced of sin and earnestly groaning for redemption." Others came the next day, for their numbers increased daily, and he gave them such advice as he deemed necessary for their spiritual benefit. About this period he also formed "Band Societies," and published a volume of "Hymns and Poems" for the use of the "people called Methodists."

Mr. Whitefield had left England in August to re-visit America, and had desired Mr. Wesley to take the charge of the souls he had been instrumental in leading to Christ. The glorious work of reformation began to spread more extensively than ever. The lanes of the cities and the fields became in many places vocal with prayer and praise. Thousands flocked to listen to the sacred truths of the Gospel, and while the messengers of salvation proclaimed a full and free pardon, through faith in Jesus Christ, to every repenting sinner, hundreds would fall prostrate to the ground crying for mercy, and would soon after arise praising God for delivering grace. These mental exercises and physical demonstrations were at first condemned; but Mr. Wesley was forced, when called on to account for these strange scenes, to say, in the language of Peter, "What was I that I could withstand God?"

So rapidly did the cause of the Redeemer extend that Mr. Wesley and his brethren in the regular ministry could not supply the congregations, and in consequence lay preachers were accepted to assist in the great work. Mr. Maxfield was the first who entered the ranks of what has since become a numerous host, who, with the Divine approbation resting upon their labors, have successfully assisted in spreading scriptural holiness over the world.

John Nelson, so celebrated in Methodist history, about this time commenced to exhort and shortly afterwards to preach, and soon a multitude of itinerant lay preachers were employed in the Lord's vineyard, assisting the founder of Methodism in carrying on the great work of leading souls to Christ. At the time of Nelson's conversion he was from home, working at his trade, that of a stone-mason. He heard Wesley preach at Moorfields, and becoming convinced of sin he sought and obtained peace in believing. As soon as he could do so he returned to his family and friends in order to tell them "how great things God had done for him." Upon his arrival his friends naturally desired to learn something respecting the Methodists, although many of them were fearful that he was laboring under the delusion of the devil, and Nelson, without any preconceived idea of becoming a preacher, began to tell the people who called upon him what God was doing for the inhabitants of London. At first he sat in his house and merely conversed with those who came in, but as the crowds increased he found it necessary to stand at the door, where he first told them what he had himself seen and experienced, and afterwards strove to impress upon the minds of his listeners the great truths which he had learned, and which had been of so much benefit to him.

Upon hearing of Nelson's zeal Mr. Wesley hastened to Bristol, and was "surprised to find a society and a preacher awaiting him. He addressed them and hundreds of others on the top of Bristol Hill. He recognized Nelson as one of his 'helpers,' and his band of rustic followers as one of his United Societies."

The division of the Societies into classes, and the appointment of class-leaders originated in consequence of the debt on the chapel at Bristol. Mr. Wesley was responsible for the liabilities, and "it was decided that each member of the Society should contribute at least one penny per week in order to reduce the burden. The Society in Bristol was therefore divided into small classes," numbering about twelve persons each, one of whom was appointed to collect the amount and hand it to the stewards. This person was called the leader. The duty of the leader was to visit each member of his class once a week, to receive their contributions, and where parties were found who were too poor to pay the stipulated sum, the leader or some wealthier member would generally pay it for them. These leaders found, on visiting the members at their own homes, that some of them "walked disorderly," and needed to be reproved and to be instructed more fully in the doctrines of the Gospel. Mr. Wesley was not long in deciding what course to pursue in order to make this new adjunct to Methodism spiritually beneficial to the societies. It was determined that the classes should assemble once a week, when the leaders were to inquire of the members what progress they were making in the divine life, and was to give such admonition or advice as was deemed necessary. These meetings for Christian fellowship commonly commenced with an exhortation, singing and prayer, and after the members had spoken, the services were concluded by praise and supplication. The meeting of the class in one place saved the leader much time in collecting the contributions, and became a source of great religious improvement to the membership of the several societies. Since that period the institution of class-meetings has lost nothing of its essential religious peculiarities, but is quite as great an assistance now to a growth in grace as it was at the commencement of Methodism, and especially so to penitents or young converts.

Having found that good had resulted from the class-meetings at Bristol, Mr. Wesley called some of his friends together in London and obtained their consent to divide the society there also into "smaller companies called classes." From that time the arrangement became uniform among Methodists, and continues to exist to the present time as a vital feature of the Christian polity of the various Methodistic bodiés throughout the world.

Mr. Wesley called his first Conference on the 25th day of June, 1744. There were present six ordained clergymen and four lay preachers. The clergymen were, the Revs. John and Charles Wesley, John Hodges, Henry Piers, Samuel Taylor and John Meriton. Laymen, Thomas Maxfield, Thomas Richards, John Bennet and John Downs. The Conference was entertained by Lady Huntingdon, but met for the transaction of business in the old Foundry. Five days were spent in consultation and in arranging plans for future operations, and also in considering certain points of doctrine and discipline, when they separated, on Friday, to go forth again as luminaries spreading scriptural light throughout the land, although they were well aware that persecution and even bonds awaited them. Already they had been shut out of the National Churches, and had been mobbed while preaching in the fields and on the commons; but no fears deterred them. Mr. Wesley when shut out of the old church of his father, at Epworth, had considered it no dishonor to either the living or the dead to stand upon his father's tombstone, and from this strange pulpit call sinners to repentance. God manifested Himself to the assembled multitude in power, and many were moved by the Holy Spirit to seek the pearl of great price.

Methodism was fast spreading through various parts of England. The few clergymen of the Established Church who now itinerated with the Wesleys cordially co-operated with the "lay-helpers." Wales had shared in the glorious reformation, and now from Ireland was heard the Macedonian cry, "Come over and help us." Mr. Wesley hastened to their relief, "assuredly gathering that the Lord had called him to preach the Gospel unto them;" he reached "Dublin on Sunday, the 19th August, 1747, and went immediately to St. Mary's Church, and was permitted by the curate to preach in the afternoon to a gay and careless congregation," with apparently but little effect upon the audience. He was, however, soon much encouraged by finding Mr. Thomas Williams, a local preacher from England, who had been preaching to the people and had already formed a society in Dublin, numbering about three hundred members. Here, as in the case of John Nelson and his little flock at Bristol, Mr Wesley found a preacher and society awaiting him, which he gladly acknowledged as being in the regular and legitimate line of Methodistic succession. He met and conversed with them as he was accustomed to do with the societies in Bristol, Newcastle and London, exhorting them to "steadfastness in the faith." In his journal he "pronounced the Irish people the politest he had ever seen."

Before the visit of Mr. Wesley the Methodists in Dublin had procured the use of an old Lutheran church as a place of worship, and in it he hastened to expound the word of life, though on some occasions the throng was so great that there was not room for the multitude "no, not so much as about the door." Having spent fourteen days among them he returned to England highly delighted with the hospitality and Christian deportment of the Irish societies.

Mr. Charles Wesley, who went over to Ireland "about two weeks" afterwards, met with a very different reception, the Roman Catholic priests having stirred up their flocks against the "Swaddlers," as they called the Methodists. Extensive riots followed for quite a length of time, the preachers and society were mobbed, and several persons were killed, among whom was a poor woman who had been attending a field meeting, who was beaten to death. Unhappily, too, these scenes of violence and murder received the sanction, at least indirectly, of many Protestants, and of some of the clergy of the Church of England. Charles Wesley was not, however, to be deterred from the discharge of his duty. He preached on Dublin Green and in other places of public resort, as well as in the "preaching house," with great effect. "The word came with power irresistible, and the prayers and sobs of the people often drowned his voice." Efforts were made to bring the rioters to justice, with but partial success; the parties brought to trial were either acquitted or only punished very lightly, and after a time Mr. Wesley left the city to visit other portions of the island. Before leaving Dublin, however, he had succeeded in quelling, in a measure, the violent tumult of the people, and had collected means and procured a better place of worship for the society. In the new places to which he went Mr. Wesley was received as a messenger from God, and upon his return to Dublin he was gratified to find that there, too, the lions were comparatively tamed.

John Wesley returned to Ireland on the 8th of March, 1748, and Charles went back to England to take charge of the societies there. Methodism soon became firmly established in various parts of Ireland; though in Cork, and many other cities and towns, the little flocks suffered from violent persecution.

In 1758 we find Mr. Wesley travelling through the County of Sligo. Dr. Stevens says, "He passed to Court Mattress, where he found a colony of Germans, whose fathers had come into the country under Queen Anne, from the Palatinate on the Rhine. A hundred and ten families had settled in the town and in the adjacent hamlets of Killiheen, Ballygarrane, and Pallas, and their descendants were now numerous. Having no minister they became noted for their drunkenness and profanity, and an utter contempt for religion; but they had changed remarkably since they had heard the truth from the Methodist itinerants; an oath was now rarely heard among them, nor a drunkard seen in their borders. They had built a large preaching-house in the middle of the Court Mattress. Many times afterwards Wesley preached among them, as did also his fellow laborers, and with lasting effect. So did God at last provide for these poor strangers, who for fifty years had none that cared for their souls.

"At a later visit Mr. Wesley says that 'such towns as Killiheen, Ballygarrane and Court Mattress could hardly be found elsewhere in Ireland or England; there was no profanity, no Sabbath-breaking, no ale-house in any of them."

It is not the author's purpose to trace, at present, the history of Methodism in Europe further than to the period when it broke over the barriers of the sea-girt isles and was transplanted in the new world, through the instrumentality of a few Irish emigrants, which event occurred about fourteen years after Mr. John Wesley's first visit to the County of Sligo.

CHAPTER II.

FROM THE EMIGRATION OF MR. EMBURY TO THE ORDINATION OF BISHOP ASBURY

Extension of Methodism—Emigration of Philip Embury, the Hecks, &c.,—Prompted thereto by Barbara Heck, Embury begins to preach to his countrymen—He not among the card players—Robert Strawbridge preaches in Maryland—Which had the priority?—Captain Webb—Additions to the Society—The rigging loft—Methodism successful in New York—The rigging loft becomes too small—Mrs. Heck urges the building of a meeting-house—Old John Street Church built—Strawbridge labors with success in Maryland—The old log meeting-house—Boardman and Pillmore are sent to America—Mr. Asbury—Additional preachers sent out—The first Conference, of whom composed—William Watters the first American Itinerant—Upon the declaration of Independence the English preachers generally return to Europe—Mr. Asbury remains—Dr. Coke—First General Conference—Mr. Wesley's plan for the American Church approved—M. E. Church organized—Coke and Asbury elected General Superintendents—Asbury ordained—At the close of the Revolutionary war many Methodists remove to the British possessions.

THE work of God through the instrumentality of the Methodist itinerants had spread over the greater part of England, Ireland and Wales, had been introduced into Scotland and the West Indian Islands, and was now destined, on the Continent of America, through the instrumentality of this same Methodism, to extend still more widely. The work of reformation commenced at Oxford had not been confined to the lower classes alone. Its benign and cheering influences had reached and operated upon the hearts of many of the wealthy and noble of the land, who now contributed largely of the means at their disposal for the extension of the work in which Mr. Wesley and his co-laborers were engaged. The success of Methodism in the County of Sligo, Ireland, will be remembered. A number of these German Irish, whose fathers half a century before had left the "Palatinate on the Rhine," in consequence of a cruel war, and had found refuge in Ireland, had now determined to remove to the far off western continent. Among these emigrants was Philip Embury, a young Methodist local preacher. When the ship was about to sail, Embury stood upon its crowded deck and addressed the friends of the emigrants who had come to bid their relatives farewell. The scene was one of peculiar interest. A company leaving home and kindred to try their future in a strange land; the dangers of the mighty ocean were before them; the privations and afflictions of a new country were to be met and successfully braved, or poverty, sorrow and disappointment must be endured. The anchor was raised at last, the sails spread and the ship moved out upon the boisterous deep to contend for a time with the winds, the waves, and the tides. The land receded rapidly from view, and the loved ones on the vessel and those on the shore, with tear-bathed faces looked a long adieu to friends and kindred. Who among that group assembled there could have imagined the mighty results which were to follow the exertions of the man who had that day addressed them from the deck of the emigrant ship? The vessel reached its destined port in safety on the 10th of August, 1760, and Philip Embury, with his fellow colonists, settled in New York. This company, according to Dr. Stevens, consisted of Philip Embury and his wife, Mary Switzer, to whom he had been married on the 27th of November, 1758, in the Rathkale church; two of his brothers and their families; Peter Switzer, probably a brother of his wife; Valer Tettler; Philip Morgan, and a family of Dulmages, with Paul Heck and Barbara his wife.

In 1765 another little band of emigrants from the same

place reached New York, and with them Mrs. Heck renewed her former acquaintance. Mrs. Heck and several of these Sligo emigrants had been members of the Methodist societies in Ireland, as well as Embury, but after their arrival in this new country they hung their harp on the willow, and said in effect, "How can we sing the Lord's song in a strange land?" Embury and his associates became disheartened and lukewarm in religion, and, in consequence, some of their number backslid and became openly wicked. Mrs. Heck on one occasion, on going to visit one of these families, coming in upon them unexpectedly, found some of the party engaged in playing cards. Her righteous soul was grieved, and stepping forward she gathered up the cards and threw them into the fire, at the same time reproving the delinquents sharply. Knowing as she did that Philip Embury, who was a cousin of her own, had been a local preacher in his native land, she went directly to his house and urged him to set at once about his Master's work. He replied that he had no suitable place in which to preach, and if he had, did not know that he could secure a congregation. Mrs. Heck, however, over-ruled these objections, and having prevailed on him to consent to preach, she went out, and returned with four other persons, the five constituting his first congregation in America. Mr. Embury was not among the card players—does not appear even to have been in the same house with them.

It is a disputed point as to who formed the first Methodist Society on the American continent, some asserting that the first society was organized in Maryland, in 1760, by Robert Strawbridge, a local preacher from the north of Ireland; while others claim that Philip Embury organized the first society in 1766, in New York. The evidence seems to preponderate in favor of Philip Embury and the New York society.

Mr. Strawbridge was an active, zealous local preacher, and at a very early period in American Methodist history was instrumental in causing the erection of what was afterwards known as the "old log meeting house," in Frederick county, near Sam's Creek, in the State of Maryland.

As far as the question of priority relates to us of the present generation, it makes but little difference which of these laborious pioneers established the first society; it is the almost miraculous results which followed the exertions of both with which we are most concerned.

Upon this question the General Conference of the M. E. Church in the United States, held at Buffalo, in 1860, adopted a report from which the following paragraph is an extract:—

"As to the date of the introduction of Methodism into this country, the testimony is not as satisfactory as we might desire. The most generally recognised date has been the formation, in New York, of the first Methodist society in America, in 1766. But the testimony is conclusive, from the published communications of Rev. Dr. G. C. M. Roberts, that Rev. Robert Strawbridge, a Wesleyan preacher from Ireland, did arrive in America as early as 1760,* and shortly after began preaching and administering baptism, in the State of Maryland, and that Methodism did thus have an existence in America prior to the formation of the society mentioned above, in New York, in 1766. Your Committee feel that the Church would be doing no violence to historic truth to fix upon either 1860 or 1866 as the centenary of American Methodism."

Shortly after Mrs. Heck induced Mr. Embury to commence preaching in New York he organized a class, or society, on Mr. Wesley's plan, following the example of Nelson in England, and Williams in Ireland. The Methodists in New York were

* Mr. Shillington, who is regarded by Dr. Stevens as the "best Irish authority" in these matters, fixes the date of Strawbridge's emigration as "not earlier than 1764, nor later than 1765." Very searching investigations have been made with regard to these rival claims; and the General Conference, as is well known, finally gave the preference to 1866 for the celebration of the centenary of American Methodism.

few and at first attracted but little attention. By degrees, however, Embury's discourses drew an occasional stranger, until the house could not contain the people. It was then decided to rent a larger room for public worship, the congregation paying expenses.

About this period a new impulse was given to the efforts of the "little flock." Captain Webb, a British officer, who was stationed with his regiment at Albany, and who had joined the Methodists in England in 1765, was anxious to visit his brethren in New York, and one evening, to the surprise and alarm of the society, he entered their humble room and took a seat in their small assembly, dressed in his regimentals. All eyes were for a moment fastened on the stranger, fearful that he had come to disturb the meeting. But when they saw him kneel in prayer, and engage devoutly in the services, their distrust and sorrow at his approach was turned into joy as they recognised by his deportment that he was one with them. After the services had been concluded he made himself known to them, and as he had been a local preacher in England Mr. Embury invited him to preach when in the city—a request with which he cordially complied. A British officer standing before a congregation, clad in a scarlet coat, with his epaulets and other military habiliments, proclaiming the gospel of Christ to the people, was indeed a strange sight, and this, together with his earnest manner of speaking, attracted many to the preaching of the Methodists. A spirit of awakening followed, and several were converted and added to the society. In consequence of the numbers who came to hear the word, a still larger place of worship had to be procured, and a "rigging loft in William Street" was secured and fitted up for the purpose. Without any premeditated design Mr. Embury and the New York society were closely following the example of their co-religionists in London, England, who were worshipping in the old Foundry. Humble edifices in both instances, but destined to become famous in Methodist history.

Captain Webb now entered more fully upon his Master's work, preaching as he had opportunity to the inhabitants of Long Island, as well as in other places, extending his labors as far as Philadelphia, and his efforts were abundantly owned and blessed. While Captain Webb was thus engaged out of New York, Mr. Embury was earnestly proclaiming a full salvation to the crowds who now came to listen to him in the rigging loft. It, like the rooms before used for worship, became too small to accommodate those who came to hear, and the society, urged to do so by Mrs. Heck, resolved to build a new meeting-house. In this undertaking they were aided by citizens who were not members of the society, and John Street Church was the result of their united efforts. The Church was named "Wesley Chapel," and was dedicated to the worship of God October 30th, 1768, by Philip Embury.

While Captian Webb and Mr. Embury were leading forward the hosts of Israel in New York and its vicinity, Mr. Strawbridge was unfurling the banner of the cross in Maryland. Like other local preachers similarly situated, he commenced preaching in his own and other private houses, "and very soon a society was collected of such as desired to flee from the wrath to come and to be saved from their sins." The log meeting house was erected, and he continued to preach and to take care of the classes there until Mr. Wesley sent out preachers to take the oversight of the societies in America.

The success which had attended the exertions of Embury in New York, of Strawbridge in Maryland, and of Webb in Philadelphia, was a source of great joy to Mr. Wesley and his co-laborers in Europe. Mr. Wesley was solicited, by the American societies, to send out missionaries who could devote their whole time to the ministry of the word; and in 1769 he complied with their request, sending out Richard Boardman and Joseph Pillmore, who had offered themselves for the work. The conference was convened by Mr. Wesley in that year, at Leeds, in August; but the missionaries, having had a tedious voyage of nine weeks, did not reach their destination until

October. They landed at Gloucester Point, six miles below Philadelphia, October 24th, 1769, and were agreeably surprised on reaching Philadelphia to find Captain Webb there at the head of a society of about one hundred members, anxiously awaiting their arrival. Mr. Pillmore remained for a time in Philadelphia, while Mr. Boardman went on immediately to New York, where he found a society, under the charge of Mr. Embury, numbering about the same as the one in Philadelphia.

Mr. Pillmore, shortly after he had entered upon his work, heard of the efforts of Mr. Strawbridge in Maryland, and in consequence visited him, that he might encourage him, and the little band of believers that he had gathered round him, in the work in which they were engaged. He found the society regularly organized, and the devoted local preacher teaching them the way of salvation.

These missionaries did not, however, confine their labors to the cities already mentioned, but itinerated extensively through the country in various directions, forming societies wherever they found the people desiring that they should do so. They found the multitudes who came to hear them generally orderly, and the most encouraging success attended their labors.

As was incumbent upon them, they reported the result of their efforts to Mr. Wesley early in 1770, urging that more ministerial assistance might be sent to them. With these earnest solicitations Mr. Wesley complied the next year, sending out Francis Asbury and Richard Wright, who volunteered their services for the American work. "They landed in Philadelphia, October 7th, 1771, and were most cordially received by the people."

Mr. Asbury, who afterward acted so prominent a part in the Methodist Church in America, entered immediately upon his ministerial duties, extending his labors to the towns and country places, as well as the cities and other places in which societies had already been formed. He from the first took an honorable lead in the itinerancy, and continued to do so until the end of a long and useful life. Although in many instances he had to contend with considerable opposition from the ungodly and lukewarm, yet he was "immovable, always abounding in the work of the Lord." And to this may be attributed his unparalleled success in "turning many from darkness to light, and from the power of Satan unto God."—The preachers asssociated with Mr. Asbury followed his example, thus in a greater or less degree spreading the sacred truths of Christianity throughout the land.

In 1772 Mr. Wesley appointed Mr. Asbury "general assistant," by which office he was to have the oversight of the preachers and societies in America, and appoint the preachers to their respective circuits. In December of this year Mr. Asbury held a Quarterly Meeting Conference in Maryland, in which several subjects were discussed, the characters of the brethren examined, and the preachers appointed to their several charges. To the great joy of Mr. Asbury, Mr. Wesley, in 1773, sent over to strengthen the itinerancy, Thomas Rankin and George Shadford, and as Mr. Rankin had been travelling longer than Mr. Asbury, he was appointed the "general assistant of the societies in America." Up to this time, a period of about seven years since Methodism had had an organized existence in America, there had been no regular Conference, the business of the Church and stationing of the preachers having been attended to at the Quarterly Meetings. Mr. Rankin being now, however, "general assistant," and there being several preachers engaged in the work, it was deemed expedient to call them together for consultation. A Conference was therefore called, which met in Philadelphia on the 4th of July, 1773.

There were present Thomas Rankin, George Shadford, Francis Asbury, and Richard Wright, missionaries sent out by Mr. Wesley; John King, William Watters, Robert

Strawbridge, Abraham Whitework, Joseph Yearbry, and Robert Williams, local preachers. Mr. Williams had been a local preacher in England, and had a "permit" from Mr. Wesley to act in that capacity under the missionaries in America. Mr. King received his license from Mr. Pillmore, after his arrrival on this continent. Messrs. Boardman, Pillmore, Webb and Embury were not present at this Conference. There were, therefore, present at the first American Conference, only four travelling and six local preachers. At this Conference the local preachers were associated with the regular preachers in the transaction of business. The returns were, Preachers, 10; In society, 1,160.

Although Mr. Strawbridge had never been ordained, it appears that he had baptized and administered the Lord's Supper. Such a course of procedure was considered irregular, and consequently the Conference passed the following rule:—

"Every preacher who acts in connection with Mr. Wesley and the brethren who labor in America, is strictly to avoid administering the ordinances of baptism and the Lord's Supper." This was a timely and judicious measure.

William Watters, who attended this Conference, was the first person in America who entered the work as a regular itinerant. He continued a faithful servant of God and the Church until the end of his days, and was instrumental in bringing many souls to Christ.

In the beginning of 1774 the Messrs. Boardman and Pillmore returned to England, while the Messrs. Rankin and and Asbury continued to take charge of the work in America. The second Conference was held in Philadelphia, in May, 1774. The returns are, Preachers, 17; Members, 2,073, showing an increase of 913 in the societies. From this period the work of reformation continued to spread still more extensively, accessions being made to the Church daily. The Messrs. Rankin and Asbury worked in fellowship with each other, travelling almost continually; and although they did not see eye to eye on all matters of Church polity, they labored together in such a way that the work was not hindered.

The difficulties which had for several years existed between the American Colonies and the British Government now began to be more fully developed. There had been demonstrations of open hostility to home authorities, and upon the 4th of July, 1776, Congress declared the thirteen American Colonies "free and independent States."

At this crisis Mr. Rankin, with several of his brethren, returned to Europe, but Mr. Asbury decided to remain with the societies, and do all that lay in his power to uphold the cause of his Redeemer. In connection with many of his brethren he suffered much during the sanguinary struggle of the American Revolution; but he braved the storm, and with his associates in the ministry was at his post ready to commence the Methodist campaign as soon as the Revolution should terminate.

As is the case in every country during war, the cause of God suffered more or less during the American conflict, but through the exertions of Mr. Asbury, Freeborn Garretson, Joseph Hartely, and some others, the societies were visited as far as it was practicable, and sermons occasionally delivered while the war was in progress.

Great Britain acknowledged the independence of the United States in 1783. The following year Mr. Wesley ordained Dr. Coke as Bishop, or General Superintendent, and sent him, with the Messrs. Whatcoat and Vasey, whom he ordained Elders, to America, to organize the societies into a regular scriptural church, with its Bishops, Elders, and Deacons. These brethren Mr. Wesley furnished with their consecration parchments, and also sent with them a letter of introduction to the American Methodists, assigning the reasons for the step which he had taken preparatory to the organization of the Methodist Episcopal Church in America.

Dr. Coke, and the Messrs. Whatcoat and Vasey reached

New York on the 3rd of November, 1784, from whence they immediately proceeded to the State of Delaware, in order to meet Mr Asbury, who was associated, by Mr. Wesley, with Dr. Coke, as one of the Superintendents of the Methodist Church in the United States. After a consultation with Mr. Asbury and some others of the American brethren, it was decided that a General Conference should be summoned in order to consider the scheme proposed by Mr. Wesley. To the call thus made sixty out of eighty responded, and assembled in Baltimore on the 25th of December, 1784.

Dr. Coke presented to the Conference Mr. Wesley's plan of forming the Methodist societies in America into a Church. The measure was approved, and in evidence of their acquiescence in the scheme the Conference proceeded "to elect Dr. Coke and Francis Asbury, General Superintendents; for although Mr. Asbury had been appointed to that high office by Mr. Wesley, yet he declined acting in that capacity independent of the suffrages of his brethren over whom he must preside." Mr. Asbury was first ordained Deacon, then Elder; and before the close of the Conference he was consecrated to the office of Bishop, by the imposition of the hands of Dr. Coke, Richard Whatcoat, and Thomas Vasey, assisted by the Rev. Mr. Otterbein, a pious minister of the German Church.

Dr. Coke having been properly ordained Bishop by Mr. Wesley and other Presbyters of the Church of England, and the Messrs. Whatcoat and Vasey being Elders, they had authority to ordain Bishop Asbury, without the assistance of Mr. Otterbein; but as it was Mr. Asbury's wish that he should be associated with the others in the service, and there being no objection made, the request was complied with. At this Conference a number of the preachers were ordained Deacons and Elders, and several new rules were adopted for the further guidance of the body.

The proceedings of this first General Conference gave the

utmost satisfaction to the preachers and people throughout the country. Extensive revivals followed—the legitimate result of a united Church with a zealous and pious ministry, whose efforts were crowned with success by the Almighty.

In consequence of the Revolutionary war many members of the Methodist societies removed to the British possessions, having adhered throughout the war to the Imperial Government, and many others also emigrated shortly after peace was proclaimed. The attention of the reader will henceforward be more particularly directed to the introduction of Methodism into Canada, and to the tracing of its history in this highly favored land.

CHAPTER III.

PIONEER METHODISTS IN CANADA.

Embury removes to Ashgrove, N. Y.—Is followed by the Hecks and others—Preaches and forms a society—Death—Re-interment—The Hecks, Emburys, &c., &c., remove to Canada—First Methodist class in Canada—No preacher, either travelling or local—Mr Tuffey—George Neal—His military career—Conversion—Comes to Canada—Preaches—Persecuted—Death of the Persecutor—Continues to preach without further molestation—Forms a society—Ordained—Usefulness—Death—Mr. Lyons—James McCarty—Cast into prison for preaching the Gospel of Christ—His wife and friend Perry denied access to him—The kind Irishwoman——Sentenced to imprisonment on one of the Thousand Islands—Prevails on those who are conducting him thither to land him on the main-land—Returns to his family—Preaches the next Sabbath—Again arrested—Sentenced a second time to transportation—Reasons for believing that he was murdered—End of the persecutors.

A NUMBER of the Irish Palatines, who, under God, were the founders of Methodism in New York, were also the founders of Methodism in Canada. About the year 1769 Philip Embury and family left the city of New York and located themselves at Ashgrove. They were followed, in 1770 or 1771, by Paul and Barbara Heck, their three sons, and several others of the New York society. Here again, as in New York, Embury held meetings among the people, and formed a class, the first within the bounds of the present Troy Conference. This zealous and eminently useful man died suddenly, in 1773, from injury received while mowing; he was buried on the farm of his friend Peter Switzer; whence, after the lapse of more than half a century, his remains were removed to the Ashgrove burial ground, where they were re-interred with appropriate ceremonies; an eloquent address, suited to the peculiarly interesting occasion, was delivered by his gifted countryman, Rev. J. N. Maffit, to the large assemblage gathered together thus to evidence their veneration for the memory of the sainted Embury.

In 1774, in consequence of the evidently approaching revolutionary storm, and being ardently attached to British institutions, the Heck family, John Lawrence, who had married the widow Embury, David Embury, brother to Philip, and many more of the Irish Palatines from Ashgrove, emigrated to Lower Canada, and stopped for a time near Montreal. Not being pleased with that locality, however, they, in 1778, removed to Augusta, in Upper Canada. David Embury, with several of his friends, subsequently settled along the Bay of Quinte, where many of his descendants still live.

The first Methodist Society in Canada was formed, as nearly as can be ascertained, in 1778, and numbered among its first members Paul and Barbara Heck, their three sons, John, Jacob and Samuel, John and Catherine Lawrence—formerly Mrs. P. Embury—Samuel Embury, son of Philip, and such others as felt it a privilege to unite with the class. Mr. and Mrs. Lawrence opened their house as a place of worship, and Samuel Embury was appointed leader. Here was a class organized and a leader appointed without even the assistance of a local preacher, the necessity of the case, we apprehend, fully justifying the action of this little Christian community. Paul Heck died 1792, and Barbara in 1804. They both sleep near the old blue church in the front of Augusta.

Separated, as these emigrants were, from their brethren in New York, it is probable that nine or ten years elapsed before they enjoyed the privilege of hearing a sermon. Broad and dreary forests intervened between them and their friends, and they were surrounded by wild savages, who not unfrequently rent the air with their terrific war-whoops as they hastened to join in the deadly conflict then raging in and sweeping over the Provinces they had left. It was impossible, therefore, to send missionaries to their aid, and consequently the little band met together as they did—without a pastor—conducting their public worship in the best way they could.

Methodism was introduced into Quebec, in Lower Canada, as early as the year 1780, by means of the 44th Regiment of British soldiers, stationed there in that year. Mr. Tuffey, who had charge of the Commissariat Department, had been one of Mr. Wesley's helpers before he left the old country, and after his arrival in Canada he preached to his fellow-soldiers and to such others as were willing to attend his meetings. But although evidently a pious and useful officer, he does not appear to have formed any permanent society.

Shortly after the United States of America had achieved their independence the 44th was disbanded, and some of them returned to England, while others settled in various parts of the colony. Before, and immediately after the independence of the United States had been acknowledged by Great Britain, many of those who had adhered to the cause of the Crown during the struggle made their way from the Republic into Canada, and to these was added quite an emigration from Europe. Among the emigrants from both countries were many members of the Methodist Societies, but they became scattered abroad in the wilderness, as sheep without a shepherd.

That the labors of Mr. Tuffey resulted in good is evident from the fact that the disbanded soldiers who had settled along the banks of the St. Lawrence, and on the shores of the Bay of Quinte, were, in many instances, the first to open their log cabins to receive the Methodist preachers. The class of people, however, who most preferred Methodism were the descendants of the Palatinate Irish, whose forefathers had derived so much benefit from the preaching of Mr. Wesley and his indefatigable missionaries in Sligo; they had not forgotten the good which had resulted from the teachings of the Methodists in their father-land, and now labored to scatter, as far as was possible in the new country to which they had come, the seed which had borne such good fruit in the land they had left.

On the 7th of October, 1786, Rev. George Neal crossed the Niagara River, into Canada, at Queenston, and settled in the Niagara District. Mr. Neal was born in Pennsylvania, February 28th, 1751, but resided at different periods in North Carolina. South Carolina and Georgia, In the latter State he was made captain in the British service, to which cause he adhered throughout the war of the Revolution. He was soon promoted to a majorship, and was present at the siege of Charleston, where he narrowly escaped with his life by the timely assistance of Lord Francis Roden, who came to his support. He organized another troop. but was again overpowered by General Green, who killed or made prisoners the entire company; the Major alone. it is believed, making good his escape.

As a soldier, Mr. Neal was resolute and not easily daunted. Upon one occasion, while his company were preparing their morning meal. after a night of considerable annoyance from the enemy. a cannon ball from the American camp struck an embankment near Neal's camp-fire, where he was hastily roasting a piece of meat. A brother officer remarked, "Major, you had better move your quarters, the Americans are getting our range." Neal replied that if he was not born to be shot there was no danger of a cannon ball killing him. At that instant another cannon ball struck the embankment, covering himself and his ration with dust, which so annoyed him that he removed from the place. He had scarcely left his position when a third shot struck the very spot where he had the moment before been seated. Neal ever afterwards believed that if he had not yielded to the advice of his friend he would have found to his cost that "he was born to be shot."

After the success of General Green he was convinced that it was useless for him to contend any longer as a British soldier, cut off so completely as he was from the Imperial forces, consequently he went further into the interior of the State, where his sentiments were not so well known, and commenced teaching school. Here, for the first time, he heard a Methodist preacher, Rev. Hope Hull, through whose instrumentality he became concerned with regard to his spiritual welfare, and about a year subsequently he found peace through faith in our Lord Jesus Christ.

Mr. Neal was soon called upon to act the part of a public teacher of the doctrines he professed, being sent by the Presiding Elder to travel on the Pee Dee River, where many souls were awakened and brought to a knowledge of salvation by the preaching of the word. His British proclivities, however, being still strong, though much attached to the Methodists among whom he was laboring, he resolved to emigrate to Nova Scotia, but having missed his passage he set out for Canada, which he reached at the time before stated.

Although he was a British subject, and had proved his loyalty to the government, and his attachment to British institutions on many a well fought field, yet he found great obstacles thrown in his way when, on his arrival in Canada, he commenced preaching the Gospel. The British officer commanding at Queenston having learned that Mr. Neal occasionally held meetings among the people, sent for him and forbade him to hold any more, asserting that none but clergy of the Established Church of England should preach in the colonies. Mr. Neal, feeling that he had rights as a British subject, determined not to yield to this person's dictation without making a strong effort to maintain them, and with them his religious opinions and privileges. Finding him, therefore, immovable in his purpose, the officer commanded him to leave the Province within a given number of days. Before the time had expired, however, his persecutor was called into eternity, and Mr. Neal was suffered, without further molestation, to proceed in his labor of love, preaching in and about Niagara District. The work of the Lord prospered in his hands, as he travelled from settlement to settlement, preaching to people in their shanties, and in their barns, or the woods, the unsearchable riches of Christ.

From the commencement of his religious efforts in Canada. Mr. Neal found some who sympathized with him in his religious views. Mr. Conrad Cope, with some of his relatives, had come to Canada in 1783 or 1784, and settled for a time near Queenston. Mr. Cope had been a Methodist in the States, and in after years he served the Church in this Province in the capacity of a local preacher. He very much encouraged and assisted Mr. Neal in his early efforts in this country, and died at a good old age, in Copetown. At the time of his death, and for some years previous to it, he was a member of the New Connexion Methodist Church.

Mr. Neal, following the illustrious example of Nelson, in England, Williams, in Ireland, and Embury, in New York, collected together those who had been converted, and formed a society in Stamford, in 1790, appointing Christian Warner class-leader, an office which Mr. Warner continued to fill until the time of his death, which occurred on the 21st of March, 1833. This class was composed of a number of members who afterwards distinguished themselves as pillars in the Church of God. The work continued to spread, the leavening influence of the Gospel manifesting itself in many places, extending along the Chippewa, and up Lyons' Creek.

Here, then, as well as in Augusta, was a company of faithful men and women, regularly organized, and waiting until ministers should be sent who were authorized to administer to them the sacraments of baptism and the

Lord's Supper. The work of God in Canada was very similar, in many respects, to the commencement of Methodism in New York, under Philip Embury and Captain Webb, and in Maryland under Mr. Strawbridge. Mr. Neal's proceedings were approved of by the brethren in the United States, as well as by his brethren in Canada, and on the 23rd of July, 1810, he was ordained Deacon, by Bishop Asbury, at Lyons, in the State of New York.

Though Mr. Neal taught school for a livelihood, yet he travelled extensively, laboring as a local preacher for nearly fifty-four years, preaching after he was so enfeebled by age as to be unable to stand while delivering his discourse. There are, scattered here and there in Canada, still a few survivors of those who were taught in Mr. Neal's school, or who were brought from darkness to light through his instrumentality. Mr. Neal died at the residence of his son-in-law, J. Hutchinson, Esq., near Port Rowan, on the 28th of February, 1840, being exactly 89 years old, having died upon his birthday. The text from which this aged pioneer preached his last sermon was Isaiah xxvi. 7, 8.

In the year 1788 Mr. Lyons, who was a member of the Methodist Episcopal Church in the United States, and who held a license as an exhorter in that Church, came to Adolphustown, in the capacity of a school-teacher. Mr. Lyons taught his school during the week, but upon the Lord's day and evening he frequently held meetings among the scattered inhabitants, many of whom were awakened and converted, while others, who had been Methodists before coming to Canada, were stirred up to greater diligence in their Master's service. Mr. Lyons, however, did not attempt to form any classes. Though, like all the other Methodist U. E. Loyalists, he venerated British institutions, yet he, like them, was warmly attached to the M. E. Church in the United States, and labored diligently for its establishment along the shores of the Bay of Quinte.

While the Messrs. Neal and Lyons were at work, in their respective localities, promoting the educational and spiritual welfare of the people, Mr. James McCarty, formerly from Ireland, left the State of New York, and settled at Ernestown, in 1788. He was an earnest follower of Rev. George Whitefield, and felt impelled to preach "Jesus and the resurrection" to the destitute settlers by whom he was surrounded. The religious teaching of these humble followers of Christ resulted in the conversion of very many who had been hitherto comparatively ignorant of the plan of salvation, while others were greatly edified, and all were more fully prepared to receive the regular preachers when they were sent among them by the New York Conference.

Mr. McCarty wrote and read his sermons, after the manner of the Church of England, but by his energy and piety he attracted many to listen to his discourses. He was not long allowed to pursue his sacred calling.

In consequence of the very peculiar circumstances connected with the bitter persecution of Mr. McCarty and his subsequent mysterious death, great pains have been taken to procure accurate information upon the subject. The account of this matter given below will differ in some points from that given by Mecham and Playter. It is considered, however, the most correct, the facts which will be narrated having been obtained from John McCarty, Esq., of Cobourg, who is a son of the man whose case is under consideration.

An edict in Council had been passed before the organization of the Upper Canada Parliament, decreeing "that all vagabond characters should be banished from the Province." Certain zealots of the Church of England—officials of high standing in and about Kingston—declared Mr. McCarty to be a vagabond character, because he dared to preach the Gospel contrary to their will, and urged that he should be transported to the United States. He was accordingly informed against by a person named Church, and was arrested and imprisoned, neither his wife, nor a kind friend, named Perry, being allowed to see him or minister to his wants. An Irish woman, living in Kingston, having, however, heard of McCarty's condition, appealed to Judge Cartwright on his behalf, and obtained permission to supply him with food, although it is apparent that the Judge was *not* favorably inclined toward the prisoner. In due time McCarty was tried for the *vagabond offence of preaching the glad tidings of salvation*, was found guilty, and was sentenced to solitary confinement on one of the Thousand Islands, in the St. Lawrence. Four Frenchmen were selected to carry the sentence into execution. They placed him in a boat, with the intention of taking him to the island as directed; but he, having some knowledge of the French language, succeeded in inducing them to land him upon the mainland, when he immediately returned home to gladden the sad hearts of his wife and their four small children, who were in the howling wilderness, dependent upon the exertions of the father and husband for their daily food. But, alas! how short-lived is earthly bliss. Surely "when the wicked bear rule" the people have cause to mourn. On the Sabbath after his return he was again preaching in the house of Mr. Robert Perry, when an officer and three men, armed, who came out from Kingston, entered and again arrested him. Mr. Perry, Col. Simmons, and Col. Parrett became security for him that he would be forthcoming in Kingston next day. Upon these conditions he was permitted to remain at home until Monday morning, when he appeared, with his bail, before the authorities. He was immediately placed in one of the cells, and was shortly afterwards again sentenced to transportation, and it is said they left with him for Montreal, from whence he went into the neighboring State to seek a suitable location, where he might once more establish his family. It has been asserted by a Mr. Sherwood that he saw Mr. McCarty in Montreal, and that he was at that time returning from the

States for his wife and children, and that he passed up the St. Lawrence to a place called the Cedars, and that some short time after he had passed this place he was found dead in the woods, not far from the road side, having been stabbed in several places. Mr. Sherwood declared that he saw the clothes of the murdered man, and that he knew them to be the clothing of James McCarty.

If the statement of Mr. Sherwood is correct, then McCarty is accounted for; but, if Sherwood has not told the truth with regard to seeing him in Montreal, or if he was mistaken concerning the raiment of the man murdered near the Cedars, then the singular disappearance of Mr. McCarty will in all probability never be accounted for until the Judgment of the great day. He may have been placed on one of the Thousand Islands, according to the first sentence, and left to perish, or his persecutors may have disposed of his life in some other way. One thing is evident, he died a martyr for the cause of God in Canada.

The persecutors imagined that they had gained a great triumph in getting McCarty out of the way; but their triumph was short-lived, Divine vengeance being particularly visited upon three of the leading men most conspicuous among the persecutors; to one of whom, at the time of McCarty's commitment to prison, Mr. Robert Perry remarked, "You may kill McCarty, but a hundred will rise up at his burial. whom neither you nor your party can kill."

Captain C——, who was most active in McCarty's persecution, afterwards wrote a confession of his crime, stating that he had "wrongfully and wickedly injured an innocent man," and handed the paper to Mrs. McCarty, who had it presented to the Judge. But he said, in effect, as did the Jews on a certain occasion, that he was not responsible for the conduct of Church, he should "see to that." Captain C—— finally fell into a state of insanity, which continued until his death, a period of many years.

The Engineer closed his career in eight or ten days, and Mr. L——, also suddenly, in two or three weeks."

A strange mystery hangs over the fate of Mr. McCarty, who was thus so unexpectedly removed from a fond wife and helpless family, and from the few suffering Christians whom he had gathered together; but the waves of persecution were not permitted to swallow them up. Lyons, Perry and others continued to encourage the people to hold fast whereunto they had attained, until, by the leadings of Providence, pastors should be sent to them who would proclaim the Gospel to them, and form societies among the settlers, wherever it was practicable to do so.

That time had now arrived.

CHAPTER IV.

FROM 1789 TO 1792.

Rev. Wm. Losee visits Canada—Preaches to the little flocks in the wilderness—They, through him, request the Conference to send them ministers—Losee is appointed—His character as a preacher—The scoffer humbled—Class of persons who constituted the first societies—Progress of the work.

THE Rev. William Losee was the first itinerant Methodist preacher who came to Canada. Mr. L. was received as a probationer at the Conference held in New York, commencing 28th of May, 1789, and was appointed that year, with the Rev. David Kendall, to the Lake Champlain Circuit. This region of country was then but sparsely settled, dotted only here and there with a civilized habitation. From the most reliable information that can now be obtained it would appear that the missionaries did not succeed in establishing any societies that year. The summer months having most probably been spent in exploring the country and preaching to the scattered inhabitants, and not having met with the success which they expected there, it is supposed that the Presiding Elder, Rev. Freeborn Garrettson, recommended Mr. Losee to visit Canada, where he had relatives residing, hoping that an effectual door might be opened in the British possessions for the messengers of salvation.

The reason for assuming that the Messrs. Kendall and Losee were unsuccessful on the Lake Champlain circuit is, that no returns of members were made for that year, and at the next

Conference the name of the charge disappeared from the Minutes.

A variety of circumstances lead to the inference that Mr. Losee crossed the St. Lawrence and commenced travelling up the river, on the Canadian side, in the latter part of December, 1789, or in the beginning of January, 1790. It is asserted that he preached for the society in Augusta, and also in various places, as he passed up to the Bay of Quinte, where he found the little flocks collected by the Messrs. Lyons and McCarty, and immediately entered upon his labors among them.

How long it required for Mr. Losee to travel from Lake Champlain to the Bay of Quinte, cannot be decided; but as he had to pass through an almost interminable forest, and as he was sent on a warfare at his own temporal charges, it is reasonable to suppose that he endured severe hardships.

Mr. Kendall was sent, in 1790, to Long Island, but there is no mention made of Mr. Losee in connection with any circuit, although he was continued on trial by the Conference, which proves conclusively that he had the confidence of the Conference, his Presiding Elder, and the Bishop. How or where Mr. Losee spent the spring and summer of 1790 cannot now be ascertained, as he only remained a portion of that year in Canada. It is not likely, however, that he was idle, having most probably spent his time in some part of the United States. The facilities for travelling were not so good in those days, nor did news circulate so rapidly as in these days of steamboats, railroads and telegraphs; consequently, communication between friends at a distance was always difficult, and sometimes impossible. It required a long time to travel from Canada to New York, even when the nearest possible route was taken. At the present day, such a journey performed as the early pioneers were obliged to do it, on horseback or on foot, would be considered a great undertaking, although the roads might be good, the bridges safe, and the accommodations along the route both convenient and comfortable; but in Mr Losee's day, no matter which one of the several routes was taken, his journey through the wilderness must have been long, difficult, and not a little perilous, being obliged as he was to cut his way through the bush, follow the windings of the Indian trails, wade through creeks or swamps, and ford the larger streams, or delay long enough to construct a raft in order to cross the rivers which it was found impracticable either to ford or swim; while food was only to be procured by gathering wild roots, or by the chase.

It has already been intimated that the Canadian people had sent an earnest request to the New York Conference, by Mr. Losee, affectionately urging that body to send ministers to this Province. The petition was cordially received, and at the Conference of 1791 Mr. Losee was ordained Deacon, and sent to Kingston, Upper Canada, Rev. Jesse Lee being his Presiding Elder; though it does not appear that Mr. Lee visited the Province during the year at all. Mr. Losee reached his field of labor in February, 1791, and immediately commenced his work, preaching among the people whom he had visited the winter previous, and organizing the classes regularly, neither Mr. Lyons nor Mr. McCarty having formed any. Mr. Losee organized the first class on the Kingston Circuit on Sunday, February 20th, 1791, this being the third organized in the country; the fourth class was formed on the following Sabbath, and the fifth class in Canada, and the third on the Kingston charge, "on Wednesday, the 2nd of March, the day on which Mr. John Wesley died." The work in Canada may now be said to have been fairly commenced.

Mr. Losee was a plain and powerful preacher, and frequently very pointed in his remarks to the ungodly It is related of him that on one occasion, when preaching at Hay Bay, a powerful man, who had at different times disturbed religious worship, entered the assembly and began, as usual, to annoy all those who were near him by his irreverence and scoffing. Mr. Losee for some time continued preaching without appearing to notice the disturber, waxing warmer, however, and more eloquent, as he proceeded. At length, when the scoffer had passed all bounds, the minister suddenly paused, and fixing his dark piercing eye upon the man, and at the same time pointing his finger directly at him, said in an exceedingly solemn manner, "O Lord, smite him!" "Amen," heartily responded some of the worshippers. The "amens" had scarcely died away when, again, with still greater emphasis than before, Mr. Losee pronounced the same words, *"O Lord, smite him!"* "Amen" again rang through the congregation. The offender leaped to his feet to leave the place, but before he had taken the first step the preacher once more cried out at the top of his voice, "O LORD, SMITE HIM!" and at the same instant down the man fell, as though he had been shot. The scene which followed was indescribably solemn and impressive. Sinners trembled and wept, prayer and praise became general among believers; it was indeed a time of power. The man, as soon as he fell, had begun to call upon God for mercy, and thus he who had come "to mock, remained to pray," and was some time after added to the "number of the disciples." In this manner the word grew and multiplied in the land.

There is another Kingston circuit mentioned in the Minutes of 1791, which has been mistaken by some for Kingston, Upper Canada, but which, from its connection with the other circuits among which it is placed, clearly indicates it to have been situated in the Southern States. Rev. Francis Parker was appointed to the Southern Kingston, while Mr. Losee was sent to Kingston, Upper Canada.

There does not appear to have been any return of members from Canada up to the time of Mr. Losee's appointment to Kingston. The society at Augusta had been organized before this period, and so also had the class at Stamford. The year following Mr. Losee's appointment to the Canadian work we find the name of Kingston dropped and Cataraqui substituted, with a return of 165 members as the first fruit of Losee's labors, taken in connection with the efforts previously made by Heck and Embury in Augusta, and by Lyons and McCarty on the shores of the Bay of Quinte. Whether Mr. Losee or the Methodists in the east had any knowledge of Mr. Neal and his society about Niagara or not, cannot at this late period be determined, nor has it been ascertained whether or not the members in the Augusta or Stamford society were included in the returns.

Having organized those into societies along the Bay of Quinte who had been brought under the influence of Methodism by the exertions of his predecessors, and his own labors the winter previous, Mr. Losee commenced to form an extensive circuit east and west of Kingston.

In passing from settlement to settlement among the scattered inhabitants, the itinerant found here and there persons who had heard the Methodist preachers in Europe and the United States, prior to their removal to Canada, some of whom had been converted at their far-off homes, and others who, though not Methodists themselves, were yet favorably impressed by what they saw of them.

Many of the United Empire Loyalists who had left the United States shortly after its independence, as well as during the progress of the war, had been Methodists at home, and numbers of these, together with some of the disbanded British soldiers, and other emigrants more directly from the mother country, gladly opened their little cabins to the ministers of Christ. "Glad tidings of great joy" were proclaimed to them, and the word proved "quick and powerful." Sinners in the anguish of an awakened conscience cried out, "Men and brethren, what must we do to be saved?" while the earnest, faithful pastor exhorted them to repentance and faith through believing in Christ, and on many occasions strong men fell to the ground, apparently lifeless, and after a time returned to consciousness, praising God for a full salvation from sin.

So interested were the inhabitants by the religious services of Mr. Losee and the preachers who followed him that they travelled miles through the woods, often with their ox teams and and sleds, or on foot, not unfrequently carrying their children in their arms or upon their backs, in order that they might listen to the word of life; and upon the conclusion of the services, returned to their homes, lighting their paths in the night with their torches, illuminating the wilderness as they went, and causing the forest to resound with the songs of Zion. Souls were awakened or converted at almost every meeting, indeed at this period the declaration of the prophet was peculiarly applicable, "The wilderness and the solitary place shall be glad for them; and the desert shall rejoice, and blossom as the rose. It shall blossom abundantly, and rejoice even with joy and singing; the glory of Lebanon shall be given unto it, the excellency of Carmel and Sharon, they shall see the glory of the Lord and the excellency of our God."

The Church, however, had to pass through clouds as well as sunshine. There were stout-hearted sinners who opposed and persecuted the followers of Christ, and severely tried the piously disposed members of their own households, because of their religious principles. Even the messengers of peace themselves were frequently maltreated by men who neither regarded God nor man. But the little band of Israel moved forward in defiance of all opposing influences, "clear as the sun, fair as the moon, and terrible as an army with banners."

CHAPTER V.

FROM 1792 TO 1795.

Second year of regular missionary labor—Mr. Losee returns to the mission—Rev. Darius Dunham sent with him—The work is divided into two circuits—The first Quarterly Meeting—The Lord's Supper administered—The preachers repair to their respective fields of labor—Erection of the first Methodist meeting-house—Mr. Losee retires from the itinerancy, and subsequently leaves the Province—Canada is set off as a separate District—Arrival of more missionaries—They visit Niagara and hold a Quarterly Meeting—The people much encouraged.

Mr. Losee, at the Conference of 1792, gave such a feeling description of the lamentable spiritual destitution of the people in Canada, and pleaded their cause so earnestly, that Bishop Asbury resolved to send more laborers to his assistance. Rev. Darius Dunham, who had been ordained Elder the year previous, offered himself as a missionary, and was accepted.

After the close of the Conference, which this year commenced its session on the 15th of August, the two Missionaries set out for Canada, and reached Ernestown before the middle of the next month. The Canadian work was divided into two charges—the one east of Kingston, extending down the St. Lawrence, called Oswegotchie, and the other extending westward up the Bay of Quinte, called Cataraqui. The names of both circuits were of Indian origin, and referred more particularly to certain streams of water which ran through them, the one emptying into the St. Lawrence, and the other into the Bay of Quinte. Mr. Losee was appointed to the Oswegotchie charge, and Mr. Dunham to the Cataraqui. The preachers accompanied each other as far as Ernestown, in the vicinity of which Mr. Losee had preached the year previous.

Mr. Dunham being an Elder, as has already been intimated, and it being impracticable for the Presiding Elder, Freeborn Garretson, to visit the province at that time, it was resolved that the missionaries should hold Quarterly Meetings themselves. Accordingly, the first Quarterly Meeting in Canada was commenced on Saturday, the 15th of September, 1792. Word having been circulated in the various settlements with great rapidity that such a meeting was to be held, many came for miles through the woods, some to *see* a "Methodist Quarterly Meeting," and others to enjoy its spiritual advantages. The religious services were held in the barn of a Mr. Parrot, who lived in the first concession of Ernestown. So precious was the word of God in those days that the people were collected from various portions of six townships to attend this meeting. Can we not imagine that we see the whole scene—the people coming through the woods in small companies, men, women, and children, winding their way through swamps and round fallen trees, by means of narrow paths made through the bush. Entering the clearing they are joined by others who have travelled thither in a similar manner; other companies, and still others join them, until the whole congregation has assembled. Some to whom the thing is new stand at a distance from the barn, shy, yet curious; while others, a little bolder, come nearer and seat themselves upon the fallen logs, or upon the stumps, in order to witness all that shall take place among those strange people. But to those who have tasted the good word of life and of the powers of the world to come, it is a day of thankfulness and heartfelt rejoicing as they enter the barn, which is for the time being a sanctuary, and reverently kneeling, earnestly pray for the descent of the Holy Ghost upon themselves and upon the congregation. There are mourners in Zion there, too, fearful, yet hoping for a deliverance from sin. The preachers have taken their seats beside the small stand—the Bible and hymn-book are already upon it. At length the hymn is given out, and the assembled congregation join in singing.

> "Hark! in the wilderness a cry,
> A voice that loudly calls, Prepare!"

The melodious sound, greatly assisted by the powerful bass tones of Mr. Dunham, attracts those of the more fearful, or more careless, who have still remained at a distance, aloof. The second hymn is sung; the text is given out, and a soul-stirring sermon follows; weak believers are comforted; sinners are converted or awakened, and warm-hearted, earnest Christians rejoice.

After the religious services had been closed, and many who had gathered round the preachers and clasped their hands in friendship, had welcomed them to the country and extended to them their hospitality, a Quarterly Meeting Conference was called, and matters were arranged for the better co-operation with and support of each other. As many remained over night in the vicinity, staying in the shanties of their friends, a prayer-meeting was held in the evening, the people finding their way through the forest by the aid of their lighted torches.

The love-feast on Sabbath morning was new to many, but was solemn and impressive, and after the membership had related their Christian experience, the Methodist ministers, for the first time in Canada, proceeded to administer the sacrament of the Lord's Supper. How refreshing to the people of God, who had so long been deprived of the ordinances of the Lord's house, to be privileged thus once again to commemorate their Saviour's dying love. This was the beginning of good days among the Methodist people in Canada. Some who had come to the meeting cast down and disquieted in their minds because of their sins, returned to their homes rejoicing in God their Saviour. Others, who had been actuated by no higher motive in coming to the meeting than the gratification of an idle curiosity, were there arrested by the Spirit's power, and brought, with contrite hearts, to the foot of the cross; while bystanders exclaimed, "We have seen and heard strange things to-day."

Immediately after the Quarterly Meeting Mr. Losee set out for his circuit on the banks of the St. Lawrence, in order to visit the society in Augusta, and to open up new fields of labor; and Mr. Dunham commenced his work upon the shores of the Bay of Quinte.

Mr. Losee occasionally visited his old friends along the Bay, preaching to them as opportunity occurred, and took a very prominent part in the erection of the first Methodist meeting-house; but of this more anon. At the close of the year Mr. Losee returned 90 members in connection with the Oswegotchie circuit, and Mr. Dunham 259 in connection with the Cataraqui.

An occurrence transpired this year which, so far as it concerned Mr. Losee, was very unfortunate, as he was evidently a very pious man and devoted to his work as a Christian minister. He became ardently attached to a young woman who, it appears, did not reciprocate his feelings, and who in a short time accepted the heart and hand of another. Mr. Losee unwisely allowed this to have such an effect upon his mind as to unfit him for his work as an itinerant preacher, and he ever afterward acted only in a local capacity. After having recovered his mental equilibrium he left the country, and, so far as can be ascertained, returned again to it but once, and even then it was not till after a lapse of many years. Upon his final visit to Adolphustown he preached with great acceptability and energy, and was privileged to meet many of his old and tried friends. Though after his disappointment in love he never again resumed his place in the itinerant ranks, yet from occasional glimpses obtained of him it is evident that he maintained his integrity to the close of life.

Rev. S. Stewart, of the Niagara Annual Conference, who remembers having seen Mr. Losee and heard him preach, says: "I was present at the session of the New York Conference held in Troy, in 1821. Mr. Losee, then an old man with locks as white as wool, was invited to preach on Sabbath before the Conference. He ascended the pulpit steps with a weight of years, but delivered a powerful sermon from Mark x. 48: 'Thou Son of David, have mercy on me.'"

Dr. Stewart further adds, "Having heard much of William Losee when I travelled about Hallowell, I asked Father Vandusen, one of the first class-leaders in that section of Canada, if Losee was a good preacher. His reply was, 'He was a son of thunder, he feared no man, but warned every careless soul he met with on the Bay of Quinte to be reconciled to God.'"

After Mr. Losee ceased to travel, the care of both circuits seems to have devolved upon Mr. Dunham. It does not appear from the Minutes that any appointments were made to the Canadian work in 1793; yet, from the names of neither of the preachers sent there the previous year appearing this year in connection with any other circuit, it may be inferred that the omission was accidental. The probability is that Mr. Dunham had charge of the work, as his name appears again the next year in connection with it.

Mr. Dunham had studied medicine prior to entering the ministry, but he gave up profession, friends, and country, to come into the wilds of Canada in order to bear messages of peace to the people settled there. He united with the Conference on trial, in 1788. In 1790 he was ordained Deacon, and in 1792 he was elected and ordained Elder. During this period he travelled three circuits, viz., Shoreham, Cambridge and Columbia. He travelled the Cambridge circuit two years, and on the other two circuits one year each.

In 1792 he volunteered, as before mentioned, to come to Canada as a missionary.

The district of which Canada formed a part embraced, with that country, the region lying between it and Albany, in the State of New York, Freeborn Garrettson being the Presiding Elder. It does not appear, however, that he visited either of the Canadian circuits; it therefore devolved on Mr. Dunham, as he was an Elder, to hold the Quarterly Meetings, and administer the sacraments to the people where it was found expedient to do so.

At the Conference of 1794 Canada was set off as a separate District, Darius Dunham, P. E. The names of the circuits were again changed, and two additional missionaries sent out to supply the work. "Upper Canada, lower circuit, James Coleman; Upper Canada, upper circuit, Elijah Woolsey." As the fruits of the labors of Dunham and Losee up to this period, there were returned, members in society, 334.

It has been supposed by some that the preachers now extended their labors into the Niagara District, where Neal had previously formed one or more classes; but such a conclusion does not seem to be warranted, from the mere fact that the work was divided. It appears, however, that Mr. Dunham, as Presiding Elder, visited the Niagara country in the autumn of 1794, or in the spring of 1795, and held a Quarterly Meeting, and administered the ordinances of the Church. The first Quarterly Meeting in the Niagara District was held, it is believed, in Queenston. The people manifested the greatest anxiety to attend such a religious service; some of them had waited long and anxiously for this time to come. At length the day appointed arrived; the hour had come, and the people were assembled; but the Presiding Elder had not yet reached the place. Concern and solicitude were manifested by all; the Elder might have been taken ill upon his lonely journey, or he might perhaps have lost his way and be unable to reach his destination for several days. After some time, however, all anxiety was happily removed. "Two men upon horseback emerged from the woods. The strangers were Mr. Dunham and the preacher from the east." The people, overjoyed, ran to meet and welcome them; some wept, and others shouted for joy. The whole scene, as well as the religious services which followed, presented a touching exemplification of how highly the services of the sanctuary were prized by those dwellers in the forest. How ardently Mr. Neal and his little band had longed to see this day; and now for the first time they were to enjoy a love-feast in the wilderness, and partake of the sacrament from the hands of their own ministers. There was indeed great joy among the people.

At the Conference of 1795 the names of the circuits were again changed, as follows:—

Oswegotchie—James Coleman.

Bay of Quinte—Elijah Woolsey, Sylvanus Keeler.

Niagara—Darius Dunham.

The membership had increased to 483. The Canadian work was this year placed under the care of Rev. John Merrick, who had the charge of a very extensive District, embracing within its bounds, Philadelphia and Canada, with all the country between. No small charge this in those days when there were no railroads, few turnpikes, and, as he travelled wilderness-ward, still fewer bridges; where the only places of accommodation were the log cabins of the scattered settlers or the wigwams of the friendly Indians, and when even these failed, the shelter of the dark, deep woods, with only the blue canopy of heaven for a covering. Those were the times which tried men's faith and constancy, but they counted not their lives dear unto them, so that they might but win souls to Christ.

The Messrs. Coleman, Woolsey, Keeler, and Dunham were now travelling extensively along the margins of our lakes, bays, and larger rivers. The labors which these energetic and heroic men performed, the trials and privations they endured, and the difficulties they encountered and overcame, similar in many respects to those endured and encountered by Bishop Asbury in his labors, can never be fully known until the great day. Their efforts in the cause of God and of humanity were owned and blessed by their heavenly Father, and hundreds were converted through their instrumentality, and added to the Church.

CHAPTER VI.

1795 TO 1799.

Canada set off as a separate District a second time—The arrival of Messrs. Coate and Wooster—Commencement of the great revival—Not all sunshine—Mr. Wooster's health fails—The missionary called to his reward—Joseph Jewell arrives—Lorenzo Dow visits Canada—His labors—His eccentricities.

At the Conference of 1796 Canada was again set off as a separate District—Darius Dunham, P. E.

Bay Quinte Circuit—	Samuel Coate.
Oswegotchie "	H. C. Wooster.
Niagara "	James Coleman.

This Conference year was distinguished for a very extensive and powerful revival of religion, extending its influence to the various societies in this country, and to some portions of the United States. Dr. Bangs, in his History of the M. E. Church, vol. ii, p. 72, speaks of this gracious reformation as having taken place in 1797; but after much careful examination of the subject we have decided to follow the date of the general Minutes as that most likely to be correct, particularly so, as there do not appear to have been any appointments made to the Canadian circuits in 1797. We learn, too, from the statistics, that the returns in 1796 were 474, and that at the Conference of 1797 the members in society in Canada were 795, showing a large increase for the Conference year of 1796. The revival commenced at the first Quarterly Meeting held on the Bay of Quinte circuit after the arrival of Revs. S. Coate and H. C. Wooster. These zealous and successful servants of God suffered very severe hardships on their way to their work, having spent "twenty one days" from the time they left the Conference till they reached the Bay of Quinte. The State of New York, or at least Western New York, was as great a wilderness as Canada, and through this wilderness they travelled, lodging at night wherever they could find shelter, in the cabins by the way if they could; if not, in the woods. At last, however, they reached their destination in safety, and just in time to meet the friends gathered for the Quarterly Meeting. Gladly indeed were they welcomed by the people to whom they had come, and among whom they were to labor.

On Saturday, after the religious services, the Presiding Elder, Mr. Coate, and the official members of the Church retired to attend to the business of the Quarterly Conference, while Mr. Wooster remained to pray with some who were seeking religion. While thus engaged, the spirit of God descended upon the people in a most powerful manner; sinners cried for mercy, believers prayed for the sanctifying power of the Holy Ghost, and others fell prostrate to the floor, motionless, filled with that

> "Sacred awe which dares not move,
> And all the silent heaven of love."

Mr. Dunham, upon returning from the business meeting, entered the place of worship and found the congregation in what he considered a state of enthusiastic confusion. His piety and his patience both seem to have been brought to the test for the time; after viewing the scene a moment or two, however, he knelt down and prayed the Lord to stop what he considered to be "wild fire" from running among the people. Wooster, whose heart was "all on fire to be dissolved in love," happened to be praying near where Mr. Dunham knelt, and he at once began to pray for God to bless "Bro. Dunham," when suddenly the Spirit of the Lord descended upon Mr. D., and he fell prostrate to the floor as one slain. He soon recovered his strength, however, and joined in the exercises with hearty earnestness. Many were converted during the progress of the meeting, and some professed to have received the blessing of sanctification.

Sabbath was a day of peace and power. The love-feast was indeed a feast of love to most of those assembled there, and at the sacrament of the Lord's Supper, the Lord was manifested to his people in a gracious manner. The public services were not less interesting; the word was quick and powerful, for the preachers "spake as the Holy Ghost gave them utterance." It was a day long remembered by the people.

The Quarterly Meeting being now over, Mr. Wooster went to the Oswegotchie Circuit, scattering the "fire" as he went from society to society. Mr. Coate continued to fan the flame on his own charge, where it first commenced, and Mr. Dunham greatly assisted in the work as he passed round the District.

The increase in the societies on the three circuits has already been pointed out, but this was only a small portion of the good that resulted to the inhabitants of this province from this wonderful manifestation of God's presence. In several sections of the country the Methodists gained considerable influence, and many who up to this period had refused or neglected to attend the ministry of the word, were attracted by curiosity to hear the new preachers.

It must not, however, be fancied that all was now religious sunshine, or that the offence of the cross had ceased. On the contrary, there were many who not only blasphemed themselves, and said "these men are full of new wine," but bitterly persecuted these humble followers of Christ, and induced others to do so likewise. Upon one occasion, when Rev. Mr. Coleman was making a pastoral call upon one of his congregation who was seeking religion, her husband struck him severely upon the forehead, injuring him very much; and many of the members, also, were obliged to suffer violent persecution, for righteousness' sake.

At the end of two years it became painfully evident to Mr. Wooster's friends that he could not long continue active in his Master's work; consumption began to make rapid inroads upon his constitution. He continued to preach even after his voice was so far gone that he could only be heard in a whisper, and upon some occasions, seated on a chair, even spoke to the congregation through a second person. Mr. W. was a very earnest, devoted minister, frequently rising in the night to pray for the people of his charge.—Finding that his recovery was hopeless, he, though very weak, returned to his native land to die among his relatives. He reached his father's home in June, 1798, and died on the 6th of the following November, being in the 27th year of his age. Thus early fell Hezekiah C. Wooster, the first preacher called from the itinerant ranks in Canada to join the patriarchs and prophets in the kingdom of God. His ministry on earth was short but glorious.

The Conference of 1795 had set apart the first Friday in March as a day of special fasting and prayer, and it was recommended that the day should be observed "in all the societies and congregations with Sabbatical strictness." The ministry and the membership of the Methodist Church in those days attached much importance to the strictly religious observance of such recommendations, whether made by the Church or by the civil government; and consequently not unfrequently very beneficial results to the Church and the State followed. In accordance with the decision of the Conference, therefore, public religious services were held in various parts of Canada, as well as in the United States. The societies met in order to pray with and for each other. Self-examination was instituted, humiliation and self-denial practiced, and a spirit of reformation promoted. By such appointments the laws of God are venerated, and the statutes and authorities of the civil government respected. If the practice of fasting and humiliation were more strictly attended to in the present age it would have a tendency to elevate the standard of piety and of good morals among the people.

The gracious revival which followed the first Friday in March 1796, has already been briefly referred to; but the results of that reformation, and the revivals of the following year, both in Canada and the United States, will only be fully known when the assembled worlds are gathered together.

In 1798 the membership on the Canadian circuits was 809. Darius Dunham was again appointed Presiding Elder, and was also appointed to the charge of the Bay of Quinte Circuit; Oswegotchie, Samuel Coate; Niagara, James Coleman, Michael Coate, junior preacher. M. Coate was a brother of Samuel Coate, and had been removed from Middletown, Connecticut, to Niagara, Upper Canada. He remained but one year in this country and then returned home.

The general work continued to advance steadily, although at times the numbers remained stationary, and twice there was a decrease. This, however, instead of disheartening the missionaries, only served to stir them up to greater diligence.

In 1799 a new Presiding Elder was appointed to take charge of the Canadian work, and Mr. Dunham was thus relieved of a very heavy responsiblity. The appointments for the year were as follows, viz.:—

JOSEPH JEWELL, P. E.

Bay of Quinte—Samuel Coate.

Oswegotchie—Darius Dunham.

Niagara—James Coleman.

The membership was 866.

Mr. Jewell is said to have been a good preacher, an excellent singer, and a laborious minister. The work, as it will be seen hereafter, received a fresh impetus under his administration. New circuits were formed, the field of operations greatly enlarged, and many added to the Church. His District extended from Niagara to Prescott.

After many efforts of his friends, Lorenzo Dow had succeeded in being admitted on trial by a previous Conference. This year he was sent by Bishop Asbury to what was called upon the Minutes, Essex Circuit. Of this field of labor Mr. Dow thus speaks: "Mr. Asbury sent me into Canada to form a new circuit and break up new ground." This was a frequent method of appointing preachers in those days. They went out to *form new* circuits, and otherwise enlarge the work committed to their charge; and the preacher who was either unable or unwilling to do this was considered nothing more than a burden to the connection, and a very fit subject for a permanent location—and so he should be still.

Mr. Dow reached his new territory some time in August, but remained only until about the last of the following October, when he resolved on carrying out his project of visiting Ireland. He was, however, quite useful during his stay among the people of Essex. The "new ground" embraced portions of Vermont and Lower Canada. There were returned to the next Conference, as the fruit of Mr. Dow's labors, 270 members.

About twenty years previous to this Mr. Tuffey had preached to the British soldiers in Quebec, but Mr. Dow was the first travelling preacher in Lower Canada, appointed by the Conference to form circuits and organize societies.

Lorenzo Dow was an exceedingly eccentric but very useful man, and although he did many strange things, and made use of many singular expressions, yet, apparently in the end most of them assisted in the furtherance of his mission. The world was in the most literal sense his parish. He had no respect for order or for Conference rules, his only object being to preach, leaving others to gather the sheaves and take care of the wheat.

Mr. Dow's second visit to Canada was in 1802. He came

into the Province somewhere near Kingston, and passed down the banks of the St. Lawrence, preaching as he went. He also visited Canada a few years previous to his death, and preached in the District of Prince Edward, and in other sections of the country along the Bay of Quinte. He was now a very old man, dressed as plainly as before, and quite as singular as ever.

It is said that during this visit he had an appointment in the Methodist meeting-house in Belleville. The day being fine, so great a crowd gathered to hear him that there was not room for them in the house. In order to accommodate the concourse of people so that all might hear, Dow ordered a small waggon to be placed in the shade near one of the windows of the church, which he occupied as a stand. Temporary seats were arranged so as to accommodate as many as possible inside as well as outside the building. Among the crowd in front of the speaker was a very gaily dressed young lady, whose father being wealthy allowed his daughter abundance of means to dress as she pleased. This young person attracted considerable attention by the contempt she manifested towards both the preacher and the religious services. As soon as Dow had finished his sermon he stepped out of the wagon, and passing rapidly through the congregation suddenly touched the young woman upon the shoulder, saying abruptly, yet earnestly, "Young woman, if your head was cut off it would not be worth a cent, and your soul would go to the devil." Dow went on his way, allowing the crowd to disperse at their leisure. Miss —— left her seat bathed in tears, and on her way home and after her return, it might truly be said of her, as it was of Saul of Tarsus, "Behold she prayeth." She was in agony of soul for a time, but found peace with God and united with the Church.

CHAPTER VII.

SECULAR AFFAIRS, PIONEER DIFFICULTIES AND DANGERS.

Trials and privations of the settlers—A retrospect from 1776 to 1793—The Province divided—Quotations from Mr. Lymburner's speech in opposition to the project—Modes of travelling, and the routes taken by the early emigrants—Character of some of the hardships experienced—The first mills—A primitive bolter—The "hungry year"—Bill of fare of a pioneer preacher—Boy lost in the wilderness—The friendly Indian.

BEFORE entering upon the history of Canadian Methodism, at and since the commencement of the present century, it will perhaps interest the reader to give a few incidents illustrating the perseverance and energy of the early settlers under difficulties and privations of almost every kind. With regard to the privations of the pioneer preachers, let it be borne in mind that Mr. Losee came to Canada in 1790, and Mr. Dunham in 1792.

Prior to the Revolutionary War of 1776, but very few English families had emigrated to the upper portion of the colony. Lower Canada had not been settled by the French until 1608; for although Jacques Cartier had discovered it as early as 1534, still it required, with French management, about 74 years to succeed in planting the first permanent colony. In 1673 the French established a trading post where the city of Kingston now is, and about the same time, or shortly afterwards, commenced trading points at Niagara and Detroit.

Immediately after the conquest of Canada by the English in 1759, English as well as French traders visited the western wilds for the sake of the fur trade with the Indians; but it was not until 1778 and the following years that the upper country began to attract attention, and to be settled by loyalists from the United States. The population west of Lower Canada was in 1783 about 10,000 souls.

In 1788, under the administration of Lord Dorchester, the western portion of the Province of Quebec, as Canada was then called, was divided into four Districts, and in 1791, the year after Mr. Losee's first visit to the province, the country was divided into Upper and Lower Canada.

An idea may be formed of the state of the country at that time from the following extracts from the speech of Adam Lymburner, Esq., a merchant of Quebec, who was heard at the bar of the House of Commons in opposition to the bill providing for the division of the province:—

Mr. Lymburner observes:—"I beg leave to bring to the recollection of this honorable House that the distance from Quebec to Niagara is about 500 miles, and that Niagara may be considered as the utmost extent westward of the cultivable part of the province. For, although there is a small settlement at Detroit which is, and must be considered of great importance as a post of trade with the Indians, yet it must appear to this honorable House, from its situation it can never become of any great importance as a settlement; the falls of Niagara are an insuperable bar to the transportation of such rude materials as the produce of the land. As the farmers about Detroit, therefore, will have only their own settlement for the consumption of their produce, such a confined market must greatly impede the progress of settlement and cultivation *for ages to come*. There are, sir, between three and four thousand loyalists settled upon the banks of the river Cataraqui and the north side of Lake Ontario, in detached settlements, many of them at a great distance from the others, besides those on Lake Erie and at Detroit. Civil government cannot have much influence over a country so thinly inhabited, and where the people are so much dispersed. * * * * * We have had to encounter numberless difficulties which the pride and insolence of a set of men, whose minds were corrupted by the exercise of despotic power, have thrown in our way in every step we made. Such, sir, has been the unhappy tendency of the government of the province, that not only the people have been oppressed, and the resources of the country neglected; but almost every public building in the province has been suffered to fall into decay and perish. There is not a court-house in the province, nor a sufficient prison, nor a house of correction; there is not a public school-house. In short, the country is reduced absolutely to a state of nature. * * * *

"As British subjects who had forfeited their worldly possessions in the cause of the empire and its integrity, and had abandoned their homes in preference to an abandonment of their allegiance, and migrated to the wilderness of the north, to seek an asylum and a new country, they were worthy of the solicitude of the government and nation to whose cause they conscientiously adhered. The loyalists, as they were denominated, had located themselves principally in the western parts of the province, along the northern bank of the St. Lawrence, and in the vicinity of the Lakes Ontario and Erie, where the climate was more genial, and the soil better suited to agriculture, than in that section of the province known as Lower Canada. *The country bordering upon those great lakes was at the time a vast solitude, with but very little exception.*" * * * * * *

Such were the limited views taken at that period of the resources and importance of the great West, even by persons of intelligence and commercial experience.

"In that year, 1791, the agricultural settlements which

had been formed in the upper part of the province by disbanded soldiers and American loyalists had become considerable. Some thousands of people had spread themselves over the District of Niagara, and over lands still more remote from Quebec, particularly in the Western District. Between these new settlements and the country upon the St. Lawrence there were large tracts of wilderness intervening, which the Indians still held as hunting grounds, and through which there was no road whatever in the year 1791, nor for many years afterwards. The mail from Quebec found its way into this region but once or twice in a twelvemonth, for it was, in fact, only capable of being traversed by Indians and hunters, or by persons as active and hardy as they. The common way of travelling from the upper country to and from Montreal and Quebec was through the lakes and rivers in the summer season; and the passage was, in point of inconvenience, more formidable, and frequently occupied more time than the intercourse between Toronto and London (England) at the present day.

"On the assumption of the government by the first governor, General Simcoe, after the partition of the provinces in 1791, he issued an invitation to American settlers to come and establish themselves in Upper Canada. Well aware of the fertility of the land, the salubrity of the climate, the nature of its settlement, and extent of its capabilities, they came over in numbers, particularly from New Jersey and Pennsylvania, and some of the early settlers have said that when they first came into the township of Ancaster, they had to ride sixty miles to Niagara, through an Indian trail, for every article they required which they could not raise or manufacture."

The infant colony was steadily progressing, slowly, it is true, but not the less surely, and the facilities for communicating with other countries increasing. "In 1792 the mail between Quebec and New York was monthly, but not always regularly so. In the *Quebec Gazette* of the 10th November, 1792, it is stated that the latest news from Philadelphia and New York was to the 8th of October."

Between 1792 and 1796 postal communications seem to have increased very considerably, as a post office advertisement of that year informs the public that "a weekly conveyance by post has been established between Montreal and Burlington, in the State of Vermont." Another advertisement states that "a mail *for the upper countries*, comprehending Niagara and Detroit, will be closed at this office on Monday, the 30th instant, at four o'clock in the evening, to be forwarded from Montreal by the *annual winter express*, on Thursday, 3rd of February next;" and the *Quebec Gazette* of the 8th March, of the same year, informs its readers that "by this day's Burlington mail we have received New York papers of the 16th ultimo, they contain European intelligence to the 15th December, inclusive."*

Upon one point Mr. Lymburner's judgment was defective, viz., that the Falls of Niagara would for "ages to come" prove an insuperable bar to the progress of settlement and cultivation; but who at that date could dream of any feasible plan to surmount the formidable obstacle? The era of canals was not yet. With regard to the then condition of the country in other respects he appears to have been pretty accurate.

The three or four thousand U. E. Loyalists of whom he speaks as being located on the Cataraqui and the north side of Lake Ontario, were scattered from Prescott to York, now Toronto. Although Mr. L. does not state the number of inhabitants located about Niagara, and extending along Lake Erie to Detroit, it is estimated from other sources, as has been previously mentioned, that there were in all Upper Canada about 10,000 souls.

* See Smith's Canada.

How little did Mr. Lymburner, or his contemporaries, imagine the marvellous changes that would be wrought by persevering industry and untiring energy in less than half a century; the frail canoe discarded for the stately steam-packet, and the wearisome and dangerous journey on foot or horse-back, along the trail of the Indian, for the secure and comfortable seat in the rail-car; portages dispensed with, and communication by water obtained by means of the canal; and the *annual winter express* superseded by the lightning telegraph. Such is the march of science and civilization; onward, and ever onward.

The modern traveller, while speeding past the smiling fields of waving grain at the rate of forty or fifty miles per hour, frequently asks, "How did our forefathers reach their homes in this then wilderness waste? By what means did they transport their families and effects over hundreds of miles without either roads or bridges?" It is to be regretted that the history of those times has not been more carefully preserved. Sufficient, however, has been handed down to give us a faint idea of the sufferings and privations endured by the pioneer settlers.

Many of those who, being strongly attached to the British Government, adhered to that standard at the commencement of and during the American Revolution, having learned that Canada offered them an asylum from the bitterness of warfare and of civil strife, sold or abandoned their possessions in the United States, and bent their course thither. Placing as many as they possibly could of the more feeble old men and the women upon horseback, and having arranged large baskets or panniers in pairs, each containing a child, so that one hung on each side of the horse, while the stouter members of the party walked beside, or drove what cattle they could bring with them, companies of these loyal fugitives from the different States started *en route* for Canada. How many a longing look went back to the dear old homestead, seen now for the last time; or how many a sigh welled up from the hearts of the wanderers, as they remembered that they were leaving forever the scenes of their happy childhood, who can tell? Human joys and sorrows are the same in all ages.

The distance travelled in a day depended greatly upon the situation of the country through which they were obliged to pass. At times a temporary shelter was erected for comfort or safety during the night, or upon stormy days; but more frequently the blue vault of heaven was their only roof—the damp, cold ground their only bed. Generally several families accompanied each other, and erected their camps closely together, for mutual protection, in case of an attack by wild beasts, or by Indians, many of whom were far from friendly, their united camp fires not only promoting their safety at night, but helping in a measure to enliven the vast solitude.

The bill of fare of the immigrants would not present a very tempting appearance to an epicure, but there were few dyspeptics in those primitive times. Boiled wheat, boiled corn, or corn meal when there was time to pulverize it in the mortar, fish when near the streams, the flesh of wild fowl and wild animals, with such roots and greens as were considered fit for food, which could be gathered in the woods through which they were travelling. As these journeys were usually undertaken in the warm season the cattle and other domestic animals had plenty of food, and game was easily procured for the consumption of the family.

Frequently when there were several cows in the drove there was more milk than the travellers needed for present use; accordingly two small churns were procured, into which the surplus milk was strained; these, like the panniers, were balanced across the horse in the morning, and the motion of the beast during the day agitated the milk, so that when they stopped at night the milk was found to be churned, and they had a supply of butter for their evening's repast.

Very often several weeks were spent travelling in this manner before the party reached their destination—rivers had to be crossed on rafts, or forded, swamps to be wallowed through or a detour made round them, and miles upon miles of trackless forest to be penetrated ere they reached their new home.

The more highly favored emigrants who had resided previously on the borders of the lakes or large rivers, adopted other means of transportation. These came most part of the way from New York by water. With regard to this route Bishop Richardson has furnished the following interesting account:

"The route of transit for more than a century from New York and the settlements along the Hudson to this country, was by means of the Mohawk and Oswego rivers and their connections. By means of this highway through the wilderness, the seaboard was connected with the waters of the great lakes. This brought Oswego into note at a date coeval with the settlement of Canada. The French first built a fort at the mouth of the Oswego River, and tradition speaks of severe fighting there between them and the old British Colonists of New York and the adjoining provinces. It subsequently fell, with the other French possessions on the lakes and rivers, into the hands of the British, who erected the fort on the east side of the river, which after the Revolutionary war was surrendered to the United States.

"The route of travel was up the Hudson to Schenectady, thence up the Mohawk to Fort Sanwix, where the city of Rome now stands. Here was a short portage to Wood Creek, or as it is now called by some writers, Norval Creek, thence along the windings of this muddy stream to Oneida Lake, and through the lake to Three Rivers' Point, thence down Oswego River to Lake Ontario. This route from the Hudson was performed by means of Schenectady boats, and occupied a period of several weeks. Rich and poor, gentle and simple, young and old, families of emigrants and others, all had to contend with the stones, shoals, mosquitos, wild animals, and other annoyances, along this circuitous route, in an open six oar boat. For weeks together the voyagers had to subsist on such stores as they could bring with them, or procure from the water or the woods, sleeping as best they could in the open boat or on the shore.

"Their dangers and hardships were by no means ended on their arrival at Oswego. The best craft in those days for crossing the great lakes were schooners and sloops, from 30 to 100 tons, and these small vessels were dependent on wind and weather as to the time of their departure; and when they would go out it frequently occupied a week or two to get to the western parts of Lake Ontario. Sometimes when no rigged vessel was in port, which was often the case, on the approach of winter they would venture in open boats to reach Kingston, by coasting along the lake shore to the eastward of Oswego and the foot of Lake Ontario, at the imminent peril of their lives.

"When I was a boy, well do I remember hearing annually of one or more boats being wrecked, and numerous lives lost along that dangerous part of the coast between Oswego and Stoney Point; while others would be for days storm-bound with wind, rain, or snow in the mouths of the numerous creeks along that part of the lake.

"At the commencement of the war which eventuated in the independence of the United States, Upper or Western Canada was scarcely known to the people of the revolted colonies. The only way of coming from the States to the eastern part of Upper Canada was that above mentioned, by Oswego, and another by a rough road leading through an unbroken wilderness for more than a hundred miles, to Oswegotchie, now Ogdensburg. By way of Lakes George and Champlain, however, lay an early frequented route, but this led into Lower Canada, and communicated directly with Montreal.

"Several of the early settlers of the Home and Niagara

Districts, and about Long Point, found their way from the State of Pennsylvania, through the woods, on pack horses, encamping in the wilderness with their families for weeks together. It must be left to imagine the destitution, privations and hardships attendant on these incipient beginnings of a new settlement in an isolated wilderness, without the most ordinary means of subsistence.

"Tradition speaks of the people having to live on fish, roots and wild game; and when they had, without the ordinary implements of agriculture, cleared a small patch of ground, and raised some Indian corn, potatoes, or a little wheat sown on a newly burnt fallow, among the stumps, and dragged with a bush, or harrow composed of wooden teeth, there was no mill or other machinery to make meal or flour in many cases short of thirty to eighty miles. I have heard of persons carrying a grist through the bush on their backs fifteen or sixteen miles to and from the mill.

"To add to their privations they encountered the 'scarce year'—about 1793 or 1794—when the products of the earth having failed, and there being no means of obtaining supplies from abroad, famine stared them in the face, and indeed it is said numbers were actually famished to death, and more victims would have fallen but for an unusual abundance of fish, which Providence caused to frequent the streams during the 'hungry season.' I have heard the 'old people' talk feelingly about this year of famine.

"It was to labor and suffer in this remote region, and among the settlers in such circumstances that the first missionaries of the Methodist Episcopal Church penetrated the woods and swamps intervening between the settlements in the United States and Canada.

"I recollect conversing nearly forty years since with an aged sister, VanCamp, who was among the first fruits of Methodism in Canada. She told me that she had her residence at first in the township of Cornwall, and in the winter of 1790 or 1791 she saw through her window, one exceedingly severe day—a snow storm then raging—a man on horseback, riding through the tempest. He soon knocked at her door, and asked shelter and the rites of hospitality. Although a stranger, she took him in. He was suffering from hunger and cold, but his good hostess soon made him comfortable in both respects. He told her in the meantime that his name was Losee, that he was a Methodist missionary, and that he would preach if he could procure a congregation. Though a stranger to the Methodists, Mrs. VanCamp cheerfully consented to the proposition, and sent her boys out to notify the scattered neighbors that a Methodist preacher was at her house, and that if they would come out he would preach to them that evening. Thus was the public worship of God introduced into those parts, and Mrs. V. and some others became happy converts to the faith of the gospel of Christ, so strikingly exemplified in the life, labors, sufferings, boldness and zeal of the herald of the cross.

"The following incident in the life of my father may serve to show the dangers and difficulties attendant upon the communications by water between places adjacent to each other, yet upon opposite sides of the lake: So late as 1795 or 1796 the American troops at Fort Oswego had to look to Canada for flour, and my father contracted to furnish a supply in the fall of the year, just previous to the setting in of winter. He took in his load, purchased of the families about the Bay of Quinte, and sailed for Oswego, but just at the mouth of the river encountered a severe wind, which baffled all attempts at making harbor—no steam power for navigation purposes in those days. Being driven into the lake, and a furious snow storm ensuing, he was driven, after combatting all night with the wind, waves and snow, into the mouth of Sandy Creek, and wrecked, being now between twenty and thirty miles eastward of Oswego. My father and a seaman who was with him swam to the shore, but here was only snow and woods—no friendly roof to shelter them, no food to satisfy the cravings of hunger, nor fire to warm the poor benumbed limbs, and no settlement short of Oswego to the west, and a reported commencement of one called Rotterdam about fifteen miles, through dense woods and swamps, to the southward. They first tried the woods, but sinking above the knees in snow and slush they had to abandon that route, and take the course of the lake shore to Oswego, intersected as it was by several streams. They commenced their journey as already intimated, without food or fire. Providence, however, was kind to them in the time of their greatest extremity, for on arriving at the mouth of the Salmon River, twelve or fifteen miles east of Oswego, they discovered a boat on the opposite side with her crew, storm-bound in the creek. They called, and were immediately brought over and relieved. My father proceeded with the boat to Oswego as soon as possible, and reported the total loss of his vessel and cargo. Winter having now set in, and navigation closed for the season, he had no way left of returning home but by Schenectady or Albany, and thence by Lake Champlain and Lower Canada to Kingston. His home was not reached before the month of February. My mother in the meantime, at Kingston, had heard nothing of him further than that the vessel was wrecked and the cargo lost, and that he had reached Salmon River, and gone from thence to Oswego. Judge of her anxiety, with her little family, alone during those dreary months till my father made his appearance suddenly in the middle of the winter.

"This incident may be taken as a sample of similar disasters, and the extreme difficulty and danger of travelling in those days."

The case of Mr. Richardson was by no means an isolated one. Mr. Thomas Horner, the first settler in the now County of Oxford, came into Canada by the Mohawk route, bringing with him from Albany materials for the building of a saw-mill, which he erected near the present location of the Princeton Station on the Great Western Railroad. Mr. Horner and a Mr. Watson had been invited into the country by Governor Simcoe, and in 1793 they reached the township of Blenheim, which a party had been sent out to survey. Mr. Horner's nearest neighbors at that time on the east were in the township of Brantford, and to the west in the township of Chatham. But nothing daunted by the sparseness of the population he built the mill at great labor and expense, having been obliged to draw his machinery, after it had reached the head of Lake Ontario, the remainder of the way—through the woods—to Blenheim upon ox sleighs. The mill, however, was not completed so as to commence work until 1795.

The father of the late Bishop Reynolds, with his family, left the Hudson and came into Canada by the route above described, and after leaving Lake Ontario travelled through the wilderness to the township of Burford, and settled there in 1796. The journey from the Hudson to Burford occupied a little more than two months—it would now occupy about as many days. Here the family remained until the year 1803, when they removed to the township of Dorchester and erected a saw-mill not far from what is now the Dorchester Station.

Arrived at their new home, the hardships of the emigrants, so far from being ended at the close of their toilsome and dangerous journey, were scarcely more than commenced. Houses were to be built, forests to be cleared away, and food and raiment to be provided for large and in many instances helpless families. The style of architecture in that era was sufficiently primitive. The builders having provided a sufficient number of logs of the size required, they began their operations, laying the logs upon one another, and "notching" them with an axe at the corners, in order to make them fit firmly. When the wall had attained to the desired height a cob-roof, as it was called, was put on, *i. e.*, the gables were built up straight while the sides were drawn in by making the logs placed in the gable each somewhat shorter than the one immediately beneath it, leaving an equal length of the inequality at each end until the building terminated in a peak at the top. This was then covered either with elm bark or with clapboards of oak, ash, or pine, split out about four feet long, something like roughly rived shingles. Another method of covering the roofs was to procure basswood troughs, two of which were placed closely together and a third placed in an inverted position over them, causing, of course, the water to run into the troughs beneath. As to doors and windows, the proper openings were indeed made in the walls, but as there was neither glass nor boards to be had, a quilt in most instances answered the purpose of a door, while the place designed for a window was seldom covered with anything more weather-proof than a curtain, and that frequently an improvised substitute for the genuine article. The edifice was generally minus a chimney, the smoke making its way at will through an orifice in the roof near the gable, and the earth answered for a floor. The more enterprising of the settlers, however, those who had an eye to appearances and comfort, soon furnished their habitations with clapboard doors, floors of basswood slabs, and stick and mud chimneys. Such, as a general rule, were the houses of the pioneer settlers; some few perhaps were better than those above described, but many were vastly worse, one room frequently constituting kitchen and dining room, parlor and all. But in these rude cabins many a Methodist preacher was hospitably entertained, being upon each return cordially welcomed to a seat at the huge fireside, and as kindly invited to partake of their homely meal of Johnny-cake and venison, fish or wild fowl, as the case might be; and when bed time came, after having prayed with the family, he stretched his wearied limbs upon the earthen floor, by the fire, and slept soundly until the morning, when, refreshed and invigorated by the last night's rest, he set out again in pursuit of the object of his mission, hoping to "hunt up the lost sheep of the house of Israel." Thus for weary, weary miles did the early itinerant push his way through the forest, being guided by marked trees, or by the sun, or following the narrow Indian trail, often from morning until night, till at last tired and foot-sore he emerged into another "clearing," with its shanty in the centre, to be again warmed and fed, and permitted to occupy a bed similar to the one of the night previous.

Many of the new comers were destitute, and as they were generally very far removed from the comforts of civilization, without mills or clothing establishments—although assisted as far as was practicable by the government, for the space of two years—in many places they suffered severely from lack of the necessaries of life.

As soon as it could be done, a spot of ground was cleared, rye and wheat sown, and corn and potatoes planted, and when fit to use, the corn was roasted or boiled, and eaten as we now use "hot corn;" when it became too hard to be eaten in this way it was shaved from the cob by means of a jack-plane or jointer, and boiled until it became soft, and was used with milk or maple molasses. After it became fully ripe the corn was shelled, dried, and pulverized in a mortar.

The construction of these primitive mills was as follows:—A small hollow ironwood tree was procured, a portion of which was taken, and after the cavity had been thoroughly cleansed, one end of the hollow piece of wood was slipped over and fitted upon a stump which had been previously prepared for the purpose, the top of the stump being made to serve for the bottom of the mortar. The mortar having been made to stand firmly on its solid pedestal, a spring-pole, similar to the old-fashioned well-sweep, was fastened to the ground in such a manner that it would spring at the top, and to the top of this a piston was attached, through which, a short distance from its lower end, a wooden pin had been put, in order that the *miller* might use both hands at his work; and the *mill* was completed. The work of pulverizing now commenced; the corn having been put in the mortar, the miller caught the pin in the piston with both hands, and by means of the spring worked the piston up and down until the corn was sufficiently pounded. The meal thus prepared was then sifted, the finest being taken for bread, and the remainder, after being again put in the mortar and still further pulverized, was made into samp or sepawn.

The sieve was simple and easily constructed, being made of an animal's pelt properly cleaned and dried, then stretched upon a hoop and punctured with a hot spindle, the holes being made so small that though they allowed the meal to go through they retained the bran and the chaff.

Mr. Andrew Ostrander and his wife came to this country at quite an early day, and settled near Niagara. Having succeeded in harvesting his first crop of wheat, Mr. Ostrander proposed pulverizing some of it instead of the corn, but the common sieve, it was found, would not separate the bran from the flour. Mrs. Ostrander, however, was determined to have a loaf of "wheaten" bread once more, and set her woman's wits to work to contrive a bolt which would answer the purpose. A happy thought at last occurred to her. Her "Sunday bonnet," which she had brought to the country with her, she had laid aside, having no further use for it in the woods; to it she went, and having ripped out the millinet,* she washed it thoroughly and stretched it upon a small hoop. Her bolt being now prepared, and Andrew having pounded the wheat, the contrivance was tested, pronounced a success, and "wheaten" bread and "short cake" again delighted the eyes and the palates of the solitary emigrants.

Mrs. Ostrander was born on the 23rd of April, 1760, and died on the 25th of April, 1864, being thus at the time of her death one hundred and four years old, the last seventy of which she was a Methodist. In her day what great changes had been effected, not only in America but throughout the world.

* An article used fifty years ago or more for giving shape to bonnets; it was similar to, though not quite so close in texture as that now used in bonnet shapes

Methodism, from being a little one, had become a thousand, and the small one a great nation, since she had first been reached through its instrumentality, and had cast in her lot with its people.

At first the settlers transported nearly everything on horses, or in packs upon their backs; but after mills had been erected within ten or fifteen miles of them other methods were adopted. Sometimes three bushels of grain were placed across an ox-yoke and in this manner conveyed to and from the mill; or, if the bushes and large trees had been cut out of the way, another kind of conveyance was used; a large forked stick was procured and the thickest part hewed down to the size of a sleigh tongue. Upon the crotch of this a box was constructed capable of holding five or six bushels of grain, and with the tongue securely fixed in the ring of an ox-yoke, and the prongs dragging on the ground behind, the vehicle moved off. This was considered a great improvement upon the old methods of travelling. Other improvements, however, followed, the wooden-wheeled truck and ox-sled superseding the ox-yoke and forked stick, to be in their turn superseded by the cart and the Pennsylvania waggon.

Of the sufferings of the early pioneers, from want of proper clothing, and from want of food, we can scarcely have any adequate idea, the military and government stations being at such distances from each other, and often from the settlements, that it required days, and sometimes weeks to reach one; so that, even when supplied by the government, their families were often extremely destitute, frequently living for a length of time upon ground-nuts, acorns, hickory nuts, or leeks, and when even these could not be procured, upon the *inner bark of trees*, or wild greens, boiled. At some periods, so great was the destitution, that when the wheat and rye had reached a milky state it was frequently cut and dried sufficiently to be rubbed out by hand and boiled for food, so as to support nature until the crop came to maturity. This was especially the case during the "hungry year," when, the crops having failed the season before, hundreds nearly starved to death, and parents often heard their children crying for food, which they were not able to give them, to allay the cravings of hunger. During this year the younger children, in many instances, subsisted for days together upon milk alone; while the elder members of the families relied entirely upon such roots and greens as they were able to gather.

One case in point will illustrate, in a degree, the privations both of pioneer settlers and pioneer preachers. In 1806 Rev. Robert Perry was sent, by the N. Y. Conference, with Rev. Thomas Whitehead, to the Niagara Circuit. Mr. Perry succeeded in penetrating as far as the western part of the township of Ancaster, where a settlement had been made near what is now known as Jerseyville. Here a family named Wilson had settled. The nearest mill to the settlement was at Niagara, and the grain having been brought from the upper part of the township to the "head of the lake," it was sent on to mill, in charge of some of the neighbors, while the rest returned to their homes for a few days, and at the appointed time journeyed back to the lake to meet the boat and get their respective loads; but it not unfrequently happened that the boat was detained by foul weather, or other unpropitious circumstances, and did not return at the time she was expected, thus causing very great uneasiness to both those who had gone to meet it and those who remained at home. On one occasion Mr. Perry, upon coming to his appointment at Mr. Wilson's house, found that Mr. W. had "gone to mill," and had not yet returned. The people assembled for worship and the services were conducted as usual; but after the congregation had left, Mrs. W. told him she had nothing which she could give him to eat excepting roasted potatoes. She had had part of a loaf the day before, but expecting her husband would have returned in time for preaching she had given the piece of bread to a sick woman in the neighborhood, and since Mr. W. had left, the cows, too, had strayed away, and she and her little son—a lad of nine or ten years—had searched for them in vain, so that she had not even her usual supply of milk and butter. The preacher partook of the repast, *Lentine* as it was, which was offered in a spirit of generous hospitality, and proceeded on his way.

Shortly after the departure of Mr. Perry, as Mrs. Wilson was looking anxiously toward the point whence she could catch the first glimpse of her husband if he were returning, she heard a cow-bell, and hoping that her cows might be with the cattle whose bell she heard, she sent her little boy to see if they were there, and if so, to bring them home; charging him at the same time if they were not there to come directly back, lest he might get lost in the woods. The boy, not finding the cattle, as he expected, attempted to return, but mistook his path. Becoming alarmed at his prolonged absence his mother started towards the woods to meet him, calling him at intervals. But no answer meeting her agonized ear, and finding that despite every effort she was unable to hear him or make him hear her, she became convinced that he was lost, and hastening back to the house, she blew the horn—the mode of announcing to the neighbors that something was wrong and help needed. Word flew quickly; the neighbors rallied; every effort was made for the child's recovery, but without success. Night, in all its darkness and gloom, had set in, and further search then was impossible. Who can portray the anguish of that mother's heart during those dreary watches which intervened between that and morning light. In addition to the suspense and anxiety occasioned by the protracted absence of her husband, she has now the terrible thought resting upon her that her child is lost in the wilderness; perhaps hopelessly lost; even now he may have become the prey of wolves, or if not, he may starve to death long before aid can reach him. Next morning the search was resumed, but in vain, as far as the child's friends were concerned. To return, however, to the lad. When he reached the strange cattle, and found that his father's were not with them, he turned to retrace his steps, but getting bewildered he took a wrong course, and wandered on till he became convinced that he was lost. In his efforts to get again upon the right path he ran first in one direction and then in another, until he came upon an Indian trail, where he cried and halloed, hoping to hear some one reply, if it were only an Indian. Failing in this he continued to run on, carefully following the trail, till just at dusk he came out upon the Grand River, at a spot near which there was a large camp of Indians. Here again he called and cried till he attracted the attention of an old chief, who, seeing the child's evident weariness and distress, went to him, soothed his fears, and taking him to his tent placed food before him. Having ascertained who he was and whence and why he came, the old man told him that he must stay with him for the night, and as he had seen the cows and knew where they were, he would take both him and them home in the morning. Thus assured, the tired child slept till sunrise, when, true to his promise, the chief roused him and conducted him and his cattle back to the settlement, to the great joy of his agonized mother.

CHAPTER VIII.

FROM 1800 TO 1804.

Statistics of the Church in 1800—The itinerancy further strengthened—Formation of Ottawa Circuit—Opposition encountered—The humble disciple and the violent persecutor—Time of trial—Saul among the prophets—Camp-meetings—Upper Canada Circuit organized—Its extent—State of the work in 1801—Nathan Bangs enters the itinerancy—Sketch of his early life—1801 to 1807—Then and now—How Mr. Bangs found the work, and how he left it—Mr. Robinson is sent to Canada—After a time he locates—Becomes deranged!—Incidents of his later years.

FROM the time Methodism had been established in New York, by Embury, in 1766, up to the commencement of the present century, embracing a period of thirty-four years, the societies in the United States had increased to 63,958, and in Canada to 936, there being in both countries 287 preachers. Included in this calculation were 13,452 colored people, showing that from the first the M. E. Church manifested a deep interest in the moral improvement and salvation of the slaves.

At the several Conferences of 1800, 41 preachers were admitted on trial, 23 were received into full connection, 24 located, 3 withdrew, and 4 died. Among those who located was Darius Dunham, who had for eight years braved the trials, privations and labors incident to the life of a missionary in the wilds of Canada. This year the work in Canada was further strengthened. The appointments were as follows:

JOSEPH JEWELL, Presiding Elder.

Niagara—Joseph Sawyer.

Bay Quinte—Sylvanus Keeler, William Anson.

Oswegotchie—Joseph Jewell, James Herron.

Grand River—Daniel Pickett.

The Ottawa, or Grand River Circuit, as it was called, to which Mr. Pickett, who was a man of energy and of promising talents, was sent, was entirely new ground. Quite a number of Americans had settled on both sides of the Ottawa above the French settlements, and it was to these that Mr. Pickett directed his labors.

Many years prior to this period the French, and at a later date the Americans, had passed up the Ottawa to French River, and thence into lakes Huron and Superior, a distance of many hundred miles, in order to secure furs from the Indians; and Mr. Asbury, as was his practice, sent out preachers to instruct the people as fast as he could find a new opening and a man suitable for the work.

Referring to Mr. Pickett and his first circuit, Mr. Playter says, page 68,. "He was a useful, zealous man, and was well spoken of thirty years after by the old settlers." Mr. P. went cheerfully to his remote charge, and labored diligently to build up the cause of his Master among the people to whom he had been sent. One circumstance which occurred while he was on this circuit is, perhaps, not unworthy of record.

Here, as elsewhere, there were some who were strongly opposed to the introduction of Methodism among them, while others gladly welcomed the way-worn missionary. Belonging to the class of eleven persons which Mr. Pickett found on his arrival, (but by whom organized we are not informed), was a person whom, for convenience, we will call Stephen, and in the same neighborhood was a violent opposer whom we will call Saul. Stephen, who had but recently moved into the bush, was poor, with a family of small children depending upon him; his entire stock consisted of one cow, and from her their chief support was derived. Saul, on the contrary, having been longer in the country, was in quite comfortable circumstances, decidedly opposed to Methodism, and a bitter enemy of Stephen, whom he averred was, with all his shouting and loud professions of piety, nothing else than a hypocrite. So much did he dislike his poorer neighbor that, although he had an abundance of hay, he would not sell him any to assist him in wintering the cow; the consequence of which was that the poor beast had to live upon browse and the moss from the tops of the trees which her owner cut down for her. About the middle of the winter there came one of those fearfully stormy nights which, when they come even in cleared countries, make people gather more closely round the fire, thankful for the kindly warmth and shelter. Poor Stephen and his wife slept but little all that stormy night; sad forebodings filled their minds, for their poor cow was standing in her log shelter without one mouthful, and if she died what was to become of them? In the midst of their forebodings they strove to encourage each other by repeating such assuring promises as are given to those who put their trust in God, remembering that cheering assurance, "The Lord will provide."

As soon as the day dawned the poor man hastened to learn the fate of his cow, when, to his utter amazement, he found her eating hay, a large bundle being before her. The question now arose, "who had brought and given the cow the hay?" The falling snow had covered up the track, and no trace of the donor could be discovered. Stephen informed his wife of the circumstance, and both arrived at the conclusion that the "fodder" had not been brought through kindness, and very soon found their surmises to be too true. In a short time it began to be whispered in the neighborhood that Stephen had been stealing hay from Saul. Saul asserted that he had been informed that Stephen's cow had been supplied with hay that "awful stormy night," and he was sure hay had been taken from his mow. It was now noised about that Stephen, with all his *profession* of piety, was a *thief*, and great was the commotion in the little society, as well as among the people of the world, for truly circumstances seemed very much against poor Stephen. A charge was entered against him and presented to the preacher on his next visit. Mr. Pickett hastened to visit the accused, who with his wife was now almost heart-broken. They were poor, and had been despised before because they were Methodists, and now they were accused of theft, and had no apparent means of establishing their innocence. To add to their sorrow and mortification, too, a stigma was now fastened upon the infant society. Mr. P. listened with great solicitude to their account of the matter, and finally decided that he would postpone all Church proceedings until his next appointment, at which time the matter should be thoroughly investigated, exhorting the society at the same time to make the matter the subject of earnest prayer.

In due time Mr. Pickett returned, and as it was generally understood that Stephen was that day to have his trial before the society or a committee, the congregation was unusually large, as all were anxious to learn the result.

At the appointed hour the preacher announced his text, dwelling chiefly upon the wisdom and justice of God, and pointing out that every work would be brought into judgment, with every secret thing, whether it were good or evil, at the great day of account. He concluded by exhorting his hearers to prepare for that day by repenting of their sins and accepting of Christ as their Saviour. The speaker had unusual liberty; God was doubtless with his servant that day.

After the religious services were ended, Saul rose from his place in the congregation and requested permission to speak a few words before the people dispersed. He said he had a confession to make before God and his people; he had himself brought the hay in question to Stephen's cow, and had then reported to the class-leader that he had no doubt but that Stephen had stolen the fodder from his barn. This he had done, he said, in order to injure his neighbor and the Methodists generally in the estimation of the people; but now would ask forgiveness of both them and God, and while he had any hay Stephen's cow should not want. As may well be imagined, such a disclosure had a thrilling effect upon the congregation; Stephen grasped Saul's hand in token of forgiveness, while louder than ever he shouted "Glory to God" for His mercy. Stephen wept tears of joy, while a good old sister commenced singing, in which she was joined by the class,

> "Ye fearful saints, fresh courage take.
> The clouds ye so much dread
> Are big with mercy, and shall break
> In blessings on your head."

The penitent offered himself to the society, and the people went away saying, "We have seen strange things this day. Saul is also among the prophets."

The reformation to which allusion has already been made as having commenced at Napanee, had extended more or less all along the Canada border and across into the neighboring States. In this year, 1800, camp-meetings were commenced, and served greatly to promote the cause of God, not only among the Methodists, but among the Presbyterians and others. As, however, it is designed to devote a chapter to these meetings and their results, we will not treat the subject further in this place.

In 1801 the work had so extended that 10 preachers were appointed to the Canada District. The membership had increased to 1159, and there were 5 circuits, one of which was called Upper Canada. To this extensive charge the Presiding Elder was appointed, having a young man as an assistant. Where the P. E. was to preach besides attending his Quarterly Meetings on the four charges, extending from the Ottawa to Long Point, is left to conjecture; it may have been designed by Bishop Asbury that he should take charge of whatever field Samuel Draper should be assigned to upon his arrival in the country.

The following is the list of appointments for the year:—

CANADA DISTRICT—JOSEPH JEWELL, P. E.

Upper Canada—Josepch Jewell, Samuel Draper.
Niagara—Joseph Sawyer, Seth Crowell.
Bay Quinte—Sylvanus Keeler, Daniel Pickett.
Oswegotchie—William Anson, James Aikens.
Ottawa—John Robinson, Caleb Morris.

Methodism had now extended its benign influence into nearly every settlement in the country. Eleven preachers were travelling from the Ottawa in the east to the Thames in the west. These men preached generally twice, and sometimes three times in the day, many weary miles intervening between the preaching places. Where the people were sufficiently near to each other they collected them together, prayed with them and expounded the Scriptures to them; then, having delivered their message, they went on their way, looking up and comforting others with the glad tidings of salvation. In not a few instances the settlements were from ten to fifty miles apart, and in some instances still farther, often compelling the weary itinerant to sleep in the woods or lodge in Indian camps. Their food was generally of the coarsest description, and often of the poorest quality of that. But their watchword was, Onward—the salvation of souls their delight.

Mr. Asbury was not slow to occupy every opening which occurred, and as emigrants were fast flocking into the country he saw the necessity of sending more laborers into the vineyard. Among those who entered the itinerant ranks about this time was Nathan Bangs. Mr. Bangs had come to Canada in the spring of 1799; he was converted shortly afterwards, and here entered the Methodist ministry, in which he afterwards acted so prominent a part. Speaking of his first visit to Niagara Falls, in company with his brother-in-law, Seth Smith, and family, he says, "The day after our arrival in Canada we reached the Falls of Niagara. Here we made a halt and went down to the river's bank to view the stupendous scene. The water comes rushing and foaming down for two or three miles before it reaches the chute, where it plunges, in two immense masses, one hundred and seventy feet, into the yawning gulf, and then sweeps away, in whirling eddies and billows, about seven miles, into Lake Ontario. We stood in silent awe as we gazed on this wonder of creation. I lay down upon Table Rock, which shelved over a part of the frightful abyss and shook with the unceasing thunder of the waters; and as I looked down I became dizzy and appalled. The rock has changed much since that day. No description of this grand scene, that I have seen, approaches the reality as it thus appeared to me at the close of the last century. Its incessant thunder, heard for miles around, its solemn grandeur, its indescribable power, beauty, and sublimity, overpowered the mind, and silence was the best expression of the spectator. At that time there was no house near the Falls, on either side of the river, but they burst upon the view of the visitor in the midst of the aboriginal wilderness of nature. I have seen them perhaps a hundred times since; the Falls themselves are sacred from the hand of man, but how have their surroundings been changed! Now there are busy villages on both shores, a suspension bridge in sight, a railroad upon it, a ferry across the river almost beneath the cataract, a bridge from the American side to Goat Island. Nearly everything has changed; but the grand, the awful Falls thunder on."

Almost immediately after his conversion Mr. B. felt that he was called to preach, and following out that conviction he commenced to travel in 1801, under the Presiding Elder. Niagara, then a six weeks' circuit, was his first field of labor; his colleague, William Anson. They extended their work from the river to Long Point, but in December it was agreed that young Bangs might confine his work to the west of the Grand River. Shortly after, he found his way to Oxford, where he was well received, and where he soon organized a society. He was not, however, without severe mental conflicts, and was frequently tempted to leave his charge and go home, notwithstanding that he was blessed in his labors with the comforts of the Holy Spirit, and through its influence was made instrumental in the conversion of many souls, and in gathering them into the Church of Christ. Oxford was no exception to the general rule so far as regarded the new settlements. The roads were bad, the settlers scattered, and, in most cases, destitute. Compare the Oxford of 1801 with the Oxford of 1869. What changes have not sixty-eight years made? The wilderness has indeed become a fruitful field.

In those early days of our young itinerant a mile and a half per hour with a yoke of oxen was considered good speed, and the means of conveyance something of which to be proud; now, an ordinary car is scarcely to be endured, and we must travel at the rate of a mile a minute, or there will be impatient grumblings at the conductor and his "slow coach." A mail four times a year bringing the news, was considered a boon which could not be too highly prized; now, the lightning flashing on its track of wire across the mighty ocean is scarcely swift enough for this fast age.

In 1802 Nathan Bangs was admitted on trial by the New York Conference and sent to the Bay of Quinte, Home District. His colleagues this year were J. Sawyer and Peter Vannest; Bangs, of course, being junior preacher. Here he was severely tried both in body and mind, but his heavenly Father delivered him out of all his difficulties, and made him an honored instrument in His hand of bringing many sinners to Himself. After having labored two years very successfully here, he was, at his own suggestion, sent, in 1804, to the French settlements on the Thames—called in the Minutes of that year River la French.

Mr. Bangs had been received into full connection at this Conference, and ordained Deacon, and in consequence of his appointment to those western wilds, he was two days afterward ordained Elder. Conference over, Mr. Bangs, in company with Daniel Pickett and William Anson, left New York for Canada on the 18th June, entering the province at Kingston. Mr. Bangs parted from his travelling companions at the head of Lake Ontario*—Mr. Anson being bound for Yonge Street, and Mr. Pickett purposing to go to Niagara, while Bangs pushed on for the far West, as that part of Canada was then called. Working his way westward he reached Oxford about the first of August. On the 4th and 5th of that month he attended a Quarterly Meeting on this circuit, and then passed on towards his new charge. In this lonely and toilsome journey he was accompanied by a young man who had agreed to go with him. By the 9th they had reached Delaware, at which place they slept on a bundle of straw, and the next morning, after having partaken of a scant and hasty meal, at about as early an hour as Jacob took his departure from Padan-aram, they left Delaware and entered the "Long Woods"—a stretch of forest extending thence to the vicinity of Chatham, with only here and there a clearing. After a weary day's travel through the woods, following the marked trees as guides, they reached a Frenchman's shanty, not far from where Wardsville now is. Here they obtained shelter for the night, their supper consisting of "sepawn and milk"—their bed, as on a previous night, a bundle of straw. Next morning, the good woman of the house, "on hospitable thoughts intent," sent some distance for a "drawing" of tea. The tea on hand, the hostess found herself in a dilemma—teapot or teacup she had none; but she was not to be deterred by the lack of such utensils from offering to her guests the kindly beverage that "cheers but not inebriates." Washing her "dish-kettle" thoroughly, she steeped her tea in that, and

* See Life and Times of Bangs, page 133. Why Mr. Anson should have come to the head of the lake does not appear, that point being fully forty miles west of the one at which he should have turned northward to Yonge Street.

served it to her visitors in tin cups. Doubtless, in after years the Dr. drank his tea from costly china cup and silver tea pot with much less zest than he drank it that memorable August morning in the little shanty, with all its homely accompaniments. Bidding the kind Frenchman and his family good-bye, the travellers proceeded on their journey, and passing through the Flemming settlement stopped at Moraviantown, where he dined with the Moravian missionary. Passing down the river that afternoon, he halted at the house of Mr. Lemuel Sherman, who hospitably entertained them, and who also opened his house for preaching. Thamesville is located on a part of this farm, the remainder is still owned and occupied by descendants of Mr. Sherman. Sunday, 12th of August, was a memorable day to the people of this vicinity. Here, after a tedious journey of fifty-four days travel from New York, the young itinerant opened his mission among the scattered inhabitants along the Thames. Speaking of Mr. Sherman, and of his own first meeting among this people, Dr. Bangs says:

"This man took his horse and rode through the settlement for ten miles, notifying the people that there would be preaching at his house on Sunday at ten o'clock. At the appointed hour the house was crowded. I commenced the service by remarking that 'when a stranger appears in these new countries the people are usually curious to know his name, whence he comes, whither he is bound, and what is his errand; I will try to satisfy you in brief; my name is Nathan Bangs; I was born in Connecticut, May 2nd, 1778; I was born again in this province, May, 1800; I commenced itinerating as a preacher of the Gospel in the month of September, 1801. On the 18th of June, the present year, I left New York for the purpose of visiting you, of whom I had heard about two years ago, and after a long, tedious journey I am here; I am bound for the heavenly city, and my errand among you is to persuade as many as I can to go with me. I am a Methodist preacher, and my manner of worship is to stand while singing, kneel while praying, and then I stand while I preach, the people meanwhile sitting. As many of you as see fit to join me in this way can do so, and others may choose their own method.' I then read a chapter in the Bible, after which I gave out a hymn. When the young man who accompanied me stood up to sing, they all rose, men, women, and children. When I kneeled in prayer, they all kneeled down. Such a sight I never saw before. I then read for my text, 'Repent ye, therefore, and be converted, that your sins may be blotted out when the times of refreshing shall come from the presence of the Lord.' In explaining and enforcing these words I felt that my divine Master was with me in truth and power, every cloud was dispelled from my mind, and my heart overflowed with love for this people. I believe I preached with the 'Holy Ghost sent down from heaven.' When I had concluded I informed them of our manner of preaching, the amount of quarterage we received, and the way in which it was collected. I then said, 'All of you who wish to hear any more such preaching rise up.' They all rose, every man, woman, and child. I then notified them, that in two weeks, God willing, they might expect preaching again, and closed the meeting. Thus was my circuit begun."

After the public services were ended many of his congregation grasped him by the hand, giving him a hearty welcome. Among these was a Mr. Everett, who had seen Bishop Asbury, and who had anxiously longed for the visit of a Gospel minister. He also invited Mr. Bangs to preach at his house, which was still farther down the river, at a place now called Louisville. Thither Mr. Bangs proceeded that same afternoon and preached at 3 o'clock. At this place he met, for the first time, a John Messmore, a German Baptist, who had written to him two years previous to this, urging him to visit them that they might receive the word of life. At Mr. Messmore's he again preached, and thence proceeded to other places west and south of Chatham, working his way towards

Detroit. Some idea of the extent of this circuit may be conceived when it is realized that it embraced all that section of country from the township of Mosa, County of Middlesex, in the east, to Detroit in the west, and all the settlements along Lake Erie, through Tilbury, Romney, Mersea, Gosfield, Colchester, and Amherstburg, wherever there were settlers.

The people suffered much during the summer and autumn, nor was Mr. Bangs exempt, in consequence of the prevalence of ague and fever, produced by the miasma arising from the vast swamps of the west. Finding himself unable to withstand this deleterious influence, in November he left the circuit and returned to Niagara. On this journey he, with a man who had accompanied him, spent one night in the woods, between Mosa and Delaware. The night was cold, there being about two inches of snow on the ground, but by making a good fire they were able to make themselves comparatively comfortable, although they lacked sufficient food for themselves and their horses.

It was not till four years afterwards that this mission was again visited. The next missionary who found his way to the west was Rev. William Case, who was very successful in his labors, as were also N. Holmes, S. Hopkins, and many other equally worthy and useful men, who have since toiled and triumphed, too, in the western country.

Several amusing and striking incidents occurred in those early days, illustrative of the times, two of which, anticipating the dates of their occurrence may be related in this connection. On one occasion Mr. Case, while preaching at the house of Mr. Isaac Dolson, was portraying the fondness that possessed some men for strong drink, and its demoralizing effects upon themselves and others; warming with his subject as he advanced, and looking at the same moment towards the door, near which a very rough specimen of humanity sat, the preacher said, "There are men who will even bring whiskey to the place of worship in their pockets." "You are a wizard."

cried the poor conscience smitten man at the door, and running out of the house he broke his bottle against it, and left the place in a rage. In a few weeks, however, he returned, and sought and found salvation.

At another time, when S. Hopkins was preaching at this same place, he had occasion, in the course of his sermon, to speak of the disagreeable conduct of some ungodly men, of their revengeful dispositions, &c., &c,, and of their influence on society. At this juncture a man in the congregation, fancying the preacher had pointed directly at him, leaped to his feet, and putting himself in a threatening position, said angrily, "Sir, it is more than flesh and blood can endure to be singled out and exposed in this way before a public assembly, and if you will step outside of the door I will *dirty your shirt for you, sir,*" meaning that he would knock him down and trample him in the dust. He too, however, left the house only to reflect on his conduct, and shortly afterwards returning, sought and obtained pardon through faith in our Lord Jesus Christ.

Mr. Bangs extended the work across the Detroit River to Detroit itself, which, however, he afterward was obliged to abandon. In 1805 he was again sent east to Oswegotchie. In 1806 he was sent to Quebec. In 1807 he returned to Niagara, and in 1808, having spent seven years in the itinerant work in this country, he was sent, with Robert Dillon, to the Delaware. He left the province greatly beloved, became eminent in his native land, and died at a good old age, and full of honors.*

When Mr. Bangs commenced to travel, in 1801, the members in Canada numbered 1159, 10 preachers, and 5 circuits; when he left the province, in 1808, there were 12 circuits, 17 preachers, and a membership of 2360. During these seven years the work had extended as far as Quebec in

* See Life and Times of N. Bangs, by A. Stevens, D. D.

Lower Canada. The Lower Province was not, however, so fruitful a soil for Methodism as the west, being settled as it was with French Roman Catholics; yet, in most instances, these people treated the ministers with kindness when they found it necessary to call at their houses.

At the New York Conference of 1801, the work in Canada was farther reinforced by John Robinson, James Aikens, and Caleb Morris, who, with the other preachers for Canada who had attended the Conference, made their way to the province through the wilds of New York. During most part of their journey they were obliged to sleep in the woods, besides suffering from many other inconveniences, but after enduring much weariness, and suffering very great privations they at last reached their respective destinations. Mr. Robinson went that year to the Ottawa circuit. In 1802 he travelled the Niagara circuit, and in 1803 he was Presiding Elder of the Canada District. In 1804 he travelled Vershire circuit, in Vermont. In 1805 he located and settled upon a farm near the shore of the Bay of Quinte. While in the itinerancy he was a laborious and useful minister. Sometime after his location he became melancholy, and finally hopelessly insane. It was pitiful to see him wandering about the house and yard, as he would do for days together, in great mental anguish, particularly in the early part of his affliction. In his later years the disease assumed a milder form and he would travel about from place to place, frequently taking long journeys, not only through Canada, but into the United States, revisiting his old friends, and calling upon those of the preachers whom he thought likely to receive him cordially. His usual course was to pray with the family where he stopped, and to preach wherever he could secure a congregation. His remarks were, as might be expected, disconnected and wild, being in general nothing more than a violent declamation against fine churches, richly dressed Methodists, and well paid preachers. The manners and things to which he had been accustomed in his early days were of course, the only ones which he esteemed right, and without loud preaching he considered no good could be accomplished. In his old age he allowed his hair and beard to grow quite long, which gave him a very venerable appearance, reminding one of the ancient patriarchs. As he passed along the road with his little pack, containing some few articles of clothing, or when upon entering a house, as he leaned upon his staff and stroking his white beard with his left hand, he would say, "Peace be to this house," his aspect was dignified and impressive. During his wanderings in his later years he frequently stopped at the house of the writer. In familiar intercourse his conversation was pious, sometimes wandering, but generally witty, and always agreeable. At family worship his manner was devout, and when invited to lead in prayer his supplications were fervent and generally appropriate.

Upon one occasion, happening to be present at a love-feast, Father Robinson, as he was familiarly called, rose as if to relate his experience, and said, "If you all think as I do you will never pay any man silver or gold for preaching the Gospel," and continued for some time to enlarge upon his subject. The Presiding Elder, who, with one or more of the preachers, was in the altar, made no remark, hoping that he would soon sit down. The appearance of the crazy man, however, his ludicrous remarks, and the time selected for his harangue, caused quite a sensation in the congregation, some tittered audibly, some smiled, and many were grieved that the solemnities of the love-feast should have been thus disturbed. An elderly local preacher at length requested the old man either to desist or leave the church, but to Father Robinson his words were as "sounding brass." Finding expostulation vain, the local preacher stepped forward, and called upon another person—who refused to obey the summons—to assist in removing the old man from the church. At this stage of the proceedings Mr. Robinson, without any further compulsion whatever, walked deliberately to the door, and then turning to the Presiding Elder, with his hand uplifted, said, with great emphasis, "David, art thou a ruler in Israel and suffereth these things this day;" then turning his back upon the church he walked hastily away. Poor old man, his was a case to excite pity more than censure, and we have often thought that it would have been better if his brethren had exercised more patience towards him and his eccentricities than in some instances they seem to have done. He has years since entered into his rest.

For several years, as must necessarily be the case in so new a country, the changes on the circuits were numerous, some circuits being divided and others united, as circumstances required, or prudence dictated, while the changes of the preachers were still more frequent. Some few who were sent to Canada were not pleased with the country, the climate being too cold for their health, and the country too fearfully wild to be acceptable to their families. In such cases it was very natural for them to intimate to Mr. Asbury a preference for some other field of labor, and he in almost every case would send them in some other direction. Every change, however, had the tendency of enlarging the borders of Methodism in both countries. Onward, onward, was their watchword and reply.

CHAPTER IX.

OF CAMP-MEETINGS.

Camp-meetings—Necessity for such means of grace in the early day—How the people went to Quarterly Meetings in the beginning of this century—The origin of camp-meetings—Their results in the United States—Incorporated into the economy of American Methodism—Arrangement of a camp-ground—Order of the services—Camp-ground at night—Description of an early camp-meeting—Canadian Methodists follow the example of their fathers—First camp-meeting in Canada—Beneficial results attending it—Opposition encountered—Conversion of Peter Jones and his sister—Scriptural precedents in favor of camp-meetings—Is it desirable to hold them now—A plea for camp-meetings.

REFERENCE has been made to camp-meetings in a previous chapter; it is proper, therefore, that their origin and results should be briefly alluded to in this place; but before entering more directly upon the subject it may not be uninteresting to the reader to take a retrospect of a few years, in order to learn something respecting the remarkable outpouring of the Spirit of God upon the people at the Quarterly Meetings in the days of our ancestors, and out of which arose the necessity for holding camp-meetings.

For several years the Quarterly Meetings had occasioned the collecting of the members of the societies from various parts of the country, the services generally continuing two days. In many cases, these services were held in the middle of the week, as it was impossible for the Elder to attend all such appointments upon the Saturday and Sabbath.

In the month of January, 1776, a powerful revival broke out in that part of Virginia where Mr. G. Shadford was laboring, many sinners were awakened and savingly converted, and the membership was greatly strengthened. Gracious revivals, too, occurred among the Presbyterians and Baptists, not only in Virginia, but in Maryland also.

Among the Methodists, meetings were appointed for exhortation and prayer during the intervals between the regular appointments of the preachers, and these meetings were attended by many who had never before manifested any interest in such matters. Multitudes thus aroused to a sense of their lost condition would go for leagues to listen to Asbury and Shadford, who seemed like luminous meteors passing through the land.

Early in May, 1776, a Quarterly Meeting was held about twelve miles from Petersburg, Va., which was even more numerously attended than usual. Upon this occasion the windows of heaven seem to have been opened, salvation descending upon the people in an astonishing manner. The second day was the great day of the feast. All day the house was thronged; in every part sinners were crying for mercy, while established believers and new converts were shouting for joy; the shades of evening closed around them—lights were sent for—and it was not "until some time in the night" that the congregation dispersed. These people returned to their homes, as did the early Christians after the day of Pentecost, scattering the holy fire among their neighbors and in their families, until, like a flood of hallowed light the glorious Gospel of the Son of God spread its sacred influence in various directions, over a space of from four to five hundred miles.

Mr. Young, in his history says, "On Tuesday and Wednesday, the 30th and 31st days of July, a Quarterly Meeting was held at Mabury's dwelling house in Brunswick, now Greensville County. No meeting-house in Virginia could have held the people. We had a large arbor in the yard which would shade from the sun two or three thousand people. The first day was a blessed season, but the second was a day never to be forgotten. We held the love-feast under the arbor in the open air; the members of the society took their seats, and other people stood all round them by hundreds. The place was truly awful by reason of the presence of the Lord. Many of the members spoke, and while some declared how the Lord had justified them freely, others testified that the blood of Jesus had cleansed them from all sin." During the progress of this meeting hundreds were bathed in tears, and many were "crying to God for pardon or holiness." In this manner did the work of God extend and prevail among the people in the several States until the commencement of the present century.

Camp-meetings, like other institutions of Methodism, grew out of the necessities of the case. At the commencement of these meetings the country was new, the congregations large, and the houses of worship small, and situated at very great distances from each other. It was fitting, therefore, that the ministers should follow the example of their Master, who taught the multitudes upon the mountain and by the sea shore. This peculiar means of grace was originated by the united efforts of the Presbyterians and Methodists, under the following circumstances:—A very gracious display of God's power had prevailed among the membership of these two bodies during the year 1799, in the lower portion of Kentucky. In 1800, two brothers, one a Methodist and the other a Presbyterian, who were preaching in Logan and Christian counties, agreed to hold their meetings together. It was, however, soon found that their congregations were so large that they could not be accommodated in any of their places of worship, and in consequence, during the summer months they sought the woods as a shelter for the crowds who came to listen to their ministrations. "Many came from far," bringing food for themselves and provender for their animals, very frequently stopping out all night because "there was no room for them in the inn," or as was often the case, no inn to go to. The Rev.

William McKendree was at this time Presiding Elder, his District embracing that part of the State in which this reformation was going on. It appears, however, that he visited the middle of the State in the latter part of 1800, or the beginning of 1801, and that at a large meeting, composed principally of Presbyterians and Methodists, after preaching he gave them an interesting account of these "feasts of tabernacles." His words kindled to a flame the zeal of the people, and they longed for the period to arrive when they, too, should enjoy a camp-meeting. In due time the proper season arrived, the site was chosen, and the ground prepared; the stand was erected, tents built and furnished, and seats arranged. When all the preparations had been completed the shrill notes of a trumpet were heard resounding through the forest, thus giving notice that divine service was about to commence. The waiting, expectant multitude responded readily to the call, those who could seating themselves, while others leaned against the tall forest trees for support; all listening eagerly to the messages of mercy as they fell from the lips of the ambassadors of Christ. The zeal of the preachers, manifested upon these as well as other occasions, and the reformations following these efforts, connected with the singularity of the meetings themselves, induced many thousands to attend, although at first the preparations for the accommodation of the people were but limited. After a time, however, matters were more systematically arranged. Suitable groves having been selected, and the logs and underbrush removed, the encampments were encircled by a "brush fence" provided with gates as a means of protection against the assaults of the lawless. Within this fence the tents were arranged in proper order, and frequently so great was the multitude that there would be two or more tiers of tents completely round the encampment. The pulpit or stand was then, as now, a sort of platform covered overhead to protect the preachers from the sun or rain.

The services were conducted very much in the same manner in which they are in our more modern day. First a sermon from the stand, followed by an exhortation, which was in turn succeeded by a general prayer-meeting, either in the open camp-ground, or in a certain number of designated tents. At stated periods the people prepared and partook of their meals, though while some were thus engaged it often happened that others assembled in groups upon the ground, or in tents, to sing and pray until recalled by the sound of the trumpet to the seats in front of the stand. At dawn of day the trumpet sounded to arouse the sleepers from their slumbers, and with the new day commenced the same routine of services.

At these gatherings scores of the most ungodly men, who had come for the express purpose of disturbing devout worshippers, were smitten with conviction for sin, frequently falling like dead men, or soliciting the prayers of the righteous, and also pouring out for themselves agonizing supplications to God for mercy. Many, too, carried conviction with them to their abodes, and in their stated places of worship, or at home, found peace in believing. Thus did God carry on his work among the people.

A camp-meeting at night was indeed a picturesque scene. The fires upon the stands situated at given points in the enclosure, illuminated the whole place, and this glow of mellow light falling upon the canvass tents, and upon the deep green foliage of the forest, moved as the leaves and branches were by the gentle breezes of a lovely June night, gave to the whole scene a charm which is indescribable. Add to this, groups gliding here and there as their fancy dictated or necessity compelled, while others were engaged in worship or in praise, and it must be admitted that such a meeting—properly conducted—presented a scene at once solemn and grand. To many, of course, such meetings were places of confusion, but to great numbers the Gospel as proclaimed at camp-meeting was experienced to be the power of God unto salvation.

Speaking of the early camp-meeting, Mr. Young remarks, "In consequence of so great a collection of people it frequently happened that several preachers would be speaking at once to different congregations on the same ground. Nor were they at a loss for pulpits; stumps, logs, or lops of trees served as temporary stands from which to dispense the word of life. At night the whole scene was awfully sublime; the ranges of tents, the fires reflecting light amidst the branches of the towering trees; the candles and lamps illuminating the encampment; hundreds moving to and fro with lights or torches, like Gideon's army; the preaching, praying, singing, shouting, all heard at once, rushing from different parts of the ground like the sound of many waters, was enough to swallow up all the powers of contemplation. Sinners falling and shrieking for mercy, awakened in the mind a lively apprehension of that scene when the awful sound shall be heard, 'Arise, ye dead, and come to judgment.' But these meetings did not escape censure and opposition. It is difficult, indeed, to control a large collection of people of every description; hence it is that there might have been, and probably were, many irregularities. The enemies of these meetings, who were generally prejudiced and bigoted professors, or the wicked who had no liking for them, took advantage of every circumstance, and exaggerated every unfavorable occurrence to such a degree as to give to all a false and dreadful coloring. Some bigoted priests on these occasions were quite busy; they were much worse at misrepresentation than the wicked themselves."

The fame of these meetings had at an early season reached Canada, and inspired the people with an ardent desire to have one of their own; but it was not until the summer of 1805 that these desires were gratified, when Henry Ryan and William Case, who had been sent to Bay Quinte Circuit that year, resolved to hold one. The meeting, which was held upon the farm of Mr. Peter Huff, on Hay Bay, commenced on Friday and lasted till Monday. With the exception of the Sabbath, the attendance, as might have been expected in so very new a country, was not large. The pulpit, however, was well represented, Daniel Picket went down from Yonge Street, and Thomas Madden from Smith's Creek, while Nathan Bangs and S. Keeler came up from the Oswegotchie. The labors of these brethren, assisted as they probably were by Darius Dunham, who had located, exerted a powerful influence upon the people, many of whom had come from great distances in order to be at the meeting. To very many it had been indeed a season of rejoicing, and they returned to their homes "like giants refreshed with new wine," scattering the holy fire as they went. The success which attended this meeting induced others to make, the attempt and as the country became more thickly settled, and the circuits enlarged, camp-meetings were held as occasion appeared to justify, and as the people were able to sustain them; not in every case, however, followed by the same results.

In some parts of the province multitudes were converted at these meetings, while in other parts, the work was very greatly hindered by the ungodly rabble, who would combine together in order to disturb the worship, and persecute the worshippers. Frequently, too, these desperadoes were headed by men of influence and means, and their violent conduct sanctioned by those high in authority; but God was with his people, and in a measure restrained the wrath of the evil doers until laws were enacted protecting people in their various modes of religious worship.

But it was not upon civilized society alone that camp-meetings produced a salutary effect; the aborigines of the country shared largely in the general good. Polly Jones, an Indian girl, was the first fruit of the Gospel among the Mohawks of this country, and her brother Peter was converted the next day. Both of these children of the forest were born of the Spirit at a camp-meeting held in the township of Ancaster, in June, 1824.

In both Europe and America, at least among Methodists, the name of Peter Jones has become a household word, and both countries have been moved by his fervid eloquence, as he pleaded the cause of his race in his own peculiarly simple and dignified manner. He was long spared to be a blessing to his own people and the country, and after having for many years adorned his Christian profession by a straightforward, consistent course, he only a few years since finished that course with joy, and entered upon his rest. It is, alas! true that Christianity has not accomplished for the Indians all that it was hoped or desired that it would, but still the glorious Gospel of the Son of God has done much towards elevating the various tribes, both morally and socially.

The question is frequently asked, "Is it *now* either necessary or expedient to hold camp-meetings, when the country is settled, and the churches numerous and capable of accommodating the people?" It is, we think, for many reasons, if they are properly conducted. The necessity for out-door preaching was never greater in Canada than at the present time. There are certain classes which can be reached in no other way, and street preaching in our cities, and camp-meetings in our country places may be made to be as productive of good in the present and future, as they have been in the past. Much, very much, however, depends upon the manner in which such services are conducted; strict order should be maintained, and all the services should be conducted with an eye to the conversion of sinners, and the lasting benefit of the people, and not to a display of flowery oratory or declamation.

But it is urged that out-door preaching calls together a multitude indiscriminately, and that much wickedness is the result of such gatherings. To this it is replied that this is not the object of such meetings, but we know that in times of old "there was a day when the sons of God came to present themselves before the Lord, and *Satan came also* among them." But were the sons of God responsible for his conduct? Neither should Christians in the present day be held responsible for the misconduct of his children. The hearts of the ungodly are just as vile in the sight of heaven when at home as when they are at camp-meeting, or other out-door exercises; they only exhibit their innate depravity more publicly and fully in their collective capacity, thinking they can do so with greater impunity. Are the servants of Christ therefore to refrain from proclaiming the glad tidings of great joy to perishing man, in the wilderness or in the streets and lanes of our cities, and are the songs of praise and thanksgiving never to ascend from our majestic forests, because the wicked may manifest their wickedness? As Methodists, we think not. Now and then a lukewarm or pharisaical professor may be displeased because "a man has been made every whit whole on the Sabbath day," or, in other words, because one has been converted from the error of his ways in a noisy Methodist prayer-meeting.

That there is considerable excitement at meetings of this kind is no reason why they should not be held, the preaching of the gospel is designed to create a beneficial excitement, and it is not at all likely that there has ever been as great an excitement at any Methodist meeting as there was at that prayer-meeting long ago, in Jerusalem, when the Apostles and brethren met together upon the day of Pentecost. Some of the priests and many of the Pharisees found considerable fault with the zeal and noise of those early Christians, even accusing them of being "full of new wine;" all of which, however, did not prevent Peter from preaching an excellent sermon, and taking into the Church "three thousand souls." On one occasion when Christ cast an unclean spirit out of one possessed of a devil "he lay as one dead, insomuch that they said, he is dead." If, therefore, the Spirit of God descend upon the people when they are all with one accord in one place praying for the out-pouring of the Holy Ghost, whether it be at camp-meeting or anywhere else, we say, let them sing, or shout, or rejoice as the Spirit may incline them.

CHAPTER X.

FROM 1804 TO THE COMMENCEMENT OF THE WAR OF 1812.

Immigration continues to increase—Henry Ryan and William Case arrive in the country—Characteristics of these men—Ryan and the belligerent blacksmith—Ryan and the lawyer—Mr. Case's special work—Arrival of Mr. Whitehead—Andrew Prindle, the first Canadian itinerant, enters the work, 1806—State of the work from 1806 to 1808—John Reynolds, the second Canadian itinerant, employed—Sketch of his life—State of the work from 1809 to 1812—Canadian work transferred from New York to the Genesee Conference—Commencement of the war of 1812—Consequent departure of the American preachers—Gratifying result of twenty-two year's laborious toil and self-sacrifice on the part of the missionaries.

THE tide of emigration continued still to roll into the country, and to push further back from the banks of the rivers and margins of the lakes into the interior, thus necessitating the enlargement of old circuits, and the formation of new ones, to supply which required more preachers, who were accordingly sent out by the N. Y. Conference. The same spirit of reformation continued to attend the preaching of the word, so much so, that in 1804 the work extended from the St. Clair in the west to Montreal in the east, embracing seven circuits, with nine preachers, including the P. E., Samuel Coate. Rather an extensive District this would be called even now. What then must it have been in those days of vast wildernesses and unbridged rivers. It is scarcely probable, however, that Mr. Coate visited "Le French," the section of country between Delaware and Detroit, as the missionary, Rev. N. Bangs, only remained part of the year, the country in that region being so sickly, and his own health so feeble.

In 1805 the membership in the Canada District had increased to 1787, being an increase since 1800 of 851 souls, and an accession of 3 preachers and 3 circuits within the same period

It will be seen by the General Minutes of this year that Revs. Henry Ryan and William Case were sent out as missionaries, being appointed to Bay Quinte Circuit. These two men were destined in after years to take a prominent position among their brethren, and to stand forth conspicuously in the history of those troublous times consequent upon the war of 1812, their remarkable energy of character qualifying them for the task set before them. Almost immediately after reaching their charge they made preparation, as has already been stated, for holding the first camp-meeting in Canada. Rev. F. Reid, in an article dated August 2nd, 1864, and published in the *Northern Christian Advocate*, speaks of Mr. Ryan as follows:—

"He labored arduously and faithfully, and accomplished much for the cause of Christ in the early days of Canadian Methodism. He commenced his itinerant life in 1800, and after travelling five years in the New York Conference, was sent to Canada, in company with William Case. Thenceforth he was a Canadian, and devoted himself, with all his characteristic energy and force, to the spiritual interests of his adopted country. 'In Canada his labors were Herculean; he achieved the work of half a score of men, and was instrumental in scattering the word of life over vast portions of that new country, when few other clergymen dared venture among its wildernesses and privations. He also suffered heroically from want, fatigue, bad roads, and the rigorous winters of those high latitudes.'—[*Life of Bishop Hedding*.] 'He was well nigh six feet in height, of large, symmetrical proportions, with prodigious muscular developments, and without doubt one of the strongest men of his age. His voice excelled, for power and compass, all that I ever heard from human organs. When occasion required, and he gave it its full power, it was 'as when a lion roareth.'"

His strength of constitution, as well as his courage, was no small assistance to him in so wild and new a country; where, too, many were violently opposed to Methodism, and to Methodists, especially to the preachers, and where these people were encouraged in their deeds of violence by those high in authority. In these early days it was no unusual circumstance for the Methodist missionary to be waylaid and insulted on his routes, or to have his religious services disturbed by lawless men, encouraged and abetted by those who, from their position in society, ought to have known better, and set a better example.

Mr. Ryan, it is believed, left no journals or papers from which much can be gathered relative to his labors; but there are still many in Canada who remember well his zealous, laborious life, and who even yet dwell upon his powerful discourses with pleasure, not forgetting to mention his ready repartee when annoyed at the witticisms of the ungodly. So sarcastic was he, and caustic as well, that few cared to attempt to impose on him a second time. To fear he was a stranger. Two or three incidents relative to his wit and courage are subjoined as characteristic and amusing.

It is related upon good authority that upon one occasion as Mr. Ryan was leisurely riding past a blacksmith-shop, he was assailed by the smith, who it appears had asserted that if that "saddle-bags man" ventured to pass his shop he would beat him. Seeing Mr. Ryan coming up he dropped his hammer, saying at the same time to some of his friends who were in the shop, that he was now going to flog the preacher, and running out he seized the horse by the bridle, and ordered Mr. Ryan to dismount, or he would "knock him out of the saddle." Mr. Ryan expostulated, but in vain; the longer he reasoned the fiercer his antagonist became. Seeing that all milder measures were fruitless, Mr. Ryan leaped from his horse, and springing suddenly upon his assailant, caught him by his collar and pantaloons, and in an instant threw him over an old brush fence into a thicket of briars. He then quietly remounted his horse and rode off, leaving the belligerent smith to get out as best he might, so far as he was concerned.

Upon another occasion, while conducting a camp-meeting, at which some rowdies had given considerable trouble, Mr. Ryan was standing near the large gate, when some young gents, among whom was a young lawyer named Jones, came up and said as politely and innocently as though they had been engaged in no mischief, "Elder, may we go into the encampment?" "Yes," said Mr. Ryan, "*if you behave yourselves.*" As they entered the ground, Jones, who wished to create some amusement at the preacher's expense, said "Elder, when I was at Auburn, in the State of New York, some time since, did I not see you in the State prison?" "I think it is very likely, sir," replied Mr. Ryan, "for when last in Auburn, I was invited to preach to the convicts, and I saw a fellow among them who looked very much like you." It is scarcely necessary to add that Mr. Jones did not again attempt to try his wit upon the "Elder."

During the war of 1812, one day as Mr. Ryan was standing in his door-yard, an Indian hunter came up a with piece of venison, which he laid down upon a sled standing by, requesting Mr. Ryan to buy it. Having enquired and ascertained the price, which was half a dollar, he purchased the meat and presented an American half dollar in payment, upon discovering which the savage said, "You a Yankee, me kill you," and instantly drew his hunting knife. Ryan, as if moved by a flash of electricity snatched a stake from the sled, and ordered the Indian to put the money down and be off with his venison The Indian quailed before him as a child would before a man, and quietly obeyed the order. Numerous other anecdotes might be related of him, but the above sufficiently indicate the character of the man.

Remarking on his pulpit exercises, Mr. Reid says:—

"His preaching was often with remarkable particularity and point, and was productive of immediate and gracious results. He was preaching in New York, on one occasion, several successive evenings. A Mr. C. was present, who, though not a member at that time, was a regular hearer at the chapel, and I believe a good man. His extreme diffidence and want of confidence had kept him back from many Christian duties, especially family prayer. In one of his sermons the Elder referred to this duty with characteristic earnestness; and as if appealing to some particular individual said, 'You know your duty and do it not. In the name of God I charge you to begin this night. I warn you at your peril not to neglect it any longer.' Mr. C. really thought, as he said afterwards, that some one had informed the Elder about him, and that he meant him in particular. He left the chapel with the full purpose to do his duty that night; but his courage failed him. and he neglected. The next evening, near the close of the sermon, as if the thought suddenly struck him, Mr. Ryan earnestly exclaimed, 'Last night on your way home you promised God that you would commence family worship, but the devil frightened you from your purpose. O man! if you mean to save your soul, and hope for the salvation of your family, go and do your duty this night, even if you die in the attempt.' Mr. C. said the Elder looked him directly in the face, and he could not doubt that somehow he knew what had passed in his mind the night before. He was too thoroughly aroused this time to be driven from his duty any longer. He commenced at once."

William Case, the early colleague of Mr. Ryan in this province, and for many years a laborious minister, spent most of his itinerant life in Canada. Though a pious man, and very zealous in his efforts for the extension of his Master's kingdom, he was not nearly as powerful a preacher as Mr. Ryan. His life-long object was to do good, and though not always successful in his schemes, yet he accomplished much for the benefit of the Indians, with whose welfare he very closely identified himself from about the time of the conversion of Peter Jones and his sister till the end of his life.

In 1806 Rev. Thomas Whitehead, who had previously travelled, it would seem, under the Presiding Elder, in the vicinity of New York and Albany, in Nova Scotia and New Brunswick,* and Andrew Prindle, who was the first Canadian itinerant that entered the ranks, were received on trial by the New York Conference, and appointed to their respective fields of labor, Mr. Whitehead being sent to Niagara, and Mr. Prindle to the Ottawa.

The Canada District was this year divided into the Upper

* The information afforded by the published Minutes respecting the work in the Eastern Provinces during this period must be admitted to be exceedingly defective; all that is to be gleaned therefrom with regard to Mr. Whitehead, prior to 1806, is that in 1791 his name appears in connection with the Liverpool Circuit, Nova Scotia, W. Black, P. E. Nevertheless it is believed that he was sent as a missionary to Nova Scotia some years earlier than the above date, perhaps as early as 1786 or 1787; that he travelled extensively, and spent many years in the work there. To those who were acquainted with the unimpeachable integrity of Mr. Whitehead's character, his own assertion that such were the facts would be amply sufficient, but happily his statements are corroborated by those of persons who were acquainted with him while he was travelling there. A friend of the writer being in New York visited a very old friend, deceased many years since, but then resident in that city, Mr. Seabury, who was a brother of Bishop Seabury, of the Protestant Episcopal Church, and the father-in-law of the late Rev. Joshua Marsden, of the English Conference. The conversation naturally turning upon Canada, Mr Seabury inquired, with much affectionate interest, after Mr. Whitehead. Pleased at learning that his esteemed friend was known to and appreciated by his visitor, the old gentleman was easily led to yield himself to the recollections of the past, stirred by the mention of Mr. Whitehead, and he entertained his gratified auditor with various reminiscences of Mr. Whitehead's ministerial labors in Nova Scotia, also bearing hearty testimony to the ability, piety, zeal and usefulness which characterized his ministrations while travelling in that country.

and Lower Canadian Districts, having an addition of two circuits, viz., Quebec and St. Lawrence. Le French had been given up, so that the work now only extended from Long Point to Quebec.

The years 1806 and 1807 were seasons of great prosperity to the infant church in Canada. Notwithstanding the thinness of the population and the opposition with which the Methodists had to contend, in 1808 the societies numbered 2360, showing the considerable increase, since 1805, of 563 souls, while nearly every year brought new preachers into the field, in consequence of the addition of fresh circuits.

In 1808 John Reynolds, the second itinerant raised up in the country, was sent out by the Conference. Mr. Reynolds was born in the State of New York, near the city of Hudson, on the 9th of February, 1786. In 1796 his parents removed to Canada, and the year following located themselves in the township of Burford. They finally settled in Dorchester, at a place still known as Reynolds' Mills, on the east branch of the River Thames, where some of the family connection yet reside.

When about seventeen years of age Mr. Reynolds, in 1803, experienced religion, under the labors of Rev. N. Bangs. In November, 1807, he was sent out as an assistant on the Niagara Circuit, travelling under the Presiding Elder, Joseph Sawyer. The appointments given in the Minutes for the Niagara Circuit that year are, N. Bangs, T. Whitehead, and N. Holmes. It appears that there was an understanding between Bishop Asbury and the Canadian Presiding Elders that the latter might arrange the work as they thought best. Accordingly the appointments were re-arranged, the Presiding Elder of the Lower District—it is presumed with the consent of the other Presiding Elder—requesting Mr. Bangs, instead of going to the Niagara Circuit, to return to Montreal, where he had labored the greater part of the previous year. Mr. Bangs complied with the request, and Mr. Madden, who had been appointed to Montreal, went to Quebec. Thus a vacancy occurred on the Niagara Circuit, to supply which young Reynolds was called out into the work.

In 1808 he was admitted on trial by the N. Y. Conference, and sent with Daniel Pickett to the Augusta Circuit. Although unordained he was, in 1809, appointed to the Yonge Street charge, where he was well received. The year following, viz., 1810, the work in Upper Canada became part of the newly formed Genesee Conference. Mr. Reynolds was that year admitted into full connection, ordained Deacon, and appointed to the Smith Creek Circuit, which embraced what is now known as Clark, Port Hope, and Cobourg.

In 1811 he was appointed, with Rev. John Rhodes, to Augusta, where he had preached with considerable success three years before. The hardships of the itinerant life rested with great weight upon a man as delicately constituted as Mr. Reynolds, still he continued to travel until after the war of 1812. In 1815 he located, and settled in what is now known as the town of Belleville, then an extensive cedar swamp, only slightly reclaimed from its primitive wildness. Here he entered into mercantile business, but continued to preach as his health and circumstances would permit, assisting, also, the infant church very materially with his means.

At the Hallowell Annual Conference, held in 1824, Mr. Reynolds was ordained Elder by Bishop George. At the Conference held in Belleville, in 1835, he was re-admitted, and at a special General Conference, held the same month, at the same place, he was elected General Superintendent, *pro tem.* This step was rendered necessary in consequence of the secession, in 1833, of a large number of the preachers, including the then General Superintendent, Mr. Case; they having effected a union with the Wesleyan Conference in England, formed themselves into a body since known as the Wesleyan Methodist Church in Canada.

At the Conferences held in June 1834 and in Feb. 1835 an

Elder had presided, in accordance with the provisions of the Discipline of 1829, Section 5th, pages 25th and 26th. At the General Conference held in Palermo, in June 1835, Mr. Reynolds was duly elected to the episcopal office, and on the Sabbath following his election, June 28th, 1835, he was ordained according to our consecration service. For the validity of his election and ordination, see Journals of 1835, and the Discipline of 1829, pages 23 and 128 to 138.

As a business man Mr. Reynolds was very successful. After the re-organization of the Conferences his liberal contributions were a great assistance to the struggling Church. He aided very considerably in the erection of the new church in Belleville, and also gave liberally to the building of the Seminary—now Albert College. For his services to the Church as General Superintendent he would never receive any remuneration whatever.

Since the Bishop's death his enemies, and those of the M. E. Church in Canada, have industriously circulated a report to the effect that at one time he was connected with a distillery, and also other slanders equally prejudicial to his character as a Christian minister. Very great pains have been taken to ascertain the truth in relation to these statements, but no foundation has been found upon which the fabrication might rest. If Mr. Reynolds had been engaged in any disreputable business transactions between 1815, when he located, and 1824, when he was ordained, how came it that such conduct, which must have been well known if it had ever occurred, was passed over without censure, and he suffered to receive ordination? How was it that the Christian Indians had such confidence in his integrity as to choose him, with the approbation and by the advice of Mr. Case, as one of the Trustees of Grape Island, if he was or had been, as has been asserted, instrumental in the corruption of their tribes; or how was it that even up to 1833, Rev. Egerton, now Dr. Ryerson, could speak as highly of him as he did in the public papers, if such transactions had taken place? That no charges were preferred against Mr. Reynolds at the time these things are represented to have occurred, and that the violent opposers of Methodism in and around Belleville did not blazon abroad such a grave dereliction from rectitude, as they certainly would have done had it been in their power to do so, is a sufficient refutation of the slander.

In 1809 there were 5 preachers stationed in Lower Canada, and in Upper Canada 13. The District in Lower Canada extended from Ottawa to Quebec, the Upper Canada District from Cornwall in the east to Detroit in the west. The Presiding Elders were, for Lower Canada, Samuel Coate, for Upper Canada. Joseph Sawyer. The membership in 1810 was, in Lower Canada, 192, in Upper Canada, 2603. How five preachers were sustained by so small a membership as there was in Lower Canada it is difficult to understand, but as they were mostly single men it is to be presumed that they lived with the people. This year the Rev. Daniel Freeman was sent to the Ancaster Circuit, Rev. Joseph Gatchell to the Niagara, and S. Luckey to the Ottawa. In 1811 there was a slight decrease in Upper Canada, and in Lower Canada a small increase.

In 1812 the entire* Canadian work was placed under the Genesee Annual Conference. Henry Ryan, who had been appointed to the Upper Canada District in 1810, was continued in the same relation, and Nathan Bangs was appointed to the Lower Canada District in place of Joseph Samson, who had been the Presiding Elder the year previous. In consequence, however, of the war which this year broke out between England and the United States, Messrs. Bangs, Luckey, and others did not go to their respective fields of labor. These brethren, who, during their career in Canada,

* Dunham and Stanstead charges were border circuits, and therefore are not included in the Canadian work, as they were never connected with the Lower Canada District.

had conducted themselves with remarkable prudence, did not leave the province at this juncture because of any misunderstanding between them and the people, but because, being citizens of the country with which England and the colonies were at war, they found themselves looked upon with suspicion by those who were not Methodists, and in consequence their power to do good circumscribed; and in addition to this, the Canadian Government had issued an order commanding all American citizens to leave the province by the 3rd of July, 1812.

There were in Upper Canada, at the Conference of 1812, 13 preachers and 2550 members; in Lower Canada there were 5 preachers and a membership of 295, making in all, including the preachers, 2863 souls, the result of twenty-two years of laborious toil on the part of the self-sacrificing missionaries. Of deaths and removals no proper record had been kept.

CHAPTER XI.

FROM THE COMMENCEMENT OF THE WAR TILL THE DEATH OF BISHOP ASBURY

The war cloud bursts—Madison's recommendation—Canadian retaliatory order—Meeting of the New York and Genesee Conferences—Reasons why the American preachers did not come to their work—Names of preachers standing to their posts—Hibbard's fate—Canadian special Conferences during the war—Necessity for them—David Culp called out—How the work was supplied—State of the societies at the close of the war—Genesee Conference resumes control of the work—Death of Dr. Coke—Bishop Asbury visits Canada—Extracts from his journals—He returns to the United States—His death—The effect of the death of Dr. Coke and Bishop Asbury on Canadian Methodism.

THE dark cloud which had for some time been gathering over the horizon of both nations, as has been intimated in the preceding chapter, now burst forth in all its fury upon the devoted heads of the inhabitants.

Four days previous to the meeting of the New York Conference, which was convened, according to Dr. Bangs, on the 5th of June, 1812, at Albany, President Madison, in his message to Congress, had recommended war with Great Britain. Congress acquiesced, and on the 18th of the same month war was formally declared. The news reached Lower Canada on the 24th, and Upper Canada on the 26th; and, as a consequence of this proclamation, the Canadian Government issued the order mentioned before, that "all American citizens should leave the country by the 3rd day of July, 1812." This decree was to go into effect just twenty days before the meeting of the Genesee Conference, so that it will be readily seen that these two Conferences assembled this year under a pressure of great anxiety respecting their Canadian brethren. Appointments, however, were made to the Canadian work by both. The Upper Canada District had in 1810 been placed under the care of the Genesee Conference, but the Lower Canada District remained connected with the New York Conference till the close of this year. The appointments were as follows, to Lower Canada:—

LOWER CANADA DISTRICT—NATHAN BANGS, P. E.

Montreal—N. Bangs.

Quebec—Thomas Burch.

Ottawa—Robert Hibbard.

St. Francis River—Samuel Luckey, J. F. Chamberlain.

But, though these appointments were made, but two went to the fields assigned to them, viz., R. Hibbard and Thomas Burch, it being considered unsafe for the others to come into the province, in consequence of the proclamation, Mr. Burch supplying Mr. Bangs' place in Montreal, where, being a British subject, he was permitted to remain.

For Upper Canada the appointments were as follows:—

UPPER CANADA DISTRICT—HENRY RYAN, P. E.

Augusta—J. Rhodes, E. Cooper, S. Hopkins.

Bay Quinte—Isaac B. Smith, John Reynolds.

Smith's Creek—Thomas Whitehead.

Yonge Street—Joseph Gatchell.

Niagara—Andrew Prindle, Ninian Holmes.

Ancaster and Long Point—Enoch Burdoch, Peter Covenhoven.

Detroit—George W. Densmore.

As Detroit could be supplied from the American side, Mr. Densmore remained for a time in Canada. The preachers who were engaged in the work in Canada during the war were, H. Ryan, T. Whitehead, John Reynolds, A. Prindle, E. Burdock,

G. W. Densmore, who remained for a time, David Culp, who was called out by Mr. Ryan as a supply early in 1812, David Youmans, William Brown and Ezra Adams, who all entered the ranks between that time and the close of the war.

Just prior to the war the statistics for both Canadas were as follows:—2 Districts; 11 circuits, with a membership, including the preachers, of 2863. Alas! that cruel, ruthless war should retard a work so graciously begun; but it was permitted so to be. Two nations of kindred blood rushed to arms. "Greek met Greek" in the open field, and in the sanguinary conflicts which followed, many brave and good men, some of them near relatives or warm personal friends, others brethren in the Church of Christ, who had bowed together at the same altar, now engaged on opposite sides, fell to rise no more till earth and sea shall give up their dead.

It is not the province of a work like this to give a minute detail of all the important historical events connected with the war of 1812; nor is this the place to enter into any argument upon the subject. Suffice it to say that its disastrous effects on both countries were felt for several years after its close; and it is to be earnestly hoped that no such calamity may occur in the future. There are many interests common to both England and the United States which should unite them so closely together in the bonds of amity, as to render such a contingency impossible. Originally they were of the same blood, and more recently there has been such a constant interchange of immigration and emigration going on between the two nations, especially between the British Colonies and the United States—British subjects going thence, and Americans coming into the provinces—that the people may almost be said to be one, and a war between them would be in reality fratricidal. Commercially, they are mutually, to a very great extent, dependent on each other. But more than all this, and above it, they are the two great Protestant nations in the world—the only nations that stand forth as champions of civil and religious liberty, and the only ones who stand ready at all times to succor the distressed and downtrodden of other nations. Surely then, in view of all these circumstances, it behoves the statesmen of both countries to exercise a mutual forbearance towards each other, and this done their petty differences will be adjusted without recourse to arms.

As the breaking out of the war had so entirely disarranged the work that it was impossible to proceed without new plans, Mr. Ryan, Presiding Elder of the Upper Canada District, called a Conference of the preachers who remained in the country, which met at Mr. Benjamin Corwyn's, near Lundy's Lane, in the summer of 1812, and here they arranged the Upper Canadian work. There were present at this Conference, H. Ryan, Thomas Whitehead, A. Prindle, John Reynolds, E. Burdock, G. W. Densmore, J. Rhodes, E. Pattie, and David Culp. It will be seen from the above that all the preachers remaining in the country were not present at this Conference, perhaps because in the then disturbed state of the country it was not possible for them to attend. Lower Canada, probably in consequence of the distance, as well as the danger of travelling in such troublesome times, was not represented at all. Indeed there were not many to represent, and scarcely any one to come. The Messrs. Burch and Hibbard had, it is true, gone to their respective fields of labor, Mr. Burch supplying the place of Mr. Bangs in Montreal, and Mr. Hibbard going to Ottawa; but unhappily, in October of the same year, while visiting the societies on the St. Francis Circuit, which were without a preacher, in consequence of Mr. Luckey not thinking it safe to come, he, in attempting to cross the St. Lawrence on the ferry, by some mischance fell into the river and was drowned, though his horse escaped. Mr. Hibbard was last seen with his arms extended to heaven and then sank to rise no more till he shall be summoned by the great archangel; thus adding another name to the list of faithful missionaries who have fallen while laboring to advance the interests of the

Redeemer's kingdom. Although diligent search was made, his body was never recovered.*

In consequence of the war pressing so heavily on certain localities, a few of the preachers stopped travelling, but almost all acquiesced in Mr. Ryan's arrangements and cheerfully went to their work. Financially, the preachers were often in very great straits, though where all spiritual life was not pressed out of the people, they gave of their means for the support of their ministers to the extent of their ability. Every effort was made by Mr. Ryan and his little band of co-laborers to supply the people with the word of life, and to do this the more effectually, several of those circuits nearly adjoining each other were united, so that they could be under the supervision of the regular preachers, who visited the various appointments at stated periods, as nearly as they possibly could, while the intervals were, as far as was practicable, filled by the local preachers, or when in, or approaching near to the vicinity in which they lived by those brethren who had located, and had not re-entered the effective ranks. These were Daniel Pickett. Darius Dunham, Daniel Freeman, Robert Perry.

† Mr. Ryan summoned a second Conference in 1813, which met at Bowman's church in the township of Ancaster; and, the war still continuing to rage, in the spring of the year following, 1814, he called a Conference which assembled at the "6th Town Shore meeting-house"—District of Prince Edward—near a Mr. Conger's. Here, as well as at the former Conferences, the state of the societies was carefully considered.

* Another authority says that it was in the Richelieu River that Mr. Hibbard was drowned, and that some time after that sad event a body was found, which being supposed to be that of Mr. Hibbard his friends caused it to be buried.

† No regular record of these Conferences has been preserved, but the deficiency has been supplied, as far as was practicable, by the kindness of our aged veteran, David Culp, who was present at all of them, having been called out by the Presiding Elder, Mr. Ryan, early in the year 1812, and who is therefore the oldest Methodist preacher in the country.

and such changes made in the itinerancy as was judged best for the cause in the country. There were present at the Conference of 1814, Henry Ryan, Thomas Whitehead, E. Burdock, John Reynolds, A. Prindle, J. Rhodes, E. Pattie, T. Madden, Daniel Pickett, and David Culp. Ezra Adams—who had been admitted into society by David Culp—was this year employed by this Conference, but was not, it appears, present.

John Reynolds, whose health had been greatly enfeebled by his excessive labors, located either in the latter part of 1814. or the beginning of 1815, and commenced teaching school, but finding his lungs continuing weak he entered the mercantile business, as has been before mentioned. Several others of the preachers, besides Mr. Reynolds, located during or immediately after the war.

It will have been observed by a previous paragraph, that some of the preachers who had formerly located were present at this Conference of 1814, having been called into active service by Mr. Ryan, as the necessity of the case required.

Throughout the course of the war high churchmen, and other interested politicians, had sought to "evil affect" the minds of the Methodist people of Canada against the American preachers, urging that the societies in the province ought not any longer to be dependent upon ministers who owed allegiance to a foreign government. This plea, which at first sight appeared plausible, led some astray. A few Methodists about Kingston withdrew and formed themselves into a body called Provincial Methodists. The body was small and short-lived, the preachers and most of the people returning to the old fold.

The war of 1812 terminated by the treaty of Ghent, on the 24th of December, 1814, but so slowly did news travel in those days, it was not until the 17th of February, 1815, that the treaty was ratified at Washington, and the tidings were not officially announced in Canada until the 1st of March.

On the 29th of June the Genesee Conference met at Lyons, N. Y., and resumed the control of the societies in Canada; and again, with the consent of the Canadian Methodists, sent out heralds to assist in proclaiming the glad tidings of peace through the country.

It has been previously stated that the membership of the Church, just prior to the commencement of the war numbered 2863. At its close there were returned, at the Genesee Conference of 1815, only 1765; this, however, does not include Lower Canada, from which there were no returns. Such are the sad effects of war, whether it is undertaken justly or unjustly. There had been not only a fearful loss of life and property occasioned by this war, but also a very great declension of religious feeling among the inhabitants generally.

The Canadian work was once more divided into two Districts, viz., Upper and Lower Canada, the Upper Canada District extending from the Bay of Quinte in the east to Detroit in the west, including six circuits. The appointments were as follows:

UPPER CANADA DISTRICT—WILLIAM CASE, P. E.

Bay Quinte—David Culp, Ezra Adams.
Smith's Creek—To be supplied.
Yonge Street—John Rhodes.
Ancaster—Thomas Whitehead, David Youmans.
Niagara—William Brown.
Detroit—Joseph Hickcox.

The Lower Canada District extended from Augusta in the west to Quebec in the east, to which the following appointments were made:

HENRY RYAN, PRESIDING ELDER.

Augusta—Thomas Madden, Andrew Prindle.
St. Lawrence—Israel Chamberlain, John Arnold.
Montreal and Quebec—To be supplied.

Two of the old circuits were this year left out of the

Minutes, namely, Long Point in the west, and St. Francis in the east, but the societies on the Long Point Circuit, including Oxford and other places west of the Grand River, were supplied with preaching, as far as was practicable, by the preachers on the Ancaster Circuit.

The death of Dr. Coke, which occurred at sea, May 3rd, 1814, while on his way to establish a mission in Ceylon, occasioned great sorrow among both the Methodists of Europe and America. It was announced at the various Conferences of 1815, and a brief but interesting account of his life and labors was published in the Minutes of that year. As first Bishop of the M. E. Church, he was enshrined in the hearts of American Methodists; and as a zealous and indefatigable missionary, he was equally and deservedly popular throughout England, Ireland, and Wales. His death was sudden, but we have no doubt glorious. He had retired to his cabin at the usual hour; in the morning it was found that his spirit had taken its flight. Like Enoch of old, "He walked with God, and was not: for God took him." Thus, unattended by any but the angelic host, this eminent servant of God passed away to his rest.

Bishop Asbury did not long survive his friend and co-laborer, Dr. Coke, having died in less than two years after. Mr. Asbury was born in England, on the 20th of August, 1745. In 1771 he came to America, landing at Philadelphia, Oct. 27th of that year. At the General Conference of 1784, which was held in Baltimore, he was ordained Bishop of the M. E. Church. From the time of Mr. Asbury's arrival in America until his death, a period of forty-five years, he allowed himself no relaxation from his excessive labors; travelling continually from north to south, from south again to north, publishing alike to *bond* and free the glad tidings of salvation. In the year 1811 Mr. Asbury made a short visit to Canada. A few extracts from his journals of that date will suffice to show the estimation which he had of the country, as well as his own severe toils and suffering while laboring among the societies in this province. He says:

"At the Indian village I led my horse across the pole bridge; careful as I was, he got his feet in an opening and sank into mud and water; away went the bags—books and clothing wet, and the horse yet fast. We pried with a pole at the stern, and he, by making a desperate effort at the same time, plunged forward and came out. The mosquitoes were not idle while we were busy. * * * At eight o'clock we set sail and crossed the St. Lawrence by rowing; the river here is three miles wide. We rode through Cornwall in the night, and came to Evan Roy's, making fifty-four miles for the day's journey. It is surprising how we make nearly fifty miles a day over such desperate roads as we have lately travelled. * * * I suffer much from my lame feet and the great heat, and no small inconvenience because I have not been instructed how to prepare my mind and body for the change I discover on this side. * * * Why should I have new feelings in Canada? Friday I preached at the German settlement. I was weak in body, yet greatly helped in speaking. Here is a decent, loving people; my soul is much united to them. I called upon Father Dulmage, and Brother Hicks, a branch of an old Irish stock of Methodists in New York; I lodged at David Brackenridge's, above Johnston. Saturday we rode twelve miles before breakfast; reached Elizabethtown. Our ride has brought us through one of the finest countries I have ever seen. The timber is of noble size; the cattle are well shaped and well-looking: the crops are abundant, on most fruitful soil; surely this is a land that God the Lord has blessed.

"Upper Canada, Sunday 7th. I rose in pain. We have a large, unfinished house in which we congregated for love-feast, at eight o'clock, and sacrament. I could not speak long. We had about one thousand souls together. Monday, we took the path to Mallory's, where we dined, and continued on to

Baldwin's, and from thence to Joel Stone's, at the mouth of Canadiguk. The pain in my foot is so severe that I cannot much enjoy the great kindness of these people. Tuesday, a heavy ride brought me to Elias Dulmage's. My foot is much inflamed, and my whole body disordered. Wednesday, I preached in the new chapel at Kingston. I have applied a poultice to my foot; I must do something to hasten a cure, or I shall scarcely reach Conference in time."

Mr. Asbury remained in Canada till the 15th of July, when he crossed from Kingston to Sackett's Harbor, and proceeded thence to Conference. He continued to labor faithfully to the end, and may almost be said to have "ceased at once to work and live," having preached his last sermon on the Sunday previous to his death. He expired in peace on Sunday, the 31st of March, 1816, in the 71st year of his age.

Shortly before Bishop Asbury's death he wrote to the British Conference remonstrating with its members on their action in sending their missionaries to Canada, and taking up work already occupied, thereby creating ill-will and division in the societies. His English brethren, however, did not heed his gentle remonstrance, and thus was entered the dividing wedge, which has since so riven and marred the Canadian Church. Before the matter could be brought before the General Conference of 1816, the Bishop had passed from the ranks of the Church militant to those of the Church triumphant.

The death of Bishops Coke and Asbury was greatly lamented by the American Church, and the Canadian Methodists had as much reason to regret their demise as any other section of the church on this continent. Indeed, as subsequent events proved, they had much more reason to deplore it, for had they lived they possibly might have prevented, by their prudent counsels and remonstrances, the inroads made in after years upon the societies in Canada by the English missionaries

CHAPTER XII.

DIFFICULTIES WITH THE ENGLISH MISSIONARIES.

Sanguine hopes dashed to the ground—Arrival of English missionaries—Consequent dissension and division—Charges of disloyalty—By whom the dissensions were fomented—The reason why—Correspondence between the American and English Conferences in 1816—No beneficial result—Another four years—Correspondence between the two bodies in 1820—Its result—The division of fields of labor—Letters of instruction—Arrangements carried out.

THE war being now ended it was hoped that peace would once more be restored to the distracted societies as well, and that in a very short time the Conference would be able to supply the various circuits in Canada with suitable pastors, whose labors would, as in times past, be crowned with success; but in these expectations the Canadian Church was, to a great extent, mournfully disappointed.

During the war some parties, taking advantage of the absence of the American preachers, who were prevented by it from coming to their charges in Lower Canada, invited the English Conference to send a missionary to Quebec. The request was complied with, and he was shortly after followed by one to Montreal. At a later period the English Missionary Society sent their agents into Upper Canada, and these men, arrogating to themselves the claim of *superior loyalty*, began at once sowing the seeds of discord and strife in old and long-established societies. The seed sown produced the desired fruit in due time, and an agitation commenced for a separation of the Canadian Methodists from the parent body.

Of the charges brought against the American preachers by the high-church politicians and the English missionaries, the only important ones—two in number—were most unjust. The first, that the American preachers taught their adherents disloyalty to the British Government, was utterly untrue, as the conduct of Canadian Methodists amply proved throughout the entire struggle of the war, by freely dyeing Canadian soil with their blood in its defence. The second, that the American preachers had not the proper regard for the welfare of the Canadian Societies, or they would not have left their little flocks at the first appearance of danger, and fled to the United States for safety, was exceedingly unfair, when these same accusers knew perfectly well that a government proclamation had *ordered them to leave the country* within less than a month after the declaration of war. This fact, however, was kept studiously out of sight by the unscrupulous maligners—a feat which it was not difficult to accomplish in those days, when there were few if any newspapers in the country to chronicle the proceedings of the government, or indeed any one else, and when there were a great many who could not have very well afforded to take them if there had been. It was not, therefore, a hard matter to mislead some uninformed people by such false representations as these, and thus induce them to encourage the interference of the English missionaries.

Another plea, however, was urged by the British Conference, viz., the religious destitution of the people during the war—a plea which, as far as Upper Canada was concerned, was not true; one which was evidently prompted only by political rancor. If the English Conference felt so keenly for the "religious destitution" of the Canadian people, why did they not send their missionaries to their aid at an earlier period, when the people were really destitute, and thus occupy the ground before those encroaching Americans had an opportunity, instead of waiting complacently until these same Americans, at the risk of their lives, had established flourishing societies in almost every settlement of any considerable size, from Detroit to Quebec, and then attempting to undermine them, that they might build upon the foundation which others had laid?

The cry of disloyalty raised by the enemies of all Methodism, and echoed by the English party, was without even the shadow of an excuse, as the Methodist people themselves had proved; but to remove every doubt respecting it, and to show plainly the course to be pursued by American Methodist preachers under foreign governments, the General Conference of 1820 adopted the following disciplinary rule:—"As far as it respects civil affairs, we believe it the duty of Christians, and especially all Christian ministers, to be subject to the supreme authority of the country where they may reside, and to use all laudable means to enjoin obedience to the powers that be; and therefore it is expected that all our preachers and people who may be under the British, or any other government will behave themselves as peaceable and orderly subjects."—*American Discipline, page* 26.

So far as it regarded the religious destitution of the people during the war, Mr. Ryan had supplied the vacancies occasioned by the carrying out of the proclamation, with the assistance of those preachers who showed their loyalty both to the government and to the interest of the Church by remaining in the country despite danger and difficulties, and in so doing he had supplied the work better, and accomplished more good than the few English missionaries could possibly have done, ignorant as they were of the country, and uninured to its peculiar privations. The injustice, untruthfulness, and unfairness of the charges brought against the Canadian Methodists were unworthy of the merest time-serving politician; how much more unworthy, then, were they of the character of ministers of the Gospel.

These missionaries, on coming to the province, at once entered on their work of division, pleading in justification of their conduct, that it was decidedly wrong for the Methodists of Canada to be under any foreign ecclesiastical superintendence, while, with their usual consistency, the English Conference at this very time—which fact was, however, kept carefully out of sight—was pushing forward its mission work, and sending its missionaries into foreign countries, wherever there was any opening whatever. Not that the sending out of missionaries into foreign lands was reprehensible; what was wrong, dishonorable, was, the desiring to supplant others on already occupied ground, and to deprive them of the fruit of their self-sacrificing labors.

The true reason for the conduct of the English missionaries, and for their encouragement by both the Home and Provincial Governments, was one very different from that given to the people. The members of the Methodist Episcopal Church were opposed to any *Established Church* in the colonies, while the Wesleyans of England, in those days, were not, considering themselves to be, as Mr. Alder afterwards affirmed, "a branch of the Church of England, both at home and abroad."

Bishop Asbury's letter of remonstrance to the English Conference resulted in the appointment of the Rev. Messrs. Black and Bennett, of Nova Scotia, as delegates on the part of the English missionaries to the American General Conference of 1816, but produced no beneficial effect. The speeches of the delegates were conciliatory, nothing more, and the reply of the English Conference to the Bishop's letter as follows:—

"*New Chapel, City Road, London, Feb. 7th*, 1816.

VERY DEAR SIR,—It is by the particular request of the last British Conference that we, as members of the Missionary Committee, address you, and our brethren in the United States, whom we very highly esteem as fellow citizens of the saints, and fellow-laborers in the vineyard of our common Lord; most fervently wishing that peace, righteousness, and joy in the Holy Ghost may abound in you and by you, to the praise of God and the glory of his grace.

"On reading your last very kind and affectionate letter, we sympathized with you, knowing how much it must have effected your mind, after being favored with so much spiritual prosperity, to have to lament a "decrease of members in your societies;' but we trust, since it hath pleased Divine Providence to cause the terrors of war to cease, and to restore the invaluable blessing of peace between the two countries, that by this time you hail the dawn of a more auspicious day, and see the returning glory of the Lord revealed, and the quickening power of the Spirit diffusing its reviving influence, and that the voice of joy and rejoicing is heard in the congregations of the righteous. 'Glory to God in the highest, peace upon earth, and good-will toward men.' Our united prayer and supplication for you is, 'O Lord, we beseech, O Lord, we beseech, send now prosperity.

"It is with gratitude to the Lord of all that we can say, He is still extending His kingdom among us, by the instrumentality of the preached word; and his servants have had much consolation in their labors by seeing sinners powerfully convinced of sin, penitents born of God, and believers sanctified by the Spirit. God has lately been reviving his work in various places, particularly in the city of Bristol, at Salisbury, &c.; in the former place several hundreds have been brought to the knowledge of God their Saviour. We can assure you we love this 'good old-fashioned religion,' of a deep conviction for sin, a clear sense of justification by faith, and entire sanctification of the soul from all moral pollution, as well, if not better than ever. Blessed be the God and Father of our Lord Jesus Christ, who hath blessed us, and does even now bless us, with these spiritual blessings in heavenly places in Christ Jesus; and we ever pray with increasing desire, 'Thy kingdom come.' Our blessed Lord has greatly favored us with success in our missionary efforts, particularly in our new stations in the eastern world, Ceylon, &c., though this has been attended with its afflictive circumstances. Since the death of our venerable, highly esteemed, and much lamented friend and brother, Dr. Coke, our beloved Brother Ault has been removed from a sphere of useful labor to his great reward. The other brethren are still preserved in their useful labors. A Buddhist priest of considerable learning has been converted to Christianity, and is now engaged in translating the Scriptures into two of the native languages. Several Moormen, or Mohammedans, have also received the truth, and are becoming useful preachers of the word of life; and thousands of the poor heathen flock to hear the joyful tidings of the Gospel. Our missionaries have begun to build a large chapel, house, school, printing-office, &c., at Columbo, and have received the liberal support of the inhabitants. These buildings are to cost seven thousand dollars, six thousand of which have been already subscribed by the inhabitants. We have lately sent five more missionaries to that quarter of the globe, and one more is shortly to sail for Bombay. Thus the Lord is enlarging his kingdom 'even from the rivers to the ends of the earth.'

"We rejoice in the ardent Christian affection you express toward your brethren in this country, and be assured they entertain the same lively feelings and sentiments of brotherly love toward you and your fellow laborers in the Lord; and should we be favored with a visit from you or them, it would give us inexpressible pleasure to give you the right hand of fellowship, and every expression of our sincere Christian regard.

"To preserve a mutual good understanding and the unity of the Spirit, and, as far as possible, a co-operation in promoting the good work of the Lord, we feel it our duty to state to you a subject of local difference, which to us has been painful, and which we feel a delicacy in stating, but to which we are compelled from the necessity of the case, that the word of the Lord be not hindered. In consequence of application being made to the British Conference, from a society at Montreal, a missionary was sent to that place, and received as the messenger of the Gospel of peace; but we are sorry to learn that some misunderstanding has taken place between Brothers Strong and Williams, our missionaries, and Brother Ryan, your Presiding Elder for Lower Canada. From the former we have received a statement of their proceedings, and from the latter a letter of complaint. We have also received a letter from Brother Bennett, the Chairman of the Nova Scotia District, who has visited Montreal, etc., and reported to us his proceedings. Upon a review of the whole, and from the most serious and deliberate consideration, we are led to conclude that, considering the relative situation of the inhabitants of Montreal and of Canada to this country, and particularly as a principal part of the people appear to be in favor of our missionaries, it would be for their peace and comfort and for the furtherance of the Gospel, for our brethren to occupy those stations, especially the former, and to which we conceive we have a claim, as a considerable part of the money for building the chapel and house was raised in this country. We trust our American brethren will see the propriety of complying with our wishes with respect to those places; not to mention their political relation to this country, which, however, is not of little importance, for we are conscious that their general habits and prejudices are in favor of English preachers, being more congenial to their views and feelings, which should certainly be consulted, and will tend to facilitate the success of the Gospel and their spiritual prosperity. As your and our object is mutually to diffuse the knowledge of Him whose kingdom is not of this world, and by every possible means to promote the immortal interests of men, let us not contend; we have one Master, even Christ; but give place to each other, that the word of the Lord may have free course, run and be glorified. We cannot but hope that, from the contiguity of the labors of the brethren belonging to the two Conferences, the spirit of unity and love will be promoted, and by this measure a more perfect reciprocal intercourse established. As you have kindly invited our esteemed brethren Messrs. Black and Bennett to take a seat in your Conference, we have directed them to pay you a visit at Baltimore for this purpose, and to amicably arrange and settle this business, whom we trust you will receive as our representatives and as brethren.

"Praying that our mutual love may abound yet more and more, and that we may ever enjoy and rejoice in each others' prosperity, till the whole earth is filled with the glory of God, we remain your affectionate brethren in Christ Jesus.

"Signed for and in behalf of the Committee,

JAMES WOOD, *Treasurer.*
JOSEPH BENSON,
JAMES BUCKLEY, *Secretary.*"

This communication, and other papers submitted by Messrs. Black and Bennett on behalf of the English Conference, as well as various petitions from Canada, protesting against the objectionable course pursued by the English missionaries, were referred to a committee of the General Conference, and after having given a patient hearing to Messrs. Black and Bennett, on behalf of the English Conference, and Messrs. Ryan and Case, on behalf of the Canadian Methodists, the committee presented the following report, which was adopted by the Conference:

"The Committee appointed by the General Conference to confer with Messrs. Black and Bennett, delegates appointed by the London Methodist Missionary Society to represent the British connexion to this Conference, and, if possible, to make an amicable adjustment of certain differences between our Church and the British connexion relative to Upper and Lower Canada, beg leave to submit the following report, viz.:

"1. Your committee have had several friendly interviews with the above-mentioned delegates on those subjects, and they are happy to state that there appears to be an earnest desire to have all existing difficulties terminated to the mutual peace and satisfaction of both parties, and to perpetuate the Christian union and good understanding which have hitherto existed.

"2. It appears, from written communications, as well as from verbal testimony, that unhappy dissensions have taken place in Montreal between certain missionaries sent (at the request of a few official members of the society in that place, in time of the last war,) by the London Missionary Society, and some American preachers, which have terminated in a division of that society.

"3. Although the late hostilities between the two countries separated, for some time, those provinces from the immediate superintendency of the Methodist Episcopal Church in America, yet all the circuits, (except Quebec), were as regularly supplied as circumstances would admit of with American preachers.

"4. It furthermore appears, from written and verbal communications, that it is the desire of the great majority of the people in Upper and Lower Canada to be supplied, as heretofore, with preachers from the United States.

"5. In the two provinces there are twelve circuits and one station, (Montreal), which have eleven meeting-houses, which have been hitherto supplied by American preachers.

"These things being duly considered, together with the contiguity of those provinces to the western and northern parts of the United States, your committee respectfully submit the following resolutions:—

"Resolved by the delegates of the Annual Conferences of the Methodist Episcopal Church, in General Conference assembled,

"1. That we cannot, consistently with our duty to the societies of our charge in the Canadas, give up any part of them, or any of our chapels in those provinces, to the superintendence of the British connexion.

"2. That a respectful letter be addressed to the London Methodist Missionary Society, explaining the reasons for the above resolutions."

Neither the action of the General Conference, nor the letters of explanation or remonstrance which accompanied the above

...solutions, produced, however, any beneficial result; instead of the intruders being removed, the number was increased in Lower Canada and others sent to Upper Canada, where, like their predecessors in Lower Canada, they began scattering the firebrands, arrows, and death of dissension among the already sorely tried societies. For four years longer this state of things continued, crippling the energies of the societies, retarding the progress of the work of evangelization, and giving ample opportunity for the enemies of Methodism to cry, "Ha! ha!!" But at last, in 1820, an arrangement was entered into between the General Conference and the English Connexion. Communications had been passing between the two bodies from time to time, relative to the matters in dispute between them, and at this General Conference the whole trouble was once more discussed, in consequence of the presentation to the Conference of numerous "memorials and petitions from the several circuits in Upper Canada, protesting against the interference of the British missionaries, and praying that they might still be supplied with the ministry and ordinances of religion by the American Conference." A document, of which the following is a copy, relating to the same subject, had also been received from the Methodist Missionary Society in London, and had been submitted to the General Conference by Bishop McKendree:—

"*Wesleyan Mission House*, 77 *Hatton Garden. London*, 25*th Feb.* 1819.

"DEAR SIR,—We transmit for your information the following resolutions, lately entered into by the Committee of the General Wesleyan Missionary Society in London, relative to the British missionaries in Canada, and which resolutions have been transmitted to those missionaries:—

"*Resolved*, 1. That it be recommended to the brethren in Canada to preach in a chapel which is now jointly occupied by the American brethren, and, for the sake of peace, to pursue their labor separately, and not to continue their labors in any station previously occupied by the American brethren, except when the population is so large, or so scattered that it is evident a very considerable part of them must be neglected.

"*Resolved*, 2. That they are to act under the general instruction of the Committee, of June 26th, 1818, viz.,

"1. That it be communicated to the missionaries there that the Conference and the Committee never intended that missionaries sent out by them should invade the societies raised up by the preachers appointed by the American Conference, and to divide them; but that they should communicate the benefits of the Christian ministry to those parts of the country where the inhabitants are destitute of them, and to labor in those towns and villages where the population is so large that the addition of their labors to those of other ministers is demanded by the moral necessities of the people.

"The foregoing resolutions will, we hope, satisfy yourself and the American Conference, that the British Conference and the Missionary Committee in London feel sorry that any interference should ever have taken place between your missionaries and those sent by the British Conference, who most earnestly wish that their missionaries may labor in harmony with all good men.

"Praying that Christian kindness and good-will may prevail and abound, we are, dear sir, with Christian affection, your obedient servants.

JABEZ BUNTING,
RICHARD WATSON,
JOS. TAYLOR,
General Secretaries."

After having given the whole subject a careful consideration the General Conference adopted the following resolutions:—

"1. *Resolved*, by the delegates of the Annual Conferences, in General Conference assembled, That it is the duty of the Bishops of the Methodist Episcopal Church to continue their episcopal charge over our societies in the Canadas, all except Quebec.

"2. *Resolved*, &c., That the following address be sent to our brethren in Canada:—

"DEAR BRETHREN,—We have received, and read with deep interest, the affectionate memorials and addresses from the several circuits in the Provinces of Canada, in which you have expressed your strong attachment to us, and your ardent desire for the continuance of our ministerial care over you. We most cordially reciprocate the sentiments of brotherly affection and Christian attachment you have expressed, and pledge ourselves to use our best endeavors for your spiritual and eternal interests.

"We sincerely deprecate those evils of which you complain. and which have grown out of the conduct of the missionaries sent by the British Conference to labor in Canada. Confiding, however, in the integrity of that Conference, and believing they have been misled by partial and erroneous statements sent by interested parties in Canada, we still hope that the existing embarrassments will be removed, and that an amicable adjustment of this unhappy affair may be brought about.

"We can assure you that no means which, in our opinion. will be likely to produce this desirable result, shall be left untried.

"That you may be convinced that we have neither been inattentive to your interests nor unmindful of the respect due to our British brethren, we beg leave to lay before you a brief statement of what has been done in reference to this subject.

"It is, doubtless, well known to you that your case was fully laid before us at our last sessson in this city, and impartially considered in the presence of Brothers Black and Bennett, who were sent as representatives by the British Conference; and after hearing all that could be said on both sides of the question, it was resolved most expedient, among other reasons because we understood it was your earnest desire, to continue, as we had done heretofore, our ministerial labors among you. That the British Conference might be fully apprized of the course we had taken, an address was sent to them stating the reasons which had directed our decision in relation to Canada, and requesting that some arrangements might be made for an amicable adjustment of the existing difficulties. To this communication we have received no direct answer.

"Similar communications have been since sent by Bishops McKendree and George. The letter sent by Bishop George contained a full development of the affairs of Canada; but neither has an answer to this been received.

"As some of the circuits have petitioned to have a separate Annual Conference in Canada, this subject has been considered, and it is thought to be inexpedient for the present, because, among other reasons, it might prevent that interchange of preachers so very desirable, and so essential to your prosperity.

"After assuring you of our unabated attachment to you as a branch of the Church over which we are called, in the providence of God, to extend our oversight, and of our determination, at your earnest request, as well as from a conciousness of imperious duty, to continue to afford you all the ministerial aid in our power, we exhort you to steadfastness in the faith, to unity and love, and to perseverance in all holy obedience.

"3. *Resolved*, &c., That the following note be inserted in the Discipline, under the twenty-third article of our Church, viz., 'As far as it respects civil affairs we believe it the duty of Christians, and especially of all Christian ministers, to be subject to the supreme authority of the country where they may reside, and to use all laudable means to enjoin obedience to the *powers that be*: and therefore it is expected that all our preachers and people who may be under the British, or any other government, will behave themselves as peaceable and orderly subjects.'

"4. *Resolved*, by the delegates of the Annual Conferences

in General Conference assembled, That this Conference address the British Conference on the subject of a mutual exchange of delegates, as representatives of the one Conference to the other.

"5. That the episcopacy be requested, if practicable, to send a delegate to the British Conference at their next session in July, or at any time thereafter, and furnish him with the requisite instructions, and also to draw on the Book Concern for the amount necessary to defray the expense.

"6. *Resolved*, &c., That the episcopacy, by and with the advice and consent of the Genesee Conference, if they judge it expedient, previous to the sitting of the next General Conference, shall have authority to establish an Annual Conference in Canada."

The first of these resolutions was afterwards so altered as to permit the delegate, who might be sent to represent them at the British Conference, to allow all of Lower Canada to be given up, if by this means they could obtain peace. Rev. J. Emory, afterwards Bishop Emory, was appointed delegate. He proceeded to England, and in addition to bearing the fraternal messages of affection and regard from the American Church to their English brethren, he brought before them once more the Canadian matters for adjustment. Mr. Emory was duly received by the English Conference, and a courteous address was sent in reply to that sent by the General Conference. Resolutions were also passed relating to affairs in America. Of those relating more especially to Canadian matters the following is a copy:—

"On the subject of the unpleasant circumstances which have occurred in the Canadas between the American preachers and our missionaries, referred to the Conference by the Missionary Committee in London, with their opinion that Upper Canada shall be left in possession of the American brethren, and that our missionary exertions shall be confined to the lower province, this Committee recommend to the Conference the adoption of the following principles and arrangements:—

"1. That, as the American Methodists and ourselves are but one body, it would be inconsistent with our unity, and dangerous to that affection which ought to characterize us in every place, to have different societies and congregations in the same towns and villages, or allow of any intrusion on either side into each others' labors.

"2. That this principle shall be the rule by which the disputes now existing in the Canadas, between our missionaries, shall be terminated.

"3. That the simplest and most effectual manner of carrying this rule into effect appears to us to be to accede to the suggestion of the American Conference, that the American brethren shall have the occupation of Upper Canada, and the British missionaries that of Lower Canada, allowing sufficient time for carrying this arrangement into effect, with all possible tenderness to existing prejudices and conflicting interests on both sides; the arrangement to be completed within a period to be fixed as early as possible by the Missionary Committee. But should insuperable difficulties occur in the attempt to execute this plan, (which, however, we do not anticipate) either party shall be at liberty to propose any other mode of accommodation which shall assume as its basis the great principle laid down in the first of these resolutions, and which we are of opinion should be held most sacred in every part of the world.

"4. That if hereafter it shall appear to any of our brethren there, either British Missionaries or American preachers, that any place, on either side of the boundary line now mentioned, needs religious help, and presents a favorable opportunity for usefulness, the case shall be referred by the Canada District Meeting to the General Conference, or by that body to the Canada District; and if either shall formally decline to supply the place on their own side of the boundary, then the other shall be at liberty to supply the said place, without being deemed to have violated the terms of this friendly compact.

"5. And it shall be explicitly understood in this arrangement, that each party shall be bound to supply with preachers all those stations and their dependencies which shall be relinquished by each of the connexions, that no place on either side shall sustain any loss of the ordinances of religion in consequence of this arrangement.

"6. That the Missionary Committee be directed to address a letter to the private and official members, trustees, &c., under the care of our missionaries in Upper Canada, informing them of the judgment of the Conference, and affectionately and earnestly advising them to put themselves and their chapels under the pastoral care of the American preachers, with the suggestion of such considerations, to incline them to it, as the committee may judge most proper.

"7. That the Bishops of the American connection shall direct a similar letter to the private and official members, trustees, &c., under the care of the American preachers in the Province of Lower Canada, requesting them to put themselves and their chapels under the care of the British missionaries."

The English Conference also sent a letter of instruction to their missionaries in the provinces, of which the following is a copy:—

"Copy of a letter of instructions from the Missionary Committee in London, to the Rev. Messrs. R. Williams and others in the Provinces of Canada:—

"Dear Brother,—Herewith we transmit you a copy of resolutions, passed at our late Conference, on the subject of the disputes which have unhappily existed between our American brethren and us, relative to our missions in Canada.

"The preceding resolutions are general, and refer to the renewal of the intercourse, by personal deputation, between the American and British Conferences, by the visit of Mr. Emory. We have given you the resolutions in full, that you may see that we have recognized the principle that the Methodist body is ONE, throughout the world; and that, therefore, its members are bound to cordial affection and brotherly union.

"The resolutions of the Committee, passed some time ago, and forwarded for your guidance, prohibiting any interference with the work of the American brethren, would show you that the existence of collisions between us and them gave us serious concern, and that the Committee were anxious to remove, as far as they, at that time, were acquainted with the circumstances, every occasion of dispute.

"Certainly the case of Montreal chapel was one which we could never justify to our minds, and the Committee have, in many instances, had but partial knowledge of the real religious wants of the upper province, and of its means of supply. The only reason we could have for increasing the number of missionaries in that province was the presumption of a strong necessity, arising out of the destitute condition of the inhabitants, the total want, or too great distance of ministers.

"On no other ground could we apply money raised for missionary purposes for the supply of preachers to Upper Canada. The information we have had for two years past has all served to show that the number of preachers employed there by the American brethren was greater than we had at first supposed, and was constantly increasing.

"To us, therefore, it now appears, that though there may be places in that province which are not visited, they are within range, or constantly coming within the range, of the extended American itinerancy; and that Upper Canada does not present to our efforts a ground so fully and decidedly missionary as the lower province, where much less help exists, and a great part of the population is involved in popish superstition.

"We know that political reasons exist in many minds for supplying even Upper Canada, as far as possible, with British missionaries, and however natural this feeling may be to Englishmen, and even praiseworthy, when not carried too far, it will be obvious to you that this is a ground on which, as a missionary society, and especially as a society under the direction of a committee which recognizes as brethren, and one with itself, the American Methodists, we cannot act.

"1. Because, as a missionary society, we cannot lay it down as a principle that those whose object is to convert the world shall be prevented from seeking and saving souls under a foreign government, for we do not thus regulate our own efforts.

"2. To act on this principle would be to cast an odium upon our American brethren, as though they did not conduct themselves peaceably under the British Government, which is, we believe, contrary to the fact.

"3. That if any particular exceptions to this Christian and submissive conduct were, on their part, to occur, we have not the least right to interfere, unless, indeed, the American Conference obviously neglected to enforce upon the offending parties its own discipline. Upon any political feeling which may exist either in your minds or the minds of a party in any place we cannot, therefore, proceed. Our objects are purely spiritual, and our American brethren and ourselves are one body of Christians, sprung from a common stock, holding the same doctrine, enforcing the same discipline, and striving in common to spread the light of true religion through the world.

"In conformity with these views we have long thought it a reproach, and doing more injury by disturbing the harmony of the two connexions than could be counterbalanced by any local good, that the same city or town should see two congregations, and two societies, and two preachers professing the same form of Christianity, and yet thus proclaiming themselves rivals to each other, and, in some instances, invading each others' societies and chapels, and thus producing party feelings. The purposes of each, we are ready to allow, have been good, though mistaken; and we rather blame ourselves for not having obtained more accurate information on some particulars, than intimate any dissatisfaction with the missionaries in the Canadas, with whose zeal and labors we have so much reason to be satisfied.

"A part of the evil has also arisen from the want of personal communication, by deputation, between the two Conferences, now happily established. These considerations had long and seriously occupied our minds before the arrival of Mr. Emory, charged by the General American Conference to bring these matters under our consideration. The Committee, previous to the Conference, went with him fully into the discussion of the disputes in the Canadas, and recommended those principles of adjustment which the Conference, after they had been referred to a special committee during the time of its sitting, adopted, and which we now transmit to all the brethren in the Canada station.

"You will consider these resolutions as the fruit of a very ample inquiry, and of serious deliberation.

"None of the principles here adopted by us do indeed go further than to prevent interference with each others' labors among the American and British missionaries, and the setting up of 'altar against altar' in the same city, town, or village; but knowing that circumstances of irritation exist, and that too near a proximity might, through the infirmity of human nature, lead to a violation of that union which the Conference has deemed a matter of *paramount* importance to maintain, we have thought it best to adopt a geographical division of the labor of each, and that the upper province should be left to the American brethren, and the lower to you. The reasons for this are:—

"1. That the upper province is so adequately supplied by the American Conference as not to present that pressing case of necessity which will justify our expending our funds upon it.

"2. That Mr. Emory has engaged that its full supply by American preachers shall be, as far as possible, attended to.

"3. That this measure at once terminates the dispute as to Montreal.

"4. That it will prevent collision without sacrifice of public good.

"5. That Lower Canada demands our efforts rather than Upper, as being more destitute, and the labors of the brethren there being more truly missionary.

"A transfer of societies and places of preaching will, of course, follow. Our societies in Upper Canada are to be put under the care of the American brethren; theirs in the lower province under yours.

"It is clear that this, under all the circumstances, will require prudent and wise management, and we depend upon you to carry the arrangement into effect in the same spirit of kindness and temper in which the question has been determined by the Conference and Mr. Emory.

"Feel that you are one with your American brethren, embarked in the same great cause, and eminently of the same religious family, and the little difficulties of arrangement will be easily surmounted, and if any warm spirits (which is probable) rise up to trouble you, remember that you are to act upon the great principle sanctioned by the Conference, and not upon local prejudices. The same advices Mr. Emory has pledged himself shall be given to the American preachers, and you will each endeavor to transfer the same spirit into the societies respectively. When the preachers recognize each other as brethren the people will naturally fall under the influence of the same feeling.

"We have appointed our respected brethren, Messrs. Williams and Hick, who are to choose as an associate a third preacher in full connection, to meet an equal number of preachers to be appointed by the American Bishop, who shall agree upon the time in which the chapels and societies shall be mutually transferred, and the arrangements of the Conference be carried into effect. The place of the meeting they are to fix for their mutual convenience, but the meeting is to be held as early as possible after the receipt of the instructions of the Committee, that the report of the final adjustment of the affair may appear in your next District Minutes.

"We conclude with our best wishes for your personal happiness and usefulness. May you ever go forth in the 'fulness of the blessing of the Gospel of peace,' and be made the honored instruments of winning many souls to the knowledge and obedience of the faith of our Lord Jesus Christ.

"We are, dear brother, yours very affectionately,

JOS. TAYLOR,
RICHARD WATSON, } *Secretaries.*

Wesleyan Mission House, 77 *Hatton Garden*,
23*rd August*, 1820."

It had been agreed between Mr. Emory, on the part of the M. E. Church, and the English Conference, that similar instructions should be sent by the Bishops to the American preachers stationed in Canada, to whom the task of carrying out the above arrangement should be committed; consequently the following communication was addressed by Bishop McKendree to Rev. William Case:—

Alexandria, *D. C.*, *Oct.* 16*th*, 1820.

DEAR BROTHER,—I transmit you herewith a copy of the resolutions of the late British Conference, received through Brother Emory, our representative to that body, on the subjects embraced in his mission; and also of the instructions of the Missionary Committee in London to the Rev. Messrs. R. Williams and the other British missionaries in the Provinces of Canada, predicated on those resolutions.

"From these documents you will perceive that the desire of our General Conference, both for the establishment of a personal intercourse by deputation, between the two connections, and for the amicable adjustment of the afflicting differences in the Canadas, has been happily accomplished. Indeed, it appears, not only from those papers, but from the communications of our representative, that this desire was met, both by the British Conference and the Missionary Committee, with a promptness and brotherly affection which we should take equal pleasure in acknowledging and reciprocating.

"This it now devolves upon me (my colleagues being necessarily at a great distance, in the discharge of their official duties in the south and west) to enjoin it upon you to do, and to promote the same spirit of kindness towards our British brethren, among all the preachers, travelling and local, and all the official and private members within your District, to the utmost extent of your power.

"To remove the prejudices and allay the unpleasant excitements existing will, no doubt, require much prudent care. But 'in this labor of love,' I expect in you a ready mind. Let the difficulties you may meet with only stimulate you to the exertion of your best and most persevering efforts in this behalf. Remember, 'Blessed are the peacemakers;' '*Seek* peace, then, and *ensue* it.' If it even seem to flee from you, follow it.' 'Looking *diligently*, lest any man fail of the grace of God; lest any root of bitterness, springing up, trouble you, and thereby many be defiled.'

"In the present state of things (your acquaintance with which renders detail unnecessary) we have thought it best to agree to a division of our field of labors in the Canadas by the provincial line. In the expediency of this measure you will see that the Missionary Committee in London and the British Conference have concurred, so that our labors there are to be confined, in future, to the upper province, and those of the British missionaries to the lower.

"A transfer of societies and places of preaching will, of

course, follow. Our societies in Lower Canada are to be put under the care of our British brethren, and theirs in the upper province under ours.

"For the execution of these arrangements I have appointed Brother Ryan and yourself, with authority to associate with you a third preacher in full connection, to meet the Rev. Messrs. R. Williams and Hick, appointed by the Missionary Committee, and such other preacher as they may associate with them. The time and place of meeting you will agree on with them, for your mutual convenience. The Missionary Committee have instructed their agents that the meeting is to be held as early as possible, after the receipt of the instructions of the Committee, that the report of the final adjustment of the affair may appear in the next District Minutes. In this we concur. You will, therefore, immediately on the reception of these instructions, in conjunction with Brother Ryan and your associate, correspond with the Rev. Messrs. Williams and Hick and their associate on this subject; and fail not to use every means in your power for the prompt execution of the arrangement in the best faith, and in the most harmonious and affectionate manner. In the language of the Missionary Committee, we cordially unite to say, 'Feel that you are one with your British brethren, embarked in the same great cause, and eminently of the same religious family, and the little difficulties of arrangement will be easily surmounted, and if any warm spirits rise up to trouble you, remember that you are to act on the great principles now sanctioned and avowed by the two connexions, and not upon local prejudices.' If each endeavor to transfuse this spirit into the societies respectively, the people will much more easily be brought under the influence of the same feeling, when it shall be found to possess and actuate the preachers. In any event, let there be no deficiency on your part in spirit, word, or deed. We commit to you a sacred work, which you are bound to perform, not only as to the matter, but in the manner, in the temper, in which, as these instructions are intended to show you, we ourselves would perform it, could we be present. Attend strictly to this, that we may have joy and consolation in your love, the bowels of the saints being refreshed by you; and forward to us, as early as possible, regular and full copies of all your correspondence and proceedings in this business.

"Should it be found practicable to complete the arrangements previously to the next Genesee Annual Conference, you will, of course, take care to provide for the supply of those circuits, societies, and places of preaching in the upper province which may be transferred to us by our British brethren, as they are to provide for those which are to be simultaneously transferred to them in the lower province. You will also take care, from time to time, to extend supplies to any remaining places which may be found destitute in the upper province, as far as possible.

"There are several circuits, I believe, in Lower Canada attached to the New York and New England Conferences. These are included in the arrangement. You will, therefore, forward a copy of these instructions to each of the Presiding Elders in whose Districts those circuits are embraced, and request them to be prepared to co-operate with you in the final execution of the business, and to report the same at their ensuing Annual Conferences respectively.

"The Missionary Committee in London having kindly furnished us with a copy of their instructions we shall transmit a copy of these I now send you to them. You will also show them, when you meet, to the Rev. Messrs. Williams and Hick, and their associate, and, if they desire it, give them a copy, that you may go on in this good work as we have happily begun, with that frankness and kindness which become brethren in such a cause.

"By the sixth resolution of the British Conference on the Canadian business, it is provided that the Missionary Committee be directed to address a letter to the private and official members, trustees, etc., under the care of the missionaries in Upper Canada, informing them of the judgment of Conference, and affectionately and earnestly advising them to put themselves and their chapels under the pastoral care of the American preachers, with the suggestion of such considerations to incline them to it as the Committee may judge most proper. And by the seventh resolution it is provided that we shall address a similar letter to the private and official members, trustees, &c., under our care. I accordingly enclose a letter which you will use for that purpose, after you have met with Messrs. Williams, Hick, &c., and agreed with them on the time of making the transfer of the societies, chapels, &c., but not to be used before. At the same time, after this meeting and agreement, you will also forward a copy of this letter to each of the Presiding Elders in the New York and New England Conferences whose Districts embrace circuits in Lower Canada, to be used by them.

"Confiding in the faithful discharge of the several trusts committed to you, I commend you to the Lord and remain, dear brother, Yours in love,

WM. MCKENDREE.

The address to the "private and official members" in Lower Canada, mentioned by Bishop McKendree in the above letter, was as follows:

"To the private and official members, trustees, &c., of the Methodist Episcopal Church in Lower Canada:

"VERY DEAR BRETHREN,—You are aware that for several years past very unpleasant collisions have occurred in various parts both of the upper and lower provinces, between the British missionaries and some of our brethren. This has been a source of great affliction to us, and has led to the adoption of various and successive measures for the correction of the evil.

"Our late General Conference, being earnestly desirous of restoring the amicable relations of the two connexions, authorized the deputation of a representative to the British Conference for this purpose. One was accordingly sent. And, after a deliberate investigation, it has been mutually thought best, for the sake of peace and love, under all the circumstances of the case, to divide our labors in the Canadas in such a manner as to guard effectually against all collisions in future.

"With this view it has been agreed that our British brethren shall supply the lower province and our preachers the upper; yet so that no circuit or societies on either side shall be left destitute by the other. This has been sacredly attended to, and mutual pledges for the performance of it have been passed. It now becomes our duty, therefore, to inform you of this agreement, and to advise you in the most affectionate and earnest manner to put yourselves and your chapels under the care of our British brethren, as their societies and chapels in the upper province will be put under ours.

"This communication to you, we confess, is not made without pain; not from any want of affection for our British brethren, but from the recollection of those tender and endearing ties which have bound us to you. But a necessity is laid upon us. It is a peace offering. No other consideration could have induced us to consent to the measure. Forgive, therefore, our seeming to give you up. We do not give you up in heart, in affection, in kind regards, in prayers.

"The British and American connexions have now mutually recognised each other as one body of Christians, sprung from a common stock, holding the same doctrines, of the same religious family, and striving in common to speed the light of true religion through the world, and they have agreed to keep up a regular intercourse by deputation, in future, for the maintenance of this brotherly union.

"Let any past differences, therefore, be forgotten; let them be buried forever. Confirm your love toward our British brethren, and receive them as ourselves; not as strangers, but as brothers beloved. By this shall all men know that we are Christ's disciples, if we love one another. Love is of God, and he that dwelleth in love dwelleth in God, and God in him. May the God of love and peace be with you, and crown you with the blessedness of contributing with us to heal the wounds of the Church, and to establish that 'fellowship of the spirit' which shall make us to say, 'Behold how good and how pleasant it is for brethren to dwell together in unity! It is like the precious ointment upon the head, that ran down upon the beard, even Aaron's beard, that went down to the skirts of his garments. As the dew of Hermon, and as the dew that descended upon the mountain of Zion, for there the Lord commanded the blessing even of life for evermore.'

"For any further information that you may desire, I refer you to the Presiding Elder, to whom it is given in charge to make this communication to you; and remain, dear brethren, with the same affection for you in the bonds of the Gospel of peace, and the best wishes and prayers for your happiness and salvation.

"WM. MCKENDREE,

Alexandria, D. C., October 16th, 1820.

Such was the arrangement effected between the two bodies; which, if it had been carried out in good faith by the English missionaries, would have almost immediately restored peace to the disturbed societies, and caused the ruinous agitation to cease. The Americo-Canadian Methodists kept to their part of the agreement to the very letter, removing their men entirely from Lower Canada, while the British missionaries only partially performed theirs, still allowing their agents, in defiance of the agreement, to occupy a station of importance in Upper Canada.

What was accomplished, however, secured comparative peace—for a few years—to most of the societies in Upper Canada, which had been distressed and injured by the unseemly contention; and in 1824, the General Conference once more remonstrated, gently, with the English Conference, on their behalf, and passed the following resolution on the subject:—

"That a respectful representation be made to the British Conference of those points in the agreement between the two connections, which have not, on the part of their missionaries, been fulfilled."

CHAPTER XIII.

FROM THE DEATH OF BISHOP ASBURY TILL 1819.

State of the work just prior to 1817—Conference of 1817—Where held—Bishop George presides—Preparation for the Conference—Result of preparation—Special subject of prayer—The answer—Danger of listening to Methodists—Parental injunctions—Temporary result—Conversion of a Calvinist, and his subsequent life and labors—General revival of 1817—Fresh interference of English missionaries—Consequent trouble—Reason why—Turmoil of 1818 and 1819—Result of the contention, and its effect upon the cause.

NOTWITHSTANDING all the difficulties with which the Church had had to contend during these years of trial, the societies continued steadfast, and in Upper Canada, with very few exceptions, remained strongly attached to the original connexion and to their faithful pastors, the American preachers. Congregations and societies steadily increased. Suitable places of worship were in many places erected, and the power of God in the conviction and conversion of precious souls was manifested on every charge.

The year 1817 was remarkable for the most extensive revivals that had yet taken place in the country. The Genesee Conference held its session this year at Elizabethtown, Upper Canada, commencing June 21st, 1817, Bishop George presiding. An Annual Conference in Canada was a new and strange thing indeed. It was, in fact, an epoch in the history of the province. Anxiously the people awaited the day of its commencement, anticipating with delight the pleasure to be derived from the visit of the Bishop and the other American preachers whom they had never before seen; and many and earnest were the petitions offered up in faith by the people of God, that He would be pleased to pour out His Spirit, not only upon the Conference and themselves, but also on such as might, from mere motives of curiosity, come to see and hear. Some, more earnest even than the others, singled out *particular individuals* of their acquaintance, and made them especial subjects of prayer, for some time previous to the sitting of the Conference. How many sessions of Conference are now preceded by this spirit of earnest supplication, on the part of the people in whose vicinity it is to be held, for the descent of the Holy Spirit, the "baptism of fire?" Among those who had been specially named in these exercises was a young man formerly from Delaware County, State of New York, but then residing not far from Elizabethtown. The individual in question was strictly moral and upright in his deportment, but unconverted, and, therefore, an object of solicitude to faithful Christians. Educated a Calvinist, he had a strong dislike to Methodists, and from what he had heard concerning them, considered their manner of worship very objectionable. At the time he left the parental roof, among many other cautions from his careful parents, he had received one, above all others, to "shun the *Methodists*," as they believed there was some "demoniacal influence about their preaching; it was dangerous to even hear them; those listening might be *bewitched*." The young man carefully attended to the advice of his parents, given, no doubt, with the best intentions, and though deprived of any other means of grace, in consequence of there being no minister of the denomination of which he was an adherent within his reach, he would not for a long time expose himself, as he supposed, to a dangerous influence, by going to hear a Methodist. Finding, however, in his intercourse with these people, that they were peaceable and well-disposed, and that their walk and conversation was not that which he would have expected from people having dealings with the enemy of souls he began to look on them more favorably, and was at length induced to go to their meetings and listen for himself. Having gone for a few times and scrutinized proceedings closely, and being unable, notwithstanding his prejudices against them, to see anything wrong or unscriptural in their manner of worship, he came to the conclusion that the Methodists in Canada must be different from those of whom he had been warned, and that therefore he might attend their meetings in safety. He had attended the Methodist meetings a few times before the Conference met, and being desirous of gaining all the information he could concerning these strange people, influenced, no doubt, by the Holy Spirit, in answer to prayer on his behalf, he attended the meetings held in connection with it, and before its close the word had taken such a hold upon his mind that he then and there sought and experienced a change of heart. He at once cast in his lot with the once despised Methodists, and has since devoted a long and honorable life to the promotion of their interests and the advancement of his Master's kingdom. He became himself a Methodist preacher, and was admitted into the Genesee Conference at the session held in 1820, at Lundy's Lane, having been employed by the Presiding Elder the previous year. The *young* man has grown *old*, both in years and in labors, but the scenes of the Conference of 1817 continue green in his memory. In the seventy-fourth year of his age, and fifty-first of his ministry, Rev. Philander Smith, D. D., senior Bishop of the Methodist Episcopal Church in Canada, still lives a life of usefulness, the fruit of earnest, importunate, faithful prayer. Bishop Smith is the oldest Methodist minister in Canada *now effective*.*

The Elizabethtown Conference is memorable as a spiritual birth-place, not only to Bishop Smith, but to many others still

* As these pages are being put into type the melancholy intelligence reaches us that the venerable Bishop Smith has finished his course. He died at his residence, Brooklin, Ont., March 28th, 1870. Truly a prince and a great man has fallen in Israel.

living in the country. The religious services on the Sabbath commenced at eight o'clock in the morning, and lasted with but little intermission till eight at night. There were five sermons preached, besides the exhortations given. Bishop George delivered a powerful discourse, and it is estimated that over one hundred souls were awakened and led to seek salvation at this Conference, or immediately after its close.

The reformation spirit kindled at this Conference was not confined to Elizabethtown alone, but was carried by the preachers to their respective circuits. Hallowell, Bay of Quinte, and Niagara shared largely in the revival influences. So wide-spread, indeed, was this revival that, despite the interference of the English missionaries, and the opposition of the Executive, influenced as it was by high churchmen and the Family Compact, an increase of 1624 members was reported at the Conference of 1818. In few countries did Methodism spread so rapidly, or take so deep root among the people as it did in Upper Canada prior to the coming of the English missionaries. Up to this time the people were *united*, and the work of evangelization made almost miraculous progress; after this there was dissension and strife, and a corresponding declension in the progress of the Gospel.

The state-paid priesthood of Canada, together with the faction denominated the "Family Compact," had from the first looked with disfavor upon Methodism, and had striven by every means in their power—legal or otherwise—to prevent its introduction, and cripple its movements, and having almost unbounded influence with the Executive, they contrived to make the Methodist societies labor under many civil disadvantages; but this opposition had very little effect upon the masses. Notwithstanding the disabilities under which they labored, the people gladly opened their houses to the self-sacrificing ministers of the pure word, and scores upon scores were converted through their instrumentality, and so remarkably well-conducted, peaceable, and orderly had they proved themselves to be, as subjects of the realm—both preachers and people—that when unjust charges of disloyalty were made against them by designing and unscrupulous politicians, the *parliament* of Upper Canada, in 1828, after a careful inquiry into the conduct of these men, and the influence they had exerted upon the people, from the time of their first entrance into the country, by a vote of the House 22 to 8 publicly vindicated their character from these aspersions.

The principal reason of the bitter hatred of the high church party to the original Methodists of Canada, was their unswerving opposition to church and state connection. This was the "head and front of their offending;" and it was because of this that they were stigmatized as "*rebels*" by their opponents, who were themselves seizing that which did not belong to them, and trampling both law and justice under their feet.

Finding that they could not stop the onward march of Methodism by the means to which they had hitherto resorted, these parties eagerly seized upon this new agency. If they could only succeed in getting the societies divided, so that there would be contention among brethren, a good part of what they desired to accomplish would be done. They hated bitterly Methodism in any form, but if there must be Methodist societies in the province, it would be better for the Church of England if those societies were under the control of the English Conference, as the views of that body, with regard to church and state connection, were more in unison with their own, and by encouraging them to occupy the ground, one of two objects might be gained—perhaps both. Either the English missionaries would crowd the original body out of the field, and thus stifle the opposition to the establishment of the Church of England as *the* Church of the provinces; or the division and strife engendered by the interference of these missionaries in the societies, would so cripple their energies that Methodism would cease to be respected, and having so fallen, its influence would cease to be feared as a power for good in the nation. Accordingly, inducements were held out, and probably some misrepresentations made to the English Missionary Society to influence that body to send out missionaries to Canada. The Society complied, and their agents upon their arrival joined in the false and dishonorable cry of disloyalty, which had been raised against their brethren, and "setting up altar against altar," they divided the societies and congregations wherever they could obtain a foothold, thus accomplishing the end so ardently desired by the enemies of Methodism.

In order to justify their conduct in opposing the original societies the English missionaries united with the high church party and the Executive—not the parliament, be it remembered, but an irresponsible government, influenced by the Family Compact—in the plea that it was inconsistent with true loyalty for the Methodists to be under what they were pleased to term the control of a foreign church. The self-sacrificing ministers who had come to the country when it was a howling wilderness and had endured all manner of harships, in order that they might convey to the destitute and scattered inhabitants the tidings of salvation through the merits of a risen Redeemer—many of them, too, actually British subjects, and attached to British rule—were accused of being political agents, sent here to teach the people sedition. It is not surprising that such calumnies and misrepresentations of the motives of worthy men should have created great excitement, and stirred up much ill will, especially when it was so well known that the original preachers were laborious and pious men, who had served the people faithfully, without meddling with politics, and who had received only the scanty support voluntarily contributed by a poor but willing people; while the new comers, at the same time they were impugning the motives of their brethren, and were striving to enter upon their labor, that they might build on the foundation which others had laid, were to be, in a measure, independent of the societies, being assisted by the influence of the government, and deriving their support from the Missionary society at home, while they were themselves merely the tools of those who cared only that party spite might be gratified, and true Methodistic principles subverted.

The course of procedure of both classes of assailants was noticeably inconsistent. The government, at the very time it was raising such an outcry against Methodists, as being bad subjects, because they were connected with a body the majority of whom were resident in a foreign land, was *giving aid and encouragement* to the Roman Catholic Church, a body that is not only under the temporal and spiritual control of a foreign power, but that *holds itself amenable to no other,* when there is a difference between the civil jurisdiction and the order of the supreme Pontiff; this aid, too, given from the public chest. While the English Conference, at the same time its agents were re-echoing the cry of "no foreign control for Methodists," was, as it afterwards acknowledged in one of its own reports, sending its missionaries into *foreign countries* wherever there was any opening for them.

The year 1819 was one of contention and strife, even worse than the preceding one. Eight more missionaries were sent out from England, so that now they were spread from Quebec to Niagara, and the continual contention between them and the original occupants of the ground greatly retarded the work of the Lord among the people, as it might have been foreseen that it would by those who had planned the scheme. The disastrous results of these dissensions were manifested at the close of the year. The Canadian circuits were only able to report to the Conference of 1819 an increase of 501, while the year previous the increase had been 1624, thus showing conclusively how the work had been retarded by the contention which had sprung up.

In the western portion of the country the commotion had not been so great as in the east, principally because the settlements being newer, especially in the interior, they were more difficult of access, and the work was more laborious. Where there were real hardships to be borne, and real difficulties to be encountered, the original body was still left as before to pioneer the way; after that had been cleared, and the ground broken up, then the others might come in and reap the fruit which their brethren had sown amid toils and hardships almost inconceivable. West of the township of Ancaster there had as yet been no interference, consequently the societies had not been disturbed, the facilities for the transmission of news being so few and irregular that they knew, even by report, very little of what was taking place further to the east, and happy and contented with their relations to their faithful shepherds, they were united and in proportion prosperous.

Societies had been formed along Westminster Street, and on a road known as North Street, running north from Kettle Creek—where St. Thomas is now situated—to the River Thames; and appointments taken up in the townships to the east and the south-west, besides one in the township of Delaware. With the exception of an occasional appointment taken up, or one dropped, the Westminster Circuit remained, so far as geographical boundaries were concerned, in about the same position for several years. Out of reach, for a time at least, of the evil influence of contention and turmoil, these societies kept gradually increasing their numbers, swelled from time to time by conversions among themselves, or by the coming in of immigrants, from the British Isles or from the United States, who had been Methodists in their dear old native land. Here even yet "the desert and solitary place" were "made glad," and the joyous songs of Zion rose to heaven without the comfort of the worshippers being marred by discord and envy. Happy would it have been for the entire work if as much could have been said of it all.

CHAPTER XIV.

INTRODUCTION OF METHODISM INTO THE VICINITY OF LONDON, ETC.

Settlement of new townships in the west—A Methodist ex-Commissary settles in Westminster—He introduces the Gospel into Westminster, Lobo, St. Thomas, and the west of London—Sketch of life and labors of Mr. Pettis—Eastern part of London settled—Arrival of a Methodist family—Mr. Webster finds a class—First sermon preached in London Township—The preacher and text—Mr. Webster finishes his course in peace—Casualty at Hay Bay.

IN a country such as Canada was about this period, new portions of the province were being continually opened up for settlement, and hardy pioneers were constantly taking advantage of the opening thus offered to make themselves homes, and to lay the foundation of future success for their children, and the future greatness of the land of their adoption.

A settlement had been made in Westminster shortly before, or about the time of the war, and of those coming hither a few were Methodists, some from the neighborhood of Kingston, and some from about East Flamboro. Among these was a local preacher, named Charles Pettis, who came to Westminster after the war, and who was destined then and afterwards to do good service in his Master's cause; a short sketch, therefore, of his conversion and subsequent labors will not be uninteresting.

Born in the town of Ashford, State of Massachusetts, in the year 1777, at the age of eleven he, with his parents, removed to Prescott, near which his father settled. In 1794 Mr.

Pettis was awakened under the preaching of Rev. J. Coleman, who was then travelling the Upper Canada Lower Circuit. At this time the whole province was included in two circuits, which were travelled by Messrs. Coleman and Woolsey. On New Year's eve, while Mr. Coleman was conducting the services, Mr. Pettis, then in his 18th year, was converted, and commenced the New Year of 1795 rejoicing in God his Saviour. The year following he was licensed as an exhorter by Rev. S. Keeler, and held meetings among the people in the vicinity in which he lived. In 1809 he removed to East Flamboro, where he continued to exhort and do all he could to benefit the souls of those among whom he lived.

The war breaking out in 1812, Mr. Pettis was called out in the service of his country. He held the office of sergeant, but being connected with the commissariat department, he was not present at any of the engagements. His position, however, gave him considerable influence with the men, and he was allowed to hold meetings among them, and very frequently he administered religious consolation, as well temporal comfort, to the wounded and the dying on the field of battle.

After the termination of the war he removed, with his wife and four other persons, from Flamboro to North Street, Westminster. Here he again commenced holding meetings among his neighbors, and being now a local preacher he went to work more systematically. Like most of his brethren, Mr. Pettis was a pioneer preacher, having been the first to introduce the Gospel into the township of Lobo, and into the western part of the township of London; indeed he was quite as zealous in the cause of his heavenly Master as he was in the service of his country, and he was by no means deficient in love for it, as he had already proved.

Some months after his arrival in Westminster he learned that there was to be a ball on Christmas eve at a place called Dingman's Creek. On hearing of the anticipated party, Mr. Pettis became impressed with the idea that he ought to go to it, and, if possible, get it changed to a religious meeting. He mentioned the matter to his wife, but she, fearing that his zeal was not according to knowledge, tried to persuade him not to go, arguing that it was not probable he could do any good, and he might give serious offence. They, however, both made the subject a matter of earnest prayer, and the impression still continuing, Mr. Pettis at the proper time set out for the place of amusement. Arrived there, he found that several had already assembled, and he at once made known the object of his visit to the proprietor of the house, telling him he had been so forcibly impressed with the idea that he ought to come and preach to the people assembled there that night, that he could not resist the impression, and had come accordingly.

Mr. Dingman informed him, very kindly, that he could use his house on some future occasion as a preaching place, but that this evening there was to be a dance; the people were even now assembling, and would not like to be disappointed; still, if he could obtain the consent of the party, he might preach if he chose. Mr. Pettis conversed with the manager, repeating what he had told Mr. Dingman, and requesting his permission to address the people. The manager was considerably amused at the earnestness of Mr. Pettis, but after consulting with a number of the company, he consented that Mr. Pettis might speak, or as he termed it, "open the ball," and after the meeting, they would go on with their amusement.

The company having now fully collected, Mr. Pettis, placing, a chair before him, arrested their attention by relating the impression which, resting so forcibly upon his mind, had brought him there. He wished, he said, to give them advice which he thought would do them good, and trusted none of them would be offended. Having thus introduced himself and his mission, he commenced singing a beautiful hymn, and afterwards engaged in prayer. During the progress of these exercises some of the audience became melted into tenderness, even the preacher himself was moved to tears, and when he commenced exhorting, the Holy Spirit seemed to descend upon the people. Those who were determined to resist the gracious influence quitted the place, and the rest remained to pray. A glorious revival followed, and with the assistance of the circuit preacher, who came to his aid in a little more than a year after his singular meeting, some seventy members were added to the Church.

In 1819, a small settlement was commenced in the western part of London township, in what was afterwards known as the Jacobs and Morden settlement. This was quite separated from a similar one commenced a short time previous in the east of the same township, there being an untracked forest and the river Thames between them, and as a consequence the people forming the two settlements knew nothing of each other for a length of time.

Mr. Pettis commenced holding meetings in the Morden neighborhood late in the summer of 1819, according to the date he has given, but a Mr. Wm. Warner, of London Township, who made one of the first congregation, places it in 1820. The following is the substance of Mr. Warner's letter on the subject:—

"Our first meeting began in August, 1820. Some of us met at the house of Nathan Jacobs to sing hymns. On the Sunday following we met again; after singing, Mr. Jacobs proposed to have prayer; Jacobs, James Mitchell, and myself prayed. This was the first time I ever prayed in public. Local preachers and exhorters now came from Westminster, whenever they could cross the river on horses. The names of these men were Charles Pettis, John Sutton, and Aaron Killburn. We agreed to meet together on Thursday evenings, for prayer-meeting, and others soon united with us."

Which is right in the date of the commencement of this society, Mr. Warner or Mr. Pettis, cannot now be definitely decided. Mr. Pettis, however, visited them as frequently and as regularly as it was possible to do, until it was taken charge of by the nearest circuit preacher. Not long after Mr. Pettis' first visit to the Jacobs settlement, a class of twenty-three members was organized. Mr. Pettis is believed to have been the first preacher who addressed a religious meeting in the township of Lobo, and also at Kettle Creek—now St. Thomas. He preached a funeral sermon in the latter place in the summer of 1815.

Before the disruption of 1833, Mr. Pettis had travelled the following circuits, under the Presiding Elder:—1st. The London Circuit, his colleague, Rev. M. Whiting. 2nd. Oxford, colleague, Rev. John Bailey; this circuit then embraced Stratford and Goderich within its bounds, these towns being just commenced. 3rd. Dumfries. 4th. Thames; and 5th. The Dumfries a second time. He was travelling this circuit at the time of the consummation of the "Union," so called.

He was strongly opposed to the arrangements entered into between the English and Canadian Conferences, utterly refusing to give the least countenance to the movement, consequently he co-operated heartily with those brethren who were, in the latter part of this year, holding meetings, and once more collecting the scattered societies together, in order that they might be re-organized. At the Conference of 1834 he was admitted on trial, and after travelling several years, and doing the Church good service, he finally took a superannuated relation. A few years since, having lived an exemplary and useful life, and seen his beloved Church restored to prosperity, at a good old age he entered his rest.

While Mr. Pettis and his associates from Flamboro were struggling to reclaim Westminster from its native wildness, London Township was also being settled slowly. About a year preceding the arrival of the Jacobses and Mordens a few emigrants had commenced a settlement in the eastern part of the township. In March, 1819, Mr. Robert Webster, formerly of the County of Wicklow, Ireland, but more recently from the State of New York, whence he had emigrated to

Canada, in consequence of his preference for British institutions, settled with his family in the south-eastern part of the same township, his making the second household between the east and north branches of the river Thames, though there was an unmarried man, several miles further up the north branch, who had commenced a clearing. The townships further to the north, between London and Lake Huron, at that date were an unbroken forest, not having as yet been even surveyed, while where the now flourishing city of London stands the wild beasts roamed at will, and the dismal howl of the ravenous wolf might have been heard night after night, if there had been any human inhabitant to hear him. which, however, there was not, unless, perhaps, a wandering Indian. Such were the difficulties of travelling at that period, and the unfavorable season of the year, that it took Mr. Webster and his family three days to travel from what is now Dorchester Station to within about four miles of what is now London City. To those from the highly cultivated fields and beautiful scenery of the south-east of Ireland, or even from the more recently civilized State of western New York, the view was desolate and dreary beyond description. Who could have imagined the almost magic change which would be wrought there in less than fifty years?

Mr. and Mrs. Webster had both been Methodists in their native land, Mr. Webster having united with society at the early age of twelve, and Mrs. Webster at eighteen. Upon emigrating to the United States they had cast in their lots with the Methodists there, and while residing in that country he had received license to exhort. Coming, as they did now, into a new land, it was not strange that they should pine for congenial society, and almost despair—especially Mrs. Webster—of finding any. It was not long, however, till Mr. Webster found out a little class in Westminster. Thenceforward Sabbath after Sabbath found him wending his way—when it was at all practicable—through forest and swamp, and across the unbridged river, to the place of meeting, a distance of six miles, making a Sabbath day's journey of twelve miles, in order to attend the public worship of God. This course was faithfully persevered in till his own house could be opened for public worship; it had from its first erection been a *home sanctuary*. The Rev. Alvin Torrey, the preacher on the Westminster Circuit, had already too large a field to cultivate properly, and could not, therefore, take up any fresh appointment, but the public ministry of the word in London was not long delayed. Rev. Samuel Belton, a nephew of Mr. Webster's, had this year, 1819, been stationed in York, and having business in Oxford he determined to visit his uncle, and if a congregation could be secured, to preach to the settlers. Accordingly he sent his uncle a message to that effect, and the appointment was duly announced. In due time Mr. Belton arrived and fulfilled his appointment, thus preaching the first sermon that was delivered in the township of London. This was in June or July, 1819, and was therefore prior, by some weeks at least, to the first meeting held by Mr. Pettis in the Morden neighborhood. The congregation was large, considering the number of inhabitants, the people coming many miles, for the word of the Lord was precious in those days. The day was fine, the scene novel. Not half a year had elapsed since the first tree had been felled in that dense forest where now stood the yet unfinished humble dwelling, for the time being to be honored as a place of worship, and even in that short period see what the industry and enterprise of man had accomplished. The congregation having been accommodated with seats as well as was possible—those who were unable to get in standing outside—and the introductory services over, the preacher, his tall head nearly touching the chamber floor, rose to give out his text, one which in the light of history, looking at it from this date, may almost be termed prophetic. Opening his Bible at the 35th chapter of Isaiah, he read those delightful words, which have so often given comfort to the way-worn and weary child of God:—"The wilderness and solitary place shall be glad for them; and the desert shall rejoice and blossom as the rose. It shall blossom abundantly, and rejoice even with joy and singing; the glory of Lebanon shall be given unto it, the excellency of Carmel and Sharon, they shall see the glory of the Lord, and the excellency of our God." The text itself was encouraging, and the sermon based upon it greatly comforted and edified the listeners, several of whom, who had been brought up under religious influences in Ireland and other places, not having heard a sermon for many months. But of those present that day, probably none felt to rejoice more fully in the "words of this salvation" than did Mrs. Webster, who when she entered the wilds of Canada thought she was cut off from the house of the Lord and from the congregation of His people forever. How different this delightful summer Sabbath from her first Sabbath in those dreary woods the March previous.

Thenceforward religious meetings were established at the house of Mr. Webster, changing occasionally to the house of Mr. Cooper Pixley, who had come into the township shortly after Mr. Webster, and had located himself about two miles from where the city of London now is. In the long intervals between the appointments of the regular preachers, Mr. Webster kept up the religious services in these places for several years, acting as an exhorter. Though frequently urged by his brethren to take a license as a local preacher he steadily refused to do so, but complied with their request so far that he would change appointments with the local preachers, often travelling many miles to speak with the people. He continued in his course of usefulness till the year 1836, when he was called home. As he had lived a child of God, so he died, his last words being:—

"Jesus my advocate above,
My friend before the throne of love."

Mrs. Webster survived her husband many years, and having lived to see the literal fulfilment of the text first preached in her house, she, too, passed over the flood.

The year 1819 was a memorable one to the people on the Bay Quinte, not, however, as in the case of Westminster and London, for the introduction of the Gospel—that had been introduced many years previously—but for a casualty the most deplorable that had ever occurred in their locality. Revs. Isaac Puffer and James Wilson had this year been stationed on that circuit, and had appointed a Quarterly Meeting at Hay Bay meeting-house, to be held on the 19th and 20th of August. Sabbath morning rose clear and beautiful, all nature seemed alive with joy and harmony, people from a distance were thronging to the house of God, as they journeyed thitherward uniting their voices with those of the feathered tribes in songs of grateful praise to the Most High; the hour of worship was nearing, and some of those who had already reached the sanctuary had commenced a prayer-meeting. Alas! that joy should so soon give place to bitter grief, that songs of prayer and praise should so soon be changed to lamentation and wailing. Those who lived on the north side of the bay were obliged to cross it in boats in order to reach the meeting. A company of young people—most of them professors of religion—eighteen in number, got into a boat, intending to cross, and as they settled themselves for what they thought would be a pleasant sail, they too, like their friends who had been travelling toward the meeting by land, began to sing a soul-reviving hymn. They had not proceeded far, however, when they found their boat had sprung a leak. The water increased rapidly, and the poor voyagers had no way of baling it out. Every effort was made to reach the shore, but in vain; the weight of so many in the boat tended to hasten the catastrophe; they sank within sight of the horror-stricken worshippers, who had rushed from the church upon the first cry of alarm, to render what assistance they could, but help of man was of little avail. Out of the eighteen living, joyous young people who half an hour before had been engaged in singing, but eight reached land alive. A seine was procured in as short a time as possible, and nine of the bodies drawn to land, the tenth was not recovered till the next day. The dreadful scene on shore beggars description.

Monday was a day of lamentation, and mourning, and woe. The news had been spread far and wide the day previous, and hundreds attended the funeral. At the time appointed the concourse of people met near the scene of the disaster; the nine coffins were placed in a row outside the church, and Mr. Puffer improved the solemn event by preaching an earnest and impressive sermon to a deeply affected audience. The tenth corpse was not buried with the others, nor in the same grave-yárd. Thus suddenly—while on their way to worship—perished ten persons, eight young women and two young men, while yet in the bloom of early youth.

CHAPTER XV.

FROM 1819 TO 1823.

Conference of 1820—Conference Scenes—Contrast between 1812 and 1820—First Canadian mission proper—The missionaries—How they lived—Mr. Peale—Novel method of crossing Hay Bay—Its results—Progress of the work—Sabbath schools in 1822—Marriage Bill brought before the House, 1823—It passes the Lower, and is rejected by the Upper House—Cause of its rejection—What the "Family Compact" was—Struggle to establish the Church of England in Canada—Consequent persecution of Methodists—Alvin Torrey's mission—Arrival of Seth Crawford—Conversion of Peter Jones—State of the work in 1823.

THE Genesee Annual Conference held its session for the second time in Canada in 1820, commencing July 20th, Bishop George presiding. It appears from the Minutes that the Conference was appointed to be held at Niagara, but for some cause it was convened in the old red meeting-house at the west end of Lundy's Lane. From a letter written by Messrs. Ryan and Case to Rev. N. Bangs, after the close of the Conference, it would appear that 100 preachers attended this Conference, 18 were admitted on trial, 30 ordained, and 122 appointed to circuits and stations, 28 of whom were sent to Canadian charges, including Detroit, then connected with that work. There seems to be a slight discrepancy between some of the statements of Messrs. Ryan and Case, and the account in the General Minutes, there being only 25 named there as having been ordained; both accounts are, however, probably correct, as 5 of the 30 may have been local preachers, whose names would not, therefore, appear in the Minutes.

Sunday of this Conference, like the one three years before at Elizabethtown, was indeed a high day. The people thronged the bush and corduroy roads from St. Davids, Lyons Creek, the Beaver Dams, and the surrounding country, all intent on reaching the place appointed for worship. The church was within hearing of the thunders of the ever roaring Falls of the majestic Niagara, and thus the devout worshippers were constantly reminded of Him whose "voice is as the sound of many waters."

In the morning the services were held in the church, though it was filled to overflowing, but in the afternoon the crowd had increased to such a degree that it was judged best to remove to a beautiful grove which was convenient to the church. Thither, accordingly, the Bishop and ministers repaired, followed by the assembled host. The scene was solemn and impressive, the ordination of twenty, out of the thirty, young heralds of the Cross, in this leafy temple, beneath the azure vault of heaven, alone adding not a little to its interest.

How very different the meeting of the Canadian and American people on that occasion from the last meeting of the representatives of the two nations in that locality, though at the opposite end of the Lane, six years before. Then, while nature was clothing herself with the mantle of darkness, to hide, perhaps, the blood of the slain, the forces of these two nations had met in deadly conflict. The field was to be contested with carnal weapons; the lovely country adjoining to be over-run with fire and sword. The grand old voice of the mighty cataract mingled for the time with the clamorous sounds of martial music, the clash of arms, and the horrid din of war; and when, the furious combat over, its deep tones could once more be heard, as if moaning in unison with the wounded and the dying on the gory field.

Now, in full view of that dreadful field, which must call up most harrowing recollections, British subject and American citizen were met again, not as before to grapple in deadly strife, as enemies, but as brethren, united in the same glorious warfare, the Bishop and his band of itinerants leading on to sure and certain victory in a bloodless contest; their watch-word, "Little children, love one another."

Though not followed by as extensive revivals as the former session held in Canada, in 1817, three years previously, still much good was accomplished, and the advancement of the Church furthered by this session of Conference. The report of the Canadian work for the year was, 2 Districts, 17 circuits, 28 travelling preachers, 47 local preachers, 65 exhorters, and 5557 members.

The year 1821 was not distinguished by as many, or as extensive revivals as some of the previous years, but the societies enjoyed comparative peace, and the work continued to progress, though more slowly, yet steadily. New appointments were taken up on old charges and a fresh circuit formed in the more recently settled townships north and west of York, now Toronto. This field of labor extended from York, on Lake Ontario, to Lake Simcoe, not, however, interfering with Yonge Street circuit, but running in a north and north-westerly direction, through the destitute portions of the front townships, and the inhabited townships of the second and third range. This appointment was recorded on the Minutes, thus:—"York, and mission to the new settlements, U. C., Fitch Reid, Kenneth M. R. Smith, missionaries."

This may be styled the first mission field proper in Canada, under the charge of the M. E. Church, as it was the first under the direction of the Missionary Society of the M. E. Church, then but recently established in New York. Before this period the preachers were sent out "*to make circuits*," and were expected to obtain their scanty allowance among the people with whom they labored, except a small pittance sometimes procured for them by Bishop Asbury, and as most of the itinerant preachers of that period were unmarried, they managed to accomplish their task and live, but that was about all. The people were poor, but such as they had, they gave freely in return for the services rendered by their pastor, and he, knowing this, but being anxious to do them good, lived with them, faring and dressing as poorly as they did. As the preachers began more generally to marry, however, some provision had to be made for their families, and hence the necessity of forming new plans, and making new arrangements.

This year, James G. Peale was sent to introduce the Gospel into the new settlements of the Rideau country, but had no claims on the mission fund for support. Indeed, there was but little money as yet in the missionary treasury to assist any one, and that little had to be divided among so many destitute circuits, not only in Canada but in the United States, that but a very small portion fell to the share of each missionary.

Mr. Peale had been a soldier, and was therefore able to endure hardship better than many less inured to it; and now he was as zealous in the cause of his divine Master as he had previously been in the cause of his king and country. Many of the disbanded soldiers, after the war, had located themselves in and about Perth, and these had been joined by a large number of immigrants from Scotland and other parts of Europe, and among these Mr. Peale labored; but though he and Messrs. Reid and Smith worked hard and endured many privations, they were not nearly so successful as they had hoped to be, nor, indeed, were any of the preachers as successful as in some of the previous years, for at the Conference of this year there is a decrease reported of 396 members.

In 1822 the Grand River Mission was commenced, and Alvin Torrey sent to till the new field. The mission extended from the mouth of the river, at Dunnville, to Brant's ford, a rapid in the river at which the Indian chief, Brant, and his warriors, used to cross the stream, and which is now known as Brantford. Here and about the borders of the reservation, at that time extensive, some whites had located themselves, and these came within the bounds of Mr. Torrey's charge. He also extended his labors along the borders of Lake Erie, through Rainham, and to other townships on both sides of the river, gathering up in all thirty members during the year. Mr. Torrey had not found his charge an easy one; his routes were long, his fare poor, and his lodgings frequently uncomfortable; but —his heart was in his Master's work—he labored on "as seeing Him who is invisible."

The circuits commenced the year previous about Perth, and north and west of York, were beginning to yield fruit, though the preachers were still subject to many hardships and privations. This was especially the case with Mr. Smith, who was frequently obliged to carry an axe with him, in order to fell trees across streams, so that he could pass over, and to chop paths for himself through the swamps, being guided through those perilous wastes by his pocket compass.

This year, (1822,) Mr. Peale had been sent to the Bay Quinte Circuit, where he became a martyr to imprudent zeal. Mr. Peale had an appointment at Switzer's church, and while he was on the opposite side of Hay Bay, in December of that year, the ice closed over the Bay. The ice was not strong enough to bear up his horse, and it was too smooth for him to travel over with his boots on; he, therefore, not wishing to disappoint the people, removed his boots, and crossed the Bay—a mile and a half—in his stocking feet. In order to keep from freezing he was obliged to run all the way, and when he reached the church he was in a profuse perspiration. He preached to the assembled congregation, but a violent cold was the result of his race on the ice. The Sabbath following he walked several miles against a severe wind, which added to his indisposition: after worship he was much worse; his illness increased rapidly, and in a few days more his toils were over, he had entered his rest. During his illness he suffered very much, but, while reason lasted, he triumphed in the prospect of immortality and eternal life.

While these laborious servants of God and of the Church were pushing through swamps, and fording rivers, hunting up the lost sheep in the wilderness, Messrs. Ryan and Case were by no means idle, but were actively engaged in holding Quarterly Meetings on their respective Districts, which extended from Ottawa to Detroit. They were assisted in the work of evangelization by such men as David Culp, Isaac Puffer, Philander Smith, and others equally zealous and laborious, who were travelling immensely large sections of country, called circuits, which had already been organized, and where societies had been formed. Mr. Case, in the report of his District this year, 1822, mentions that there were forty Sunday schools in connection with the Church, showing unmistakeably that the *children* were neither forgotten nor neglected by the Church in those days, dark as were the times. Another mark of the progress of the people, and of their liberality, may also be gathered from the same report, viz., the fact that on his District alone there were twenty places of worship already built or in process of erection, and this—be it remembered—at a time when it cost not a little effort on the part of the people to do these things. The membership in 1822 was 5601, making an increase over the preceding year of 440.

In 1823 a bill authorizing Methodist ministers and the ministers of the several other hitherto disqualified denominations, to solemnize matrimony, was brought before the Upper Canada Parliament, which passed the House of Assembly, but was thrown out by the Upper House, composed as it was, almost exclusively, of members of the high church Family Compact, or those influenced by them, and quite independent of the people.

The high church party were at this time straining every

nerve to procure the establishment of the Church of England in Canada upon the same footing as in England, and this party was greatly aided by a clique—chiefly resident in Toronto, then York—which has already several times been referred to as the Family Compact, a name applied to it in consequence of the frequent intermarriages of those composing it with each other's families. At the head of this faction was the .Rev. Dr., afterwards Bishop Strachan, a prominent minister of the Church of England, who though a Scotchman by birth, had attached himself to the Compact, several of the younger members of which had been educated by him, and through their influence he had been promoted to a seat in the Legislative Council. Such an undue influence had this man attained in this irresponsible Assembly—its members not being elected by the people, but appointed by the Crown—that at this period, and for some years subsequent, he might with truth have been styled the dictator of the province, succeeding as he did in obtaining complete control of the government, through his influence with the Lieutenant-Governor, and through him, in a measure, the control of the Home Government, as far as its legislation concerned Canada.

These men had always looked with jealous eyes upon Methodism, treating the denomination with the utmost injustice, and where it was in their power, with the foulest tyranny; no wonder, then, that they should mark the unparalleled success of the laborious efforts of the Methodist preachers, in the increasing numbers and influence of the societies, with astonishment and rage, and stretch their power to its utmost verge in multiplying legal disabilities upon the men who had done so much to promote the spiritual, and in consequence, the temporal welfare of the masses, and whose influence for good they feared.

Some Methodist ministers had at a former period solemnized matrimony, but the government had refused to acknowledge such marriages legal, and in consequence the authorities had given the ministers who thus officiated, considerable annoyance. Rev. Joseph Sawyer had been obliged to leave the country for a time, in order to escape the vengeance of the bitter enemies of Methodism, though he was a *regularly ordained* minister, and at the time Presiding Elder, simply because he had ventured to solemnize marriages in his District, and that at a time when there was no law of the land, passed by the representatives of the people, forbidding it. Rev. Henry Ryan was sentenced to banishment to the United States, by an obsequious judge, for a similar offence, but the sentence was not carried into execution against him, in consequence, it is said, of his well known loyalty. The Rev. Isaac B. Smith was prosecuted for marrying a couple on his charge. He protested against the claims of superiority set up by the would-be "Established Church," stood his trial, pleaded his own case, and, notwithstanding all the legal advantages of his opponents, the technical skill of adverse lawyers, the exertions of the prosecuting council, and the very apparent partiality of the judge, he won the suit, the jury deciding in his favor. To avoid further trouble, expense, and persecution, however, the Methodists afterwards refrained from performing marriages till a specific act, authorizing them to do so, could be obtained from Parliament, which led to the introduction of the "Bill" before mentioned to the Parliament of 1823, the fate of which has already been recorded.

Many persons, however, sooner than be married by a minister of the Church of England, preferred to go to the United States, where they could enjoy the privilege of being married by their own minister, or any other clergyman whom they might choose, while others, unable to take so long or expensive a trip, would, where it was at all possible, secure the services of a magistrate. Even this last, however, could not always be accomplished, as no magistrate could solemnize matrimony within fourteen miles of the residence of an English Church minister. Such is priestly usurpation wherever it can have its way.* The Methodists were harassed in every possible way by the dominant faction, not even being allowed to hold, in their own right, a lot on which to bury their dead, or build a church; and they, and other bodies similarly situated, were insolently termed dissenters, when there was not—either then or since—any church established *by law*, from which to dissent, and *rebels* against the government because they claimed their rights as British subjects. This ever ready cry of disloyalty was the one raised by the Compact and its abettors against every opponent, that they might the better cover up their selfish policy, and secure the Clergy reserves—amounting to one-seventh of the lands of the entire province—for the Church of England.

All this opposition, however—except in the matter of disabilities—affected the Methodist people but little; neither ministers nor members slackened in the least their efforts for the salvation of souls, and the work continued to prosper mightily in their hands. This year, 1823, the boundaries of the old Westminster Circuit were somewhat changed, and London Circuit formed, embracing not only London Township, but portions of several others. There were fifteen appointments, to be filled every two weeks, and that at a period when both branches of the Thames were unbridged. Between fording streams and following bush roads, the preacher, Rev. Robert Corson, did not have particularly easy or comfortable times on the new charge, and on several occasions lost his way in the forest, and did not in consequence reach his appointments in season, he, however, generally at such times arrived before the congregation had dispersed. On one occasion, while crossing the river at one of the fording places, he got out of the direct

* So strong was the feeling upon this subject, that instances have been known of persons residing within the prescribed distance of a Church of England minister, going from their homes far enough to put fourteen miles between him and them, so that they could be married by a magistrate, rather than submit to the assumptions of the Church of England in this matter.

line, into a deep hole, and both horse and rider went under the water. It was with great difficulty he succeeded in getting out and reaching the opposite bank in safety. The salary received by Mr. Corson, in compensation for his labors on this charge was *one hundred and sixty dollars.* He was a married man.

Rev. Alvin Torrey, who had the year previous been sent to labor on the Grand River, had opened up an extensive field of usefulness in that locality, both among the whites and Indians, being greatly assisted in the work by Mr., afterward Rev. Edmund Stoney, then a local preacher. Mr. Stoney made himself useful principally in establishing spiritual worship among the Indians in the vicinity of Brantford, holding his meetings at the house of a chief named Thomas Davis, who lived at the Mohawk village, near the old Mohawk church, the oldest edifice of the kind in the province.

Most of the Mohawks were nominally members of the Church of England, but were very immoral, and addicted to the curse of their race, strong drink. Thomas Davis also adhered to that Church, but in the other respects mentioned was an exception to the rest of the tribe. He had learned to read the Scriptures, and was in the habit of reading the Church of England prayers in his family: and on Sundays, in the absence of the clergyman officiating at the old church, of reading them with the Indians who would collect to hear him. Thus his heart was operated upon and inclined to listen to the earnest counsels given by Mr. Stoney, and to offer him his house, in which to teach his (Davis') poor benighted brethren.

The work among the Indians was very much furthered this year, too, by the arrival of an earnestly pious young man from the United States, named Seth Crawford. This young man, being desirous of being useful among the Indians, had come hither for the double purpose of making himself more perfectly acquainted with their language, and of imparting what instruction he could to them, including adults as well as children.

He pursued his course steadily, acquainting them with their lost condition, and presenting before them the plan of salvation, and after a time a few of the adults became truly awakened.

Among those who were benefitted by the example and instruction of Mr. Crawford, was Peter Jones, to whom reference has before been made. Jones could not properly be called a pure blooded Indian, his father—a government surveyor—having been a white man. Augustus Jones, Peter's father, had, in his employment as an official of the government, been brought into intimate association with the Indians, and becoming attached to them he had chosen a daughter of the forest for a wife.

Peter Jones was born on Burlington Heights, which are situated at the western extremity of Burlington Bay, on the 1st of January, 1802. These Heights were, at the time of Jones' birth, and indeed till within a few years, since which they have been marred by the hand of man, a most romantic spot. It was, on the first settlement of the country, before it had been at all changed by man, a high narrow strip of land, starting from the Bay from which it takes its name, and running in a northerly direction between it and an immense marsh which lay east of the present site of Dundas. A portion of these Heights comes within the present bounds of the city of Hamilton, part of which has, within a later period, been laid out as a city for the dead, what is now the most picturesque part being inclosed in the beautiful Burlington Cemetery.

Upon these Heights the British had, during the war of 1812, an almost impregnable stronghold, the fortification being protected on three sides by natural barriers, the great height of the banks, whose sides were precipitous, almost, as a wall, and from which every tree, bush, and protuberance that might aid the climber had been carefully removed, preventing any danger being apprehended of approach of the enemy by the Bay on the east, and the deep and very extensive marsh to the north and west, afforded additional security against approach in that direction, while the south, the only place at which an entrance need be feared, was covered by strong breastworks running all the way from the bay to the marsh. The native grandeur of the place was, of course, much marred by the troops during its occupation as a military post, but in the lapse of years it had regained much of its original beauty, when in running the line of the Great Western Railroad a deep cut was put through the northwest portion of the Heights, and another nearly in the centre, to make a shorter passage for the Desjardine canal, thus ruining forever its primitive loveliness.

Born in such a romantic spot, and reared as he was among the children of the forest, it is not surprising that young Jones grew up an ardent lover of nature, and identified himself in his after years more closely with the interests of his mother's rather than with those of his father's race.

At the age of fourteen he was sent by his father to an English school in Saltfleet, some few miles east from the now city of Hamilton, where he made considerable proficiency for the time he attended. The knowledge acquired at this school was, at a somewhat later period in his life, of no little value to him in assisting to qualify him for his career of usefulness.

Though surrounded by the evil influences of savage life and heathenism, he was strictly moral and upright in his deportment, never falling into the besetting vice of his race—an excessive use of strong drink. At the age of eighteen years he was, by his father's request, baptized by an Episcopalian minister, in the old Mohawk church, near Brant's ford, now Brantford, to which vicinity Mr. Augustus Jones had removed. Here, in 1823, he became acquainted with Mr. Crawford, whose counsel and religious instruction resulted in so much good to him and to others.

On Friday, 1st of June, in that year, Peter, in company with his sister Polly and some others, attended the camp-meeting on the Ancaster Circuit, which has been before mentioned in the chapter on camp-meetings, and before its close both were soundly converted. Returning home to their friends, these young converts, happy in the enjoyment of their new found peace, and a consciousness of a Saviour's love, set at once to work to do what good they could among their own people, and a reformation commenced which spread rapidly among the various tribes along the Grand River, until some hundreds of the wild sons of the forest were brought into the Christian Church. This revival among the Indians gave a very great impetus to revivals among the whites.

The state of the general work in Canada, for this year, was as follows:—2 Districts, 21 circuits, 32 travelling preachers, and 5450 members.

CHAPTER XVI.

FROM 1823 TILL THE CONFERENCE OF 1826.

General Conference of 1824—New Conference—More trouble—Reasons for Mr Ryan's dissatisfaction—Unwarrantable proceedings—First Canada Conference—Bishops George and Hedding present—Mr. Ryan takes fresh offence—His subsequent conduct—Conference of 1825—James Richardson and Egerton Ryerson admitted on trial—David Culp locates—Sketch of his labors—Incident connected with the early settlement of the country—The Church and the temperance movement—Conference of 1826—*Christian Advocate* started—Mr. Case and the Indians—Statistics.

In 1824 the city of Baltimore was again favored by the session of the General Conference being held there, the Conference commencing on the 1st of May. The Canadian interest was represented by Revds. Wyatt Chamberlain and Isaac B. Smith, who had been appointed delegates by the Genesee Annual Conference of 1823, in the customary manner. Their appointment, however, gave serious offence to Rev. Henry Ryan, who considered that he should have been elected, as he had for so many years led the van in Church affairs in Canada, and endured so much in building it up. But though still a laborious and energetic man, and in many places much beloved for his past labors, he was gradually becoming—and had been for some years—very unpopular among the preachers, in consequence of his arbitrary assumption of superiority and control over them.

During the war he had in reality been the temporal head of the Canadian Church, and after its close for many years he had been foremost in fighting her battles, having arrayed against him the combined influence of both the English missionaries and the high church party. Their continued and clamorous cry of disloyalty, though he knew it to be false, stung a man of Mr. Ryan's impetuous temperament to the quick. His national pride roused, he became possessed by a strong desire to be freed entirely from the control of the American body, desiring that a separate and independent Church might be organized in Canada; perhaps, too, cherishing the, not altogether unfounded, idea that, as a reward for previous services he would be placed at the head of the new organization, and accordingly he began to agitate with a view to such a consummation. Not being included among the delegates to the General Conference, annoyed him still more, although his fellow-laborer and companion in toil, Mr. Case, was, like himself, not elected to this session of the General Conference. Mr. Case did not seem to have taken any umbrage at the choice of delegates, but, though almost equal with Mr. Ryan in abundance of labors, with quiet Christian dignity submitted to the will of his Conference, and went to his appointed work. Mr. Ryan, on the contrary, however, continued to try to inflame the minds of those on his District to such a degree that they would listen to nothing but absolute separation.

Though up to this time he had strongly opposed lay delegation, he now began to favor the holding of conventions among the laity, and although well aware that the General Conference could not in the nature of things receive as legitimate delegates persons chosen in so irregular a manner, he induced a highly respectable local preacher named Breckenridge, who had connected himself with the movement, to consent to be appointed as a delegate to that body by such a convention, and permitted himself to be chosen as another. At the time for the meeting of the Conference they proceeded to Baltimore, whither also the regularly elected delegates, Messrs. Chamberlain and Smith, had gone. Messrs. Ryan and

Breckenridge, though not admitted to seats in the Conference as delegates, were allowed a respectful hearing before the committee on Canadian affairs, but were unsuccessful in obtaining the object of their misssion. The petition of the Canadian Methodists presented by the regular delegates, Messrs. Chamberlain and Smith, had only asked for a separate Annual Conference, while that presented by Mr. Ryan urged for a separation from the parent body, complete and entire.

After mature deliberation the General Conference granted the request of the petition presented by Messrs. Chamberlain and Smith. The action of the Conference is embodied in the following resolutions, adopted at this session:—

"1st. That there shall be a Canada Conference, under our superintendency, bounded by the boundary lines of Upper Canada.

"2. That a circular shall be addressed to our preachers and members included within the bounds of the Canada Conference, expressive of our zeal for their prosperity, and urging the importance of their maintaining union among themselves.

"3. That a respectful representation be made to the British Conference of those points in the late agreement between the two connexions, which have not, on their part, been fulfilled."

Mr. Ryan returned home very much incensed at the action of the General Conference, both in regard to the formation of the Annual Conference and its reception of himself, and set himself more decidedly in opposition to it than ever.

On the 25th of August, 1824, the Canada Conference was duly organized, in conformity with the above resolutions. Bishops George and Hedding were both present, and presided alternately. The Conference was small, numbering only thirty-three preachers, including those received on trial and the two Bishops. The strong attachment of the American Methodists for their brethren in Canada was manifested by this visit of the Bishops in the then state of the country. Bishop George entered the province in the eastern district, and travelled westward, preaching as he had opportunity, till he reached Hallowell; while Bishop Hedding, accompanied by Dr. Bangs, crossed at Niagara, going east to the seat of Conference. In this way they could, better than in any other, learn the views of the societies concerning Mr. Ryan's scheme of separation; and finding, upon a careful investigation of the matter, that a majority, both of the preachers and the members, had drifted with the tide, and were anxious for an entire separation from their American brethren, the Bishops consented to favor the plan at the next General Conference, which concession gave general satisfaction. The episcopal visitation was attended with very beneficial results, explanations having been given to the people at the various stopping places of the Bishops, during their respective journeys, and their urbanity of manner, and concessions to the Conference tended still more to calm the disturbed spirits, and give assurance of peace to the societies.

During the interval between the session of the General Conference of 1824 and the meeting of this Conference, Mr. Ryan had been industriously sowing dissension among the societies under his charge; it was thought best, therefore, to remove him from the Presiding Eldership, a position which he had held since 1810. He was accordingly appointed to a mission, and Mr. Case placed in charge of the Bay Quinte District, while Thomas Madden was sent to the Niagara District.

Mr. Ryan, although at first apparently satisfied with the explanations and assurances given by the Bishops, took fresh offence at his appointment, and not long after the Conference recommenced his crusade against the intervention or control of the American General Conference or Bishops, going the length of leaving his legitimate work before the end of the year, in order that he might the better continue the work of agitation.

The reformation among the Indians continued to progress with power, notwithstanding the agitations in the Church, and very great good was accomplished. A log church was built at a place called Davisville, and a mission school of from 20 to 30 scholars established, Davis—the chief mentioned before—having given up his comfortable residence to the school, and removed, with his family, into a small log house, in order that the Indian children might enjoy the benefit of religious instruction. The interests of the Sabbath-school were looked after, too, with commendable earnestness, and as a result several children, whites as well as Indians, were among those converted and added to the Church. The preachers—with the exception of Mr. Ryan—continued to manifest the same zeal which had characterized them previously, Messrs. Case and Madden working faithfully on their respective Districts. The Quarterly and camp-meetings were continued seasons of refreshing, the societies, both new and old, sharing more or less in the revival influence.

The first Canada Conference had entered on its course with 2 Districts, 21 circuits and missions, 33 preachers, and a membership of 6186, being an increase over the year previous to it of 736.

The second session was held in Saltfleet, on the Fifty Mile Creek, September 14th, 1825, Bishop Hedding presiding. Two candidates were admitted on trial at this Conference, who were destined at a future period to occupy distinguished positions not only in the Church, but in the country—the native land of both—viz., James Richardson and Egerton Ryerson. They were sent together to the Yonge Street and York Circuit, Mr. Richardson in charge. Both were able writers and good preachers, and soon rose to eminence in the Church; each at an early period became editor of the *Christian Guardian*, and each received the degree of D. D. from American colleges. Mr. Ryerson was one of the chief promoters of the so-called "Union" with the English Conference, in 1833, and also of the disruption between that body and the Canadian Wesleyans, in 1840. Later in life he accepted the situation of General Superintendent of Education for Upper

Canada, which he still holds, retaining, however, a nominal relation to the Wesleyan Conference.

Mr. Richardson had been an officer in the navy during the war of 1812, in which struggle he had lost an arm, but had now exchanged carnal for spiritual warfare, and entered on the work of an itinerant. He very reluctantly gave in his adhesion to the projected "Union" of 1833, and for a time went with that movement, but after a short trial of the new organization he returned to the old fold, where he has since remained. For a series of years he was the accredited agent of the Bible Society, a situation the duties of which he performed with credit and ability; and for several years past he has been the junior Bishop of the M. E. Church in Canada.

At this same Conference, 1825, Rev. David Culp located, after thirteen years of laborious toil. Though closely connected with Canadian affairs he was not by birth a Canadian, having been born in Lancaster County, Pennsylvania, in 1784. His parents belonged to that class of people known as Pennsylvania Dutch, and were both religious, his father being a Methodist and his mother a Lutheran. The elder Culp had, with some of his neighbors, watched the struggle of the Revolution with considerable anxiety, and after its termination had, for a time, determined to abide the result and continue to occupy their lands under the new order of things; but being enthusiastic "King's men" they found their situation exceedingly irksome, and after trying this kind of life for five or six years, they finally resolved to try and make their way to the *King's* country—to emigrate to the dread wilds of Upper Canada. This exodus of Mr. Culp, accompanied by thirteen of his old neighbors and co-patriots, was undertaken when David was five years of age, and their mode of travelling was somewhat similar to that of other immigrants to the country at that period

There being a number of horses and considerable stock, comprising nearly all the available property of the wanderers, it was necessary to take especial care of them, and consequently part of the company travelled by land, while the rest—as soon as they could avail themselves of it—came by water, their conveyance being a kind of boat propelled by setting-poles.

Accompanying the immigrants was a Methodist local preacher, named Webster, who having some sympathy with the others, desired to look at the country; but with more prudence than many, not bringing his family with him. The interminable forests, and general wildness of the country disheartened him, and after penetrating but a very little way from the frontier, he resolved to return, and continue to abide beneath the folds of the starry flag. The rest, however, being true loyalists, averred their determination to *make* both a *country* and a *home* in the king's dominions. What if there were huge forests!—man could cut them down. There would be a market as soon as there was anything to sell, &c., &c.

Some of the Butler's Rangers had located themselves along the southern frontier, and others of them, indisposed for work, after years of lawless life, incident to the part they had borne in the war, were still lounging about. Anxious to make capital for themselves with the government, and thus get more at its expense, these men kept up a strict surveillance on all crossing the boundary line, and in consequence became cognizant of Mr. Webster's intention of returning, which they chose to construe into an act of disloyalty. Although the two countries were then at peace, they professed to believe him an American spy, followed him, caught and searched him, to see if he carried despatches; failing to find anything of the kind they, on the pretense that something objectionable might be secreted in them, broke up the biscuits with which the women of the company—Mrs. Culp in particular—had provided him for his sustenance during his journey through the wilderness. Happily for him, nothing amiss was found, and he proceeded on his homeward journey without further molestation.

The immigrants had entered the province at the Niagara, not far from its mouth, and for a time encamped near old Niagara town. In a few days, however, Mr. Culp found a location which pleased him in the township of Clinton, and as it was on the lake shore, the boat brought the family to the exact spot which was to be their home after so many days of weary journeying. Having been a Methodist in Pennsylvania, Mr. Culp naturally longed for the society of those like-minded with himself, and hearing of Mr. Neal he sought him out and invited him to preach in his house. Mr. Neal did so, and it became a regular preaching place, forming the nucleus round which a society grew; even after this lapse of years, it is a standing appointment, there having been a church built upon a part of the old Culp farm. The ground upon which this church stands was donated for the purpose by the grandson of the original occupier, and very material assistance was given to the building of the house itself by Mrs. Culp, widow of the late Jonas Culp, and mother of the present proprietor.

The circumstance of his father's house being a preaching-place brought young David, at an early day, into intimate relations with the Methodist preachers then in the country, the more especially as there were few comfortable stopping places to be found. In his childhood and early boyhood, therefore, he listened to the ministrations of such men as Neal, Dunham, Coleman, Harris, Vannest, Anson, Sawyer, Jewell, Bangs, and others whose names and teachings are still fresh in his memory. It was not, however, until the year 1807 that he yielded to the influence of the Holy Spirit operating upon his heart. In that year the Rev. Robert Perry was travelling the Niagara Circuit, and was instrumental in the conversion of Mr. Culp. Shortly after his conversion the young convert began to exhort, and after a time received license as a local preacher. He had been employed in the work as a supply before 1812, and in that year, in consequence of the impossibility of the American preachers filling the work, he was urged out into the regular itinerant ranks by Mr. Ryan. That year he was sent to Bay Quinte and Smith's Falls Circuit; in 1813 he was appointed to Ancaster and Long Point Circuit, with Mr. Rhodes; in 1814 he was returned to the same appointment, but before the end of the year was changed to the Niagara Circuit. Some of the circuits travelled then would comprise nearly an entire Conference now. The war being over in 1815, the preachers had once more the privilege of going to and from the United States, and consequently attended the session of the Genesee Conference of that year, at which time Mr. Culp was ordained Deacon by Bishop McKendree. He was ordained Elder at the Elizabethtown Conference in 1817, and thenceforward continued to labor as perseveringly in his Master's cause as he had done previously. But toils and excessive travel had begun to wear upon him, and being pressed with the weight of a large family, in days when it was impossible for the preacher's salary to meet the demands of a household, he, as before remarked, determined to locate, for a time at least, which he accordingly did, at the Conference of 1825. He, however, continued to preach, as he had opportunity, in the vicinity of his home.

Rev. James Wilson, who had been superannuated in 1824, became again effective in 1825, and Mr. Ryan took a superannuated relation. From this time he may be said to have ceased to travel in connection with the M. E. Church.

Of those connected with this Conference only two are now in the effective work, viz., Bishops Smith and Richardson, and only a few old veterans are living.

The excessive use of intoxicating liquors at this period, and its demoralizing influence upon society, had begun to attract the attention of Christian philanthropists, and their action resulted in the formation of temperance societies. The Methodist Church in Canada having had ample opportunity for observing the deplorable effects of intemperance in the country, had from the first taken a decided stand against the evil, and now favored the temperance movement accordingly. The

Quarterly Meeting Conference of the London Circuit, which met in the township of Westminster, July 12th, 1825, Thomas Madden, P. E., in the chair, and E. Stoney, P. C., present, with an official board of twelve members, passed the following resolution relating to the matter.

"*Resolved* by the Conference that spirituous liquors at bees, raisings and trainings have a deleterious effect upon the morals of the community, and that the members of this Conference will hereafter discourage the use thereof upon such occasions."

Though the action of the Quarterly Conference had not touched upon *moderate* drinking, at home, or in society, and its members had not yet discovered the better plan of *total abstinence*, yet, for the light they then had, a long stride in the right direction had been taken.

The statistics of the Canada Conference for 1825 were as follows:—Districts, 2; circuits, 24; preachers, 40, including superannuates; with a membership of 6875, giving an increase for the year of 731.

This year Bishop Mountain, of Quebec, who had come to Canada in 1795, as first Bishop of the Church of England in the province, died; and upon the occasion of his death, Dr. Strachan, on the 3rd July, 1825, delivered an elaborate discourse. In this sermon his bigotry and wilful misrepresentation of facts, so far as it concerned other denominations, manifested itself very clearly. While proceeding to enumerate the varied and strenuous exertions of Bishop Mountain to further the interests of his Church, and the difficulties which had had to be overcome, the Doctor went on to state that at the time of Bishop Mountain's arrival in the province "there were but *five Protestant congregations* within the whole diocese," in other words, within the bounds of the two Canadas. This assertion Dr. Strachan made, knowing full well that at the time of which he spoke, 1795, the Methodists had in the province three extensive circuits. These were, Oswegotchie, Bay Quinte and Niagara, and were supplied by four preachers, James Coleman,

Elijah Woolsey, Samuel Keeler and Darius Dunham; and there was a membership of 483. Each of these preachers had at least six appointments every week, and thus must have imparted religious instruction to at least one thousand souls, in the course of their rounds.

In the course of his remarks, the Dr. further stated that up to 1825 there were only about fifty Protestant congregations in the Canadas; whereas at this time the M. E. Church alone had 24 circuits, 35 ministers, and 220 congregations, with a membership of 6875. Besides the Methodist congregations there were also at this latter date quite a respectable number of congregations belonging to the Presbyterians and Baptists. as well as to other Protestant bodies.

The entire sermon was a labored effort to mislead the home government, that his party, by representing the country to be in such a fearful state of religious destitution, might gain the sympathy of the British public, and thereby secure the establishment of the Church of England in these colonies, and obtain, if not the whole, at least the lion's share of the Clergy Reserves.

According to Dr. Strachan's own showing, it was at a time when the Church of England numbered but *five* congregations in *both* ***Canadas*** that Bishop Mountain was desirous of having it made the established Church of the provinces; and that he himself was working for the same object, when his church numbered only about *fifty* congregations, or a little over. Here, with not one quarter of the number of the congregations which adhered to the Methodists alone, not counting those of the Presbyterians or Baptists, or other Protestant denominations, Dr. Strachan, with his then inconsiderable church membership and ministry, had the assurance to ask for, indeed to claim as a right, the entire control of *one-seventh* of all the lands in the province, in order that his Church might be built up at the expense of the nation, and that, too, against the express wishes of the majority of the people.

The reason of Dr. Strachan's resentment against the Methodists—especially those belonging to the original body—was sufficiently obvious: his favorite project, the establishment of the English Church in Canada upon nearly the same basis as in the mother country, was so strongly opposed by them that it was found impracticable, even after he had secured the aid and co-operation of the English missionaries, and, at a later date, of Mr. Ryan himself.

This sermon was reviewed very ably by Rev. Egerton Ryerson, then quite a young man. The reviewer was himself reviewed, but he nobly maintained his position, again reviewing his reviewer. The liberal press lent their assistance, and the controversy lasted many months, doing good service to the cause of equal religious rights and privileges.

The Annual Conference of 1826 was held in the township of Hamilton, a short distance from Cobourg, commencing Aug. 31st, Bishop George presiding. There was but one preacher received on trial; K. McK. Smith located, and James Jackson received a superannuated relation.

The work of grace among the Indians had continued to progress astonishingly, and a large number of the sons of the forest, having just returned from a camp-meeting in Cramahe, encamped near the seat of Conference, where they held meetings and received religious instruction from the various ministers assembled. Quite a number of pagan Indians were also present, as well as the Christians from Rice Lake, Grand River, Credit and Belleville, many of whom were awakened and converted during the progress of these meetings. It was a time of power, and of great rejoicing among the people of God.

Dr. Bangs, as one of the agents of the New York Methodist Book Establishment, made an official visit to this Conference, and announced the projected publication of a weekly paper, to be entitled the *Christian Advocate*, soliciting the countenance and support of the preachers to aid in its circulation in Canada.

The Conference, approving of the enterprise, accordingly passed the following resolution:—

"*Resolved*, That we highly approve of the publication of said paper; and we pledge ourselves to encourage its circulation."

The first number of the *Advocate*—the eldest of the family of *Advocates*—was issued on the 9th of September, 1826, and in a short time obtained a circulation, the largest at that time of any paper in the United States, of 30,000 copies per week. Hitherto the *Methodist Magazine* had been circulated to a considerable extent, but the *Advocate*, being a weekly, soon, in a great measure, superseded it.

The year previous a new mission had been opened on the Mississippi and Ottawa rivers, to which Rev. Samuel Belton had been sent; this year that work was added to the Perth Circuit, and called the Perth and Mississippi Mission, to which two preachers were appointed.

So rapidly and so widely was the work of God extending, and so numerous and urgent were the calls for preaching from the newer settlements, that it was with great difficulty that the work could be filled. In consequence of this, the whitening harvest, the Conference, with devout gratitude for the past, and longing desires for the future, passed the following resoultion:—

"*Resolved*, That the first Friday in November be set apart for *fasting and prayer* for the promotion of internal holiness, and the spread of the work of God in general; and particularly for an increase of laborers in God's vineyard."

From the time of the conversion of Peter Jones, Mr. Case had taken a deep, almost absorbing interest in the religious welfare of the Canadian aborigines, more especially those settled about the Grand River, Credit, Rice Lake, and Belleville. After consulting Rev. John Reynolds, William Ross, and other prominent men in and about Belleville, Mr. Case selected Grape Island, in the Bay of Quinte, on which to collect the Indians, in order to bring the adults under religious influences, and to instruct the children in the rudiments of an English education; hoping also to induce them to abandon their nomadic habits, and take to agricultural and mechanical pursuits. The island was, however, quite too small for the purpose designed, and had finally to be abandoned, and as the government could not be prevailed on to allow the Indians any land on Big Island, those who had been collected on Grape Island were removed to other missions. For a time, however, Mr. Reynolds, who took nearly as deep an interest in the Indians as Mr. Case, bore the expense of the support and tuition of one of them while he was attending school.

In the case of Big Island, as indeed in many instances since, no matter which party was in power, where these poor people have been concerned, Mr. Case, and all who took a friendly interest in them, considered that the government treated the Indians very badly, showing no regard whatever for their permanent good.

At this Conference, 1826, the work was divided into three Districts, the Presiding Elders being:—Niagara District, Thomas Madden; Bay Quinte, William Case; Augusta, Philander Smith. Statistics were as follows:—Districts, 3; circuits, 26; preachers, including superannuates and supplies, 37; membership, 7501, giving an increase for the year of 460 whites, 20 colored, and 146 Indians, making a total increase of 620.

CHAPTER XVII.

EVENTS OF 1826-27.

Withdrawal of Mr. Ryan—Aided by Dr. Strachan—Canadian Wesleyan body organized—Usefulness of Peter Jones and John Sunday—Attempts to coerce the Methodist Indians into adherence to the Church of England—Inducements offered to the Brothers Jones—John Sunday's reply—Refusal of the Joneses—Dr. Strachan's Chart—Its falsity—Testimony of the House to the character of the Methodist ministers and the tendency of their teachings—Address to the king—Result of the misrepresentations—State of Methodism in Canada at this Conference.

THE Conference of 1827 was held at Hamilton, and commenced its session 30th of August, Bishop Hedding presiding. Five preachers were received into full connection, nine were admitted on trial, and two located. Rev. Henry Ryan withdrew from the Church, and Alvin Torrey returned to the States, where he united with the Genesee Conference; David Breckenridge, also, who had been on trial, left at the end of the Conference. Rev. John Ryerson was appointed to the Niagara District, Mr. Madden was sent to Ancaster Circuit, having for a colleague, Anson Green, who had this year been admitted into full connection.

Mr. Ryan, having now severed all connection with the Church, set to work to more perfectly arrange the plans which he had for a time been forming, of effecting such a division in the Church as should eventuate in a general disruption. To this course he was urged by the counsel, and encouraged by the aid of parties who, high in authority, were still, as ever, the bitter, uncompromising enemies of Methodism, and judged this one of the best methods of retarding its progress in the country. Among those who thus urged Mr. Ryan on, were the Hon. John Wilson, the then Speaker of the House of Assembly, who had formerly been a member of the M. E. Church, but who had become disaffected, and Dr. Strachan, Mr. Ryan's former opponent, who took this opportunity of manifesting his contempt for, and hatred of the Methodist Bishops, and of that form of Methodism which had accomplished so much for the Canadian people by its opposition to the establishment in Canada of a State Church, by sending Mr. Ryan the sum of $200.00 to assist in what he professed to consider the praiseworthy effort to break up and destroy those Yankee Methodists.

The old cry of "disloyalty and foreign ecclesiastical control" was revived, and all the various changes rung upon it, as in 1812, and throughout the troubles with the English missionaries, though the falsity of the statement had been proved over and over again.

Mr. Ryan, in connection with Messrs. Jackson and Breckenridge, with some others, having separated themselves from the parent body, proceeded to organize a new church, which was called the Canadian Wesleyan, afterwards known as the New Connexion Methodists. The new organization commenced its career by inflaming, through its leaders, the political prejudices of certain classes of the Canadian people against the Bishops and the American Methodists, asserting that they exercised undue control over their brethren in Canada, and were, in fact, desirous of subverting the government; and with those who knew no better such slanders had the desired effect.

But, while thus assailed on every side, the valiant leaders of the original body did not slacken in their efforts for the spiritual welfare of their flocks. Though maliciously maligned and subjected to much vexatious annoyance, still they kept on steadily at their legitimate work—the evangelization of mankind. Peter Jones and John Sunday, also an Indian, travelled extensively among their own people, and were instrumental in bringing many hundreds to Christ. But this work was not carried on without much opposition from Dr. Strachan and the government. Only the year previous very high-handed measures had been attempted by those high in authority, in order to coerce the Indians into coming to their terms, with regard to their adherence to the Church of England. How far these threats were carried, will be seen by the following extract from the journal of the late lamented Peter Jones:—

"Monday, August 7th, 1826.—Received a message from Col. Givins, requesting the chiefs and principal men to meet him in Council at York, His Excellency the Lieutenant-Governor having a communication to make to us. We accordingly set off early in the morning.

"Tuesday, 8th—About 10 o'clock Col. Givins took us before the commanding officer of the garrison, at which place he (Col. Givins) delivered to us the following message from the Governor, Sir Peregrine Maitland:—He stated that he was requested by the Governor to inform us that he (the Governor) was very much opposed to our attending the Methodist camp-meetings, and that if we persisted in going to any more of them he would cast us off, and have nothing more to do with us; that we could now take our choice, either to desist from attending camp-meetings, and retain the good-will and aid of the Governor, or persist in going and lose his friendship and assistance. This was indeed a great trial to us, and I was for a few moments quite confounded and astonished, having been taught to believe that man was a free agent, and had a right to worship God according to the dictates of his own conscience; and also that the King's laws granted all his subjects liberty to worship God as they felt it their duty; so that if a man thought it right to retire to the woods to pray, who had a right to prevent him? or if he felt it his duty to confine his religion to the church, who had a right to judge him? Is not God the Judge of all men, and are we not accountable to him for our Stewardship? After a long consultation between ourselves, the chiefs thought it advisable, for the sake of what the Governor had done and was doing for us, not to oppose his will in this matter, particularly as we were just commencing a settlement, and endeavoring to improve in civilization.

"I abstain from giving further comments on this affair, but leave others to judge for themselves."

The question naturally arises "What had the government done for the amelioration of the aborigines prior to this, and what did they do subsequently?"

Before the Methodists had been providentially led to take an interest in their condition, the government had troubled itself very little about them, excepting when they were desirous of obtaining some particular hunting-grounds from them, and then, a paltry sum in money, or some *presents* of blankets, and gorgeous "calicoes," guns, tomahawks, ammunition, and other trifles, were considered ample remuneration for the grounds thus taken possession of. The government agents, and other traders, were allowed, too, to supply the poor creatures with the maddening fire-water at will, thus enabling those who chose to do so, to cheat them with impunity, not only out of their peltries, but out of the very presents just received from the government.

After the breaking out of the reformation among the Indians, through the instrumentality of the Methodists, they were, for a brief period, let alone, but soon, as is to be seen from the foregoing quotation from Mr. Jones' journal, they were to be tried even as others had been before.

The special kindness of the government referred to by Mr. Jones, was the erection by the government of twenty log houses at the Credit, and the promise of still further assistance to the permanent establishment of a settlement for the Indians there, that they might be instructed in the arts of civilized life.

The further aid was not found forthcoming when it was expected, as will be seen from the following quotation, also from the journal of Mr. Jones, which, although belonging to a later date, is given here in consequence of its connection with the preceding.

"January 30th, 1828.—After the council Colonel Givins desired my brother John and me to go to the Governor's office, as the Governor's secretary had some communications to make to us. We accordingly went, and after waiting an hour were informed that owing to a multiplicity of business, they could not make the communications that day, but desired us to call to-morrow at 11 o'clock. Various were our conjectures about this strange government proceeding.

"Thursday, 31st.—John and I called this morning on Dr. Strachan; he was very friendly, and made some enquiries about the general state of the Indians, and requested me to give him, in writing, a short statement of the condition of the Belleville and Rice Lake Indians, which I promised to do. At 11 o'clock, a. m., we again appeared at the Government House, but waited till 1 o'clock before any communications were made to us, when we were summoned into the presence of Major Hillier—the Governor's secretary—Dr. Strachan, the Attorney-General, and Col. Givins. To our astonishment we were now informed by Dr. Strachan that the Governor did not feel disposed to assist the Indians so long as they remained under the instruction of their present teachers, who were not responsible to Government for any of their proceedings and instructions; he was therefore unwilling to give them any encouragement. But should the natives come under the superintendence of the Established Church, then the Government would assist them as far as laid in their power. When stating their reasons for wishing us to come under the teaching of the Church of England, the Dr. and Attorney-General said that the Indians were considered by the Government to be under the war department, and therefore it was necessary that they should be under their instruction; and that another reason was, that it would make the missionary establishments more permanent; whereas at present they were liable to fluctuation, the only resource of the Methodists being that of subscriptions. It was proposed to my brother and me that if we would assist them in this undertaking, and come under their directions, our salaries should be increased, and we should have access to the contemplated college. We told them that their request would cause much dissatisfaction to the Methodists, as they claimed the Indians for their spiritual children, having been the first to teach them the Christian religion. They replied they could not help what the Methodists would think about it, as it was necessary the Indians should be responsible to them for their conduct. We then told them that it was not in our power to say one way or the other, but that we should leave it for the Indians to decide themselves. They requested an answer as soon as possible. Colonel Givins gave us to understand that the request of the Credit Indians would most likely meet with the approbation of the Governor, and desired John to make out a return of the number of families residing at the river Credit. We then proceeded to the quarters of the chiefs, who were waiting for answers to their petitions. When we told them what had been communicated to us they sighed deeply, and after a long silence said, 'Then all our labors have been in vain with our great father the Governor;' but John Sunday, with an air of disdain, replied, 'We have heretofore made out to live from year to year, even when we were sinners, and shall not the Great Spirit whom we now serve take care of us and preserve us from all harm?' I cautioned them not to be too much troubled about it, but to leave it to God in prayer, to which they assented.

"Friday, February 1st.—This morning I carried into Dr. Strachan the statements he requested respecting the Belleville and Rice Lake Indians, of which he approved. Our conversation turned upon the proposals made yesterday, when I gave him to understand that I should not take any influential part in the business, but leave the matter altogether for the Indians to decide. He then told me that the government would accomplish their design, whether my brother John and I were willing or not, but added that if they had our assistance it could be accomplished sooner."

The brothers Jones would not lend their countenance to the scheme, and the Dr. was thus left to work out his own plans.

Dr. Strachan finding that in spite of every effort of his to the contrary, the anti-Church and State party were gaining strength year by year, hastened to England with a chart which he had prepared, showing what he chose to represent as the relative strength of the various denominations in the province. Accompanying this somewhat famous chart was a letter which he addressed to the Home Government; and in this as well as in the chart, the reverend gentleman grossly misrepresented nearly all the other religious bodies, excepting his own, that were in the province. But it was more especially at the *Methodists* that his most venomed darts were thrown His never-ceasing and hackneyed cry of disloyalty was brought into requisition, as it had frequently been before, in order—no matter how false it might be—that it might do him good service in gaining the end he so much desired; and in addition, too, to his misrepresentation of other denominations, both as regarded numbers and *nationality*, he very greatly magnified the numbers and influence of his own community.

The subject matter of these documents was brought before the notice of the Upper Canada House of Assembly, and a committee was appointed by it to enquire into the accuracy, or inaccuracy of the statements therein contained. Fifty-two witnesses were examined before the committee, and after a very thorough investigation the Assembly adopted a report of which the following is an extract:—

"The insinuations in the letter against the Methodist clergymen the committee have noticed with peculiar regret. To the disinterested and indefatigable exertions of these pious men this province owes much. At an early period of its history, when it was thinly settled, and its inhabitants were scattered through the wilderness, and destitute of all other means of religious instruction, these ministers of the Gospel, animated by Christian zeal and benevolence, at the sacrifice of health, and interest and comfort, carried amongst the people the blessings, and consolations, and sanctions of our holy religion. Their ministry and instruction, far from having, as is represented in the letter, a tendency hostile to our institutions, have been conducive—in a degree which cannot be easily estimated—to the reformation of their hearers from licentiousness, and the diffusion of correct morals—the foundation of all sound loyalty and social order. There is no reason to believe that, as a body, they have failed to inculcate, by precept and example, as a Christian duty, an attachment to the sovereign, and a cheerful and conscientious obedience to the laws of the country. More than thirty-five years have elapsed since they commenced their labors in the colonies. In that time the province has passed through a war which put to the proof the loyalty of the people. If their influence and instructions have the tendency mentioned, the effect by this time must be manifest. Yet no one doubts that the Methodists are as loyal as any other of His Majesty's subjects. And the very fact that, while their clergymen are dependent for their support upon the voluntary contributions of their people, the number of their members has increased so as to be now—in the opinion of almost all the witnesses—greater than that of the members of any other denomination in the province, is a complete refutation of any suspicion that their influence and instructions have such a tendency. For it would be a gross slander on the loyalty of the people to suppose that they would countenance, and listen with complacency, to those whose confidence was exerted for such base purposes."

A copy of the above report, with a chart prepared in accordance with the evidence given before the House, was ordered by vote of the Assembly to be transmitted to the Home Government, in addition to which an address was also sent to the King, George IV., from which the following is an extract:—

"*To the King's Most Excellent Majesty:*

"MOST GRACIOUS SOVEREIGN:—We, Your Majesty's dutiful and loyal subjects, the Commons of Upper Canada, in Provincial Parliament assembled, humbly beg leave to represent to Your Majesty that we have seen, with equal surprise and regret, a letter and ecclesiastical chart, dated 16th of May, 1827, and addressed by the Honorable and Venerable Doctor Strachan, Archdeacon of York, a member of Your Majesty's Legislative and Executive Councils of this province, to the Right Honorable R. J. Wilmot Horton, at that time Under-secretary of State for the Colonies, for the information of Lord Goderich, then at the head of the Colonial Department; as they are inaccurate in some important reports, and are calculated to lead Your Majesty's Government into serious errors.

"We beg leave to inform Your Majesty that, of Your Majesty's subjects in this province, only a small proportion are members of the Church of England, and there is not any peculiar tendency to that Church among the people, and that nothing could cause more alarm and grief in their minds, than the apprehension that there was a design on the part of Your Majesty's Government to establish, as a part of the state, one or more Churches or denominations of Christians in this province, with rights and endowments not granted to Your Majesty's subjects in general of other denominations, who are equally conscientious and deserving, and equally loyal and attached to Your Majesty's Royal Person and Government. In following honestly the dictates of their conscience, as regards the great and important subject of religion, the latter have never been conscious that they have violated any law, or any obligation of a good subject, or done anything to forfeit Your Majesty's favor and protection, or to exclude themselves from a participation in the rights and privileges enjoyed by Your Majesty's other subjects.

"We humbly beg leave to assure Your Majesty that the insinuations in the letter against the Methodist preachers in this province do much injustice to a body of pious and deserving men, who justly enjoy the confidence, and are the spiritual instructors of a large portion of Your Majesty's subjects in this province. We are convinced that the tendency of their influence and instruction is not hostile to our institutions, but, on the contrary, eminently favorable to religion and morality, and their labors are calculated to make their people better men and better subjects, and have already produced in this province the happiest effects.

"While we fully and gratefully appreciate Your Majesty's gracious intention granting a royal charter for the establishment of an University in this province, we would beg most respectfully to represent that, as the great body of Your Majesty's subjects in this province are not members of the Church of England, they have seen, with grief, that the charter contains provisions which are calculated to render the institution subservient to the particular interests of that Church, and to exclude from its offices and honors all who do not belong to it. In consequence of these provisions its benefits will be confined to the favored few, while others of Your Majesty's subjects, far more numerous, and equally loyal and deserving of Your Majesty's paternal care and favor, will be shut out from a participation in them. Having a tendency to build up one particular Church, to the prejudice of others, it will naturally be an object of jealousy and disgust. Its influence, as a seminary of learning, will upon these accounts be limited and partial. We, therefore, humbly beg that Your

Majesty will be pleased to listen to the wishes of Your Majesty's people in this respect, and to cause the present charter to be cancelled and one granted free from the objections to which, emboldened by a conviction of Your Majesty's fraternal and gracious feelings to your loyal subjects in this province, as well as by a sense of duty to the people, and a knowledge of their anxiety upon the subject, we have presumed to advert.

"We would also beg leave to state that it is the general desire of Your Majesty's subjects in this province, that the moneys arising from the sale of any lands set apart in this province for the support and maintenance of a Protestant clergy, should be entirely appropriated to the purposes of education and internal improvement. We would most humbly represent that to apply them to the benefit of one or two Christian denominations, to the exclusion of others, would be unjust as well as impolitic, and that it might perhaps be found impracticable to divide them among all. We have no reason to fear that the cause of religion would suffer materially from not giving public support to its ministers, and from leaving them to be supported by the liberality of their people."

* * * * * * * * *

The principal effect accomplished by Dr. Strachan's mission to England—as far at least as Canadian affairs were concerned, was, that, through the letters and addresses correcting his gross misrepresentations, a more general and more correct knowledge of Canadian denominational strength outside the Church of England, was gained by English statesmen of the higher order; while in Canada itself, the publication of the various addresses, charts, &c., &c., caused the friends of civil and religious liberty to set themselves even more determinedly and energetically than before against every encroachment of the would-be supreme ecclesiastical power; and to show very unequivocally that no connection between Church and State would be tolerated in the country.

Notwithstanding all the conflicts through which the Methodists had had to pass during this momentous year, the state of the Church was found at the following Conference to be as follows:—

Districts, 3; preachers, 44, and circuits 30, with a membership of 8,633; making an increase for the year of 846 whites, and 272 Indians. There was a decrease among the colored people of 24.

CHAPTER XVIII.

General Conference of 1828—It complies with the wishes of the Canadian body for a separate organization—Annual Conference of 1828—The M. E. Church in Canada becomes an independent body—Civil rights still withheld by local government—Marriage Act—It passes both Houses—Royal assent refused by the Governor—Granted by the King—Prosperity of the cause—Indian Missions—Gratifying results—Address to the Governor—Reply—Communication to the English Conference—No response—Statistics.

THE General Conference of 1828 was held in Pittsburgh, commencing, as was—and is—the invariable custom, on the 1st of May.

The interests of the Canada Conference were represented by Messrs. Wm. Ryerson, Samuel Belton, John Ryerson, William Slater and Wyatt Chamberlain.

These brethren, at a suitable period, as soon as possible after the commencement of the session, presented the following memorial from the Canada Conference upon the vexed question of ecclesiastical independence:—

"*To the Bishops and members of the Annual Conferences of the Methodist Episcopal Church, in their several Conferences assembled:*

"The memorial of the preachers in Canada, in Conference assembled at Hallowell, Upper Canada, the 25th August, 1824, respectfully sheweth:—

"That petitions to the late General Conference having been forwarded from a numerous body in this country, praying for a separate connexion in Canada; that the General Conference did not think it expedient to grant the prayer of the petitioners, and offered their reasons, at the same time leaving the petitioners yet to hope for such an event, by saying that 'however expedient such a measure may be considered at a future period, the proper time for it has not arrived;' and that the Canada Conference being of opinion that the plan of becoming a separate body ought, at a future period, to go into effect, they beg leave to submit the same to the deliberate examination of their respective fathers and brethren in the several sister Conferences, with a view to a favorable decision at the next General Conference and that the reasons which have influenced the Canada Conference, in favor of such an establishment are as follows:—

"1st. The state of society requires it. The first settlers having claimed the protection of His Brittanic Majesty, in the Revolutionary war, were driven from their former possessions to endure great hardships in a remote wilderness. Time, however, and a friendly intercourse, had worn down their asperity and prejudice when the late unhappy war revived their former feeling, affording what they considered new and grievous occasion for disgust against their invading neighbors. The prejudices thus excited would probably subside if their ministry were to become residents in this country, as would be the case in the event of becoming a separate body in Canada.

"2nd. A separate establishment appears to be expedient and necessary on account of the insulated and extended situation of the societies in this country from the general superintendency. The national line is marked by a vast sheet of water stretching the whole length of the province, either in broad lakes or rapid rivers; so that, in our insulated situation, and the difficulties in passing, it was nearly thirty years after the introduction of our ministry, before one of our Bishops visited this country. Two other Bishops lived and died without setting foot in Canada: and if two others, by forced labor, have kindly stepped over, these visits have been few and transitory; consequently, inconveniences have been felt for want of ordinations, and a more particular and immediate oversight of the general superintendency. A Superintendent, therefore, to reside in the country, to attend to these important duties, would greatly remedy those inconveniences, and have a most salutary influence upon the cause of religion.

"3rd. A separate establishment appears necessary and expedient, on account of existing jealousies, lately awakened by the government of this country. On the arrival of the missionaries from Europe efforts were made to establish them in our cities and societies, by raising objections to our ministry, as coming from the United States. These objections were urged to the people here, and to the Committee at home; but when the measure proved unsuccessful, and the British Conference refused to sanction the request made to them from political motives, these objections were then urged against us to the government of this country. Natural as it was for political characters to listen to alarms on such a subject, some excitements were produced on the minds of men high in the Executive Department, and some events have rather increased than allayed these excitements. To us, therefore, it appears proper to apply for a separation, that by yielding to what might be thought to be the reasonable wishes of the government, we may obviate the objection, and remove all suspicion of the purity of our motives in preaching the Gospel in this country.

"4th. To us it appears expedient and necessary that the societies here should be set off as a separate body, because that in the event of war between the two nations, the difficulties of intercourse between this country and the United States would render it extremely hazardous, if not totally impracticable, as we are now situated, for the superintendents to discharge their duties in Canada.

"5th. To us it appears expedient that the societies here should become a Church separate from the body in the United States, in order to secure privileges which are of importance for the prosperity of religion here. At present we are not permitted to perform the rites of marriage to our members; nor, indeed, have we any legal security for one of our numerous chapels in this province, and we have been assured that in our present relation we must not expect any extension of privileges. Though we cannot assure ourselves of such advantages by becoming a separate body, yet we can apply for those privileges with more confidence; and we think we have reason to hope that when petitions shall be presented to the government from an independent Church in this country our privileges will be granted and our property secured.

"These, brethren, are the reasons which have been presented to our minds, and which appear to us of weight and moment in favor of a separation, and in order to preserve the body of Methodists in this country from the most disastrous of all events—that of divisions among ourselves."

The above memorial, as will be observed from the date, had been prepared at, and received the sanction of the Canada Conference of 1824. A copy of it had been laid before each of the several other Annual Conferences during the four years' interval between the first session of the Canada Conference and the session of the General Conference; so that the whole question was pretty generally understood, and was, therefore, brought up at this Conference for final adjustment.

The document was referred to a committee, who, after due deliberation, taking all the circumstances of the Canadian Church into consideration, finally reported in favor of the separation. The Conference accordingly adopted the following preamble and report:—

* "*Resolved*, by the delegates of the Annual Conferences, in General Conference assembled, That whereas the jurisdiction of the Methodist Episcopal Church in the United States of America has been heretofore extended over the ministers and members in connection with the said Church in the province

* Journals of General Conference, 1828.

of Upper Canada, by mutual agreement, and by the consent of the brethren in that province; and whereas the General Conference is satisfactorily assured that our brethren in the said province, under peculiar and pressing circumstances, do now desire to organize themselves into a distinct Methodist Episcopal Church, in friendly relations with the Methodist Episcopal Church in the United States; therefore be it resolved, and it is hereby resolved, by the delegates of the Annual Conferences in General Conference assembled:—

"1. That if the Annual Conference in Upper Canada, at its ensuing session, or any succeeding session previously to the next General Conference, shall definitely determine on this course, and elect a General Superintendent of the Methodist Episcopal Church in that province, this General Conference do hereby authorize any one or more of the General Superintendents of the Methodist Episcopal Church in the United States, with the assistance of any two or more Elders, to ordain such General Superintendent for said Church in Upper Canada, provided always that nothing herein contained be contrary to, or inconsistent with the laws existing in said province; and provided that no such General Superintendent of the Methodist Episcopal Church in Upper Canada, or any of his successors in office, shall at any time exercise any ecclesiastical jurisdiction whatever in any part of the United States, or of the territories thereof; and provided also that this article shall be expressly ratified and agreed to by the said Canada Annual Conference before any ordination shall take place.

"2. That the delegate who has been selected by the General Conference to attend the ensuing Annual Conference of the British Wesleyan Methodist Connexion be, and hereby is instructed to express to that body the earnest and affectionate desire of this General Conference that the arrangement made with that Connexion in relation to the labors of their missionaries in Upper Canada may still be maintained and observed.

"3. That our brethren and friends, ministers or others, in Upper Canada, shall at all times, at their request, be furnished with any of our books and periodical publications, on the same terms with those by which our agents are regulated in furnishing them in the United States, and until there shall be an adjustment of any claims which the Canada Conference may have in this connection, the book agents shall divide to the said Canada Church an equal proportion of any annual dividend which may be made from the Book Concern to the several Annual Conferences respectively; provided, however, that the aforesaid dividend shall be apportioned with the Canada Church only so long as they may continue to support and patronize our Book Concern as in times past."

In direct reply to the petition of the Canadian memorialists the General Conference directed that a copy of the foregoing resolutions, containing the decision of that body with regard to Canadian affairs, be given to the delegates from Canada, which was accordingly done.

This adjustment was not arrived at without an earnest and somewhat protracted debate. It was very natural that the American preachers should enquire the reason of all this outcry against themselves, and their jurisdiction over a Church which they had planted, and over which they had exercised a paternal care for more than thirty years. During the progress of the debate it was fully proven that they had broken no law of the land; that in every place in which, for the time being, they had resided while preaching in Canada, they had behaved themselves as became peaceable subjects of the British crown, in no way striving to subvert purely British institutions. The Canada Conference complained of no injustice at the hands of their American brethren, simply asserting that outside pressure impelled them to ask the separation, as they hoped thereby the sooner to secure certain rights and privileges which were denied them by the arrogant faction at the time in power, on the alleged ground of their connection with the American body. But subsequent events proved that this same faction were not more favorably disposed towards the purely Canadian Church than they had previously been towards the Americo-Canadian, against which they had so successfully raised so much unfounded prejudice.

The question was one of very great importance, in other respects than this. There had been no similar crisis in the history of the Church, consequently they had no precedent by which they might be guided in their deliberations. Dr. Bangs, in his History of the M. E. Church, thus ably sums up the whole matter:—

"There is an important principle involved in the above agreement to dissolve the connection which had so long subsisted between the Methodists in the United States and Upper Canada, which it seems expedient to explain. When the subject first came up for consideration it was contended, and the committee to whom it was first referred so reported, which report was approved of by a vote of the General Conference, that we had no constitutional right to set off the brethren in Upper Canada as an independent body, because the terms of the compact by which we existed as a General Conference made obligatory on us, as a delegated body, to preserve the union entire, and not to break up the Church into separate fragments. Hence to grant the prayer of the memorialists, by a solemn act of legislation, would be giving sanction to a principle, and setting a precedent for future General Conferences, of a dangerous character—of such a character as might tend ultimately to the dissolution of the ecclesiastical body, which would be, in fact and form, contravening the very object for which we were constituted a delegated Conference, this object being a *preservation*, and not a *destruction* or *dissolution* of the *union*. These arguments appeared so forcible to the first committee, and to the Conference, that the idea of granting them a separate organization on the principle of abstract and independent legislation was abandoned as altogether indefensible, being contrary to the constitutional compact.

"But still feeling a desire to grant, in some way, that which the Canada brethren so earnestly requested, and for which they pleaded with so much zeal, and even with most pathetic appeals to our sympathies, it was suggested by a very intelligent member of the General Conference, the late Bishop Emory, that the preachers who went to Canada from the United States, went, in the first instance, as missionaries, and that ever afterward, whenever additional help was needed, Bishop Asbury and his successors asked for *volunteers*, not claiming the *right to send* them in the same authoritative manner in which they were sent to the different parts of the United States and territories; hence it followed that the compact between us and our brethren in Canada was altogether of a *voluntary* character—*we* had offered them our services and *they* had accepted them—and therefore, as the time had arrived when they were no longer willing to receive or accept of our labors and superintendence, they had a perfect right to request us to withdraw our services, and we the same right to withhold them.

"This presented the subject in a new and very clear light, and it seemed perfectly compatible with *our* powers as a delegated Conference, and their privileges as a part of the same body, thus connected by a voluntary and *conditional* compact, either expressed or implied, to dissolve the connection subsisting between us without any dereliction of duty or forfeiture of privilege on either part. *It was on this principle alone that the above agreement was based.*"

The separation of the Canadian work from the American—so far as the action of the General Conference was concerned—was accomplished. Nothing now remained unfinished but the ratification of the articles of separation by the Canada Conference, when the tie which had bound them so closely together for thirty-seven years would be completely severed.

The Canada Conference of 1828, which was to inaugurate a new era in the history of the Methodist Church in the province, held its session in Switzer's meeting-house, in Ernestown; commencing on the 2nd of October. Bishop Hedding was present and presided. The action of the General Conference in answer to their memorial was brought before the Conference for their approval or rejection, when the whole subject was referred to a committee of nine, who in due time reported favorably, and the following resolutions concerning it were adopted :—

"Whereas the jurisdiction of the Methodist Episcopal Church in the United States of America has, heretofore, extended over the ministers and members in connection with the said Church in the province of Upper Canada, by mutual agreement, and by the consent of our brethren in this province; and whereas it has been and is the general wish of the ministers and members of the Methodist Episcopal Church in Upper Canada to be organized into a separate and independent body, in friendly relations with the Methodist Episcopal Church in the United States; and whereas the General Conference has been pleased to comply with our wish in this respect, and has authorized any one or more of the General Superintendents of the Methodist Episcopal Church in the United States, with the assistance of any two or more Elders, to ordain a General Superintendent for the said Church in Upper Canada:

"*Resolved*, 1st, That it is expedient and necessary, and that the Canada Conference of the Methodist Episcopal Church do now organize itself into an independent Methodist Episcopal Church in Canada.

"*Resolved*, 2nd, That we adopt the present discipline of the Methodist Episcopal Church as the basis of our constitution and discipline, except such alterations as may appear necessary from our local circumstances."

Immediately after organizing themselves into an independent

body the Conference proceeded to elect William Case General Superintendent, *pro tem.* Bishop Hedding, as soon as the election was made, proposed to vacate the chair, as he was no longer, in fact, their chairman, by virtue of his office as Bishop of the M. E. Church in the United States; but, at the urgent request of the Conference, he was induced to preside during the remainder of the session. Before its close the Bishop gave them such instruction and counsel as he considered necessary or applicable to their situation and circumstances. Thus amicably was severed the connection between the two bodies. On the part of the Americans the arrangement hitherto existing had been one of purely disinterested benevolence and Christian zeal. Their labor had been bestowed without the hope of receiving any corresponding pecuniary advantage, and in return for these unselfish exertions, they had been subjected to the most unscrupulous and malignant calumny, and in some instances to persecution. Now, however, when the cause which they had, with so much toil, planted, and so carefully and successfully nurtured, deemed itself strong enough to stand alone, and seemed desirous of cutting itself loose from the parental control and support, they, with equal disinterestedness, allowed them to make trial of that strength.

With regard to the political tendency of the connection, Mr. Playter very justly remarks:—"Nor was the connection ever injurious to the allegiance of the people to the British Crown, although manifold have been the charges to the contrary." The preachers had faithfully adhered to the rule in the Discipline—laid down for their guidance in this very matter—which forbade them to meddle in the politics of any foreign power. There is not a single instance recorded, even by the enemies of Methodism—who would have been glad of the opportunity of blazoning it abroad if there had been—of any of the preachers having disregarded this rule.

It had been urged as a reason in favor of separation, while the negotiations were pending, that by becoming independent of the parent body, the Canadian section of the Church might the sooner prevail on the Provincial Government to sanction the act by which the Methodists, and other Protestant Denominations, would be allowed to hold church property and also to consent to the passage of the act permitting them to solemnize marriage. While the act of separation was still under discussion, the law entitling them to hold church property, came into effect, thus doing away with part of the disability under which the Church, as then constituted, labored. The other point, the Canadian Executive still refused to yield, even after the separation, thus proving beyond the possibility of question, that it was *Methodism*, more even than Americanism, against which they entertained such bitter hostility. The Marriage Bill, which finally accorded their just rights to the Methodists, after having passed the House of Assembly, secured the royal assent not only without the consent of the Provincial Executive, but in spite of all the influence it could bring to bear against it, as the following facts amply prove:

This, or similar Marriage Bills, had been laid before the Provincial Legislature for six successive years, and was passed by the House of Assembly, only to be contemptuously thrown out by the Legislative Council, or, having passed that body in one instance, it was refused the Governor's sanction, without which it could not become law.

Late in 1828, or early in 1829, the Marriage Bill in question passed the House of Assembly, and on the 30th of January, in the latter year, it passed the Upper House with some alterations, to which, after some delay, the Lower House consented. The Bill as amended was finally passed on the 4th of March, 1829; but as usual, the Governor refused his sanction, and the Bill was sent to England to be laid before the King. There it remained nearly two years, until the Whigs came into power, when the King having given it the royal assent, it was returned to Canada in March 1831, just as a much more liberal act was about being passed by the

Canadian Legislature. It will readily be seen, therefore, that the rights of Canadian Methodists were not obtained any the more speedily because of the Church having become independent of the parent body.

Another reason that had been urged, and that had been considered of some weight, was that such a concession would satisfy Mr. Ryan and his friends, and thus prevent division in the Church. Nothing, however, was gained in this respect, as Mr. Ryan had gone too far, and had become too thoroughly estranged from his brethren to be willing to retrace his steps.

The manner in which the separation from the parent body had been effected gave general satisfaction, and greatly endeared the American Methodists to their Canadian brethren.

The summer and autumn of 1828, up to the very time of the Conference of 1828, had been a season of more than usual revival among both whites and Indians. Peter Jones had been appointed, the year previous, general missionary to the native tribes. He was accompanied in his travels by John Sunday, and their ministry was attended with great success, in the awakening of their brethren and the ingathering of them into the Church, besides bringing many Indian children under religious instruction.

Mr. Richardson, who had been the missionary to the Indians on the Credit during the year 1827–1828, gives the following account of the efforts of the Indians to erect a school-house and place of worship:—

"The Indians, men, women and children, were collected together by the sound of the horn, and the matter was explained to them by Peter Jones, and a subscription paper presented. In half an hour one hundred dollars (lacking 4d) were subscribed, and (it being the time for catching salmon) forty dollars were paid at the time. Many of the Indian women, when they saw others go forward and present the widow's mite, (for they gave all they had, which was from one shilling to three dollars), expressed their sorrow that they had nothing to give; but added they would have some soon. They immediately applied themselves to the making of baskets and brooms, and soon presented their dollars and half dollars, and had their names set down among the others. Little boys from eight to twelve years brought their shillings and two shillings, the product of their little fingers, to help in building a house where they could learn to be wise like white boys, and pray to Re-sha-mun-ne-to (the Great Spirit). How astonishing the contrast! A short time ago these Indians would sell the last thing they had for a tenth of its value to get a little whiskey; but now they will labor and exercise economy to get something to build a house where they can worship the Lord of Hosts."

The anniversary of the Missionary Society was held on the third day of the Conference, when the most gratifying results were reported. There were at this time, connected with the Methodist Church in Upper Canada, 10 Indian missions, 12 schools, having an attendance of 300 scholars, and a native membership of 915. Seeing that the Indians were so earnestly desirous of being benefitted by Christian instruction, and that they were really trying to help themselves, the Methodists on Yonge Street, as well as some from the London District, assisted them in building their meeting-house, and furnished them with a stove. Benevolent persons from the United States, also, did what they could to assist in the conversion and civilization of the aborigines, and thus much good was accomplished—more, in fact, considering the amount of means employed, than has ever been done since.

The new Governor, Sir John Colborne, had but a short time previously arrived in the country, and the Conference took this opportunity of vindicating the character of its ministers from the charge of disloyalty which had so often been made against them, by welcoming the King's vicegerent in the following address:—

"*To his Excellency, Sir John Colborne, K. C. B., Lieut.-Governor of the Province of Upper Canada, Major-General commanding His Majesty's forces therein :*

"MAY IT PLEASE YOUR EXCELLENCY,—We, His Majesty's faithful and loyal subjects, the ministers of the Methodist Episcopal Church in Canada, in our Annual Conference assembled, respectfully beg leave to offer to your Excellency our most cordial congratulations on your Excellency's appointment to the Governorship of this province, and your safe arrival amongst us.

"We hail it as a propitious event, and it affords us peculiar pleasure, to present to the representatative of our sovereign our assurances of loyal attachment to His Majesty's mild and beneficent government, and to the constitution of our country.

"We shall ever consider it amongst our most important duties, as religious teachers, to inculcate the principles of fidelity and obedience to the Governor and lawfully constituted authorities of our highly-favored country: and we assure your Excellency that these feelings of conscientious attachment to the British Government, cherished by us as Christian ministers, and dear to us as British subjects, pervade and animate the people of our pastoral care.

"As the ministers and representatives of our Anglo-Canadian Church, unconnected with the civil and ecclesiastical authority of any other country, we rejoice that by the kind and merciful Providence of God we form a part of the British Empire.

"We pray Almighty God that your Excellency may be guided and assisted in the discharge of the arduous duties of your Government, and that your residence among us may be equally gratifying to yourself, and beneficial to the best interests of the loyal inhabitants of this colony, and that under your Excellency's wise and equitable administration and fostering care, the general interests of this province may prosper; that the benign influence of religion and education may be widely diffused; and that our civil and religious liberties—the strongest bonds of perpetual union between this colony and the mother country—may be established on the best and surest foundations.

"We request that your Excellency will be pleased to accept of our expressions of personal respect, and best wishes for the uninterrupted health and prosperity of your Excellency and family.

"By order of the Conference.

WM. CASE, *President, pro tem.*
JAS. RICHARDSON, *Secretary.*

Ernestown, Oct. 7th, 1828.

The address was favorably received, and the following reply sent in answer to it:—

"GENTLEMEN,—Your loyal address I receive with great satisfaction, and in thanking you for your kind wishes, I must observe that the labors and zeal of ministers with your pious sentiments cannot fail of being profitable in a colony where the temptations are many, the pastors few, and the flocks scattered; particularly living, as you do, under the government of a sovereign solicitous that all should be equally protected in the conscientious discharge of their religious duties."

But though the reply of the governor was thus favorable, Dr. Strachan and his party in a short time succeeded in influencing him to such a degree that he did but little for the Indians, and gave no further countenance to the M. E. Church in Canada.

Being desirous of carrying out in good faith the arrangement entered into between the English Conference and the American General Conference, in 1820, with regard to the occupation of the Canadas by their respective ministers, the Conference before its close appointed a committee, consisting of William Case, George Ryerson, and James Richardson, to enter into a correspondence with their English brethren, and thus establish—if possible—a friendly relation and intercourse between the two connexions. This courteous communication, however, met with no response from the English Conference.

The session of the most important Conference that had ever been held in Canada was approaching its termination. The state of the work, as reported in the Minutes, was as follows:—Districts, 3; travelling preachers, 47, superannuated, 7; circuits, 32, with a membership of 9678. There was an increase in the membership of 690 whites, 343 Indians, making in all a total increase of 1033. The Presiding Elders for the ensuing year were John Ryerson, William Ryerson, and Philander Smith; and Mr. Case was appointed to the oversight of the Indian Missions.

The Church did not lack now, as it had done in the earlier years of its history, for able defenders from among its own ranks, having at its command, at this time, the ready pens and masterly minds of such men as James Richardson, Franklin Metcalf, and Egerton Ryerson, the last named of whom stood forth then, and for some years afterwards, as the champion of equal civil and religious rights, and was for a time one of the boldest and most able advocates for the secularization of the Clergy Reserves.

From this Conference of 1828, the preachers went home to their circuits with high hopes and expectations, which were, for a few years, more than realized.

CHAPTER XIX.

Conference of 1829—James Jackson—Death of William Slater—Establishment of the *Christian Guardian*—Views respecting connection between Church and State, &c.—Sunday School Union formed—Glorious success of the mission work—Statistics—Canadian Wesleyans—Great religious prosperity—Commencement of Temperance movement in Canada—Found earnest advocates in the Methodist ministers—Hon. John Rolph and Marshall S. Bidwell

THE Conference of 1829 commenced its session on the 26th of August, in the old Bowman meeting-house, in the township of Ancaster, Rev. W. Case presiding, Rev. James Richardson secretary. Being now an independent body it entered upon the business of the session without assistance from the American Church. Mr. Case, the Superintendent *pro tem.*, was a man of considerable experience, and was therefore capable of presiding with ability, which he did to the general satisfaction of those with whom he had to do.

At this Conference there were five candidates received on trial; three of the old preachers continued to hold a superannuated relation; George Sovereign located; Isaac B. Smith withdrew, and James Jackson was expelled. The charges on which Mr. Jackson was tried and upon which he was expelled were, misapplication of mission funds, and wilful slander of his brethren. With regard to the first accusation Mr. Jackson always asserted that he had a perfect right to use the funds as he had done. He had been, he said, wrongfully accused, and his life, even, had been sought—an assertion for which there does not appear to have been the least foundation in fact. Mr. Jackson was a man of very strong feeling, and a violent, indeed, abusive disputant. He had taken an active part with Mr. Ryan in his crusade against the Church and his former brethren and co-laborers, and in the course of the controversy a great amount of ill-will had arisen, and many bitter things had been said which the facts in the case did not warrant, and which in the end led to this unhappy termination.

It was reported at this Conference that since their last session one of their number had fallen in the field, the first instance of the kind that had occurred since their existence as a separate body. William Slater had died during the year. He was born in Derbyshire, England, Dec. 1st, 1787, and emigrated to Canada at an early day, the precise date is not known. Having been a Wesleyan local preacher in England, he was not long in finding work to do for his Master in the new country to which he had come; and in 1822 he was admitted into full connection in the Genesee Conference. During the few years he was permitted to live he travelled extensively, and was made the honored instrument in the conversion of many souls. He was seized with his last illness, which was but of ten days duration, when about sixteen miles from home, to which he was not able to be removed. Though much exercised with regard to the future of his little family, consisting of his wife and two helpless infants, he was enabled to cast even this care upon the Lord, and his end was emphatically peace. The Conference expressed their appreciation of his worth and services, and their sorrow at his loss, in a lengthy obituary, which was inserted in the Minutes of that year.

One imperative want which the Church had long felt, was that of a connexional paper. No merely secular paper could fully understand the wants, or enter into the interests of the religious community, nor could it so ably defend the Church from the ungenerous and untruthful assaults of its enemies. Besides being an able weapon for self-defence, it would not only chronicle the various proceedings of the body, but would be the medium through which much moral and religious, as well as scientific, instruction might be conveyed to the masses at large. The feasibility of the project of starting such a paper was brought up at this Conference, and a committee appointed to consider and report whether or not the scheme were practicable. The following is the report of that committee, which was adopted by the Conference :—

"1st. That it is the opinion of your Committee that a weekly paper should be established under the direction of the Conference, of a religious and moral character, to be entitled the *Christian Guardian*.

"2nd. That its place of location be the town of York.

"3rd. That the sum of $700 is sufficient to purchase all the apparatus for a printing establishment.

"4th. That the sum of $2050 will meet the annual expenses of such a paper.

"5th. That the annual income of the office will be at least $2800, leaving a balance of $750 annually.

"6th. That stock to the amount of $2000 be raised, by dividing it into one hundred shares of $20 each, half of which to be paid immediately, and the remainder subject to the call of the persons who may be appointed to superintend the publishing of the paper; said stock to be repaid with interest, as soon as the avails of the concern will admit of it.

"7th. That the members of the Conference do take up the shares among themselves; but if all be not disposed of in that way, that they use their influence with their friends to have the remainder taken up immediately.

"8th. That a committee of five persons be appointed annually by the Conference, to superintend the publishing of the paper and other printing that may be done in the office; and that the General Superintendent of our Church, and the preacher in charge of the Station of York, be *ex-officio* members of said committee, three of whom shall form a quorum for the transaction of business.

"9th. That the Conference appoint an editor, or editors, annually, by ballot, without debate, who shall be responsible for his, or their, conduct as editor, or editors, to the Publishing Committee, in the interval of Conference.

"10th. That the editor be appointed an agent to procure the apparatus and materials necessary for commencing the paper.

"11th. That the price of the paper be 12s. 6d., currency, per annum, if paid in advance, or 15s., if not paid previous to six months from receiving the first number, exclusive of postage.

"12th. That all our ministers, travelling and local, be agents to the paper; and every agent who may procure fifteen subscribers, and use his best endeavors to make collections and obtain subscribers annually, shall be entitled to paper gratis.

(*Signed,*) F. METCALF, *Chairman.*"

Rev. Egerton Ryerson was appointed editor, and Rev. Franklin Metcalf—who was stationed in York—assistant. The necessary material was purchased, and the arrangements for commencing operations as speedily as possible were carried out. The first number of the new paper, the *Christian Guardian*, was issued at York—now Toronto—Nov. 21st, 1829, and in a few weeks had quite an extensive circulation for those days. Though it did not realize the financial expectations of its originators, it—for a number of years, at least—did the Church and the country good service by its uncompromising opposition to Church and State connection in every form, and its fearless advocacy of civil and religious freedom, especially reprobating special grants of public money to certain, numerically small, but favored denominations, as an injustice to the great mass of the people, and, therefore, a moral evil.

What the principles of the Methodist Church in those days were, as expressed in its organ, or by its accredited champion, may be gleaned from the following extracts from the pen of Mr. Ryerson, taken from his "Claims of Churchmen and Dissenters," and from the early volumes of the *Guardian* :—

"With respect to the support afforded to religion by the civil government, matter of fact proves that it can answer no beneficial purpose. The Church of Christ never was so prosperous and so pure as she was in the first three centuries. She was not only without the aid of civil government, but was most violently opposed by it. Did this extirpate her from the earth, or retard her progress? The former part of the Doctor's sermon (meaning a sermon preached by Dr. Strachan on the death of Bishop Mountain) abundantly proves that even 'uneducated, itinerant men, without human aid or influence, can, in the strength of the Lord, strew their way from country to country with the wrecks of Satan's kingdom. Did not the religion of the Redeemer spread her victories with almost inconceivable rapidity against the united intrigue and and force of Jews, Greeks, and Romans? Why is not the manner of propogating the Gospel in the first days of its glory the most judicious manner of propogating it now? Are her evidences less clear and forcible? Is her influence less upon the heart? If she, without civil support, nay, even opposed by the civil government, rose triumphant over the powers of earth and hell, and extended her influence so wide that, as Tertullian informs us, Christians were in the forum, the senate, and in every place, except the theatre, why is her influence and extension now depending on legislative influence? If there be any power in Christianity, it operates on the *consciences* of men; resting solely on the belief of *invisible* realities. She can derive no weight or solemnity from human sanctions. "The kingdom of God,' says Jesus, 'is within you.'—(Luke xvii. 21.) It is divested of that external pomp and splendor which are calculated to excite the admiration of the world; why then should a union with worldly men and worldly policy be considered essential to its diffusion and establishment? Is it not plain that whoever insists on this heterogeneous union degrades the religion of Jesus, and displays an ignorance of its gracious power? Is this not making Christianity a pensioner upon political benevolence, rather than the 'power of God unto salvation,'—(Rom. i. 16); a tool of state more than a 'bright emanation from heaven?' No wonder, then, that the power of religion, when clogged with the selfish contrivances of men is always weakened. No wonder that those divines who are constantly dabbling in politics are a disgrace to the Church and a pestilence to their parishioners.

"When was it that the Church of Christ began to degenerate from her primitive purity? When religious establishments were first contemplated. When did popish and corrupt doctrines receive countenance and support in the Church? When religious establishments commenced their existence. When did papal domination, which has crimsoned the Christian world from age to age, commence her infernal sway? When religious establishments got the vogue."

* * * * * * * * *

"Were not the first ministers of Jesus Christ supported by the free-will offerings of Christians? The apostles had not found out the art of forcing men to support religion. This was left to the fertile genius of some of the 'venerable' successors; and by them has been displayed to admirable advantage for many centuries."

* * * * * * * * *

"The Doctor, having shot his pointless darts at the 'sectaries of Canada,' (as he was pleased to call those who differed from him) explored his 'dreary wastes' and severely reproached the lukewarmness of the English clergy, commences hostilities with the Imperial Parliament, against which he brandishes his little dagger with a great deal of vehemence and ability. However, it does not yet appear that he has cut his way to the money chest; and as we think that the Imperial Parliament are quite capable of defending themselves and taking care of their purse, we shall not step forward in their defence.

* * * * * * * * *

"He (the Doctor) may trust in legislative influence; he may 'pray to the Imperial Parliament.' But we will trust in the Lord our God, and to Him will we make prayer. And under His auspices we fondly hope that the day is not far distant 'when the banners of the Lamb will wave triumphantly over the blood-stained car of Juggernaut; when the Shaster and the Koran shall be exchanged for the oracles of truth;' when the plundering Arab, the degraded Hottentot, and the inflexible Chinese, with the polished European, and uncultivated American, will sit down under the tree of life, and all acknowledge 'one Spirit, one Lord, one faith, one baptism, and one God.'*

"The constitution of a Church and State Establishment is not suited to the atmosphere of Canada. Such a monster, whether with one, two, or three heads, must very soon share the fate in this country which he has lately met with in France —for the unobstructed air of free discussion is his mortal poison, and never can he long maintain a successful contest against the deathly piercings of that triple sword of *truth, justice, and Puritan independence,* 'which is turning every way,' guarding the intellectual citadels of the good people of Canada against his blasphemous approach. 'Many are running to and fro, and knowledge is increasing;' and it is too late in the day to attempt to introduce into British North America the policy of Portugal and Spain, or that of Charles the tenth."†

With such principles as these for their watchword, it is not to be wondered at that the M. E. Church found no favor with, but rather encountered the bitter hostility of such open

* Claims of Churchmen and Dissenters.

† *Christian Guardian,* vol. 1, No. 48.

advocates of repression as were Dr. Strachan and the Family Compact.

The Conference of 1829 was noted, also, for another very important arrangement which was entered into at that session, viz., the formation of a Sunday-school Union, with its constitution and by-laws. Although the attention of the Church had been called to the good that might be accomplished by this agency, and individual efforts had been made to establish Sabbath-schools in certain localities, with partial success; yet, up to this year, there had not been the interest taken in this branch of Christian work that ought to have been taken, either by the Church or by Christian people at large.

From this Conference, however, the preachers returned to their circuits resolved more fully than ever to devote a portion of their time to this part of their legitimate work, and the happy fruits were soon apparent on many of the circuits, as the reports of these newly formed schools, which were published in the first volume of the *Guardian*, abundantly proves. Not only were the larger scholars brought, by these means, to a saving knowledge of Christ, but many young persons who had commenced to teach in the schools, though unawakened, became convinced of their own inefficiency as teachers while yet unconverted, and of the necessity of an experimental knowledge of religion to ensure their own happiness here, and safety hereafter; and thus hundreds were added to the Church through the instrumentality of Sabbath-schools.

The mission work, it was reported, was advancing most gloriously, especially among the natives among whom Peter Jones, with several of his Indian co-helpers, were laboring so diligently. Mr. Case, more generally termed Elder Case, with the other missionaries, were also leaving no effort untried that it was in their power to make, to induce the poor pagans to cast aside their idols, and the worse than pagans, the semi-christianized savages, to cast from them their deadly foe, the fire-water, that was consuming them both soul and body;

urging all alike to come and drink of the fountain of living water. At the camp-meetings, and almost every place where the Indians remained any length of time, there were gracious awakenings among them, and scores and hundreds converted. The mandate of Governor Maitland, in 1826, referred to in a previous chapter, had not deterred the Christian Indians from attending the camp-meetings and other Methodist services, and some of these having considerable influence with the pagans, the effect was very marked on both.

A mistake occurs in the printed Minutes for this year, the name of the Niagara Circuit being omitted altogether in the list of stations, as is also the name of James Richardson, among the stationed. Mr. Richardson had been appointed to the Niagara Circuit in 1828, with Joseph Gatchell as colleague, and at this Conference he was re-appointed to the same circuit. This year Mr. Richardson resided in St. Catharines. His circuit, he states, "was large, extending to the Grand River, south-westerly, by the way of the Chippewa, Smithville, and Canboro, and to the Fifty Mile Creek, on the Hamilton road; and easterly to Warner's, near St. Davids."

Notwithstanding the opposition from every quarter, with which the Church had had to contend during the year, a very creditable increase was reported. The state of the work was as follows:—Districts, 4; circuits, 33; preachers, 52, and a membership of 10,231, making an increase over the preceding year of 403 whites, 137 Indians, and 13 colored; total 553.

The last remaining tie which had bound Mr. Jackson to the Church having been severed, he and Mr. Ryan at once proceeded to establish, upon as firm a basis as possible, the organization which had been brought into being through their instrumentality. This new branch of the Methodist family was organized in 1829, and named the "Canadian Wesleyan Church." Discussing this subject at some length, Rev. T. Goldsmith, in his "Manual," remarks: "Though the number of those who sympathized with Revs. Henry Ryan and James

Jackson and their coadjutors was very large, yet when the time of secession and organization came, and friendly pretensions were put to the test, the majority fell off like autumn leaves in a tempest." The sanguine expectations entertained by the projectors of the new body were not fully realized, and in consequence, proportional disappointment and some sourness of feeling ensued. After giving several reasons why the Canadian Wesleyans did not succeed better, Mr. Goldsmith continues: "In 1835 the Connexion," Mr. Ryan's adherents, "reached about the maximum of its numerical strength and influence prior to the union of 1841. Then it possessed 21 preachers, 42 local preachers, 13 circuits, 2481 members. * * * * Some idea may be formed of the connexional crisis by comparing the statistics of 1841, the time of the union, with the foregoing statistics of 1835. In 1841 we had only 14 circuits, and 1915 of a membership. Notwithstanding a considerable number was added by the union, who belonged to the New Connexion in Eastern Canada, still in six years we lost 566 members. General discouragement seized all hearts, and paralyzed our energies,"

From the above extracts it will be seen that the secession of Mr. Ryan and his friends, and their organization of what was intended to be a rival branch of the Church, deeply as it was to be deplored, had not accomplished as much in injuring the parent body, as it had been feared, on the one side, and hoped on the other that it would do, and had not the Canadian Wesleyans succeeded in forming a union with the Methodist New Connexion of England, they must soon have ceased to have had an existence as a Church. The effect of the secession upon the older body was, as far as numerical strength was concerned, very slight indeed, the loss being more than made up by additions, through the instrumentality of revivals.

In the latter part of this year (1829) gracious outpourings of the Holy Spirit visited nearly every charge, and general peace and prosperity appeared once more to prevail.

The twilight of the temperance movement in Canada, had, for some time been struggling with the deep darkness that had preceded it, and now its sun began to gild the moral horizon. Most of the preachers belonging to the M. E. Church fell in with this reformation movement at once, and for several years became its steadfast champions, the *Guardian* for a length of time occupying an honorable pre-eminence in its earnest advocacy of the cause; afterwards, unhappily, the zeal slackened.

From their first entrance into the country the Methodist preachers had opposed the *immoderate* use of intoxicating liquors, but most of them—preachers as well as people—used ardent spirits as a *beverage*, thinking that if not taken to excess, it was not only not sinful to use it, but really beneficial. Good and great men reasoned thus, tampered with the soul-destroying evil, till they were ruined both in body and estate, utterly unfitted for the duties of time, and unprepared for eternity. Having witnessed the sad effects of the drinking usages upon society, it is not to be wondered at that earnest Christian men and women should have hailed the dawn of this brighter day with delight.

As the light became stronger the old "reformation pledge," which prohibited only the use of ardent spirits, thus permitting indulgence in the use of milder, more refined decoctions, was superseded by the out and out "total abstinence pledge," which left no room for tampering.

The new reform, like all other reforms, received no countenance or quarter from the *extra loyal* Church and State party. It had originated in the "States," and that was sufficient. No need of anything further to condemn it.

Among those who at an early day took an active interest in the promotion of the cause, and who have since become eminent in Canada, as divines or statesmen, were Revs. Philander Smith, James Richardson, and the brothers Ryerson, the Hon. John Rolph and Marshall S. Bidwell. The two last mentioned gentleman ranked at this period among the ablest lawyers in the province, if, indeed, they were not *the ablest*.

It is but justice to notice in this connection, that though they occupied the foreground, the Methodists were not alone in the advocacy of temperance principles; the Baptists, the Congregationalists, and quite a creditable number of Presbyterians, also, from its commencement, took an active part in urging on this reformation, the beneficial results of which were very soon apparent in the moral and social improvement of the people generally throughout the province.

CHAPTER XX.

Conference of 1830—Bishop Hedding's visit—He ordains the candidates—Allusion to the arrangement of 1820—The English missionary visits the Conference—Projected seminary—Resolutions and proceedings relating thereto—Resolution with regard to temperance—An unhappy change—Revivals throughout the country—Good work among the Indians—Statistics—The institution of learning to be located at Cobourg, and called Upper Canada Academy.

THE Conference of 1830 commenced its session at Kingston, on the 17th of August, being opened in the usual form by Mr. Case, General Superintendent *pro tem.* Rev. James Richardson was re-elected Secretary, and the Conference proceeded to the transaction of business. But before the usual routine of business was entered upon another matter was brought before the attention of the preachers. Their old and tried friend, Bishop Hedding was once again in their midst. In order to prove conclusively that his attachment to his Canadian brethren had suffered no abatement in consequence of the recent separation, and that he was still interested in what concerned them, the Bishop had revisited Canada, coming in several days before the one announced for the opening of the Conference, that he might visit the mission on Grape Island. By a personal inspection he could the better judge what progress was being made in civilizing and Christianizing the Indians there congregated. After having examined the schools, and made what other inquiries he considered necessary concerning their present position, he declared himself not only pleased with the efficient management of the mission, but surprised that so much had been accomplished. The Bishop preached to them on Sabbath, the 15th of August, and by the 17th he reached the seat of Conference. It was a source of great satisfaction to these way-worn itinerants to meet again their former faithful counsellor, and they at once, before proceeding to other business, availed themselves of his superior experience and wisdom, by passing resolutions requesting him to take a seat in the Conference, and assist in their deliberations. The following is a copy of the resolutions referred to:—

"1st. That this Conference feel highly gratified with and grateful for the visit of the Rev. Bishop Hedding amongst us.

"2nd. That he is invited to take a seat in this Conference, and assist by his counsel and advice.

"3rd. That he is most respectfully requested to preside during the religious services of the Sabbath, and ordain those preachers who may be presented to him as suitable persons for ordination."

The Bishop cordially consented to comply with the request, observing that he "felt happy in being permitted to visit and observe the proceedings and order of the Conference, and although he did not consider himself possessing or holding any authority over this Conference, that authority having ceased by mutual consent of the Canada and General Conferences when the Methodists in this country became a separate and independent Church; yet he would cheerfully lend any assistance in his power, and would willingly perform the ordinations; for he felt himself fully authorized so to do, provided he was requested by this Conference. He considered himself justified in ordaining such of the preachers as might be eligible and presented for ordination, by several considerations. First, there was nothing in the Discipline of the Methodist Episcopal Church in the United States that required him to confine his ordaining to ministers of that Church. Secondly, Bishop Asbury formerly ordained English missionaries for Nova

Scotia, the West Indies, &c., &c. This example, he thought, was in point, and felt himself fully authorized to follow it. Thirdly, he had been authorized by the General Conference to ordain a Superintendent for the Methodist Church in this country, provided one should be appointed by the Canada Conference. His having authority to ordain a Superintendent, he thought, obviously implied his having authority to ordain other preachers. For these reasons, and others that might be offered, and as he was now requested, he should have no objections to perform the ordinations of such preachers as might be, or had been, elected to the sacred office."

Accordingly, on the Sabbath the Bishop proceeded with the ordination of the candidates, six of whom had been elected to Elder's orders, and twenty-one to Deacon's. The number of preachers ordained this year was greater than usual in consequence of there having been no ordination since the Conference of 1828. Mr. Case, though President of the Conference and an Elder, had no authority, according to the established law of the M. E. Church, to *ordain* the preachers, this authority being then, as now, invested in the Bishop.

The several candidates had, at the proper time, been received into full connection with the Conference, but their ordination had been delayed until a Bishop from the United States could visit the country and perform the service for them.

The English missionaries had, notwithstanding the arrangement of 1820, and in defiance of it, still continued to occupy a station in Kingston. Their agent, however, Rev. Mr. Turner, visited the Conference, and, despite all that had occurred of an unpleasant nature between the two societies, he was invited to take a seat within the bar. He accepted the invitation, and declared himself pleased with what he saw and heard.

The education of the people at large, and more especially the education of young men who designed entering the sacred office of the ministry, had long been the subject of much deep and anxious thought upon the part of many of the more far-seeing preachers. The establishment of a seminary had long been talked of among them, as something highly to be desired, but scarcely yet attainable. But at this Conference it was thought the time for action in this important matter had arrived. The project was presented for the consideration of the preachers, and after some discussion the following resolutions concerning it were adopted :—

"*Resolved*, 1. That it is expedient to establish a Seminary of learning, to be under the direction of the Conference of the Methodist Episcopal Church in Canada.

"2. That the plan and constitution of said seminary be published, and that each preacher belonging to the Conference be furnished with the same, and a form of subscription also, and that he be requested to use his best endeavors to obtain funds for the institution.

"3. That a committee of nine persons be appointed by the Conference—three from each Presiding Elder's District—to fix upon the location of the said seminary—to meet at Hallowell, January 27th, 1831, at 9 o'clock, a. m.

"4. That the above committee have authority to determine the place at which to locate said seminary ; and if, in the judgment of the committee, the amount secured by subscriptions, or otherwise, be sufficient to justify the undertaking, they shall have full power and authority to purchase, or otherwise obtain, a suitable situation for a site ; to choose trustees for the time being ; to appoint a building committee, and to transact all other business necessary to forward the building as far as practicable before the session of the next Conference."

In accordance with the above resolutions a committee was appointed, consisting of the following leading men in the Connexion :—Niagara District—Thomas Whitehead, John Ryerson, Samuel Belton ; Bay Quinte District—William Ryerson, D. Wright, J. Beaty ; Augusta District—William Brown, Thomas Madden, James Richardson. The naming of the institution was also left to the committee appointed for locating it.

On the 23rd, for some reason not explained in the Minutes, the Conference adjourned, to meet in Belleville, where it resumed the transaction of business on the 27th of the same month. Bishop Hedding returned to the United States from Kingston.

By the action of the Conference the attention of the societies generally was further called to the subject of the temperance movement still going on; the following resolutions, with the exception of the fourth, having passed that body *unanimously*. Upon the fourth a very animated debate took place. Some of those who entered into the discussion, though lovers of the cause in the abstract, contended that the resolution was quite too sweeping in its out-and-out condemnation of the use of ardent spirits under any circumstances. That the ministers composing this Conference were far in advance of many of their religious contemporaries is notably demonstrated by the fact that, after a full and dispassionate debate, of some length, this resolution was also carried, it being decided,* "that as far as it related to the members of the Conference, as ministers of a pure Gospel, and examples to their flocks, they would not recognize the deleterious drug, even as a *medicine*, to be taken *inwardly*—acting in accordance with the example of St. Paul, that should it be as beneficial to them as meat might have been to the Apostle, yet if their using it could be made the pretext or occasion for others to offend, it was their duty not to use it while the world standeth, lest they should cause a weak one to offend."

"*Resolved*, 1st. That viewing the evils of intemperance—its ravages upon the healthful constitution of the body—its destruction of the religious feeling and moral principles of the mind—its blighting influence upon the domestic comforts and opening prospects of life, and its fearful prevalence in many

* *Christian Guardian*, Oct. 2nd., 1830.

parts of this province, this Conference feel it to be an imperious duty to use their best endeavors, both by precept and example, to check its progress, and finally, in connection with the efforts of their brethren of other religious denominations, to deliver the country from the fatal scourging of so dreadful a plague.

"*Resolved*, 2nd. That this Conference believe that (what is termed) the moderate or temperate use of 'ardent spirits,' is the fruitful source of all the intemperance which abounds in this country, and which is the cause of so much immorality, misery, and destruction, both as it regards the baneful influence of the so-called 'moderate drinker's' example upon the morals of others, and the almost inevitable effects of such a vitiating indulgence upon himself.

"*Resolved*, 3rd. That this Conference view what are called temperance societies to be one of the most judicious and effectual instruments which can be used for the suppression of intemperance.

"*Resolved*, 4th. That the members of this Conference do now form themselves into a temperance society; and they hereby agree to abstain entirely from the use of ardent spirits, to enforce upon the members of our Church, and also upon our congregations, the important caution and duty of *entire abstinence;* and to use every lawful means in our power to establish temperance societies in our respective circuits and stations throughout the province.

"*Resolved*, 5th. That this Conference do decidedly disapprove of any members of our Church distilling or retailing ardent spirits."

Such was the action of the Conference of 1830, and well would it have been for the Church and the country, as well as for some of the preachers themselves, had they maintained the firm stand which at this time they took against this monster evil which had, and has brought so much suffering into the world and dishonor upon the cause of God. Some years sub sequent to this Conference adverse influences were brought to bear against the cause of temperance in some parts of the Methodist Connexion, the baneful effects of which were painfully manifested in the Church as well as in the country generally. Adherents to old landmarks, however, struggled in this crisis to keep the subject before the people, and by their efforts greatly assisted the lovers of good order and sobriety in arresting the tide of intemperance that was again threatening to sweep over the land.

By the reports from the various circuits, it appeared that there had been a general and gracious time of revival through the work. The preachers, and in fact nearly the entire membership seemed to be all alive in the cause of God. In some sections, especially in the newer settlements, the reformation spread in a remarkable manner. The camp-meetings were still honored and effectual means of grace. People flocked to them hungering and thirsting after the word to such a degree that, not unfrequently, one tier of tents around the inclosure was not sufficient to accommodate the people, and therefore the tents were arranged in successive tiers. These honest, earnest Christians came *expecting* a work of grace to follow, and they were not disappointed. In those days of power it almost seemed that one man's conversion was the sure precursor of the conversion of his neighbor, often it was the means of scattering the holy fire through an entire settlement. The Quarterly Meetings were seasons of refreshing from the presence of the Lord; and at the ordinary means of grace, prayer and class-meetings, conversions were of general occurrence.

Amid all, the interests of the Indians were neither forgotten nor neglected. The work of God continued to spread among them with amazing success. Peter Jones and John Sunday, with others of their brethren, were passing from tribe to tribe, striving with unwearied diligence to point out, alike to heathen and nominal Christian, the way of salvation, and the result was a very marked change in the deportment of the Indians themselves, and quite an ingathering of them into the Church.

This year the state of the Church was as follows:—3 Districts, 62 preachers, 36 circuits, and a membership of 11,348, showing an increase over the year preceding of 1,117; among the Indians alone there had been an increase of 101.

On the 30th the Conference closed its lengthy session, and the various committees set themselves to work at once to perform the tasks assigned them there. Of these the most important, this year, was the Committee on Education, which, as soon as was practicable, began making preparations for carrying out the project of locating and erecting a seminary which should be under the supervision of the Church. This was no slight undertaking in a country so new as Upper Canada then was, but the urgent need of such an institution was so keenly felt by the intelligent part of the community that those more nearly interested set to work with a will to accomplish so noble an object. It had been estimated that the land could be procured and the necessary buildings erected for about $24,000, but this calculation was found, upon getting to work, to have been quite too low for the accomplishment of the end desired.

The committee met, according to appointment, in Hallowell, on the 27th of January, 1831, and after receiving all the information they could obtain respecting the various places nominated, and deliberating carefully on the matter, they finally gave the decision in favor of Cobourg, naming the projected seminary the "Upper Canada Academy."

CHAPTER XXI.

Dr. Strachan's opposition—Donald Bethune's petition—Action of the House thereon—The Clergy Reserves—Rev. E. Ryerson's able advocacy of equal rights—Prominent statesmen of the period—Scheme of the Governor and the Family Compact for creating internal dissensions among the Methodists—The English missionary Committee assert that the contract of 1820 is no longer binding—Their views on the great questions agitating the people of Canada—Peter Jones' mission to England—Its results—Communication of the English Missionary Secretary to the Canada Conference—Their reply—Extensive revivals—Sabbath Schools—Statistics.

THE astonishing progress made by Methodism, compared with that made by the Church of which he was a leading minister, had from the first been an eye-sore to Dr. Strachan and those with whom he acted. Notwithstanding all that he, or they had done, and no stone had been left unturned, no scheme—no matter how unscrupulous—untried, to stop its onward march, the despised Church grew and prospered. Men feeling themselves called of God—not by the secular government—to the work of the Christian ministry, would preach, and souls hungering after the bread of life would listen, despite all the anathemas thundered forth against them by the Rev. Dr. and his satellites. Affairs, they judged, were becoming desperate. Some decisive measure against them must once more be attempted, or these "uneducated itinerants would overrun the province. Accordingly, early in 1831, a petition was presented to the Provincial Assembly, signed by Donald Bethune, and others, of Kingston," praying that a law might be enacted with the following provisions:—"First, To prohibit any exercise of the functions of a Priest, or Exhorter, or Elder of any denomination in this province, except by British subjects. Secondly, To prevent the assembling therein of any religious society or societies in Conference who shall be in society or conference with any foreign body calling themselves a religious society or otherwise; and, thirdly, To prevent the raising of money by any religious, or pretended religious, person or body, for any pretended charity, mission, or fund, the objects of which are not strictly British." This petition was referred to a committee of the House of Assembly, who in due time brought in their report, from which the following is an extract:—"In taking into consideration the application thus made" (by Bethune and others) "your Committee had no hesitation in coming to the conclusion that it is inconsistent with the benign and tolerant principles of the British Constitution to restrain, by penal enactments, any denomination of Christians, whether subjects or foreigners, in the free exercise of their religious worship; and that it is equally inconsistent with the fundamental principles of civil liberty to control by law the voluntary contributions of any man, unless made with an intent to accomplish some unlawful purpose."

The report from which the above quotation is extracted gave such evident proof of the liberality of the House of Assembly, and the uselessness of presenting such narrow and intolerant petitions that nothing of the kind was again attempted by Mr. Bethune and his prompters. The intolerance, however, and the insolent assumptions of the "High Church" party, created sympathy for those whom it designed to damage and to crush, and really, in the end, increased the influence of Methodism in the province.

Other claims and assumptions of this same party were also agitating the public mind. It is already a matter of secular history that under the reign of George the Third the British Government had set apart one-seventh of the lands of the province for the support of a Protestant clergy. These lands were now becoming valuable, and to them the ministers of the Church of England, with their usual arrogance, laid exclusive claim, contending that as the Church of England was the Established Church in England it must, of necessity, be the Established Church in the colonies, and as such entitled to the exclusive enjoyment of all funds arising from the Reserves. Upon these points the advocates of free institutions joined issue with their assailants, and Mr. Ryerson, the then editor of the *Christian Guardian*, being fully committed to the popular movement, by his controversies with Dr. Strachan, did the cause good service. The historian, in looking over the first and second volumes of the *Guardian*, and also the "Claims of Churchmen and Dissenters," must admire the earnestness and industry Mr. Ryerson at this time manifested in maintaining the rights of the people. In these views he was supported by by such able statesmen as M. S. Bidwell, Peter Perry, Dr. Rolph, and W. L. McKenzie, who, in those days of oligarchical rule, were considered as extremely radical. What changes time works! Responsible government has brought about enactments more radical—with the exception of the complete secularization of the Clergy Reserves—than any they ever advocated.

After the failure of Bethune's scheme the Lieutenant-Governor, urged thereto by the Family Compact, and hoping to lessen Methodist influence by still further engendering division in its ranks, sent home a dispatch requesting that the English missionaries might again be sent to Upper Canada, recommending that aid should be given from the public funds. With this request the English Conference resolved to comply, thus throwing the weight of its influence into the scale in favor of the Church and State party. The pretext of the Government was to establish missions among the Indians, and this, to the uninitiated English public, appeared quite plausible.

Like the fable of the wolf and the lamb, an excuse was not long in being found by the English Conference in defence of their course of procedure. It was argued by them that the contract entered into in 1820 was made with the American General Conference, and not with the M. E. Church in Canada, and hence the English Conference was in no way bound to respect the rights of the latter body; and further, that the Methodist Episcopal Church in Canada had sustained the editor of the *Christian Guardian* in his opposition to the claims of the Church of England in Canada, thus making their Church and organ "unacceptable with a part of the Canadian people," while on the other hand, the English Methodists claimed to be but *"a branch of the Church of England, both at home and abroad," and as such might expect a share in the division of the Clergy Reserves. This claim of being a branch of the Church of England was, however, repudiated by that body, and treated with unmitigated contempt, except when they hoped to make use of English Wesleyanism to raise and prop up their oppressive Establishment in the Colonies. Even at a much more recent date this has been the case. Writing upon this subject, in view of recent events, the editor of the New York *Christian Advocate* very aptly observes:—"The virtual adhesion of Wesleyan Methodism to the National Establishment has often been the occasion of severe criticism on the leaders of the 'Connexion.' Their policy seemed recreant to the popular interest as contrasted with that of the aristocratic classes. It wore an aspect of 'flunkeyism' which could not be disguised, even by appeals back to Wesley, or the early antecedents of the body. For was not Wesley a progressionist? Did any man advance more manfully in the correction of his old opinions; and if he died loyal to the Establishment, is that any reason why his successors should not, in their more advanced day, apply to the Establishment itself the progressive criticisms with which he had treated and abandoned some of the fundamental principles of the Establishment?"

* Dr. Alder's evidence before a Committee of the House of Commons, in 1828.

Had the "flunkeyism" of some of the leading members of the English Conference been confined to the Established Church of England and Ireland, where it had existed as such for generations, their sycophancy might have been excused on the ground of early and deeply rooted prejudice in favor of an old and long established institution. But in Canada the case was altogether different. Here there was, in point of fact, no Establishment, and a minority, aided by unprincipled politicians, were attempting to foist one upon the people, in direct opposition to the well understood and plainly expressed wishes of a large majority of that people. With those who were trying thus to subvert the rights of the colonists, the English Conference—for a consideration—united in friendship; and, though the contrary was asserted, for political purposes quite as much as out of concern for the religious destitution of the Indians, they consented again to send their agents into Upper Canada, to raise again the old hackneyed cry of disloyalty, and breed dissension in the societies. Such quibbling as was engaged in by the English Conference would have been a reproach to a country village lawyer. It was an unparalleled outrage upon brethren of the same origin and faith, deserving the unqualified reprobation of every candid Christian.

The pretext made by the English missionaries for coming to Upper Canada was, as has been stated, the establishment of missions among the Indians and destitute settlers. But had these been neglected by the ministers of the Methodist Episcopal Church in Canada? Not at all. It had been emphatically a missionary Church from the beginning. The destitute settlers had been supplied by its ministry when the country was so new that other ministers did not care to face its hardships, and the newer settlements were being supplied as fast as possible. The Indian missions—upon which so much stress was laid—had also been established by the Methodist Episcopal Church, and were in a remarkably prosperous condition, though, as a matter of course, the funds were not large. Mr. Case, some time prior to this movement of the English Conference, visited the city of New York, and other places in the United States, for the purpose of collecting funds for carrying on the Indian missions, taking with him a number of the converted natives. They were successful in their enterprise, and returned home well pleased with their reception.

After the return of Mr. Case and his companions from the United States, it was suggested by some persons about York, U. C., that if Peter Jones were to go to England he could collect more guineas there than Mr. Case could dollars in the States. It seemed quite probable that he might, as England was so much the richer country, and Mr. Case very readily consented for him to go. Rev. George Ryerson was about to leave for England, having been appointed an agent for the "Reformers," and sent home by them with numerously signed petitions against the arbitrary and unconstitutional proceedings of the Canadian Executive, and it was determined that Peter Jones should accompany him. Accordingly, on the 4th of March, 1831, they started upon their journey from Credit Mission, near York—now Toronto. They reached New York on the 17th of the same month, and landed in Liverpool on the 30th of April following. On Monday, May 2nd, they reached the city of London, and immediately presented their papers at the Wesleyan Mission Rooms, 77 Hatton Garden. Very shortly after their arrival they were informed that the Missionary Society would not consent to allow them to hold meetings, or collect funds among the Methodist societies in England; but if they would consent to attend the regular missionary meetings, and r frain from collecting anything privately among the Methodists, the Society would give them a grant of £300. The parties in authority at the Mission Rooms took this opportunity of informing the Messrs. Jones and Ryerson of the contem lated establishment of missions of their own in Upper Canada as soon as practicable, and at the same time read these gentlemen a homily on the exceeding impropriety of the course pursued by the Methodist Episcopal Church in Canada, and especially that of Mr. E. Ryerson, in his opposition to the claims put forth for the English Church by Dr. Strachan.

If Mr. George Ryerson ever had been very zealous in the cause of Methodism and the Indian missions, his ardor soon cooled. He shortly after severed his connection with the Methodist body, and returned to Canada an Irvingite. Mr. Jones, after remaining in England a year—lacking two days—returned to his native land, reaching York on the 19th of June, 1832. The following is a list of the sums obtained by by him while in England:

From the Wesleyan Methodist Missionary Society	£300	0	0
From benevolent persons	557	19	0
From Quakers	174	1	6
In tools and goods	500	0	0
Total	£1532	0	6

As the amounts here mentioned are given in sterling money it will be seen that counting tools and all Mr. Jones obtained about $7,660. Besides this, the British and Foreign Bible Society printed and contributed to the Indians a thousand copies of the Gospel of St. John in the Chippewa language. Mr. Jones was kindly entertained by the pious and benevolent of other denominations besides the Methodists, and was admitted to an audience with the King and Queen, who very graciously received from him a copy of the "Gospel of St. John in the Chippewa language," and who questioned him at some length concerning his people and religion. So small were the donations to the Indian missions from the Wesleyan Societies, compared with what he received from other sources, it is evident that Mr. Jones would have done much better had he not entered into any arrangement with the Missionary Society at all, but held meetings and visited the people on his own account alone. Still, at the time, both he and his friends supposed he was taking the wiser course. Then, and ever after, Mr. Jones was a faithful steward of his Lord's money, as well as an earnest and devoted Methodist minister. While he lived he worked unweariedly for the best interests of his race, and did much towards keeping them from relapsing again into barbarism. Now he rests from his labors.

In 1831 the Conference was held, according to appointment, in the town of York (Toronto) commencing on the 31st of August, Rev. William Case presiding, and James Richardson continuing to act as Secretary. Five candidates were admitted on trial, and five into full connexion. There were no ordinations, however, in consequence of there being no Bishop present. There were no withdrawals and no deaths. One was expelled, and nine, some of them old veterans, and some comparatively young men, but worn down with hard toil, received a superannuated relation.

The intentions of the English Conference relative to their design of violating the pledges made in 1820, were made known to the Conference by a communication from one of the English secretaries—Rev. James Townley—accompanied by resolutions concerning the matter passed at a meeting of the Missionary Board on the 11th of May previous.

These communications were laid before the Conference, and referred to the Missionary Committee of the M. E. Church in Canada, which met at York, to answer them and to protest against the contemplated interference. The Canadian Mission Board met according to appointment, and after due deliberation forwarded to Mr. Townley and his brethren an able paper, wherein they deprecated the action of the English Missionary Board, and kindly but clearly set forth the danger there was of creating a division, and lessening Methodist influence by such a step, giving the English Conference assurance that there was no necessity for sending their agents into the province, as it was already supplied with ministerial laborers. This document was dated "York, U. C., October 4th, 1831," and signed by John Ryerson, President of the Society, and Thomas Vaux, Secretary.

But expostulation and remonstrance were in vain; the English Conference seemed to believe that none but themselves were competent judges of what true loyalty was, and that consequently they alone, of all the Methodist bodies, were capable of teaching it to the poor, benighted Canadians.

This year, like the preceding, had been one of great spiritual prosperity. There had been several very extensive revivals. Two-days and four-days meetings had been held on many of the circuits, and so great had been the interest evinced by the people, so earnest their desire to listen and be profited by the pure word, that in several places these meetings had been protracted for ten and fifteen days.

Many of the four weeks circuits had from 25 to 30 appointments; great efforts were made by the preachers to establish Sunday-schools in new settlements, and encourage those already in the older ones. Temperance societies were organized wherever it was practicable, and the Church generally was overlooked with a careful eye. The result of all this labor was abundantly seen in the large accessions to the numbers of those in Church fellowship. There were reported to this Conference a large number of local preachers, many of them exceedingly active, who did not always wait until the circuit preacher found work for them to do, but themselves hunted up destitute neighborhoods, and held meetings among the people until the regular ministers could supply the work All honor to such men; they were worthy of their name.

The state of the Church this year was as follows:—4 Districts, 38 circuits, 65 preachers, and 12,563 members, being an increase over the preceding year of 1,130 whites, 80 Indians, and 5 colored, making in all a total increase of 1215.

CHAPTER XXII.

Cause of the ill-will of the English Conference to the M. E. Church in Canada—Its Organ too liberal—Scheme to counteract Methodist influence in Canada—Purport of the plans of Sir P. Maitland and Sir John Colborne—English Wesleyans fall in with the scheme—They send out their agent in 1832—Mr. Alder's course of procedure—Invited to meet the York Missionary Board—Disastrous results of this interview—Union between the two bodies proposed—Resolutions on the subject adopted by the Conference of 1832—Delegate appointed to negotiate the union—Mr. Alder's letter to the Governor—Resolutions opposing the measure—Mr. Ryerson's article before leaving—Errors and misstatements corrected by Mr. Richardson—Course of Mr. Case and others to lull suspicion—General work prosperous.

It has already been shown that the vigorous opposition of the Methodist Episcopal Church in Canada to the establishment, by law, in the colony, of the Church of England—or of any other Church—had given serious offence to the English Conference, who were just at this juncture looking for an excuse by which they might vindicate, or at the very least, extenuate their dishonorable infringement of the agreement entered into in 1820. To this opposition of the Methodist people generally was also added, to the great displeasure of their English co-religionists, the out-spoken advocacy of free institutions by the editor of the *Guardian*, which the dominant faction determined to silence, if possible.

In order to counteract, as far as was practicable, the influence and usefulness of the original body, Sir Peregrine Maitland, as early as 1828, had written home to the authorities recommending that a grant of public money should be offered to the English Missionary Society to induce it to send missionaries into the province, ostensibly to Christianize the Indians, but the real purpose being that they should, wherever they could, supplant the Canadian preachers in the affections of the people. After his arrival in the country Sir John Colborne also recommended the same thing, and the result of these negotiations was made apparent in the reception which the Committee vouchsafed to the Messrs. Jones and Ryerson, on their arrival in England some time after. Some of the preachers had, through their connection with the Missionary Committee, become cognizant of the intention of the English Missionary Committee to send its agents into Upper Canada, but that they were moved thereto by the Canadian Government for party political purposes, was known at the time to but very few.

In 1832 the Missionary Society in England sent out the Rev. R. Alder, as its accredited agent, to accomplish the work which they designed to do; in which enterprise, as the sequel proved, he, unhappily for the Church and the country, but too well succeeded. The Missionary Committee of the M. E. Church, finding that the English Missionary Society utterly disregarded their remonstrance, and was encroaching further and further, with the now openly avowed intention of taking and keeping the ground, in a measure succumbed under the pressure brought to bear upon them, and invited the English missionaries who were, for reasons of their own, then in the town, to attend a meeting of the Missionary Board, in order to see if any agreement could be arrived at between them. The foreign missionaries, nothing loth—indeed it would appear to have been part of their plan—accepted the invitation so unwisely given. The names of these gentlemen were Rev. Mr. Alder and the Revs. Messrs. John Hicks, Thomas Turner, and John Hetherington.

At this meeting a plan of *union* was proposed, and, unfortunately for Methodism in Canada, Rev. Egerton Ryerson, who had hitherto stood up so manfully in the defence of the

Church against her assailants, fell in with the proposed measure. It had been better for all concerned if, as Paul did with Peter, he had withstood these men to the face because they were to blame. Instead of this, however, the leading members of the Canadian Missionary Board struck their colors, and recommended the Annual Conference, which was just about to meet, to seek an alliance with the English Conference. Whether the Messrs. Ryerson and the other leading members of the Committee were aware of Mr. Alder's communication with the Governor and the Home authorities, or not, it is difficult to determine; Christian charity would lead to the hope that they were not.

The Conference of 1832 commenced its session on the 18th of August, at Hallowell, Mr. Case, as usual, presiding, and Mr. Richardson continuing to be Secretary. Seven candidates were received on trial; two were admitted into full connexion, and there were now eight superannuated men whose names were upon the Minutes. The state of the work was very encouraging, there being 4 Districts, 41 circuits and stations, and 71 preachers, besides 6 employed under the Presiding Elders. The membership was 14,999, making an increase of 3,716 whites. There was a decrease of 63 among the Indians, which reduced the total increase to 3,651. Rev. James Richardson was appointed editor of the *Guardian*, and Rev. Egerton Ryerson elected as a delegate to the English Conference.

In order to carry out successfully the scheme entered into between his employers and the Governor, Dr. Alder attended the Conference at Hallowell, and having gained what he desired from the Canadian Missionary Board, it was not difficult to set the train in motion at the Conference. In due time the project of a union with the English Conference was proposed, and the advantages which it was supposed would be derived therefrom dwelt upon at some length by the advocates of the measure. The disadvantages were not quite so ably put, nor indeed were some of the most objectionable features of the measure then even hinted, except, perhaps, to a few. Had these been generally known to the preachers, before they were committed, it is probable the resolutions on the subject of union which were adopted by the Conference of 1832 would never have received their sanction. The resolutions in question were as follows:

"That this Conference, concurring with the Board of Missions on the inexpediency of establishing two distinct Methodist Connexions in Upper Canada, and deprecating the evils which might arise from the collision, and believing that the cause of religion generally, and the interests of Methodism in particular, would, by the blessing of God, be greatly promoted by the united exertions of the two Connexions, it is resolved:—

"1. That a union between the English and Canada Conferences, duly securing the rights and privileges of the societies in this province, is an object highly important and desirable.

"2. That in order to accomplish this object the discipline and economy of the Wesleyan Methodists in England be introduced into the societies in this country, as far as circumstances and prudence will render advisable.

"3. That episcopacy be superseded by an annual presidency, unless it will jeopard our Church property, or as soon as it can be legally secured.

"4. That the usages of the English Conference be adopted in the admission of candidates into the itinerant ministry amongst us.

"5. That ordination be administered amongst us after the same form as that in which missionaries are set apart to the office of the ministry in the English Conference.

"6. That the English Conference shall have authority to appoint, as often as they see fit, a President from their own body in England to preside over this Conference; provided the same shall not be eligible oftener than once in four years, unless desired by this Conference.

"7. That when the English Conference does not appoint a President as aforesaid, one shall be elected by this Conference from amongst its own members.

"8. That the missions which now are, or may be hereafter established by this Conference, be considered missions of the Wesleyan Missionary Society, under the following regulations: the Wesleyan Missionary Committee in London shall appropriate the amount necessary to carry on the missions, but this amount shall be applied to the support of the several mission stations, by a committee of seven or nine persons (one of whom shall be the President of the Conference) members of and appointed by this Conference. The Methodist Missionary Society in Canada shall be auxiliary to the Wesleyan Missionary Society, and the funds raised be transmitted to the Treasurer of the Parent Society, and appropriated as aforesaid. The missionaries shall be appointed by the Canada Conference, subject to the sanction of the Wesleyan Missionary Committee.

"9. That, in pursuance of the arrangements above proposed, it is understood that all missionaries sent by the Wesleyan Committee into Upper Canada shall be members of this Conference.

"10. That nothing contained in the foregoing resolutions shall be understood or construed so as to affect the rights of our General Conference, or the standing and privileges of our itinerant and local preachers.

"11. That none of the foregoing resolutions shall be binding on this Conference, or of any force whatever, until they shall have been acceded to on the part of the Wesleyan Committee and Conference, and the arrangements proposed shall have been completed by the two Connexions.

"12. That a representative be sent home to England to negotiate with the Wesleyan Committee and Conference on the several subjects embraced in these resolutions."

Until after the adoption of the above resolutions Mr. Alder had very modestly kept in the back-ground, allowing the friends of the measure in the Canada Conference, especially the Messrs. Ryerson, who were fluent and *plausible* speakers, to take the lead in carrying out his plans. But when the Conference, as a body, was once fully committed in the matter, he became somewhat bolder, though he still took care not to thow off all the disguise. He told them openly that the English Conference would, he apprehended, require some further concessions; although, from perusing the resolutions, one would imagine the Canada Conference had, in committing themselves to these so fully, conceded much more than was consistent with its own self-respect. One of these further concessions, it will be seen a little further on, was the discontinuance of camp-meetings—the one means of grace which had been so especially honored of God in the conversion of souls in the province, and for this reason the means *most especially hated* by the Governor and the intolerant faction by whom he was surrounded.

His mission to the Conference having been accomplished, Mr. Alder took his departure from the *hotel* at which he and his friend Mr. Hetherington had chosen to stop, and proceeded immediately to Montreal, whence he dispatched the following letter to the Lieutenant-Governor of Upper Canada, reporting the progress of their scheme:—

"*Montreal*, 27*th August*, 1832.

"Sir,—I beg permission to inform your Excellency that I have attended the Conference of the Methodist Church of Upper Canada, and to state confidentially, for your information, the result of the interview with that body—a result much more favorable than I allowed myself to anticipate.

They have resolved that their disciplinary system shall be so altered as that it may be made to agree in all its parts with British Methodism, *as speedily as prudence* and a due regard *to the safety of their chapel property*, will allow. The Conference has already agreed to the abolition of episcopacy, which was a great barrier in the way of the entire union. They have consented to place the whole of their Indian missions under the exclusive management of our Missionary Committee. In addition to these, and other concessions of importance, I have required that no man who continues to pursue a secular calling shall be ordained to the office of the ministry; *that the British Conference shall send to Canada such ministers as it may see fit to appoint*; that no preachers shall be taken out in Canada without the consent of that body; that Kingston shall be exclusively occupied by a missionary from the British Conference, as it is a central station between the two provinces; that the propriety of continuing camp-meetings shall be seriously considered, and that the *Christian Guardian* shall, for the future, be an exclusively religious journal. The Canada Conference has appointed a representative to proceed to England, where the whole matter will be finally settled. Rev. E. Ryerson has been appointed to this office. This, your Excellency, was done at my earnest request, as he and his brothers were the most eloquent advocates of the proposed alterations.

From these statements your Excellency will perceive that I have *rigidly adhered to those great principles to which I had occasion to advert during the* SEVERAL *interviews with which you were pleased to honor me*, and it is only an act of justice to the Canadian Conference to state that my frankness in stating my sentiments and principles, *and my firm adherence to them*, contributed to procure for me, in no small degree, the confidence of a large portion of that body, of which a strong proof is furnished in the fact that an unanimous request has been addressed to the British Conference, that in the event of the proposed arrangement being carried into effect, I may be appointed as their first President, with the understanding that I shall remain for two or three years, and exercise a general superintendence over the Methodist societies in both provinces. I feel a strong conviction that, for many reasons, I should accept of such an appointment, especially as I possess a degree of local knowledge and influence which it would require a stranger some time to obtain. *May I venture to ask your Excellency's opinion of such an arrangement, as it would have great weight with our Missionary Committee as well as with myself.*

I shall return to England by the way of Halifax, in which place I shall remain till the middle of September; after which my address will be, 8 Portland Street, Kingsdown, Bristol.

I remain, &c.,

(*Signed*,) R. Alder.

*His Excellency Sir John Colborne.**

The above letter contrasts rather strangely with the remarks of Mr. Ryerson upon these same union resolutions, as published in the *Guardian*, just before he resigned the editorial chair to his successor. His article of the 29th August, 1832, shows conclusively that he either could not at the time have understood the true situation of affairs, or that he misrepresented them to his readers.

After making a few preparatory remarks upon the resolutions, Mr. Ryerson continues: "It has been intimated in some of the provincial journals that the general principles of this measure

* If further corroborative proof be needed to convince the sceptical of the "Union" scheme having been a plot between the then Government and the English Wesleyans, it is supplied in a letter of Mr. Alder's to Lord John Russell, dated "Wesleyan Mission Rooms, Hatton Garden, London, 29th April, 1840," from which the following is extracted:—

"In consequence of proposals which were made in the year 1832 by the Earl of Ripon, then principal Secretary of State for the Colonies, to the Wesleyan Missionary Committee, to *induce* them to extend their missionary operations in Upper Canada, they resolved to do so, and arrangements were immediately made for carrying that resolution into effect. My Lord, the Government of Earl Gray was moved to make this offer to the Wesleyan Missionary Committee by patriotic, as well as by religious considerations; and if the testimony of Lord Seaton" (Sir John Colborne) "and other distinguished individuals may be depended upon, a wiser arrangement could not have been proposed. On the ground of this arrangement an annual grant is secured, on the faith of the Royal were submitted to the consideration of the Canadian Conference by the representative of the Wesleyan Missionary Committee, and that he attended the Conference for that specific purpose. This is a mistake." Here follows a long explanation of how Mr. Alder *happened* (?) to attend this Conference at Hallowell, after which the writer proceeds, "He" (Mr. Alder) "accordingly attended the Conference, but did not express his own views, nor the probable views of the Wesleyan Committee on the question of *union*, until it had been investigated and prepared in committee, discussed and agreed upon in Conference. Hence the above resolutions were not the result of measures submitted to the Conference by the representative of the Wesleyan Committee, but the free and spontaneous opinions and proposals of the Conference itself."

Mr. Alder, in his communication to the Governor, mentions that the "*result of*" his "*interview with that body*" has been the making of the desired "*concessions*," in addition to which he had further "*required*" certain other concessions, &c., &c. These further concessions, however, were not mentioned in the plan of union made public to the societies, and the country. Unpopular as the measure was in the form in which it was presented it would have been much more so had the whole

word, to the Wesleyan Missionary Committee, to assist them in meeting the expense which it necessarily involves.

"The *union* which now exists between the British Conference and the Conference in Upper Canada, took place about *a year after I had*—as the representative of the Wesleyan Missionary Committee—*completed*, at Toronto, with Lord Seaton, *all the arrangements connected with the offer made by Lord Goderich to the Committee*, having proceeded from England to Canada *for that purpose*. * *

"At the time that the union took place it was stated most distinctly to Mr. E. Ryerson himself, who came to England in 1833, as the representative of the Upper Canadian Conference, to negotiate the union, that it must be clearly understood that the *union could not be permitted by us to interfere in any way with the arrangements that then existed between His late Majesty's Government and the Committee, especially with the receipt and appropriation of the grant*, which fact must be in the recollection of Mr. Ryerson." See Stinson's and Ritchey's pamphlet, pages 37, 38.

truth been known. It is apparent from the tenor of Mr. Alder's letter that the entire "union" scheme had been duly considered upon in the various "conversations" with which the Governor had "honored" him before he or his colleagues had met either the York Board of Missions or the Canadian Conference; and that at least some of the concessions which were further required had been proposed at the Government House, and been one condition of the bargain with the Wesleyan Committee. Else why so much stress laid upon the serious consideration of the "*propriety*" of holding camp-meetings, and on the course to be pursued by the *Christian Guardian*. And this demand of the Government was, after the so-called consummation of the union, for several years faithfully carried out by the Wesleyan body. Mr. Alder further assured his "Excellency" that he had "*rigidly* adhered to those great principles to which" he had "had occasion to advert" in the various interviews which they had had together. What an interest the Lieutenant-Governor must have taken in the advancement of Methodism about that period! His desire for its welfare must have been rather surprising, and highly gratifying to the leaders of the Connexion.

Which made the correct report of the proceedings of the Conference of 1832, Mr. Alder or Mr. Ryerson, it is left to the judgment of the intelligent reader of the history of those times to decide.

Not only had Mr. Alder had the resolutions of union arranged according to his own wishes and those of his employers, but he had completed the scheme set on foot at the Government House, by means of which he obtained large sums from the provincial chest to aid in carrying out their plan. This, the monetary consideration, was kept carefully out of sight by Mr. Alder, and the Messrs. Ryerson mentioned in his report as "eloquent advocates" of the measure—if, indeed, the latter gentlemen knew of it—until after the majority of the Conference were fully committed to the union, because it was well known that the reception of "Government grants," for the sustentation of their preachers, whether they were on missions, or on what had hitherto been self-sustaining circuits, would be extremely objectionable to the Methodist societies themselves, besides placing them in a false position before the liberal parliament which had done so much to protect them from persecution, and lowering them in the estimation of the people of the country generally.

Rev. Egerton Ryerson, as has already been stated in the synopsis of the work of this Conference, was duly appointed as a delegate to negotiate a union upon the terms proposed in the resolutions of the Conference. The further concessions required by Mr. Alder were not made public, but notwithstanding this, the dissatisfaction with the proposed measure, even as it appeared in the resolutions, was so strong that the Methodist people generally refused to contribute sufficient means to defray the necessary expenses of the delegate to and from England. He therefore had recourse to other measures in order to raise it.

Although everything had been kept as quietly as possible before the session of the Conference, still some hints of what had passed at the meeting of the Missionary Board had transpired, and some opposition to the contemplated measure had commenced even before its meeting; but it was not until after the announcement in the *Guardian* that a union of the two bodies was under consideration, that the people generally took the alarm.

The Local Preachers' District Conference, however, which met in Trafalgar meeting-house, on July 6th, 1832, having received information, from a member of the Missionary Board, of some of the objectionable features of the contemplated plan of union, adopted the following resolution concerning them:—

"*Resolved*, That, as it appears from the *Christian Guardian* that an union between the missionaries from Great Britain and our Church is contemplated, we address our Annual Conference on the subject of our privileges as local preachers; and Bros. Pickett, Culp, and Brown be the committee to draft such address and forward it for presentation."

As early as November following the Conference of 1832, the following resolutions, disapproving of its action in the matter, were drawn up and forwarded to Rev. William Case.

"We, the undersigned local preachers of the Methodist Episcopal Church in Canada, beg leave to address you on the subject of the contemplated union of the Methodists of this country with those of England and respectfully to call your attention to the same. In doing this we have concluded that the following resolutions would embrace some of the most important material objections wherewith our minds have been, and still are exercised against it.

"1st. We consider that every man, and body of men have been endowed by their Creator with certain natural inalienable rights and privilges. And that the commission of high crimes or misdemeanors alone can justify an invasion upon them.

"2nd. That it is an acknowledged principle of all good governments (and sometimes, from necessity or policy, of despotic ones also) that in all important matters, relating to the public good, the voice of the people should, in greater or less degree, be heeded and respected.

"3rd. That in the government of the Church in the apostolic days this was the acknowledged principle of action in matters of great importance to the Church. See Acts xv: 22.

"4th. That this principle has been adopted by the Methodist Episcopal Church as a disciplinary rule in the same. We refer to one of the limitations, restrictions, or conditions required of that body in its legislation, contained in Discipline, pp. 18, 19.

"5th. That it is a matter of extreme doubt with us, to say the least, whether the 'Resolutions' adopted by the late General Conference are not illegal altogether, inasmuch as we are credibly informed that Elders elect, as well as those who were Elders in the proper sense of the word (we mean by ordination) were admitted as members of that body, and voted on the 'Resolutions' aforesaid—a thing we believe unprecedented in the annals of Methodistical legislation. See Discipline, page 17, answer to the question, Who shall compose the General Conference?

"6th. That setting aside the legality or illegality of the measure, *courtesy*, at least, required that in a matter fraught with such mighty consequences as the contemplated union, the people, or at least the Quarterly and District Conferences, should have been consulted. We would add, 'be courteous' is a divine command, and one of the leading principles of the Gospel itself. We would, when under this head, further state that when a separation from the Methodist Episcopal Church in the United States was contemplated courtesy was so far regarded that the Quarterly Conferences debated and decided on it by vote previous to its final accomplishment by the General Conference itself. We contend that a contemplated union with another body requires the same civility; and we apprehend disastrous consequences if it be not adopted, even at this late date. It should not be forgotten that the private members and others can take their leave of us without asking our consent; that they were free-born, and may not choose to be transferred to another body without some choice of their own in a matter of such importance as the present.

"7th. The pledge required by the American General Conference of the Canadian delegates before, or without which they would not grant the infant Canadian Church their share of the funds as a heretofore branch or component part of their Church, justifies them, in our opinion, from the further payment of said fund, except the contemplated union be abandoned.

"8th. The probable lack of funds at the disposal of the British Conference, and the extreme difficulty, if not the utter impossibility of raising them in Upper Canada.

"9th. The hazard to our Church property and of the right of solemnizing matrimony.

"10th. The danger of the total suppression of the Local Conference, and at any rate the deprivation of ordination to our younger successors in office, and consequently of the right of solemnizing matrimony and administering the ordinances.

"There are other reasons which might be assigned in the form of resolutions, or otherwise, which, for delicate reasons, we would not enter upon at the present time.

"In conclusion, we desire you to convene the General Conference, if you think it advisable, expedient, and legal, or take such other measures as you may see proper to adopt for the preservation of the Church and the prevention of the evils herein stated and apprehended by us.

"We have the honor to be, reverend and dear sir, your affectionate brethren in the Gospel of our common Lord,

DAVID CULP, HENRY GILMORE,
ELIJAH A. WARREN, JOHN W. BYAM.
DAVID GRIFFIN, CALEB SWAZEY,
ARNON C. SEAVER.

Smithville, Nov., 1832.

Comment upon the above is needless; though remarkably mild, these resolutions clearly indicated the feeling of opposition in the Niagara District at least.

Before Mr. Ryerson took his departure for England, which he did on the 4th of March, 1833, he prepared a long article for the *Christian Guardian*, which, in the absence of the editor—Rev. James Richardson—was published in that journal two days after Mr. Ryerson had left for Europe. From this document the following extracts are taken, as they bear internal evidence that there was considerable opposition to the measure—a fact which Mr. Ryerson afterwards denied, declaring that the union scheme was viewed without a scruple for more than a year after its consummation.

Mr. Ryerson's communication commenced with a quotation

from a letter written by Mr. Alder, after which he continued: "While transmitting to you the above extract for insertion, I beg to avail myself of the occasion to vindicate the proceedings and character of our Conference in this affair from certain misrepresentations which have been currently circulated; especially those contained in an officious and ungenerous attack made upon that body by a political editor who professes to be a 'lover and friend of the society.' By this writer the Conference is represented as *diposing* of the societies in Upper Canada without their consent—placing them under a 'jurisdiction *foreign* to that under which they voluntarily placed themselves when they were enrolled as members of that society.' The same writer calls the 'act of the Conference on this measure *unauthorized*'—'legislating *without authority*,' '*infringing* upon the rights which the people are unwilling to *surrender*, and in the maintenance of which they show a praiseworthy jealousy.'

"It will be perceived that the Conference is *charged* with transferring to a foreign jurisdiction—of doing so without authority, and of infringing upon rights too sacred to be given up, and the *inference* is that the societies would act a praiseworthy part in resisting the Conference in this affair. I have no hesitation in pronouncing the *charges* as *false* as the *inference* is wicked. * * * * * *

"Now, sir, if our Conference electing a *Bishop* from the United States to preside *permanently*, not only over the Conference, but over the societies in Upper Canada, and that without their consent, was no transfer of them to a 'foreign jurisdiction,' or 'infringement of rights too sacred to be given up,' can its authorizing the British Conference to send out a President, eligible once in four years, to preside over its own deliberations, be considered so? I leave it to the unbiased judgment of the candid reader to answer."

It would be difficult to pen a paragraph of similar length in which a greater amount of sophistry could be made use of.

What analogy could there be between the election of a Bishop chosen by themselves according to the arrangement entered into between the American General Conference and the Canada Conference in 1828, and *consented to by the societies* BEFORE *it was finally ratified*, and the *appointment* of a President by the English Conference to take the oversight of the Church? In the latter there was no right of *choice* whatever left even to the Conference, while it is equally worthy of remark that in the former case the Canada Conference was not restricted, in their choice of a Bishop, to the ministers of the Methodist Episcopal Church in the United States; but, on the contrary, had been counselled by those in high position in that Church to select one of *their own number* as their "*permanent*" superintendent.

Further on Mr. Ryerson continues:—"For the *tenth* resolution in the plan of agreement, above referred to and already published, declares, 'that nothing contained in the foregoing resolutions shall be understood or construed so as to affect the rights of our General Conference, or the standing and privileges of our present itinerant and local preachers.' Here is a body possessing, as ever, independent legislative and executive power, and yet it is represented as not only having conceded it, but as having 'infringed upon the rights' of the societies, and even disposed of them to a 'foreign jurisdiction,' and which they are virtually called upon to resist in a tone of manly and Christian independence!! * * *

"Again, says this champion, 'the British Conference is not self moved in this affair.' Gratuitous as is this assertion it is charitable when compared with the crimination of the Canadian Conference—and may therefore be passed without further notice—our author adds yet again, 'The *Government* has had its share in this doubtful measure.' Of some of the *measures* of the 'Government' I have heretofore expressed my opinion, but as to its having 'its share in this doubtful measure,' the sagacity of our polemic is very extraordinary, when Mr. Alder himself had no idea of anything of the kind until the measure was suggested in an interview with our Missionary Board."

It is only necessary to compare the above with Mr. Alder's letter to the Governor. From the comparison it will be seen that the editor of the *Cobourg Reformer*—the paper assailed—and his correspondent, were quite as sagacious, and rather more truthful than Mr. Ryerson in this instance.

Near the conclusion Mr. Ryerson remarks:—"Only let every friend and lover of the society suspend his judgment on the results and *effects* of the measure until the report of the representative to the British Conference shall have been laid before the public. Until then evil surmising can do no one any good, and may do much harm to many."

Mr. Ryerson's request that the Church would suspend judgment until after he could have time to make a report to the ensuing Conference of 1833 clearly indicated how much he dreaded the open investigation of the scheme by the people, until after all should have been arranged so that there could be no possibility of failure.

But so glaringly incorrect and deceptive was this article of Mr. Ryerson's, that the then editor of the *Guardian*—Rev. James Richardson—was compelled by sense of duty to notice some of the erroneous statements the following week, in which he also explained the reason why communications in opposition to the measure had been refused insertion. The following is an extract:—

"As we expected a variety of opinions, among a body of people so numerous as the members and friends of the Methodist Episcopal Church in Canada, in relation to the measures of our late Conference to obtain an union with the the English Conference—and considering the discussion of the question in the *Guardian* might lead to at least unpleasant results, we resolved to avoid it if possible; and, therefore, refused admittance to some communications from those who manifested a disposition opposed to those measures; and notwithstanding we observed a letter in the *Reformer* on the subject, containing some hard things, addressed to Rev. E. Ryerson, we judged it most prudent to let it pass unnoticed. But an answer from this gentleman having appeared in our last number it seems but proper, for the sake of consistency, to say it was published in our absence—it did not even meet our eye before it appeared in the paper.

"We regret this because, in our opinion, some parts of it are so worded and connected that it may mislead those who are not better informed with respect to some former proceedings of our Conference. We therefore deem it our duty to notice some particulars, and give such information as may remove these erroneous impressions which we fear the communication alluded to would otherwise leave.

"In combatting the charge of the *Reformer* that the Conference had 'transferred the societies to a foreign jurisdiction,' Mr. Ryerson observes:—'If our Conference in electing a Bishop from the United States to preside *permanently*, not only over the Conference, but over the societies in Upper Canada, and that without their consent, was no transfer of them to a 'foreign jurisdiction' or 'infringement upon rights too sacred to be given up,' can its authorizing the British Conference to send out a President, eligible once in four years, to preside over its own deliberations, be considered so?'

"Now, it appears to us, that worded as this is, and connected as the former act of the Conference is with the latter, so that the same inference is drawn from both, it conveys the idea of similarity; that is, that as the President from England would continue his connection with the Conference from which he came, and be subject to their jurisdiction, so would the 'Bishop from the United States.' But in fact no similarity between the two cases exists, as will appear from a bare statement of the proceedings of the Conference, relative to choosing a person to serve them as Bishop.

"By mutual agreement between the Canada Conference and the General Conference in the United States, in the year 1828, the former became a distinct and separate Connexion, in '*friendly relation*' only, to the latter—wholly at liberty to select a person as their Bishop from any part they might think proper, whether from Europe, the United States, or Canada; but it was expressly understood that the person who should be elected, come from where he might, should become one with the Canada Conference—subject to its discipline, and *wholly* and *solely* under its jurisdiction and control; and that he should be, in his *civil relation*, a subject of His Majesty, if not by birth that he should become naturalized; and it was further declared, by an express resolution of the Conference, that he should not, at any time, exercise any ecclesiastical jurisdiction whatever in any part of the United States, or of the territories thereof;' so that, in fact, he was to have no foreign relation whatever, ecclesiastical or civil. It therefore clearly appears that no application can properly be made of this circumstance to the question of 'foreign jurisdiction,' any more than to the supremacy of the Pope.

"The next particular in Mr. R.'s letter we are called upon to notice is, what he says relative to our Missionary Society. He states that 'the first part of the above resolution gives the Wesleyan Missionary Committee in London no more jurisdiction, even over our *Missions*, than was possessed by the Missionary Committee in New York as late as the year 1831.' If this be so, then it gives them *none whatever*, for the Missionary Committee in New York, never did, nor could exercise jurisdiction over the Missions in Canada or elsewhere. They make no appropriations at all, these are made by the several Conferences, and paid on the draft of the Bishop; whereas the Wesleyan Committee in London has the sole power of appropriating the 'amount necessary to carry on the missions,' and consequently of controling the work.

"As to the Canada Conference Missionary Society being

'auxiliary to that of the Methodist Episcopal Church in the United States up to 1831,' we would observe that although its auxiliary relation was not *formally* dissolved, yet it was *virtually* so, by reason of the separation of the Conference. Since the separation of the Conference, our Treasurer has not accounted to theirs, no reports have been made to them as a Parent Society, and they have exercised no jurisdiction over our missionary work, either through their Bishops, or Conference, or Committee; neither as an auxiliary have we had the privilege of drawing on their funds to the amount of our appropriations, as was the case previous to 1828; all the aid we have had from them was an annual grant, limited to $700, by their General Conference, and such was the strictness of this limitation that their Treasurer expressed his regret that they could not allow us any more, as their funds were ample enough to afford us twice or thrice the amount, which we might have drawn had our society been auxiliary to theirs."

During the summer it was not known whether the union would be actually effected or not, and hence very great uneasiness was manifested by the membership of the Church—some, as a matter of course, for the measure, and others against it. In order to quiet the apprehensions of those opposed to it, and to prevent the dissatisfaction from spreading further among the people, Mr. Case, and others who with him were favorable to the scheme, referred all who questioned on the subject to the tenth resolution, which they assured them should be rigidly adhered to by their delegate, and in the meantime the preachers generally were using their utmost skill and tact in persuading their flocks that the union could not fail to be a "good measure," and that they ought to remain "silent" until they would see what was really "going to be done." "The union might not after all be effected." And at any rate it was better to say nothing until after the return of the delegate from England." "It would be premature," they said, "to get up petitions against it, to send to the approaching Conference, when they did not know what was to be done," &c., &c. In this way hundreds were cajoled into silence until after the scheme was ratified by the Conference. Others, however, were not so easily satisfied, and refused, even before Mr. Ryerson's return, to consent to or accept the situation on any terms, until they should know more about the conditions.

Notwithstanding all this agitation and turmoil, however, there was this year, as there had been for years previous, a very great degree of spiritual prosperity in the societies, though among the Indians there was again a decrease. When, in the history of the entire Methodism of Canada, were such gratifying returns again to be seen? When again were such remarkable manifestations of the outpouring of the Holy Spirit to be witnessed? Echo answers, "When?"

CHAPTER XXIII.

Conference of 1833—Statistics—Mr. Ryerson's report—Articles of Union—Union consummated—New disciplinary rules—Legality of the proceedings questioned—Grounds of objection—The restrictive regulations—Dr. Bangs' remarks thereon—Emory—Macaulay—Sherwood—No government has a provision in its organization for its own dissolution—The binding character of the first and third restrictive regulations admitted, while that of the second is denied—They are equally binding—Rights of the people—Deviation from Mr. Wesley's views—Ordination of Mr. Mather—The polity adopted by the English Conference after Mr. Wesley's death not that designed by him—The Methodist Episcopal Church the *true Wesleyan Church*—The relation existing between the President and the Conference altogether different from that existing between the Conference and a Bishop chosen by and amenable to it—Divers orders in the ministry according to Scripture—The new organization not identical with the old—The Wesleyan Conference in Canada a mere appendage of the English Conference—Facts denied at this time publicly acknowledged at the disruption—Enquiry stifled—Pretense.

According to previous appointment, the Conference of 1833 convened at York, commencing its session on the 2nd of October. It was commenced in the usual manner, Mr. Case presiding. This year Rev. Egerton Ryerson was appointed Secretary in place of Mr. Richardson, who had for several years occupied that position. It was found, on comparing the reports, that the increase among the whites, though very encouraging, was not quite so large as for some years previous, and that there was a still larger decrease among the Indians than there had been the year before. Still there was a total increase for the year of 1040. There was, then, at the commencement of the Annual Conference of the Methodist Episcopal Church in

Canada, in this year of 1833, a total membership of 16,039. There were, as before, 4 Districts and about 70 preachers, not counting those who had superannuated or located.

Shortly after the opening of the Conference, preliminaries having been arranged, Mr. Ryerson proceeded to give an account of his mission to England, with its results. The union could, in his opinion, be formed at once by the Conference if it consented to the ratification of certain articles submitted by the English Conference, and insisted upon by them, to which he, as the representative of the Canadian body, had already given his assent. These articles were as follows:—

"ARTICLES OF UNION

"*Between the British Wesleyan Methodist Conference and the Conference of the Wesleyan Methodist Church in British North America.**

"The English Wesleyan Conference, concurring in the communication of the Canadian Conference, and deprecating the evils which might arise from collision, and believing that the cause of religion generally, and the interests of Methodism in particular would, under the blessing of God, be greatly promoted by the united exertions of the two connexions; considering also, that the two bodies concur in holding the doctrines of Methodism, as contained in the Notes of Mr. Wesley on the New Testament, and in his four volumes of Sermons, do agree in the adoption of the following resolutions:

"I. That such a union between the English Wesleyan and Canadian Connexions as shall preserve inviolate the rights and privileges of the Canadian preachers and societies, on the one hand, and on the other, shall secure the funds of the English Conference against any claims on the part of the Canadian preachers, is highly important and desirable.

"II. That (as proposed in the second and third resolutions

*A new name, it will be seen, even before the ratification of the "articles."

of the Canadian Conference) in order to affect this object the Discipline, economy, and form of Church government in general of the Wesleyan Methodists in England be introduced into the societies in Upper Canada, and that in particular an annual presidency be adopted.

"III. That the usages of the English Conference in reference to the probation, examination, and admission of candidates into the itinerant ministry be adopted.

"IV. That preachers who have travelled the usual term of probation, and are accepted by the Canadian Conference, shall be ordained by imposition of the hands of the President and of three or more of the senior preachers, according to the form contained in Mr. Wesley's 'Sunday Morning Service of the Methodists,' by which the Wesleyan missionaries in England are ordained, and which is the same as the form of ordaining Elders in the Discipline of the Canadian Conference.

"V. That the English Conference shall have authority to send, from year to year, one of its own body to preside over the Canadian Conference, but the same person shall not be appointed oftener than once in four years, unless at the request of the Canadian Conference. When the English Conference does not send a President from England, the Canadian Conference shall, on its assembling, choose one of its own members.

"The proposal of the Canadian Conference is understood to include, as a matter of course, that the President of the Conference shall exercise the same functions generally as the present General Superintendent now actually exercises; he shall not, however, have authority to appoint any preacher to any circuit or station contrary to the counsel or advice of a majority of the Chairmen of Districts, or Presiding Elders. associated with him as a Stationing Committee.

"VI. That the missions among the Indian tribes and destitute settlers, which are now, or may be hereafter established in Upper Canada shall be regarded as missions of the English Missionary Society, under the following regulations:—

"1. The Parent Committee in London shall determine the amount to be applied annually to the support and extension of the missions; and this sum shall be distributed by a committee consisting of the President, the General Superintendent of Missions, the Chairmen of Districts, and seven other persons, appointed by the Canadian Conference. A standing board or committee, consisting of an equal number of preachers and laymen, shall moreover be appointed, as heretofore, at every Conference, which, during the year, shall have authority, in concurrence with the General Superintendent of Missions, to apply any moneys granted by the Parent Committee, and not distributed by the Conference, in establishing new missions among the heathen, and otherwise promoting the missionary work.

"2. The Methodist Missionary Society in Upper Canada shall be auxiliary to the English Wesleyan Missionary Society, and the moneys raised by it shall be paid into the funds of the Parent Society.

"3. The missionaries shall be stationed at the Canada Conference, in the same way as the other preachers, with this proviso, however, that the General Superintendent of Missions shall be associated with the President and Chairmen of Districts in their appointment.

"4. All the preachers who may be sent from this country into the work in Upper Canada, shall be members of the Canadian Conference, and shall be placed under the same discipline, and be entitled to the same rights and privileges as the native preachers.

"5. Instead of having the annual stations of the missionaries sent home to the English Missionary Committee and Conference for their 'sanction,' as is the case with our missionaries generally, and as the Canadian Conference have proposed, the English Conference shall appoint, and the Parent Committee shall meet the expense of supporting a General Superintendent of Missions, who, as the agent of the Committee, shall have the same superintendence of the mission stations as the Chairmen of Districts, or Presiding Elders exercise over the circuits in their respective Districts, and shall pay the missionaries their allowance as determined by the Conference Missonary Committee, on the same scale as the Canadian Book of Discipline lays down for the preachers on the regular circuits; but who being at the same time recognized as a member of the Canadian Conference, shall be accountable to it in regard of his religious and moral conduct. This General Superintendent of Missions representing the Parent Committee in the Canadian Conference, and in the Stationing and Missionary Committees, the appointments at the Conference shall be final.

"VII. That the Canadian Conference, in legislating for its own members, or the Connexion at large, shall not, at any time, make any rule, or introduce any regulation, which shall infringe these articles of agreement between the two Conferences.

"Signed by order, and on behalf of the Conference,

RICHARD TREFFRY, *President.*
EDMUND GRINDROD, *Secretary.*

Manchester, August 7th, 1833."

The glowing description given by Mr. Ryerson of his very cordial reception in England, and of the ardent love which he said was evinced by the English Misionary Society for the welfare of Canadian Methodism, quite captivated the hearts of most of the preachers, several of whom had been previously doubtful of the wisdom of the measure. The scheme was hurried through the Annual Conference with all possible dispatch, so as to leave no time for further consideration, or for consultation among the people at large. At the close of the afternoon session of the first day it was moved by Rev. Egerton Ryerson and seconded by J. E. Davidson,* "That the Canada Conference cordially concurs in the resolutions of the British Conference, dated Manchester, August 7th, 1833, as the basis of union between the two Conferences."

The resolution carried, there being no very active opposition among the preachers present, and the vote was declared to have been unanimous. The testimony of some of the preachers themselves, however, given afterwards, was that though they did not vote against the measure, neither did they vote for it.

Next morning, after the opening of the Conference, Mr. Case resigned his position as General Superintendent *pro tem.*, and on a motion made by him, (Mr. Case), the Rev. Mr. Marsden, the appointee of the English Conference, was called to the chair, *simply by a vote of the Annual Confernce.*

Thus was the union—as it was called—finally consummated by the preachers composing the Annual Conference; and that, too, in open violation of the tenth resolution of the General Conference of 1832, which the people had been repeatedly assured should be held inviolate, and without any vote of the societies having been taken in the matter.

The Conference having—so far as it was in their power to do so—abolished the government and distinguishing features of the Methodist Episcopal Church in Canada, it became necessary for the new organization to adopt another name—it could no longer be Episcopal, since episcopacy was entirely done away with. In consequence of this, therefore, they styled themselves and their followers the Wesleyan Methodist Church in British North America, and at once proceeded to adopt a new and entirely different set of disciplinary rules and regulations, which had already been prepared for their reception.

The legality of the action of the General Conference of 1832, relative to the union resolutions, had been seriously questioned by many before the Conference of 1833, and the attention of

* See *Christian Guardian*, October 16th, 1833.

Mr. Case and others called to that fact. The question had arisen principally in consequence of preachers being allowed to sit and vote in that body who were not entitled by the Discipline of 1829 to do so. Of the preachers composing this Conference one-third, or nearly so, were ineligible,* never having been ordained Elders; and in addition to this it was doubted whether the General Conference—even if it had been properly constituted—had the power to do away with the constitution of the Church, or to subvert the order of its ministry.

Against such revolutionary movements as these, and infringements of their disciplinary rights many of the membership, as well as a very respectable number of efficient local preachers, strongly protested, and their views were sustained by a number of the old located and superannuated preachers, pioneers who had been members of the New York, Genesee and Canada Conferences. These objectors were, however, coolly informed that they had no choice left in the matter, and must submit to the decision of those composing these two Conferences (1832 and 1833). This they refused to do, contending that they were justified in their course of procedure on the following grounds:—

1st. The illegal composition of the General Conference, in admitting those not eligible to a seat there.

2nd. Its legal inability to do away with the episcopate, the order of its ministry, and the form of church government agreed to between the Canada Conference and the Methodist Episcopal Church in the United States in 1828, as there was certainly an infringement of the rights of the membership.

3rd. If the legality of the action of 1832 had been admitted—which, however, was not—the violation of the "tenth resolution," which had been the only hope for the independence of the Canadian body, justified the rejection of the measure.

* See Mr. Ryerson's sworn testimony before the court in the Belleville chapel suit. Page 48 of Fowler's report.

4th. The privileges of the local preachers were, by the articles of union, legislated away from them without their consent, and without their ever having forfeited them.

5th. The matter had not been laid before the societies, and their action taken upon it prior to its consummation by the preachers, and therefore that the preachers composing this Conference had merely legislated themselves, and those who chose to go with them, out of the Church; and their action though passed by a large majority, being a violation of the restrictive rules forming the constitution of the Church, was of no force whatever, and was therefore not binding upon any excepting those who chose to accept it.*

* The restrictive rules are as follows:—

Question.—Who shall compose the General Conference, and what are the regulations and powers belonging to it?

Answer 1.—The General Conference shall be composed of all the travelling Elders who have travelled four full calendar years last past, and have been received into full connexion.

2. At all times when the General Conference is met it shall take two-thirds of its members to make a quorum for transacting business.

3. One of the General Superintendents shall preside in the General Conference, but in case no General Superintendent be present, the General Conference shall choose a President *pro tempore.*

4. The General Conference shall have full powers to make rules and regulations for our Church, under the following limitations and restrictions, viz.,—

1. The General Conference shall not revoke, alter, or change our articles of religion, nor establish any new standards or rules of doctrine contrary to our present existing and established standards of doctrine.

2. They shall not change or alter any part or rule of our government so as to do away episcopacy or destroy the plan of our itinerant general superintendency.

3. They shall not revoke or change the general rules of the United Societies.

4. They shall not do away the privileges of our ministers or preachers of trial by a committee, and of an appeal. Neither shall they do away the privileges of our members of trial before the society, or by a committee, and of an appeal.

5. They shall not appropriate the produce of the Book Concern, or of the Charter Fund, to any purpose other than for the benefit of the travelling, supernumerary, superannuated, and worn-out preachers, their wives, widows, and children.

6. No new rule, or regulation, or alteration of any rule or regula-

The preachers, it was contended, had over-stepped the bounds of the power given them in the Discipline, in thus making an entire *revolution* in the manner of Church government, and therefore the people were free either to remain in the old Methodist Episcopal Church in Canada, or to go forth with the Wesleyan Methodist Church in British North America. The *societies* had been consulted, and their advice taken, in the changes which had occurred at the time of the separation from the parent Church in the United States, even though these changes had affected no material rights or privileges of the

tion now in force respecting our temporal economy; such as the building of meeting-houses, the order to be observed therein; the allowance to the ministers and preachers, their widows and children; the raising annual supplies for the propagation of the Gospel (the missions excepted); for the making up the allowances of the preachers, &c., shall be considered of any force or authority until such rule, regulation, or alteration shall have been laid before the several Quarterly Conferences throughout the whole Connexion, and shall have received the consent and advice of a majority of the members (who may be present at the time of laying such rule, regulation, or alteration before them) of two-thirds of the said Conferences.

7. Nor shall any new rule, regulation, or alteration respecting the doctrines of our Church, the rights and privileges of our members; such as, the receiving persons on trial, and into full connection, the condition on which they shall retain their membership, the manner of bringing to trial, finding guilty and reproving, suspending, or excluding disorderly persons from society and Church privileges, have any force or authority until laid before the Quarterly Conferences and approved as aforesaid; provided, nevertheless, that upon the joint recommendation of three-fourths of the Annual Conference, or Conferences, then the majority of three-fourths of the General Conference shall suffice to alter any of the above restrictions except the sixth and seventh, which shall not be done away or altered without the recommendation or consent of two-thirds of the Quarterly Conferences throughout the Connexion.

8. The first General Conference of the Methodist Episcopal Church in Canada shall be held the last Wednesday in August in 1830, in Belleville, and henceforward, once in four years, at such times, and in such places, as shall be fixed upon by the General Conference from time to time; but the General Superintendent, with or by the advice of the Annual Conference, or Conferences, or if there be no General Superintendent, the Annual Conference, or Conferences, respectively, shall have power to call a General Conference if they judge it necessary, at any time.

laity. Why, then, had they not been consulted in the same manner before it was attempted to transfer them to the control of a foreign body whose head was four thousand miles distant, and whose polity was so different in every essential?

For the perpetuation of the Church, the General Conference might, it was argued, *alter* certain rules—subject to restrictions—but it certainly could have no power, human or divine, to alter a rule so that they might admit men into it in order to assist them to revolutionize the Church by abolishing the orders of the ministry, and to destroy its own existence. To abolish, at one fell swoop, five out of the seven restrictive rules, was, it was affirmed, something more than a mere alteration such as the proviso of the seventh restrictive would allow It was upon this proviso that the advocates of the "union" forced such a construction as would make their action in the matter appear legal, insisting that the laity should only be consulted in regard to financial, or kindred matters.

That the adherents to the old paths were not without authority in claiming that the General Conference had no right to *abolish*, even though the majority might desire to do so, is evident from the opinions expressed by Bishop Asbury and others, as given by Dr. Bangs. "They," he remarks, "clearly saw the necessity of adopting some plan by which the *doctrines* of the Church, *its form of government*, and its general rules might be preserved from deterioration." Commenting further upon the rules adopted by the General Conference, of which he had before been writing, he observes:—"Call these rules, therefore, *restrictive regulations* or a *constitution of the Church*, for we contend not about names merely, they have ever since been considered as *sacredly* binding upon all succeeding General Conferences, limiting in *all* their legislative acts, and prohibiting them from making inroads upon the *doctrines, general rules*, and *government* of the Church."*

* Bangs' History of the M. E. Church. Vol. 2, commencing on page 231.

Again, in his History of Methodist Episcopacy he continues: "It is true, however, with *these exceptions*, the General Conference have full and ample powers to modify, alter, or change, or to make any additional rules they may deem expedient and necessary for the benefit of the community." And in Emory's "Defence of our Fathers," it is observed, "Whenever the powers of the present delegated General Conference are spoken of in this work it is, of course, to be understood agreeably to the *principles of the restrictive limitations*."

It was upon such principles as those quoted above that the members and friends of the Methodist Episcopal Church in Canada, who remained true to their colors, based their claim to the church property acquired prior to 1833, claiming as they did that in superseding its prerogatives, as it had unquestionably done, the Canada Conference had forfeited all right thereto. In this view they were sustained by Judges Macauley and Sherwood, as well as by other men of legal standing and ability, and it was not until after political influence had been brought to bear upon the subject, and the creation of new judges, whose political proclivities were well-known, that an adverse judgment was given upon the question.

It is, and was then, a fundamental principle, firmly held to by both British and American statesmen, that no government has, or ever had, a provision in its organization for its own dissolution or utter abolishment,* and this is quite as applicable to ecclesiastical as to civil governments. To argue, therefore, that the proviso in the seventh restrictive rule in the "Constitution of the Church" gave the General Conference the right to *abolish* any one of the other five, because it gave

* Lincoln, the late lamented President of the United States, and an eminent lawyer as well as statesman, made the following remarks, in his first Inaugural Address, which are relevant to the matter under discussion :—"Perpetuity," said he, "is *implied*, if not expressed, in the fundamental law of all national governments. It is safe to assert that *no government proper* ever had a provision in its organic law for its own termination."

a certain amount of liberty to make *alterations*, and because these are not definitely mentioned, was perfectly absurd.

The foregoing are some, among many others, of the reasons given by the opponents of the "union" platform. The following is a specimen of the reasoning employed by those in favor of it. Rev. Egerton Ryerson, who was its most plausible and indefatigable defender and advocate, in an editorial in the *Guardian* of March 12th, 1834, remarks as follows:—"We have, however, heard of one objection against this measure, or to the principle involved in it, to which we have not heretofore adverted, and which it may be proper to notice. 'If (says the objector) the Conference had a right to form a union with the British Conference, it has a right, and may form a union with the Church of England, or with the Church of Rome.' This objection is as true as to say that because an individual has a right to form one marriage union he therefore has a right to form a dozen; or because a person may recognize the relation of his own kindred, he may therefore recognise the relationship of strangers and foreigners; or, because a man, after a period of absence, may return to his own household, he may therefore fly to the moon. The Discipline provides that no alteration shall take place in the *Articles of Faith, the standards of doctrine, or the general Rules of the Society* without the concurrence of the whole Church."

The absurdity of the above is too apparent to need much comment. In it, however, two points were admitted, one of which—the fact of open opposition to the measure—was afterward strenuously denied; the other attempted to be explained away. The writer admitted that the General Conference had *no right*, on its own mere motion, to do away with the first and third articles of the constitution. Were the rest not as *sacredly binding?* If the first and third of the restrictive rules or articles of the constitution were binding upon the Conference, prohibiting it from altering "the *Articles of Faith*, the *standards of doctrine, or the general Rules of the Society*,"

&c., surely the *second* article was as securely guarded from innovation, and as binding upon the Conference. It provides that " *They shall not change or alter any part or rule of our government so as to do away episcopacy.*" * * * The restrictive rules encompass the Articles of Faith with no stronger barriers than those which also embrace the government and the episcopacy. Mr. Ryerson admits, in the foregoing extract, that the Conference was not competent to change the Articles of Faith, neither was it competent legally to change the government of the Church, nor to do away the episcopacy. (See restrictive rules on a former page.)

Have the laity no right to insist that the form of church government existing when they united with the Church should be retained? It certainly was a right *claimed* by the Presbyterians of Scotland, one which they maintained to the death, sealing their faith in "martyrdom," and one which all history, both sacred and profane, has conceded to them. It was asserted by the preachers, on their return from this Conference, that no vital change had been made in the government of the Church, and by waiting patiently the people would see for themselves. As soon as practicable, the quarterly tickets were issued with the new title, and *sent* or handed to each person who had been a member of the old Church, and wherever the ticket was *allowed to remain* in the possession of the person to whom it was given or sent, they were claimed—despite their own protestations to the contrary—as members of the "Wesleyan Methodist Church in British North America."

The abolishment of the episcopacy, and substitution of an annual presidency, besides being considered illegal, was objected to very seriously upon other grounds, one of which was that it was a deviation from the evident designs of Mr. Wesley himself, who, at the time he made provision for the organization of the Methodist Societies in America, had not only *appointed* Dr. Coke to preside over the deliberations of the body which he with others was commissioned to organize, but had also consecrated him to the sacred office of a Bishop, by the imposition of hands, and by a solemn and specific service, giving reason for so doing; and he also requested that Mr. Asbury should be consecrated to the same office by the Doctor in the manner in which he himself had been consecrated. Neither were the opinions nor prejudices of the American people interfered with in the carrying out of Mr. Wesley's plan, it was not only accepted, but approved of by the people themselves. Indeed some of them had urged the matter upon him even before he sent out Dr. Coke. With regard to the societies in America he was entirely untrammeled in his actions concerning the organization of them into a Church. In England he was somewhat differently situated, both by his position in the Establishment, and from his having to contend with the opposition and prejudices of his brother Charles. But some time previous to his death, he made what he believed was provision for the ordination of those English preachers who had not received episcopal ordination in the Establishment, nor been ordained by himself, so that after his decease they might be properly qualified to administer the sacraments of the Lord's Supper and baptism to the societies. For this purpose, therefore, he ordained the Rev. Alexander Mather a General Superintendent, or Bishop, designing him to stand in the same relation to the English Wesleyans that Dr. Coke and Mr. Asbury did to the American.

The English Conference, after Mr. Wesley's death, refused to accept Mr. Mather as their General Superintendent, according to Mr. Wesley's plan, the Church Establishment having more influence among their leading men than had Mr. Wesley himself, as the following extracts from a recent work will show:—*"While the agitation was raging and extending the Conference of 1792 met in London, on the 31st July. The venerable Alexander Mather, who had preached thirty-

* Stevens' History of Methodism. Vol. 3, pp. 40, 51 and 52.

five years, and whom Mr. Wesley had ordained as Superintendent, or Bishop, was elected President, Dr. Coke was chosen Secretary. Kilham was censured by a formal vote for his pamphlet, Bradburn and others vindicated him, but Coke moved for his expulsion. He made some qualified acknowledgements, and was continued in the Conference."

The controversy respecting the administering of the sacraments was continued with as much acrimony after this session of the English Conference as before it, and in the latter part of 1793, Mr. Pawson, the President, expressed himself respecting the condition of the Connexion as follows:—

"At present we really have no government. It will by no means answer our ends to dispute one with another as to which is the most Scriptural form of church government. We should consider our present circumstances, and endeavor to agree upon some method by which our people may have the ordinances of God, and at the same time be preserved from division." Adverting to Mr. Wesley, he continues:—"He foresaw that the Methodists would, after his death, soon become a distinct people; he was deeply prejudiced against a presbyterian, and was as much in favor of an episcopal form of government; in order, therefore, to preserve all that was valuable in the Church of England among the Methodists he ordained Mr. Mather and Dr. Coke Bishops. These he undoubtedly designed should ordain others. Mr. Mather told us so at the Manchester Conference, but we did not then understand him. I see no way of coming to any good settlement but on the plan I mentioned before. I sincerely wish that Dr. Coke and Mr. Mather may be allowed to be what they are, Bishops. We must have ordination among us at any rate." Mr. Pawson's plainly expressed sentiments were approved by and apparently coincided with those of a later Wesleyan authority, who thus expresses himself with regard to church polity:—*"The constitution of the Methodist Epis-

* Dr. Dixon's Methodism in its Origin.

copal Church is only a development of Wesley's opinion of church polity; and it may be added that an imitation of that great transaction in this country would be perfectly justifiable on the ground assumed by Wesley himself and held sacred by his followers. * * * * If we mistake not, it is to the American Methodist Episcopal Church that we are to look for the *real* mind and sentiments of this great man."

So thought, and so reasoned those who foresaw the evils likely to be brought upon the Church in Canada by the innovations sought to be introduced into it by the parties favoring the consummation of the union; for to those who were students of Methodist history it was well known that the constitution of the English Conference was not what Mr. Wesley would have desired, or what Mr. Pawson and other eminent leaders of the body had recommended.

Another and very serious objection to the articles of union was, that the English Conference not only could, at its own option, send out whom it pleased to preside over the Canadian Conference, but that, so long as he was a member of the English Conference he might, or *might not* be a minister in orders, just as the case happened to be. It was afterwards proved that this objection was not without grounds, as some of the first Presidents who were sent from England to preside over the Canada Conference *had really not been themselves ordained*, though, despite this disqualification, *they proceeded to ordain* the Canadian preachers. Neither was this President to be a *bona fide* member of the Canada Church; he was amenable only to the authorities of the Church in England, and as independent of the Church in Canada as is the Czar of Russia of his subjects, and yet this man was for the time being to control the entire Connexion. And in addition to this, even if such a person had been qualified to administer the ordinances and ordain the preachers, it could not reasonably be expected that he, a stranger in the country, and unused to the circumstances and peculiarities of the people in a new country, could understand their wants, or that the association and intercourse with the preachers which the few days of the Annual Conference afforded him would inspire him with the same interest in the societies that might be expected from a Bishop who was a permanent resident of the country, who was one with his brethren, amenable to them, and to them only, for his conduct, and who, Asbury-like, would travel more or less throughout the entire work.

Another radical innovation, it was urged, had been made by the abolishment of the orders of Elders and Deacons in the Church, and the substitution of one called ministers instead. This was considered an usurpation of power, an act unauthorized by the laws of the Church or the word of God; especially as the order of Deacons had been established by the Apostles themselves, and approved of by the primitive Church, (see Acts vi: 5, 6). It had been adhered to by the ancient fathers, preferred by Mr. Wesley and received by both the Methodist Episcopal Church in the United States and in Canada, and the authority for its abolishment at this particular juncture was more than questioned. It was denied.*

* For a full consideration of the scriptural order of Deacons, the reader is referred to Bangs' "Vindication of Methodist Episcopacy," chap. 1, and to second edition of the "Union Considered," pp. 36, 37, 38, 39. An extract or two from Dr. Bangs will be sufficient in this place:—"Here then," the Doctor remarks, "are enumerated all those duties of a deacon which the Holy Scriptures have authorized him to perform. In this part of our ministry, therefore, we have not *followed a cunningly devised fable*, but the word of the living God, and which Church is most according to apostolic order, that which has preaching Deacons, going to and fro, sowing the seed of eternal life; or that which has *but one order of ministers*, by whatever name they may be called?"

In his "Original Church of Christ," pp. 309, 310, he argues the case still further:—"What greater proof should we require," continues he, "that those Deacons were regular preachers of God's word? Yet they were not Elders or Presbyters. They were, therefore, an inferior order in the ministry, which *proves that those err who confine themselves* to one order only. * * * Allowing the soundness of this conclusion, it will follow that those churches which admit of no distinction in ministerial order, but reduce all

Judge Macauley, commenting upon this innovation, in his opinion on the Waterloo Chapel case, remarks as follows :—"It is true the Discipline of 1834, in the Ordination Service (designedly or accidentally) acknowledges, in the same language as that of 1829, the appointment by the Holy Spirit of divers orders of ministers in the Church of Christ. Still I do not find that the British Wesleyan denomination contains more than one, like unto Elders, styled Ministers, contrary to the Episcopal discipline, which provides for three (exclusive of lay preachers) Bishops, Elders, and Deacons, without any designated by the general term ministers. The dissentent members of the Methodist Episcopal Church may feel repugnant to such arrangements. They may not look upon the union as a mere change of name, but as indicating a serious deviation in church government and the calls to the ministry—and in my construction of their discipline I cannot deny them the right to do so on plausible grounds. The American Connexion is professedly episcopal—the British is practically presbyterian, and whatever distinguished the one from the other would equally distinguish the Methodist Episcopal Church in Canada from the British Wesleyan Church in Canada."

It was objected, too, that by the articles of union the Canada Conference, and through them the societies would become a mere dependency of the English Conference, and that, in a much less liberal sense than the Province of Canada was a dependency of the British Government. Such a requirement on the part of the English Conference, made through their agent, Mr. Alder, was considered unreasonable. That it should be

to a level, *have departed from the apostolic model.* In their intemperate zeal against episcopacy, which broke out with such violence among the Independents in the days of the Stuarts, they seem to have run into the opposite extreme, by introducing a perfect parity of ministerial order as well as jurisdiction, and thus have impaired that beautiful symmetry which we behold in the orders, powers, and harmonious subordination of the several grades of officers in the primitive Church."

assented to by the Canada Conference was deemed too humiliating a degradation to be borne by the original societies in this country without an effort to prevent it.

Many, it is true, were quieted on this head by the positive denial of the fact on the part of the friends of the movement, but—to anticipate a date—when the disruption between the British and Canada Conferences took place, in 1840, then the facts before asserted by those opposed to the union, and denied by those in favor of it, were admitted by the organ of the Wesleyan Church in Canada, as well as in their almanac, and in several pamphlets published by their leading men.

It will be remembered that Mr. Alder had, in 1832, secured the government grant, which amounted to between $4,000 and $5,000 annually. This amount was drawn from the Provincial chest by the English Missionary Society, but part, if not all, was paid to the preachers of the Canada Conference laboring on mission fields; so that, though the English Missionary Society drew the money, the Canadian missionaries enjoyed the benefit of the greater portion of it. At, length, however, leading men in the Canadian Connexion, among whom were the Messrs. Ryerson, resolved to secure, if possible, the entire grant for their Canadian mission work, and draw it *themselves* directly from the government. The English Conference would allow their dependents no such liberty, and in this dispute arrangements hitherto strenuously denied were publicly acknowledged, and facts which had previonsly been concealed, as far as it was in their power to do so, by those interested in having them hidden, were brought to light.* The whole affair proving most conclusively what had been asserted by the opponents of the measure, that the articles of union, if carried out, would

* The controversy between the British and Canadian Wesleyans terminated in the reunion, the government grant having been withheld during the time of their dispute and separation.

degrade the original societies to the position of a mere dependency of the English Connexion.

Another very serious objection to the manner of the consummation of the union, was that the Church had been allowed neither voice nor choice in the matter. Enquiry had been stifled before the Conference of 1833, and after that the people were coolly informed that there was nothing left for them but *submission*. They were treated much as slaves were at that day, being allowed no more choice than they, in their transfer to a new superintendent. To such an ultimatum the adherents to the old landmarks refused to *submit*, and joined issue thereupon.

In order to give a plausible coloring to their proceedings, certain changes consequent upon the *formation* of the "Wesleyan Methodist Church in British North America," which were incorporated into the new discipline, were laid before the Quarterly Meetings of the new organization. Whether these alterations were approved or not by these meetings, however, they could not affect the ratification of the union, that having already been ratified, as far as the individual members of the Canada Conference were concerned. Before the societies were consulted, even nominally, an English President had presided over the Conference, and proceeded to ordain its preachers, and the control of the Canadian missions had been given up to Mr. Stinson, as *agent* of the English Missionary Society. In this manner were the societies consulted, and in no other, equivocal assertions to the contrary notwithstanding.

CHAPTER XXIV.

Continued excitement—Shutting out the "schismatics"—Activity of both parties—Prompt measures against the union—Meetings—Saltfleet, held December, 1833—Blenheim, January 9th, 1834—Belleville, January 10th, 1834—London, January 25th, 1834—Convention at Trafalgar—Its action—Resolutions—Polite and Christian comparison—Specimens of the arguments used on the other side—Strictures on the meeting at Saltfleet—Opposition admitted and rebuked by the organ of the Conference—Action of the London Quarterly Meeting censured—Leaders in calling the convention taken to task—Personalities indulged in when argument failed—Changes admitted—Assertions that no changes had been made.

THROUGHOUT the year the excitement consequent upon the action of the Conference of 1833 continued unabated. Indeed with each succeeding month, instead of losing, it appeared to gain fresh strength and vigor.

Immediately after the close of the session of this famous Conference haste was made to obtain and keep possession of all the places which had formerly been occupied by the Methodist Episcopal Church in Canada, and thus shut out the "schismatics," as the opponents of union were called, from the very churches which in many instances they had planted.

But if the unionists were busy, neither were those who considered the action of the Conference illegal altogether inactive, although they labored under very great disadvantages. A short time only elapsed, after it was known what the action of the Canada Conference had been, till meetings were called by Rev. David Culp—an old *regularly ordained Elder*—which were approved and attended by several of his brethren about what was called the "head of the lake;" and others followed in various sections of the province. The design of these meetings was to ascertain what the remaining strength of the societies was, and to consult as to what course to take in reorganizing the Annual Conference, and in other ways repairing the breaches so ruthlessly made in the walls of their beloved Zion by those that hitherto they had esteemed as brethren and co-laborers in the Master's vineyard. Throughout the entire work, indeed, very great dissatisfaction was manifested by the people; the local preachers, as they as a class had been the most unfairly dealt with, taking the lead in the opposition.

The first meeting which took action in this matter was convened, it will be remembered, at Smithville, in November, 1832, and its able protest forwarded, with due respect, to Mr. Case, who, however, paid no attention to it. That this very useful class of men in the Church, as well as many of the membership, were strongly opposed to even the terms proposed by the articles assented to by the Conference of 1832, was well known before Mr. Ryerson sailed for England, as is abundantly proved by his letter in the *Christian Guardian* of March 6th, 1832.*

On the 18th of December, 1833, a little more than two months after the meeting of the York Conference, a public meeting was held in Saltfleet, at which a most decided stand was taken against the terms of union; and the authority of the Conference to force the societies into a union with another body without first having asked and obtained their sanction to the measure, was strenuously denied. The meeting and some of those attending it were duly animadverted upon in the *Guardian* of January 1st, 1834, but agitation could not be put down either by the personal abuse indulged in by the editor, or by the sophistry of his pretended arguments.

* Quotations from this communication are given on pp. 271 and 272.

Another meeting was held on the 9th of January, 1834, in the old meeting-house on the Governor's road, township of Blenheim, at which the proceedings of the Saltfleet meeting were discussed and sanctioned, and, if possible, an even more decided determination manifested to adhere to the Methodist Episcopal Church.*

One day later than that on which the Blenheim meeting was convened, viz., the 10th of January, 1834, another meeting was held at Belleville, in the proceedings of which sixteen local preachers from that section of country took part.† Mr. J. Lockwwod—one of these sixteen—addressed a communication to the *Christian Guardian*, which appeared—with comments—in its issue of the 5th February, from which the following is extracted:—"Now whether the Conference at Hallowell intended, in adopting a resolution for the security of the present standing of the itinerant and local preachers, that no innovation of former usages should accrue as a consequent of the union, I am unable to say; but so it appears to have been understood by all the local brethren there present, and hence it is not surprising that excitement should arise at even the appearance of departure from what they understood to be an engagement." The resolution referred to above was the tenth of the series adopted at the Conference of 1832, and which, in direct violation of the pledges given by that Conference to the local preachers, had been totally abandoned by the delegate during the progress of the negotiations in England, and by the Conference at the ratification of the "articles of union." But plain as this article was, some of the other brethren attending the meeting did not think it sufficiently strong.

Of those who took an active part in the proceedings of the meeting at Belleville was Rev. John Reynolds, who, though

* This meeting is mentioned, and its proceedings spoken of with marked disapprobation by the *Guardian* of March 19th, 1834.

† See *Guardian* Feb. 19th, 1834.

located, was an ordained Elder in good standing. Notwithstanding the position taken by Mr. Reynolds at this meeting it was afterwards asserted, by those who sought to make capital out of it, that Mr. Reynolds had identified himself with the union, and, as a consequence of that, with the Wesleyan Methodist Church in British North America, because he had consented—after solicitation—to act as Secretary at the first missionary meeting held under the auspices of that body in the town of Belleville, and had forwarded—also by request—an account of the same for publication in the *Guardian*.* This assertion was made, too, in face of the fact that in the same issue of the *Guardian* in which the account of the missionary meeting appeared there was also published a letter from Mr. Reynolds, of which the following is a copy:—

"*Belleville, Feb. 11th*, 1834.

"DEAR BROTHER,—On looking over the last *Guardian*, I was not a little surprised that you should identify Bro. Lockwoood as the organ of the local preachers in this District; not but that he may be capable of acting as our representative, yet I think my local brethren will bear me out in saying that he never was authorized by us to act as such.

"It is very possible that he may differ from his brethren in some points, which I believe is common with all bodies of men, both in Church and State, but as to the general principle I think all agree. We are decidedly opposed to the resolutions, and therefore passed a vote at our meeting (held in this place, 10th January last) that *we could not willingly consent to or comply with them*—we prefer the old rules.

"By giving the above a place in the *Guardian* you will very much oblige your old friend and brother,

JOHN REYNOLDS."

* If acting as secretary or chairman at a missionary meeting constitutes a person a member of the Wesleyan, or any other Church, or if consenting to act as collectors, or work on committees would accomplish the same purpose, how many church members would be taken with guile.

Upon this letter the editor made the following remarks:—

"In inserting the communication to which our esteemed* Bro. Reynolds refers we supposed we were complying with the wish of sixteen local preachers; otherwise, notwithstanding our respect for the author of it, we should not have felt ourselves justified to draw so largely upon our columns, and the patience of our readers, by inserting the *labored objections*, with replies to them from any one individual. * * * * We thought, however, as Bro. Lockwood's letter came backed with so high authority, and with the sole and expressed view to elicit 'explanations,' that it was advisable to insert it in the organ of the Conference (notwithstanding its many objections to the proceedings of the Conference) with such explanations and remarks as seemed necessary, and then let the question rest, so far as controversy was concerned, after this free and ample discussion of it."

On the London circuit a still more decided stand was taken than there had been at any of the places previously mentioned. Here the preachers appointed at this Conference to that circuit, were *rejected* by the Quarterly Conference, held January 25th, 1834, because, being an official board of the Methodist Episcopal Church in Canada, they deemed that they could not consistently receive as their preachers persons who were ministers of the Wesleyan Methodist Church in British North America; and accordingly, that the work might suffer as little as possible, Rev. John Bailey, who had already travelled some years in the Connexion, was solicited to supply it as far as was practicable; which he did.

The resolutions referred to above were as follows, and were adopted by a vote of eighteen out of twenty-two members:—

* Up to this date Mr. Reynolds was an "*esteemed brother.*" There was no whisper of the slanders afterwards circulated concerning him; and which, had there been any foundation for them in fact, must have been patent to the Church at that time.

"The Quarterly Meeting Conference of the Methodist Episcopal Church of the London Circuit, to the members of the said Church throughout the province:—

"DEAR BRETHREN,—The degrading and humiliating condition to which the recent arbitrary conduct of the Conference would bring us, has induced us to come to the following resolutions, while assembled in the Conference on the 25th inst., and which were carried by eighteen, with only four dissenting:—

"James Mitchel being called to the chair, and Nathan Jacobs being Secretary, it was resolved,

"1. That the powers recently assumed by the Conference, in separating themselves from the Methodist Episcopal Church, are arbitrary and degrading to the members of said Church.

"2. That we totally deny the powers of the Conference to make the late change without the consent of the members of the Church; and that unless said pretended powers are abandoned, and the rights and wishes of the members consulted and respected we can have little confidence in said Conference, and will be under the painful necessity of discontinuing their services.

"3. That until the wishes of the members of said Methodist Episcopal Church be generally known throughout the province we deem it advisable to employ some of our local preachers to administer the ordinances of the Gospel to us.

"4. That we heartily concur in the plan of having a delegation of the Methodist Episcopal Church, for the purpose of removing from our Discipline every pretended power that the Conference may have vested themselves with, and giving the members such powers in the future government of the Church as will prevent their being reduced to a like state of degradation for all time to come.

"5. That John Bailey be requested to take charge of the

circuit, with power to employ what help the circumstances of the Church may require.

JAMES MITCHEL, *Chairman*,
NATHAN JACOBS, *Secretary*.

January 25th, 1834."

On these resolutions Mr. Ryerson commented as follows, proving clearly the light in which he viewed them:—"Several resolutions have been passed by some official members, purporting to be the voice of the circuit protesting against the union; impugning the Conference; denying its authority; and refusing to receive the preachers appointed by it."*

Following out the plan proposed by the London Quarterly Meeting, a general convention was called, in order to ascertain what the state of feeling really was in the different sections of the province, for from having no organ in which to publish their views they could not obtain accurate information without some such meeting.

This convention met at Trafalgar on the 10th of March, 1834, and continued its sitting till the 12th. Though the attendance was not large, sixteen preachers only being present, the different sections of the work were pretty well represented, and the deliberations resulted in the adoption of the following resolutions:

"1. *Resolved*, That the Christian Church, according to the intent and meaning of the Scriptures, is a society of faithful believers in Christ Jesus, among whom the ordinances of the Gospel are duly observed and administered.

"2. That the Church, by Divine appointment, for the edification of God's people, and for the better observance of the law and institutions of the Christian religion, is divided into the ministry of the word and the people, and their obligations and interests are mutual, and their duties voluntary.

"3. That the Bible, as the law of God, is the only standard

* See *Guardian*, March 5th, 1834.

to which the Church in its different departments is accountable, and that no church officer, or member of the same, has any right to impose any other rule or principle than is therein required, or may be fairly deduced from the same.

"4. That any compact or association of any Methodist or other religious society, throughout the world, is voluntary, such compact being merely intended for the mutual protection of privileges and property of the said societies, and the securing among them unity of systems of faith and practice.

"5. That the societies of the Methodist Episcopal Church in Canada became, by common consent, a free and independent Church, viz., by a ratified agreement between the General Conference of the M. E. Church of the United States, and the Annual Conference of the M. E. Church in Canada, said Canada Conference being authorized by the petitions of the people of their charge to apply for and agree upon said measure, which was afterwards, at the session of the Canada Conference in Ernestown, in this province, in the year 1828, arranged and fully settled, and a compact or Discipline then formed, that became the foundation of connection between the Conference of the M. E. Church of Canada and their people.

"6. That every member of the said M. E. Church is equally interested in the said Discipline, in all its provisions and institutions, as no individual can be a member of the said Church, or any other, but by freedom of choice; the said Discipline is equally a guarantee to the members as well as to the preachers, and no alteration of institution or change of relation can take place in the same without their consent, else their freedom is invaded, and the Discipline violated.

"7. That the said Discipline has vested the General Conference of the M. E. Church with certain powers of legislation, but such power alone can extend to the making of rules for the well-being and future good government of the

M. E. Church of Canada; if they are exercised to any further extent they are null, being unauthorized.

"8. That the Conference formerly of the M. E. Church, now denominated the Wesleyan Methodist Conference in British North America, at their two last sessions, by their propositions to unite the Church to a remote body, by their negotiations to effect the union in question, and by their consummation of the same, have acted without disciplinary authority, inasmuch as the right of self-disposal is denied the people—a most sacred and conscientious principle!

"9. That the said Conference have forfeited their pastoral charge of the said M. E. Church—have alienated themselves from any right or possession in the real properties secured by law to the said Church.

"10. That we are constrained, from principles contained in the foregoing resolutions, to enter our protest against the late changes made by the Annual Conference, as subversive of all right principle, and as a dangerous precedent to be allowed in the Church, and that we hold ourselves, and those members who concur with us, still the legal M. E. Church in Canada.

"11. That this convention do now appoint a General Superintendent, whose duty it shall be to itinerate through this province, to see that the ordinances of the Church be duly administered as far as practicable, and to notify all our preachers, travelling and local, of the M. E. Church, to meet in Conference on the 25th of June next ensuing, at Cummer's meeting-house, on Yonge Street, to elect and constitute a Bishop according to the provisions of the Discipline, and to adopt such rules and regulations for the future legislation of the Church as may accord with the natural rights of the people.

"12. That the said Superintendent, with the Elders now present, do form a committee to appoint such preachers as may offer for the itinerating department, who have been ordained or licensed agreeable to Discipline.

"13. That we consider a conciliation a desirable object,

and feel ourselves bound to accede to any such conciliatory offers as may secure to preachers and people what WE conceive to be their natural rights.

"14. That the *Hamilton Free Press*, and *Reformer*, of Cobourg, be requested to give the above resolutions one insertion, and all other editors that will copy the same will confer a particular favor.

(*Signed*,) JOHN W. BYAM, *President*,
ARNON C. SEAVER, *Secretary*.

Trafalgar, March 12th, 1834."

The General Superintendent mentioned in the eleventh resolution was to be one of the Elders, and was only to act as such till the work would be regularly re-organized.

The proceedings of the convention were subjected to the usual strictures in the *Guardian*,* where the editor, forgetting what belonged to his character as a gentleman—to say nothing of the Christian or the minister of Christ—finding argument fail in his attempt to make these brethren see as he did, condescended to *abuse*, summing up a contemptuous paragraph with a quotation from another controversialist, as follows:—"*When an ass* puts on a lion's skin he ought not to *bray*."

The columns of the *Guardian* were closed against those who differed from the editor concerning the desirability, and latterly the *legality*, of the union; while he defended both with all the plausibility of which he was so abundantly possessed, and thus many were influenced, against their better judgment, to yield to his specious arguments, and give up what they were persuaded to believe would be a hopeless contest. Mr. Alder's letter to the Governor, with the "further concessions" of the Conference, was not made public.

The following specimens of the arguments used in defence of the measure by the editor of the *Guardian*, may not at this

* See *Guardian* March 26th, 1834.

date be uninteresting. Shortly after the close of the Conference,* commenting on its late action, he represents the Conference as saying:—"If ever the God of love was present in the assembly of His servants He is here; if ever He directed all good counsels, He directs now; if ever the seal of heaven stamped and ratified any negotiation of His ambassadors, it is the *articles of union between the British Wesleyan Conference and the Conference of the Wesleyan Methodist Church in British North America.*"

To oppose this compact, then, on which he asserted the "seal of heaven" was set, would be an act of such fearful wickedness that none but infidels or backslidden Methodists would be guilty of it. Such men as Rev. Messrs. Gatchel and Culp, who had the temerity to oppose the scheme, after having been ordered by the organ to keep quiet, were thus denounced; the smallness of the numbers rallying at so short a call, after such a fearful shock, sneered and scoffed at; and the work of the convention at Trafalgar compared to an "abortive tempest in a teapot." That the editor of the *Guardian* knew there was very great opposition to the union, especially with regard to the relinquishment of episcopacy, and admitted this to be so in the organ which he controlled, is proven by the following extract from that paper:—†"We invite the attention of our readers to a few observations on the question of union between the British and Canada Conferences; especially the relinquishing episcopacy. Was it done constitutionally? Was it done prudently? Did it involve the *privileges* of any member of the Church? First, was it done constitutionally? To this we answer, it was. * * * One objection has been made in a few individual instances, inconsiderately, and for want of information, mooted *against the legality* of the proceedings of the Conference in this instance, viz., that Elders elect voted in the General Conference, which was not authorized

* *Christian Guardian*, Oct. 23rd, 1833.
† *Guardian*, Dec. 25th, 1833.

by Discipline." The "information" so indispensable to the making of those proceedings *even appear* legal, Mr. Ryerson proceeded to supply, giving *his* own rendering and supplementing of the Discipline, averring that the changes *were made prudently*, and emphatically denying that the privileges of any member had been infringed.

The strictures on the Saltfleet meeting are as follows:*—"The last *Hamilton Free Press* contains several resolutions signed David Culp and Arnon C. Seaver, said to have been adopted at a meeting of local preachers of the Methodist E. Church, held at Saltfleet, December 18th, 1833. * * * The first of these resolutions states that 'Self-government is the natural right of every man, and therefore it is the right of every man to have a voice by delegation, or otherwise, in making the laws, rules, and regulations by which he is governed.'

"This is very true in a certain sense, and we can easily show that this, in all its legitimate length and breadth, is recognized and has always been acted upon in Canada. But if it be true that no man ought to obey a law that he himself, "by delegation or otherwise, has had no voice in making,' then ought Mr. Culp and Mr. Seaver to rise up in 'armed resistance' against both the colonial and British Constitutions; for we apprehend they had no voice in making either." What begging the question! But was not the voice of the people taken at the time of the framing of these bulwarks of our liberty?

The following are some of the comments with which Mr. Ryerson favored his readers upon the proceedings of the London Quarterly Meeting:—†"Various rumors, and exaggerated and erroneous statements have been of late industriously circulated by some individuals as to the disaffection of the London Circuit to the Conference. Several resolutions have

* *Guardian*, January 1st, 1834.
† *Christian Guardian*, March 5th, 1834.

been passed by some official members, purporting to be the voice of the circuit, protesting against the union, impugning the Conference; denying its authority; and refusing to receive the preachers appointed by it."* Then follows a letter from three stewards, who, though they still went with the movement, disapproved of the action of the Conference in the formation of the union, from which the editor congratulated himself that after all matters might not be so bad on the circuit as they had been represented.

The faults of Mr. Ryan, and the disastrous division in which he had taken so prominent a part, were frequently referred to; and all in opposition to the union compared to the leaders of that movement, while long homilies were read to them of the direful evils of division in the Christian Church. It would, perhaps, have been as well for the peace of the Church had Mr. Ryerson, and those who thought with him, taken these same homilies home to their own hearts before they entered upon the unconstitutional and disastrous proceedings of 1832 and 1833. After one of these editorial lectures Mr. Ryerson continued,† referring to the convention at Trafalgar: "It is likewise known that some individuals in the Methodist Church have been opposed *from the beginning* to the union between the British and Canada Conferences. Some of them have doubtless been sincere in their opposition. * * * Accordingly, after announcements in several of the public papers, calling upon the members of the Methodist E. Church throughout the province to meet on the 10th of March, at Trafalgar, Gore District, a meeting took place, and the business, we learn from a person present, commenced with seven persons. The number when our informant left, on the second day, had been increased to sixteen. * * We are

* Compare this with Mr. Ryerson's assertions in 1837 and afterwards, that there was no opposition to the measure for more than a year after.

† *Guardian*, March 26th, 1834.

forcibly reminded of the sententious remarks of Rev. D. Isaacs to the Leeds Divisionists, 'when an ass puts on a lion's skin he ought not to bray.' We answer them thus much according to their folly." How blind the people must have been, not to have been convinced at once of their "folly" by such strong arguments as this last quotation. "Here, then," he continues, "are the proceedings of the anti-unionists. Every member of the Church can now read, examine, and decide upon them for himself. The sooner each one makes his choice the better for himself and the Church." Alluding to the same convention at a later date,* Mr. Ryerson again condescended to personalities and vituperation, heading his article, "*The late schismatic* convention at Trafalgar." After discussing it in his usual sneering manner, he continues:—"Mr. Culp, the principal instigator of this campaign against the Discipline of the Church, and who has got promoted to *Bishop elect*, can do nothing, even in his own neighborhood; we will therefore dismiss this abortive tempest in a teapot." Subsequent events proved that Mr. Culp had more influence than Mr. Ryerson gave him credit for, and that the movement was not so abortive as he had hoped.

Up to this period, and for nearly four years after, Mr. Mr. Ryerson, as mouth-piece of the Canada Conference, contended that the organic changes made in the government of the Church, and the subversion of the orders in the ministry, were legally done according to the provisions of the Discipline of 1829, and that therefore, after the action of the Conference of 1833, no interval was left during which it was possible for the M. E. Church in Canada to exist. That, in fact, it *ceased to have a being* as soon as the *Conference*—not the Church through the Quarterly Conferences—passed the vote to abolish the old government and adopted the British form and polity. But when it was found that this absurdity was controverted, not

* *Guardian*, April 9th, 1834.

only by the adherents to the old Connexion, but by the decision of two separate setts of jurymen, in two separate suits, and by a majority of the judges then in the province, Mr. Ryerson, with his followers, veered round, and solemnly protested that no change had been made. The following extracts, though anticipating the date, show the course pursued,* and the reckless assertions which were made by this party in order to gain the end they had in view. Speaking of the points in dispute, he remarks:—"Not because even the form of government is changed, for that is substantially what it always has been. * * * * In the title of the Church the word *Wesleyan* has superseded the word Episcopal; the word *presidency* stands in place of the word *episcopacy*; the word *President* has got into the place of the word *Bishop*. Six words, and nothing but words, for things remain *unchanged*, essentially, substantially, practically the same." An *unordained* President the same as a *regularly ordained Bishop?* Could any thing be more preposterously untruthful?

In combatting the opinions of the judges Mr. Ryerson asserts that, "In the Wesleyan Methodist Church in Canada there are as much as ever divers orders† of ministers, Presidents, ministers or preachers, though but one imposition of hands." Quite a distinction. What was the difference between one order and the other? A President, as soon as he receives his appointment, according to this doctrine, enters into orders without any further ceremony—the mere appointment of the British Conference at once transforms a *lay preacher into a Bishop*, for the space of one year!!! The next year there is another, similarly constituted, Bishop; last year's has sunk again to his old standing and position. Thus did Mr. Ryerson first admit that there had been changes made, and that there

* *Guardian*, Sept. 13th, 1837.

† At the assizes in Kingston, in May, 1842, Mr. Ryerson admitted, *under oath*, (in answer to a question from his lordship) that in his Church there is *but one order* of ministers.

was opposition to those changes; and then, when it suited the purposes of his Church, asserted unblushingly, in the face of the arrangement with Mr. Alder concerning government grants, and of all that had been written in the *Guardian* to reconcile the people to the alterations in the Discipline, that there had been no practical changes made, and no real opposition offered till more than a year had elapsed after the ratification of the union. Whither had consistency and truth fled?

CHAPTER XXV.

The Conference of June, 1834—Where held—Contrast between that and previous ones—Preachers present—The work of this Conference—Objections raised by opponents—Objections answered and precedents quoted—Composition of the first Methodist Conference held by Mr. Wesley—Composition of the first General Conference in America—Other authorities quoted—Necessity demanded action—Who composed the General Conference of 1835—Delegates appointed to visit American General Conference—Annual Conference of 1835—Where held—State of the work—Sad effects of politico-religious scheming—The clouds begin to rise.

It had been decided at the convention to call a Conference, to meet on the 25th of June, 1834, at Cummer's Church, on Yonge Street, (now Willowdale, ten miles from Toronto) and thither the remnant of the standard bearers that was left repaired. The meeting was a sad one. What a contrast to the early Conferences in which these grey-haired veterans had taken part. Even the Conference held by Mr. Ryan, after the outbreak of the war of 1812, was not so sorrowful as this; then, a military proclamation prevented them from meeting with the brethren with whom they had before associated for consultation; now, brethren beloved, in whose integrity they had previously confided, were separated from them by their own action. The walls of the citadel were broken down, Zion languished, and *Methodism* was become a bye-word among the people. Well might they have "hung their harps upon the willows," but work, not despondency, was their motto.

Undismayed by the disadvantages under which they labored, they set themselves to the task of re-organization.

There were present at this Conference, regularly ordained Elders, Joseph Gatchell, David Culp, and Daniel Pickett; and J. W. Byam, Deacon. There were also a number of local preachers in attendance. The minutes of these Conferences were not printed, and like those of the Conferences held during the war of 1812, are not now to be found, which is very much to be regretted, as doubtless much interesting information might have been obtained from them. But the pioneers of Canada, ecclesiastical or otherwise, intent on the work before them, have left few records behind.

The Conference was re-organized, and several local preachers, who had previously travelled under the Presiding Elder, together with others who now offered themselves for the travelling connexion, were admitted. The work was re-arranged, and supplied as far as possible with the preachers at the disposal of the Conference, and every effort made to build up again the waste places—a work not easily accomplished, with every place of worship closed against them which it was in the power of their opponents to have closed.

The leaders in the Wesleyan movement at once asserted that the Conference at Yonge Street was illegally constituted, inasmuch as some of the local preachers taking part in the deliberations had not been ordained. To this it was replied, that if the pressing exigencies of the case did not justify the action of the Conference, at least the precedent afforded by both the Conferences of 1832 and 1833 did.

Mr. Ryerson asserted that the Discipline of 1829 had been amended at Belleville in 1830, so as to admit superannuated Elders as members of the General Conference, but that the amendment was not published; and that the Discipline was further amended at Hallowell in 1832, so as to admit "all travelling Elders, and Elders elect, who had travelled four years and been received into full connection."

Admitting then, that these amendments had been legally made (which, however, was not admitted) still, from a comparison of the Minutes of Conference with these amended rules, it could be proved* that both these Conferences had been illegally constituted, as parties had been allowed a seat and a vote in them who were neither superannuated Elders, ordained Elders, nor Elders elect. These persons had not even been eligible for an election to Elder's orders. Two of these were cited as instances: Mr. Thomas Bevett, who was only admitted *on trial* in 1830, would not, even according to the amended rule, have been eligible to *Deacon's* orders until 1832, and could not, therefore, have been eligible to Elder's orders until 1834—two full years after he had been admitted to vote on such an important matter as an entire revolution of the Church. But Mr. Bevett was not ordained Deacon even in 1832, there being no Bishop present. Another was the case of Mr. Charles Wood, who, though received on trial in 1828, was not admitted into the connexion in 1830, but still continued on trial till 1831, and was therefore only Deacon elect in 1832, not having been ordained in 1831 for the same reason that Mr. Bevett was not in 1832; and had he been ordained Deacon in 1831, he would not have been eligible to Elder's orders till 1833; yet he voted in the Conference of 1832. Mr. Bevett was not ordained till after the consummation of the union; Mr. Wood does not appear to have been ordained even then; they were therefore, at the time they were permitted to vote on the union resolutions, simply *laymen*. Those attending the Yonge Street Conference therefore argued —not inaptly—that in admitting ordained Deacons, and Deacons elect, to their deliberations, they had gone no farther from the letter of the Discipline than had the Canada Conference, both at Hallowell and York, when there was no exigency in the case. Consequently they felt themselves justified in pursuing the course they did, that they might keep up the old standard which open enemies and false

* See also Mr. Ryerson's evidence in the case of Belleville Church suit, Methodist Chapel Property Case, pp. 48 and 49.

friends had determined should be torn down, and though the battle was a hard one, they were enabled to keep the banner afloat, despite opposition of every kind.

But though the convening of this Conference, and the reconstruction of the work, was considered advisable, it was not really necessary for the *perpetuation* of the Methodist Episcopal Church in Canada. The Church could have existed—in fact did exist—independently of any Conference, for according to the *Discipline*, "the visible Church of Christ is a congregation of faithful men, in which the pure word of God is preached, and the sacraments duly administered according to Christ's ordinance, in all of those things that of necessity are requisite to the same." The ministry and membership together, then—not the ministry alone—constituting the "Church," their relationship is mutual; the Canada Conference, therefore, it was contended, had no more right to transfer the members belonging to the Church under its control to the jurisdiction of another body, without having *first* gained those members' consent, than the membership had to call a convention and by forming a union with some Christian body, transfer themselves and the preachers, without their consent, to its jurisdiction. The *existence* of the Methodist Episcopal Church in Canada, during the interregnum between the Conference of 1833 and that of 1834 at Yonge Street, is fully proved by submitting the facts in the case to the test of the Discipline itself. The preachers then remaining in the Church recommenced operations as well as they were able.

But who were the preachers left in the Church? They were Revs. Joseph Gatchell, a superannuated Elder, Daniel Pickett, who had travelled for years after he was ordained Elder, who was now located;* David Culp, who had been one of the little band convened by Mr. Ryan in 1812, and who

* See journal of the Niagara District for 1832 and 1833—James Richardson, Chairman, Peter Kerr, Secretary—quoted in "Union Considered."

had—not unfrequently at the risk of his life in those troublous times—carried the words of consolation to the distracted and destitute settlers, which they so much needed to hear, had been ordained Elder after the restoration of peace, and travelled for several years, but, as was customary in those days of toil, after it became inconvenient to move his increasing family, he too had located; John Reynolds, also a located Elder in good standing, and J. H. Huston, who had travelled since 1827, and was ordained Deacon in 1830. Mr. Huston was not present at the Yonge Street Conference, but was present at the convention which called it, and took part in the proceedings. Mr. Reynolds, too, though sympathizing with his brethren, was absent; but both consented to take work. J. W. Byam was a Deacon; and all these had been regularly ordained by the Bishops of the parent connexion. Of unordained men who still had travelled extensively before and up to 1833, and were now willing to take work, were John Bailey and Charles Pettis. Besides these there were, who now offered themselves for the travelling connection, George Turner, A. C. Seaver, James Mitchell, and a number of other local preachers, who were admitted on trial and stationed, thus supplying the work.

These, then, were the preachers, and this the state of the Church in June, 1834, *eight months* after the session of the York Conference of 1833. The action of the Yonge Street Conference was questioned by the Wesleyan body also in consequence of the smallness of the number of ordained preachers attending it, but their principal leader, Mr. Ryerson, himself admitted that "the spirit and rules of the Discipline, in the mode of proceeding, can be observed by three as well as by three hundred." It was objected, too, that these Elders had not travelled "the past four years." That surely would not be necessary, since, according to Mr. Ryerson, that part of the Discipline had been amended in 1830 so as to admit *superannuated* preachers, and in 1832 unordained laymen who, at the most, had travelled but *two* years, had been allowed to vote. The fact was, the necessity of the case demanded what the M. E. Conference did, and knowing the desire of the societies to have their own form of government, in the emergency they adhered as closely as might be to the letter of the Discipline, observing the very spirit of its rules in the "mode of proceeding." The Church was peculiarly situated, and unless they too would desert it there was no other course open to them. Some years later, when the Wesleyan body in Canada had quarrelled with the English Conference, the very men who so strongly objected to the course of those who convened the Yonge Street Conference, professing to doubt their *right* to hold it—the brothers William and Egerton Ryerson—themselves, after their return from England, called a Conference, and considered *they* had a *right* to do so.

It may not be improper here to enquire how near, in point of composition, the Conference which was held on Yonge Street, June 25th, 1834, resembled the first Methodist Conference which was ever held. The first Conference Mr. Wesley ever held was in London, June 25th, 1744—just ninety years, to a day, previous to the Conference held upon Yonge Street. At Mr. Wesley's first Conference there were present six ordained clergymen and a few lay-preachers, but these lay-preachers had a voice in its deliberations.

At the Conference held on Yonge Street, there were present four regularly ordained ministers, and a few lay-preachers, whose councils were considered necessary.

In the Minutes of Mr. Wesley's first Conference, dated 25th of June, 1744, we find the following questions and answers:—

"Q. 3. How far does each of us agree to submit to the judgment of the majority?

"A. In speculative things, each one can only submit as far as his judgment shall be convinced; in every practical point each will submit so far as he can without wounding his conscience.

"Q. 4. Can a Christian submit any further than this to any man, or number of men, upon the earth ?

"A. It is plain he cannot; either to Bishop, convocation, or General Council. And this is that principle of private judgment on which all reformers proceeded: "every man must judge for himself; because every man must give an account of himself to God."—See Young's "History of Methodism," pp. 136 and 137, also Watson's "Life of Wesley," chap. 9.

After transacting the business of the Conference so far, it was decided to adjourn to meet in Belleville, on the 10th of February, 1835. The adjourned Conference met at the time specified, and determined upon calling a General Conference, agreeably to the following clause of Discipline:

"If there be no General Superintendent, the Annual Conference or Conferences respectively, shall have power to call a General Conference, if they judge it necessary, at any time."*

Rev. John Reynolds was appointed General Superintendent *pro tem.*, and the General Conference was called to meet on the 10th of June, 1835, at the seat of the Annual Conference of the ensuing year. In consequence, however, of the Minutes of this Conference not having been published, the eastern preachers mistook the date, and did not assemble on the 10th, as had been appointed. The preachers who had assembled, pursuant to the appointment of the Belleville Conference, received a letter from Mr. Reynolds, requesting them to adjourn, to meet again upon the 25th of the same month, which they did, adjourning to meet at the date specified in the Trafalgar (now Palermo) meeting-house. The Annual Conference commenced its session at 2 p. m., J. Reynolds, General Superintendent, *pro tem.*, in the chair; Arnon C. Seaver was appointed Secretary.

The necessity of obtaining a Bishop, and of having him duly apppointed and consecrated according to the provisions

* Discipline of 1829, page 20.

of the Discipline was carefully discussed by the Elders in General Conference assembled on the 27th, and after due deliberation Rev. J. Reynolds was elected to that office. On the following Sabbath, June 28th, he was duly consecrated by the laying on of the hands of Joseph Gatchell, David Culp, and Daniel Pickett. The General Conference based the legality of their action, in the election and consecration of a Bishop, upon the fourth section of the Discipline,* which is as follows:—

"Q. 2. If by death, expulsion, or *otherwise*, there be no Bishop remaining in our Church, what shall we do?

"A. The General Conference shall elect a Bishop, and the Elders, or any three of them who shall be appointed by the General Conference for that purpose, shall ordain him according to our form of ordination."

The composition and transactions of the first General Conference in America, was also cited as a case in point, although in the election of Mr. Reynolds none but Elders voted. The first General Conference commenced "Christmas Eve, in the city of Baltimore, in the year 1784; sixty preachers were assembled." As none of the American preachers had, up to that date, received ordination, they were *all* lay-preachers, with the exception of Dr. Coke, Richard Whatcoat, and Thomas Vasey, and although Mr. Asbury had been appointed joint Superintendent with Dr. Coke (with the understanding that he was to be duly consecrated to the office by Dr. Coke and Messrs. Whatcoat and Vasey) yet "he prudently withheld his consent until it was obtained by the suffrages of the preachers then present, who all declared in his favor."†

The opinion of an exponent of Methodistical polity, who was received as an authority on this subject, was also quoted. The extracts referred to were as follows:—

"That very section in our ecclesiastical economy which

* Discipline of 1829, page 23.

† Bangs on Episcopacy, pp. 91 and 92.

provides for the episcopal office, and prescribes its duties and responsibilities provides for the consecration of a Bishop by the hands of the eldership, thereby clearly recognizing the principle for which I have contended; thus we read, 'If by death, expulsion, or otherwise, there be no Bishop remaining in our Church, the General Conference shall elect a Bishop; and the Elders, or any three of them, who shall be appointed by the General Conference for that purpose, shall ordain him according to our form of ordination.' This is one case of necessity, which we as a Church recognize as justifying Episcopal ordination by the hands of Elders or Presbyters."*

The same author, in referring to the local preachers who had been ordained Elders in the Methodist Episcopal Church in the United States, remarks:—

"But will any man in his senses say that because these local Presbyters have no special oversight in the Church, they are of an inferior order? Or that because a man is a travelling Presbyter he is of an order superior to a Presbyter? He is superior in *office*, not in order."† This last quotation, it was averred, was exactly in point. The Methodist Episcopal Church in Canada being pressed, as it most evidently was, by *necessity*, the "travelling Presbyters" having left it and united themselves to the English Conference, the "local Presbyters" who remained being, in point of order, equal to travelling Elders, they were justifiable, upon both Methodistical and Scriptural principles, in calling together the Conference, in their manner of calling the General Conference, and its composition, and in their election and consecration of a Bishop.

The preachers who composed this General Conference of 1835 were, John Reynolds, David Culp, Joseph Gatchell, Daniel Pickett, and John H. Huston.

John Bailey and James Powley, who had been elected to

* An Original Church of Christ, pp. 179 and 180.

† Original Church of Christ, page 48.

Elder's orders by the Annual Conference of 1835, were ordained by Bishop Reynolds, after his consecration to that office, and were appointed by the General Conference as delegates to the General Conference of the Methodist Episcopal Church in the United States, which was to meet in Cincinnati during the May following.

The Annual Conference of 1835 met also in Trafalgar, just two days before the session of the General Conference. There were reported at this time, 21 preachers, including those on trial, and a membership of 1,243. Such was the frightful havoc which division had made in the once prosperous ranks of this Church. But its sun was not set; the horizon, it is true, was overcast with clouds; compared with the past, the prospect was a sad one; but even then the mists were rising; the clouds which had settled like a pall were being gradually dispersed; the hidden light was beginning to reappear from behind its sombre curtain, to cheer and gladden the sorrow stricken. Though bowed down and deeply humbled, the crippled Church began once more to raise its head, in spite of opposition and of *persecution*. Once more it began to exercise its influence as a powerful agent for good in the province. People and preachers alike echoed the words of the Psalmist, "The Lord of Hosts is with us; the God of Jacob is our refuge."

CHAPTER XXVI.

The General Conference of the M. E. Church in the United States, Cincinnati, May, 1836—Canadian delegates repair thither—Conduct of the Wesleyan delegates—Misrepresentation—Advantage possessed by the Wesleyan delegation over the delegates of the M. E. Church in Canada—Address of the M. E. Church read and referred to a committee—Report of committee unfavorable—Report amended and adopted—Extract from report—Consequence of the action of the General Conference—Its effect on the M. E. Church in Canada—Strong in conscious rectitude of purpose, it can succeed without foreign countenance—Chapel suits—Decisions of jury—Appeals—Judges' decision—An old judge retires—New appeal—First decision reversed—Unfair questions—Replies—Other questions—Petty persecution attempted—Does not succeed—State of the work.

THE General Conference of the Methodist Episcopal Church in the United States met in May, 1836, at Cincinnati, according to appointment, and in obedience to the desire of their General Conference, the delegates from the Methodist Episcopal Church in Canada presented their credentials as representatives of their own body. Then came a bitter struggle. The strong evincing their determination to *crush* the weak—no matter by what means—upon the maxim of the old despotic nations, "*might makes right.*" The Wesleyan body had also sent delegates, and they were determined that, if they could prevent it, the representatives of the M. E. Church should not be recognized. Accordingly, they represented not only the delegates, but the entire Church, to be composed of a set of arrogant, ambitious, dissatisfied local preachers, with a few uninformed people whom they had induced to follow them, almost too insignificant and contemptible to be noticed at all.

The word "local preacher" was used as though in itself it were a synonym for everything detestable or out of order. It was represented that only those were opposed to the union with the English Conference who were opposed to all rule and wholesome discipline; and that the delegates, and in fact all the preachers composing the Conference, were utterly unworthy the confidence or respect of the American Methodists, or indeed of Christians in that or any other country.

The Wesleyan delegates possessed one very great advantage over the others, from their having an intimate personal acquaintance with so many leading men in the American Connexion, while Messrs. Bailey and Powley were personally known to but a few, and could not, therefore, exercise so great an influence upon the Conference. Though received cordially by many members of the Conference, as Christian brethren, it was soon apparent to both that the influence exerted against them by the personal friends of the Wesleyan delegates was so strong that they would not be received as an accredited delegation. Their address was, however, presented and read before the Conference, and a committee of five appointed, to whom it was referred. The names of this committee were, D. Ostrander, A. Griffith, Charles Elliott, Levi Scott, and Z. Paddock. On the 16th of May the committee brought in their report, taking a decidedly Wesleyan view of the matter. The following day, through the exertions of friends of the struggling Church, Messrs. Bailey and Powley were introduced to the Conference, and permitted to speak in behalf of the claims of their body. The Wesleyan delegates replied, repeating their old slanders, and asserting some new ones, besides bringing all their plausible rhetoric to bear against the position taken by the delegates of the M. E. Church in Canada. An animated debate followed, and the report of the committee, slightly amended, was adopted. The concluding paragraph of the report was as follows:—

"In view of all the circumstances, as far as your committee

has been able to ascertain and understand them, they are unanimously of opinion that the case requires no interference of this General Conference."

There the action of the General Conference ended for the time, the question, however, being left an open one. In the United States it did the Methodist Episcopal Church in Canada much harm, and in Canada it was productive of a very great deal of injury, being used with advantage against the interests of that Church during the progress of the church suits which almost immediately ensued.

Among the many reasons why the Wesleyan delegation were so anxious that the delegation from the Methodist Episcopal Church should not be received or countenanced, one was, lest if it were recognized, it might receive a share of the missionary funds from the parent Connexion, and also of those of the Book Concern, which—not content with receiving aid from England, and from the provincial government—they were anxious to secure for themselves.

At the time of the separation of the Canadian Methodists from those in the United States, in 1828, the American General Conference had generously recommended that the constitution of the Missionary Society should be so altered as to enable the Society to make an appropriation to the Canadian Indian missions; and had also intimated a willingness to divide the produce of the Book Concern at New York, in proportion to the number of preachers, the same as with their own preachers. At the American General Conference in May, 1832, the matter was again brought up and discussed, when it was decided that when the consent of the several Annual Conferences should be obtained, the funds, amounting to $413,-566.93½ should be "divided according to the proportion that the number of travelling preachers in the Canada Conference bears to the number of travelling preachers in the Methodist Episcopal Church in the United States, including in both estimates the superannuated preachers and those on trial."

Before the Annual Conferences could take action on the above resolution, however, the majority of the Canada Conference had determined upon another change of relation, and commenced negotiating a union with the English Conference, through Mr. Alder, and, probably in consequence of this, they (the American Conferences) decided against the division of the funds of the Book Concern.

In 1836 the matter was once more brought before the Conference, but although the delegation from the Methodist Episcopal Church in Canada was not officially recognized, in consequence of the representations of the Wesleyan delegates, yet the fund was not divided with the Wesleyan Church, as their delegates had hoped it would be. It was agreed, however, that the New York Book Room should sell the Canada Conference books at 40 per cent. discount, while the discount to ordinary purchasers should remain as it then was. The same liberal arrangement, it may be remarked, *en passant*, was entered into by the New York agents with the book agent of the Methodist Episcopal Church in Canada, on the re-establishment of their Book Concern, some years after.

The Annual Conference met, according to appointment, in Belleville, commencing its session on the 16th of June, 1836, Bishop Reynolds presiding. The preachers learned, with no little pain and some surprise, that their representatives to the American General Conference had not been officially received, and that the countenance so much needed in their bitter emergency had been withheld. The news, for a time, cast a cloud over the spirits of these toiling ones, who had already borne so much, but sustained by a conscious rectitude of purpose, and by the support of the membership, who, when they found the Church was not destroyed, nor yet absorbed in another, had begun to rally, and were now rapidly gathering under the old banner, they determined to work on bravely and faithfully, and since countenance had been withheld, prove to the Church and to the world, that strong in the strength of *right*, they would, by divine help, succeed without it.

The usual routine of Conference work was attended to, and it was found that, notwithstanding the action, or rather lack of action, of the American General Conference, the position of the Church was much more satisfactory than it had been at the previous Conference. Like the preceding one, the session was harmonious throughout. There were no laggards, no idlers, all were both ready and willing to *work* and to suffer for the perpetuation and well-being of their beloved Church, and the good of their country. True Christians, and true patriots, these.

This year the number of preachers had increased to 24, and there was reported a membership of 2390, giving an increase over what had been reported in 1835, of 1,147. Notwithstanding they were harassed in many ways, disappointed in some expectations, maligned by their enemies, and looked coldly on by those on whose sympathy they had counted, they still saw that, despite *all these* untoward circumstances, they had much reason to be encouraged, and trusting *now* on the arm of the Omnipotent alone, they started afresh to their work.

Among the numerous sources of annoyance, one very serious disadvantage under which these heroic men labored, was their ejection from the churches wherever the Wesleyan preachers had gained possession of them—and that was almost everywhere. In country places this inconvenience was remedied by occupying school-houses, or in some instances private houses, but from the towns they were shut almost entirely out, in consequence of their having no place of worship in which to meet their little flocks. In consequence, the Church lost position in these places, and thus hundreds were lost from her ranks. Many, though dissatisfied with the terms of the union, and still more dissatisfied with the working of the new organization, and therefore anxious to adhere to the M. E. Church, had no place of worship which was their own—since the other party claimed what had been theirs—and they were unable to build again, consequently they were scattered in different directions. Some, after standing aloof for a length of time, finally acquiesced in the new arrangement. Some, unable to receive the ordinances at the hands of the ministers of the Methodist Episcopal Church, and grieved at the duplicity of some of the leading men in the other Connexion, united in Church fellowship with other Christian communities, and, with their families, were lost to Methodism forever. And many, very many, dissatisfied on the one hand and discouraged on the other, halted between the two, till, their first love having cooled during the progress of the contention, they made shipwreck of faith altogether.

In some localities where the people had means, sooner than contend more for their rights, new churches were erected, but in other sections the old trustees were not willing to yield so submissively, thus the matter was brought before the civil courts for adjudication.

Some time after the union, a suit was brought by the trustees belonging to the Methodist Episcopal Church, to recover possession of the Waterloo chapel, a place of worship near Kingston. The case was tried in the Court of Queen's Bench, and the jury decided that the property belonged to the plaintiffs. The Wesleyans appealed to the judges, when two out of the three then upon the bench sustained the decision of the jury, Judge Robinson standing alone in favor of the Wesleyans. The sheriff was therefore ordered to put the old trustees again in possession of the church, which he accordingly did. Soon after, the old trustees of the church at Belleville brought a similar action for its recovery. This case, too, after a long and careful investigation, was decided in favor of the M. E. Church. From this decision the Wesleyans again appealed; this time with more hope of success. Since the decision in the Waterloo chapel case one of the old judges had retired from the Bench, and new ones of known political proclivities had been created. So well were the political affinities of the new judges known that scarcely a doubt was entertained as to what decision would be given by the new judges, with Judge Robinson as a colleague. The decision of the remodelled Bench was in favor of the Wesleyans, thus they were permitted to keep possession of the Belleville church. A new suit was also granted them in the matter of Waterloo chapel. The case again came on at Kingston, and was tried before Judge Macau'ey, one of the old judges. After reverting to his former decision in this case, and stating that he had not in the least changed his opinion on the merits of the case, he remarked that as his brother judges differed from him, and they being the majority had so decided in the Belleville case, he would advise the jury to give the new plaintiffs *one* shilling damages, and then the defendants could appeal to England for a final decision, there being at that time no Court of Chancery in Canada. This the trustees had not the means to do, and there the matter rested, it being cheaper to build another place of worship than to carry the case through the law courts of England. Had the matter been brought before these courts it is more than probable that the decision of Judge Robinson and his colleagues would have been set aside, as it was in the more recent cases of the suit of the Toronto corporation against Hincks and Bowes; and still more recently the case of the escaped slave Anderson.

One thing that militated against the old trustees was that while these suits were pending before the judges an agent was sent by the Wesleyan body to present their view of the matter to certain leading men in the Methodist Episcopal Church in the United States. These men were believed to be favorable to them, and they determined, if possible, to secure answers to carefully put questions directed by themselves. Having secured interviews with some of them and succeeded in getting them committed on the subject, the agent proceeded to get answers to his own questions, and these, with comments on them by himself, he laid before the judges so as to influence their decision.

A specimen of these productions may not be uninteresting. In a letter to Dr. Fisk it is remarked:—"A question of law is at issue in Upper Canada, which involves the chapel property held by the Wesleyan Methodist Church in that province. The principal points in the case on which there are any doubts relate to the views of the Methodist Episcopal Church respecting *episcopacy*, the imposition of hands in the consecration of Bishop, and the powers of the General Conference to modify the episcopal office." Here an opinion is asked about a *modification*, not an entire *relinquishment* of an office. Then after mentioning the names of Bishop Hedding and Dr. Lucky, who had also been consulted in a similar manner, the following question is propounded:—

"Is episcopacy held by you to be a doctrine or matter of faith, or a form or rule of church government, as expedient or not, according to time, places, and circumstances?"

To this, as it was very well known he would, Dr. Fisk returned the following reply:—"*I*, as an individual, believe, and this is also the general opinion of our Church, that episcopacy is not a doctrine or matter of faith—it is not *essential* to the existence of a Gospel Church, but it is founded on expediency, and may be desirable and proper in some circumstances of the Church and not in others."

It was very well known to the leaders of the Wesleyan body that the Methodist Episcopal Church did not hold episcopacy to be a *doctrine* or matter of faith, but contended that the Canada Conference had no constitutional power to *abolish* it. They did not contend that it was impossible for a pure Gospel Church to exist without a Bishop, any more than that a nation could exist without a king; but superseding a kingdom by a republic, they contended, would be an act of revolution. A president was not a king, nor a king a president, neither could a mere unordained president be a Bishop.

Others of the questions put to Dr. Fisk and other leading men were so worded as to apply to the powers of the General Conference of 1784, when it was bound by no restrictive rules, and therefore at liberty to adopt what form it pleased. Such a letter* was addressed to Rev. Ezekiel Cooper, who, as a matter of course, gave the desired reply. No one had questioned the power of the American Methodists, in 1784, to adopt any form of government they deemed most expedient, any more than they had questioned the power of the Congress to adopt the form of government they judged most conducive to the public good at the time of the separation from Great Britain. But the power of a subsequent Congress, restricted by a constitution, would be seriously questioned, should those composing it attempt to subvert the republic and substitute a kingdom in its stead.

In order to have obtained a fair and impartial expression of opinion from the American Methodists referred to, the questions put should have been as follows:—

1. "Has the General Conference of the Methodist Episcopal Church in the United States, with the consent of the Annual Conferences, independently of the membership, the power, at the present time, or at any time since the passing of the restrictive rules, to abolish the episcopal form of church government, form a union with the English Conference, or any other religious body who may hold a similar form of doctrine, and transfer to the Missionary Committee of that body all their mission stations?

2. "Would it be constitutional, according to your Discipline, for your General Conference, with the concurrence of the preachers alone, to accept from another body an annual President, who, though himself *unordained*, would ordain your candidates for the ministry, instead of a Bishop regularly

* See Belleville Church Suit, page 90.

chosen by the General Conference, and specially consecrated to his office, as you now have?

3. "Have your preachers power, according to the constitution of the Church, to merge your General and Annual Conferences into one, styled the Conference?

4. "Have you power in the General Conference, the Annual Conferences concurring, to abolish the two orders of Deacons and Elders, substituting one called ministers, with but one ordination.

5. "Should your General Conference make such arrangements, would you not therefore become a dependency of the body with whom you thus united; or in such a case would you still be—*de facto*—the Methodist Episcopal Church, as you were constituted in 1784? Under such circumstances would the people be bound to follow you into this union, or forfeit their membership and Church property?"

It is more than probable, had such questions as these been propounded, that notwithstanding their personal friendship for those sending them—and friendship sometimes goes very far—the answers returned by Messrs. Fisk and Cooper would not have been quite so satisfactory to their friends.

In view of all the circumstances which had transpired, Mr. Cooper's candid letter was, after all in fact, a complete justification of the ordination of Mr. Reynolds. The following is an extract:—"Stillingfleet, in his Irenicum, and other episcopal dignitaries of the Church of England, have admitted that the power of ordination is inherent in the Elders of the Church, or Presbytery; but by certain canons, made by the ecclesiastical councils, the power was restrained, for the better order and regulation in government; and our Church holds the same opinion; therefore, if by expulson, death, or *otherwise* we should be without a Bishop, the General Conference is to elect one, and to appoint three or more Elders to ordain him to the episcopal office; so that the power of ordination is in the Elders, under restraint—but the Conference, by appointment, can take off that restraint when necessary, then the Elders have power to ordain even a Bishop." * * * * *

Further on, in trying to justfy his friends in what they had done, he remarks:—"In my opinion, the General Conference had, and has, the *power* to make the episcopal office periodically elective, and if necessary for the good of the Church, to abolish it; provided the requirements of the Discipline for making alterations be complied with; or if the restrictions be removed, which there is *power* to do, and though difficult yet not impossible to accomplish; and then any and every alteration may be made which the exigencies or circumstances may call for, and wisdom may direct." Here were two admissions made by Mr. Cooper concerning the very points on which most of this unhappy controversy hung. They had, he thought, the power to make the episcopal office periodically elective, or abolish it—"*provided the requirements of the Discipline be complied with;*" and that it was contended had not been done. The Wesleyan body asserted that the Conference had the right to do away with the restrictive rules, to which it was answered that if they had, they might form a union with the Church of England, Roman Catholics, or Mormons. This they denied. Mr. Cooper's letter, however, not only bears out the inference, but roundly asserts it:—"And then *any* and *every* alteration may be made which the exigencies or circumstances may call for, and wisdom may direct." Who were to be the judges of the exigencies, circumstances, or wisdom in the case? Certainly the entire Church. But the Conference did not choose to consult the societies, or to attempt the repeal of the restrictions; they preferred to act in defiance of both.

Besides depriving the people of the Methodist Episcopal Church in Canada of their property, and maligning both its preachers and people, another piece of petty persecution attempted by those who opposed them was the exertions made to have the preachers prevented from solemnizing matrimony, by trying to use undue influence in the Court of Quarter Sessions, where, at that time, Methodists and all ministers improperly denominated *dissenters* were obliged to apply for authority to solemnize matrimony; and by asserting, both publicly and privately, that "those pseudo Episcopals had no legal right to marry, and that marriage solemnized by them was null and void." This proved but a trifling annoyance, as those sitting on the Bench of the Courts of Quarter Sessions, excepting in a few isolated instances, where one of the magistrates happened to be a Wesleyan, proved that they knew the law of the country quite as well as their would-be advisers, and intended to act upon it.

But while all this strife was going on in the law courts, decisions, appeals, decisions sustained, and decisions reversed, how was the Church prospering spiritually and numerically? Had the work of saving souls been lost sight of in the effort to save the Church property? Not so. While the conflict was still fiercely raging, the Conference of 1837 met for its annual session at Yonge Street, in the Cummer's church, according to appointment, on the 21st of June, Bishop Reynolds presiding. Arnon C. Seaver, who had so well and faithfully served as Secretary for the several past years, was numbered with the fallen. He had left a world of strife for one of peace, having departed this life, May 1st, 1837. The Conference felt his loss very deeply; humanly speaking they could ill afford to lose one of their number at this time; but they remembered that their loss was his infinite gain, and were comforted. George Turner was appointed Secretary, and the Conference proceeded to the transaction of business.

34 preachers, including those received on trial, were appointed to circuits, and there was reported a membership of 3522; an increase over the previous year of 1132.

If their churches were being taken from them, souls were being given to them, therefore they thanked God and took courage.

CHAPTER XXVII.

OPINIONS OF HON. JUDGES MACAULEY AND SHERWOOD ON THE WATERLOO CHAPEL CASE.

THE opinions of Judges Macauley and Sherwood are such able documents, and are, at the same time, so difficult of access to the majority of the general readers of church history, it has been deemed advisable to insert them in a separate chapter, in their natural relation to the transactions narrated in the foregoing one, instead of inserting them in the form of a note or appendix.

OPINION OF THE HON. JUDGE MACAULEY ON THE WATERLOO CHAPEL CASE.*

Doe ex Dem. The Trustees of the Methodist Episcopal Church for the Township of Kingston, *vs.* THOMAS BELL.	One Acre of Land and a Stone Church in the 3rd Concession of the Township of Kingston. Lease—Entry—Ouster and Possession, admitted.

The Plaintiffs made title in a corporate name, under the Provincial Statute, 9 Geo. IV. c. 2, by which it was, (amongst other things), enacted, that whenever any religious Congregation or Society of Methodists should have occasion to take a conveyance of land for any of the uses therein-before recited, (namely, for the site of a Church, Meeting-house, Chapel or Burying-ground), it should be lawful for *them* to appoint *Trustees*, to whom, and their successors, to be appointed in such manner as should be specified in the Deed, the land requisite for all or any of the purposes aforesaid might be conveyed,—and such Trustees, and their successors, in perpetual succession by the name expressed in such Deed, should be capable of taking, holding, and possessing such land, and of commencing and maintaining any action or actions in law

* The marginal references are omitted as of little use to the reader.

or in equity for the protection thereof and of their right thereto—the Trust not exceeding five acres for any one Congregation, and the Deed to be registered within twelve months. It also provides that conveyances previously made for the like purposes should (being registered) be equally valid.

The Plaintiffs claimed the premises in question, by virtue of an Indenture bearing date the 9th day of August, 1832, and made between Daniel Ferris of the one part and John Grass, James Powley, Barnabas Wartman, Gilbert Purdy, Lambert Vanalstine, Joseph Orser, Micajah Purdy, Francis Lattimore, Senior, and Robert Abernethy of the other part, whereby, after reciting the above statute and that a religious Congregation or Society of Methodists had occasion to take such a deed of a tract of land situate in the Township of Kingston, for the site of a Church and Burying-ground, and had appointed Trustees by the name of "the Trustees of the Methodist Episcopal Church in the Township of Kingston," the said Ferris, in consideration of £3, gave, granted, sold, assigned, released, conveyed, and confirmed, into the said Trustees by the name aforesaid, and their successors to be appointed in the manner there-in-after specified, a tract of land situate in the Township of Kingston, containing one acre, and therein more particularly described:—To have and to hold the same, with the building or buildings erected or to be erected thereon, to the said Trustees and their successors in the said Trust forever, for the site of a Church, Meeting-house, and Burying-ground for the use of the Members of the Methodist Episcopal Church in Canada, according to the Rules and Discipline which then were or thereafter might be adopted by the General or Annual Conference of the said Church in Canada,—in trust and confidence that the said Trustees for the time being should at all times thereafter permit any Methodist Episcopal Minister or Preacher, or Ministers or Preachers, he or they being a Member or Members of the Methodist Episcopal Church in Canada, and duly authorised as such by the said General or Annual Conference, to preach and perform religious service in the said House and Burial-ground, according to the Rules and Discipline of the said Church. It was then declared that the full number of Trustees in the said Trust should continue to be seven, and that whenever any *one* or *more* of the Trustees therein named, or their successors in the said Trust, should *die*, or cease to be a *member* or *members* of the said Methodist Episcopal Church in Canada, according to the Rules and Discipline of the said Church, the vacant place or places of the Trustee or Trustees so dying, or ceasing to be a member or members of the said Church, should be filled with a successor or successors, being a member or members of the said Church, and to be nominated and appointed in the manner therein specified.

It was admitted that Daniel Ferris was seized and had good right to convey—that the Deed had been duly registered according to the act—that there was a congregation or society such as the statute required, as therein recited, and that the conveyance operated under the statute as a Religious Trust. This closed the Plaintiff's case.

The Defendant claimed to be in possession with the assent of some of the Trustees named in the Deed, and of others who had been appointed according to its provisions in lieu of some of the original parties who had ceased to be members of the Church, and consequently that he was no trespasser, and not liable to be turned out in this Ejectment, which was said to be brought at the instance of those who had so ceased to be members of the Church, (and were therefore no longer Trustees), in conjunction with others irregularly nominated as joint Trustees with them in lieu of those under whom the Defendant held possession, and who they contended were not legally seized of the property as such Trustees.

It appeared therefore that two sets of persons claimed to be Trustees and entitled to the possession, or to use the corporate name in which this action is brought to recover or defend it. Evidence was given in the first place by the Defendant to support the right of those under whom he held. It appeared that the Methodist Church spoken of in the Deed emanated from and was formerly in connexion with the Methodist Episcopal Church in the United States; but that with the assent of the parent establishment it was in the year 1828 separated and formed into an independent body, called the Methodist Episcopal Church in Canada. That in 1829 the Conference of Preachers belonging to such Church framed a Discipline entitled, "the Doctrines and Discipline of the Methodist Episcopal Church in Canada," such being the name adopted.

In 1833 a union took place between the said Church and the British Wesleyan Connexion in England, attended with a change of name in the first place to that of "the Wesleyan Methodist Church in British North America," and afterwards "the Wesleyan Methodist Church in Canada," and in 1834 the Conference appointed under the Discipline of 1729, framed another Discipline adapted to the altered state of things. With a view to the union, it was resolved by three-fourths of the members present at the yearly Conference held at Hallowell, in 1832, that this Conference should recommend to the General Conference to pass the third resolution of the Committee on the proposed union, which reads as follows:—"That Episcopacy be relinquished, (unless it will jeopard our Church property, or as soon as it can be legally secured), and superseded by an annual Presidency, and that this Conference recommend the Chairman to call a General Conference on Monday, a. m., at 6 o'clock." The Chairman called a General Conference meeting accordingly, and the following extract shows the course pursued by them:—"A special session of the General Conference was called and held at Hallowell on the 13th of August, 1832—voted that a Superintendent *pro tem.* be elected—William Case was duly elected. Resolved, that this Conference, on the recommendation of three-fourths of the Annual Conference, having in view the prospect of an union with our British brethren, agree to sanction the third resolution of the report of the Committee of the Annual Conference, which is as follows:—'That Episcopacy be relinquished (unless it will jeopard our Church property, or as soon as it can be legally secured) and superseded by an Annual Presidency, in connection with the 10th resolution of the said report, which says that none of the foregoing resolutions should be considered as of any force whatever until they shall have been acceded to on the part of the Wesleyan Missionary Committee of the British Conference, and the arrangements referred to in them shall have been completed by the two Connexions.' The above resolution was carried by a majority of three-fourths of the General Conference. Signed, William Case, President of the General Conference."

It also appeared that, between the separation of the M. E. Church in Canada from the Mother Church, in 1828, and the period of this union with the British Connexion, no Bishop had been nominated or ordained, and consequently that no ordinations of Ministers had taken place in the Church, unless by American Bishops; but that according to the Discipline in that behalf, there were a number of subordinate Ministers entitled to become members of the General Conference, and that at the special session in 1832 all such were, by a vote of the General Conference, admitted to the same, and allowed to participate in the proceedings touching the projected union, and vote thereon. This measure was adopted as being an act of justice towards those who would otherwise have been excluded, and towards the Church whose interests were so materially involved. It also appeared that the General Conference assembled as of course, once in four years only, but that the yearly Conference might convene a special meeting if deemed expedient, and that the meeting at Hallowell was of the latter kind and not one of those provided for by fixed appointment in the Discipline.

It was not clearly proved that all those Elders who regularly belonged to the General Conference were present. It was thought they were. But the meeting took place suddenly, and there was no time to summon any that were not actually present at Hallowell. All those qualified for Elders' orders were not present nor warned, such only as were at Hallowell attending the yearly Conference were called upon. But of the members composing such General Conference more than three-fourths of the whole and of each class, *i. e.* of Elders regularly belonging to the Conference, and of those introduced as above explained, concurred in the resolution which then passed the Board.

It also appeared that the relinquishment of Episcopacy was an indispensable preliminary to the connection with the British Conference, as Wesley had not meditated it in England—and the protocol was submitted with a pledge of compliance in this respect—and in the 2nd article of the union, the Discipline, Economy, and form of Church Government in general of the Wesleyan Methodists in England, were agreed to be introduced into the societies in Upper Canada, and in particular an Annual

Presidency was adopted. In an explanatory note it was declared to be understood on both sides, that the provisions of that article referred to no other modifications in the economy of Methodism in Upper Canada than those which took place at that Conference, and that the Canadian Book of Discipline had theretofore provided for.

There was a good deal of evidence received with a view to shew how far the Trustees named in the Deed had or had not acquiesced in the arrangement, but as their assent or dissent could not govern the main questions—namely, the effect of that proceeding upon the right of property in the cestuis-que trusts, and how far those approving of the union had or had not ceased to be members of the Church mentioned and contemplated in such Deed, the facts did not seem very material beyond what I understood to be clearly established, namely, that a majority of such Trustees approved of the union, and are adherents now to the connection with the British Wesleyans—but that a minority were dissentient, and desired to maintain the former system of Church government and Discipline, and that of such minority some, or at least one, had undeviatingly objected to the change, while others had at one period acquiesced in it, but after wavering for a time, finally dissented and joined him or those who had always continued in steadfast opposition.

Of the members of the Conference a very large majority, including all the Elders, with one or two exceptions, approved of the union, and many of the laity were equally satisfied. But one or two Elders, and a more numerous portion of inferior Clergy, and of the Laity, refused to recognize it, and denied the power of the Conference, 1st, to abolish Episcopacy, and 2nd, to form such a union, placing the Church under the auspices of the British establishment, and so far under its control as to accept, as their head, a President annually appointed by the British Conference, with authority to exercise the principal functions of their former Bishop, including ordination. Owing to the foregoing differences arising out of the union, the dissentients re-organized from the remaining fragments of the original society an Episcopal system, not in strict conformity with the discipline of 1829—rendered impossible from the secession of ecclesiastical members—but as near as might be, agreeably to its rules, and with a view to a strict adherence to that Discipline. A Bishop had been elected by the new General Conference, such as they had re-formed, but he had not been yet consecrated; also, the dissentients holding all those Trustes who espoused the union to be no longer members of the Methodist Episcopal Church in Canada, proceeded to appoint others in their place; while, on the other hand, those who had acquiesced in the union, claiming to be the same Church as before, and viewing the dissentient Trustees as nonconformists to legitimate changes, or seceders, appointed substitutes to fill the places supposed to be vacated by them, and the right to recover in this action depends upon the question, which of those two classes of Trustees are now legally clothed with such trust, and seized of the estate in question. This question is conceived to be regularly raised in an ejectment, because, by the terms of the Deed, under the Statute, the original Trustees and their successors, to be appointed as therein provided, stand seized of the estate to be protected or sued for in the collective name assigned to them, and because such Trusteeship was to cease not only at death, or by voluntary relinquishment, but also upon ceasing to belong to the Church. Wherefore it formed a subject of legal enquiry which of the parties were members of the Methodist Episcopal Church in Canada, according to the Deed in that behalf.

The first consideration is whether this forms a proper subject for investigation in a Court of Law? Religious associations of the present kind, not being regular ecclesiastical establishments, are only judicially noticed in relation to their temporal interests. The Courts exercise jurisdiction over their property as charitable trusts; and in that way their proceedings are often subjected to legal or equitable scrutiny. And throughout this opinion, when I speak of the powers of the Conferences, I wish to be understood as exclusively restricting myself to their exercise in relation to the property in question, and the members of the Church interested therein.

The only object here is to ascertain by whom the legal estate in the Waterloo Church and premises is held, under the corporate name authorized by the Statute; and if those mentioned in the deed are entitled to be regarded as Trustees, *de facto*, until ousted by some direct judicial proceeding, instituted with that view, the Defendant should succeed, for a decided majority of them side with the defence; but if it is competent to the minority to prove that such persons have ceased to be Trustees, ulterior considerations must be entertained. In the event of death or secession, any one remaining Trustee would possess the estate, without regard to the regularity of succeding appointments, but unlike ordinary trusts the legal interest is transmissable to successors when vacancies occur, and the deed provides that the trust shall be vacated by any Trustees leaving the Methodist Episcopal Church in Canada, and successors have been nominated on both sides. It is apprehended, therefore, that in a litigation like the present, between two antagonist parties, each asserting a legal right to the Trusteeship, and such right depending upon membership, a Court of Law is incidentally obliged to decide upon the competence of the General and Yearly Conferences to supersede Episcopacy and accept a President from the British Connexion. There is no avowed secession by either party, all depends upon the validity of the late union, out of which the controversy has arisen. When once the legal rights of the Conferences, as leading to a discovery of the present legal Trustees, are determined, the jurisdiction of this court terminates. Any breach or misapplication of Trust, by those legally entitled, must be redressed in Equity. A Court of Law deals with the legal estate —a Court of Equity protects the equitable interests; the one looks to the legal rights of the Trustees, the other to the equitable claims of the cestuis-que trusts. Each in its sphere confines all parties within legitimate bounds, without any arbitrary discretion belonging to either. Neither Law nor Equity go beyond or stop short of the Deed.

In this Court due effect should be allowed to its legal provisions —in Chancery to its equitable objects. Whatever the Deed legally authorizes should, at Law, be upheld—what it warrants in relation to the Trusts should, in Equity, be respected. It would seem to follow that the question of membership might arise, at law, as a necessary qualification for Trustees; or, in Equity, as essential to the privileges of cestuis-que trusts;—and to whatever extent the right of membership might depend upon, and draw into judgment, any measures of the Conferences, a Court of Law would sustain their proceeding, if conducted in adherence to the modes and forms, and within the scope and compass of their constitutional authority.

Were the legal title otherwise clear, it might then become material to look minutely into the composition of the two General Conferences held in Hallowell and Toronto, in the years 1832 and 1833, for being extraordinary, and not regular quaternal meetings; according to the Discipline it would probably be requisite that all eligible members should have actually attended, or, at least, been apprized of the time, place, and objects.

The vacancy in the Episcopal office, and its consequent want of actual representation on those occasions, and the admission of ineligble parties to the discussions might likewise merit attention, as also whether the Discipline ought not to have been amended by substantive rescision of the second restriction, previous to any vote destructive of Episcopacy. But the more important inquiry whether the Conferences could, by any steps of their own, however formal, relinquish Episcopacy and substitute a yearly Presidency to be supplied by the British Conference, against the will of some members of the Church, and more especially of such dissentients as belong to the Waterloo congregation, attracts and demands prior notice.

In taking up the question, it is proper to direct attention to the rise, progress, doctrines and discipline of the Wesleyan Methodist Church in both England and America; not to canvass the merits or the defects of practical differences, but to glean information auxiliary to the construction of doubtful rules of church government. With like object other Christian Churches, Episcopal and Presbyterian, should be glanced at—not to agitate theological discussions, nor to indulge a polemic spirit, but to collect rays converging to the subject under consideration. The merits of differing systems in themselves are not involved, and their constituent parts are only important to exhibit their distinguishing features.

1. I would in the first place premise that where the Discipline of 1829 speaks of "Our Church," I understand a Protestant sect, consisting of members Ecclesiatical and Lay, with certain known

rites and doctrines—deeming the sacraments of Baptism and the Lord's Supper of holy institution, and a duly ordained Ministry important in the administration, although not made an express article of faith.

2. That by Episcopacy I take to be meant, a settled form of church government under a superintending clergy divided into a plurality of orders, and derived from scriptural authority, which I find expressly acknowledged in those parts of the Discipline that prescribe the ordination services for Deacons, Elders, and Bishops. I think the term is used in an extended sense, not restrained merely to the Head or President of the Conference, but indicating divers clerical orders appointed for the Christian Church, of which a Bishop is the principal. Not a system devised merely by man's imagination as judicious or expedient, but sincerely believed to be deduced from sacred authority. Were it obscure on this subject a perusal of the life of the eminent and pious Wesley, and a reference to the early rise and progress of Methodism until the establishment of Episcopacy, and the promulgation of the first Discipline in the American Church, would illustrate its meaning according to this interpretation.

3. It appears to me, too, that the name used in the Discipline of 1829 denotes two things:—First, that the Church is Episcopal; and secondly, that it is seated in Canada. I think that the words "in Canada" at the end had a two-fold object:—First, to form part of the name drawn from the locality, and secondly, to qualify what went before—the whole importing that it was not only a Methodist Episcopal Church, but that Church in Canada as distinct from the main body in the United States. The name "Methodist Episcopal Church in Canada" does not merely designate an isolated society of Christians, but such a society as a portion of a more extensive community of Methodist Episcopalians, and the words in the deed of trust are capable of a similar construction —See Discipline pp. 5 and 22 at the bottom.

The Wesleyan Church in England, and the Methodist Episcopal Church in America, (of which the latter is now the largest body), though originating with the same distinguished founder, form two separate and distinct societies, not one Connexion. It is true they harmonize in Doctrine, and agree in many points of Discipline; in other respects they vary, and the history of both should be traced in the different lives of the Rev. John Wesley, and other records of Methodism, to comprehend fully the bearings of the present controversy.

What follows will display some internal differences, not immaterial, so far as this case depends upon substantial distinctions between the two communities.

The brief account of the origin of the Methodist Episcopal Church in the beginning of the Discipline shews how Episcopacy was engrafted upon that Society, and that whatever Mr. Wesley might in his own mind have contemplated, its institution was understood and received by the members of that body in its true sense, touching both ecclesiastical government, and the sacred rituals, however abridged in power and authority, or deficient in rank and distinction the Bishops may be in comparison with the English Prelates. It was that step on Mr. Wesley's part which was conceived to have formed a previous religious fraternity into an independent Christian Church. He had laid the foundation, and afterward, when the superstructure was ready, thus placed the keystone in the arch, by which it was perfected and upheld as a Church, in contradistinction to a lay association of pious brethren. His object was to cement its union as a Christian Church by an ordained Ministry, to consist of Bishops, Elders, and Deacons, through all which orders Mr. Asbury (his former assistant and a zealous lay preacher) was in America the first to pass.

In England he did not pursue a similar course, nor did he attempt to convert his adherents there into a separate Church, apart from the national establishment. He was a Presbyter or held Priest's orders in that Church, and was sincerely attached to its ordinances. He superintended the British Societies in person while he lived, and at his death the government devolved upon the yearly Conferences, by virtue of his formal *Declaration* enrolled in Chancery, executed in 1784, shortly before his ordination of Coke to the office of Superintendent in America, or to the "Episcopal office," as it is termed in the Discipline. The authority of the English yearly Conference did not result from any innate right or attribute of the preachers, nor had it existed previous to the *Declaration*, further than Mr. Wesley had been pleased to divide his power with them. History informs us that the first meeting was convened by him of his own accord in 1744, to advise upon the affairs of the societies, and explains how the preachers gradually gained influence through the increase of numbers and the "Rules of future practice" from time to time adopted, and to which all conformed as binding regulations. The American Conferences were formed under Mr. Wesley's assistants, and became clothed with power much in the same way.

Previous to the year 1784 the English Conference was not supposed to possess, in a collective capacity, and in relation to the Church property, any defined character cognizable in law. Much real estate (including chapels, &c.) had been conveyed to Trustees, to permit Mr. Wesley and such others as he should appoint, at all times during his life, to enjoy the use thereof, to preach and expound God's holy word, and after his death to permit such persons as should be appointed at the Yearly Conference of the people called Methodists, to enjoy the premises for the purpose aforesaid; and it was in order to give legal identity to such Conference that the Declaration was executed. He inserted the names of one hundred preachers, and declared that they and their successors, (therein provided for) should constitute the body meant to be designated in the Deeds of Trust, when they spoke of the Conference of the people called Methodists. It was thus that the English Conference first received its *quasi* corporate or collective character, and was perpetuated; and in whatever light Mr. Wesley's organization of a Church in America may be regarded, his arrangements for the future management of the Society in England have been respected, and it is said have been allowed and maintained in Chancery. This "*Declaration*" should be examined, for under it the Society in England have been governed ever since his death. It shews that he dictated terms to the Conference in the capacity of founder, and that with the Deeds of Trust it has, in relation to the Trust Estates, always operated like a law or charter, obligatory upon them and all the members, and so the Discipline and Deed of Trust in the case before us. Mr. Wesley's Declaration is yearly recognized, and forms a guide, in its leading provisions, as doubtless the Minutes of the Conferences will testify. It will, however, be found upon inspection that this important document is silent on the subject of ordination and the sacred ministrations. *They* are not provided for as was meditated and intended in the American Church, and the omission was no doubt designed. Herein the two, as claiming to be Churches, differ materially in their organization.

It is well known that many followers of the Father of Methodism, on both sides of the Atlantic, were members of the Established Church, and received the sacraments from the regular clergy, and not from their own preachers, unless in holy orders. Also, that in England he made no effort to suppress the practice or dispense with the necessity, and that he only adopted another plan towards America owing to the peculiar exigencies of the occasion, as set forth in his letter to Mr. Asbury and the American brethren, when he ordained Coke and others to *different offices* in the Ministry. The separation from the National Church was gradual, and not completed till after his death. Indeed up to this day (there is good reason to believe) the Methodist Clergy in England are not required to administer the sacraments, nor are the laity obliged to accept thereof from them in their own houses of worship, unless both parties are willing—it is left to voluntary choice, and any reluctance on either side warrants forbearance. It is said that in Ireland a serious estrangement and division ensued upon the Conference sanctioning the distribution of the Lord's Supper in their own meeting-houses, and by their own preachers, although only extended to such as should be willingly disposed to receive the same, it being considered an innovation upon the principles of primitive Methodism. If so, such circumstances evince the delicacy of the change proposed here; and suggest the conscientious hesitation that may be felt by the present adherents to Episcopacy, in concurring in what they may deem objectionable relaxation in a matter of spiritual concern.

It has been contended that Mr. Wesley's mode of appointing lay preachers was equivalent to ordination; yet the Episcopal Discipline preserves a marked distinction between lay preachers and those solemnly ordained to the ministry by imposition of hands, under the Superintendents dedicated by Mr. Wesley to the Episcopal office in America, and the succeeding Bishops.

In the present Discipline and distribution of power, the Methodist Episcopal Church in America is not unlike the Moravians, and some others, in which, though Episcopal ordination is deemed necessary, no elevation of rank, or pre-eminent authority is allowed the Bishop, being governed by Synods or Conferences at which he presides, and to which, as an Ecclesiastical Forum, *he* is *personally* amenable, *although the office itself is not subject.* Now the Society in this Province is a scion of the Methodist Episcopal Church, and previous to the separation in 1828 it was already an organized religious body, served by ordained ministers who received whatever sacred or ecclesiastical authority they possessed from that source. It was as a component part of that Church that the separation took place. It was by a Conference of such preachers that the Discipline of 1829 was prepared for the Church in Canada, and upon assuming an independent attitude it could not be reasonably supposed that the Conferences in Upper Canada enjoyed any higher powers in their Church than belonged to the General and Yearly Conferences in the United States over the principal establishment, although they might fairly lay claim to an equal authority. And since their printed Discipline was manifestly based upon the one which must have long obtained in the parent society, the prerogatives of the two may be justly assimilated. So that this case in effect includes the question whether the American General Conference could abolish Episcopacy throughout the whole Connexion, and reduce the Church to Presbyterian rule, without affecting the right of property, however disapproved by the lay members. It might be further asked whether that body could, in addition, and though resisted by the laity, accept a yearly President, with Episcopal powers of ordination, from the British Connexion. Politically, reasons might operate against such a measure in the United States that would weigh in the opposite scale here; but it is not a political question, and mere expediency could not determine the right.

The Disciplines of both are equally comprehensive. The General Conferences are alike empowered to make rules and regulations subject to similar restrictions, and the same proviso touching the articles and doctrines of the Church and Episcopacy, and the General Itinerant Superintendency. They are equally entitled to accept a Superintendent from without, or to make internal changes within; I therefore consider the Conferences in both countries of equal authority over their respective churches, and have not failed to reflect how the same question would be probably viewed in the American courts, should it arise there in a parallel case.

In the hope that the above represents not inaccurately the subsisting relations between the two great branches of Wesleyan Methodists, and the comparative positions of the American and Canadian Churches, I approach more nearly the consideration of the governing powers of the Conferences.

These powers must accrue to them from some of the following sources:—

First,—From the original or inherent right of the Clergy to exercise unlimited jurisdiction over the affairs of the Churches, ecclesiastical and temporal, without participation or control on the part of the laity, or—

Secondly—As select bodies appointed in the first creation of their society to govern and manage its affairs as a quasi corporation, not elected by the lay members, but established in the original foundation—or gradually invested with general legislative and executive authority, or—

Thirdly,—As placed over a voluntary religious association to rule under a settled constitution, prescribed by the founder, confirmed by usage, or adopted by connexion in the nature of an accepted charter.

But on whatever footing placed, the powers of the Conference must be inherent or conferred, and if conferred, they must have been implanted in the first organization of the Society in America, or have sprung from subsequent usage under tacit assent—or have been for the first time imparted by the Discipline ultimately published—and in tracing out their privileges, the original formation, the known usages, the acknowledged Discipline, and the deed or Trust, must all be taken into view, as together embracing and explaining the constitution.

1st. Rested upon the basis of inherent right—the early history of the Christian Church—the Councils, Synods, edicts, canons, &c., would be referred to; yet I believe that by the law and constitution of England since the Reformation, the clergy of the Established Church in Convocation are not admitted to possess inherent power to make alterations in fundamental points binding *proprio vigore* upon the laity or the property, without the sanction of Parliament, and cogent reasons would withhold from the clergy of dissenting societies a more arbitrary discretion, unless explicitly accorded to them in their domestic archives. As respects their temporal concerns, it would seem just that between the ecclesiastical governing power and the lay members, their proceedings should be regulated by some fixed and stable rules in common with other religious bodies equally entitled to exemption from secular restraint.

If the establishments need parliamentary approval, dissenting congregations require the approbation of the laws operating on vested rights.

2nd. To whatever extent the constitution of any such society expressly commissions the governing power, it may freely legislate; when obscure, legal data must form its landmarks; and it appears to me that the authority claimed by the General and Yearly Conferences on this occasion must be searched for, not in primitive recesses, but in the rules and registers of their own Church.

They are select bodies, to which the government of a religious community is entrusted, under a constitution partly written, and partly unwritten. Its written depositories are the Minutes of the Conferences and the Discipline, to which (as the foundation of our jurisdiction) may be added the deed of Trust. Its unwritten evidences repose in those early and first principles on which the Society was formed, and the Discipline founded, and the present object is to ascertain the true spirit and intent of such Discipline as unfolding the constitution and pointing out the jurisdiction of the Conferences. The Discipline may be treated as principally recording what already existed, though partly introductory of new regulations; for it was prepared for the use of an association previously organized, and its object seems to have been to reduce into digested form, and adapt to local use, the articles and rules of government already subsisting in the Mother Church, and intended to be continued in this after its amicable separation, rather than to concoct a new code. Being apparently acquiesced in by the members of the Church, it should be treated as having received their general approval. I do not know that it ought to be looked upon precisely in the nature of a subscribed document, though I am disposed so to treat it for the present, especially whenever it affirmatively introduces new regulations, or positively recognizes old ones. This case, however, depends much upon the construction of doubtful passages, not original in the Canadian Discipline, but transferred from the American edition, when revised for the use of the Church in this province, and in which they must have existed for a long series of years. Their early date in the Methodist Episcopal Church may be inferred from the mention of Superintendents instead of Bishops.

In distinguishing between what is inserted as already in force, and that which is adopted *ab origine*, it is at the same time proper also to notice those regulations of internal economy which *are embraced*, and those prominent outlines which are *omitted*. We do not perceive that it laid down as rules:—That Episcopacy should prevail; that there should be three clerical orders; or that there should be General and Yearly Conferences—all these, and much more, are assumed. They existed already as fundamentals, and formed the substratum of the Discipline. The system in its main pillars was already established, and provision was only wanted for completing and giving symmetry to its interior divisions. It must have been by the Head Conference of the infant Canadian Church that the Discipline was prepared; and they must have already had full power to make rules and regulations before the Discipline existed—at least they must have assumed, upon some previous footing, whatever authority they undertook to transfer to others *Nemo plus juris in alium transferre quam ipse habet*; for they spontaneously drew up and published it as within their province, and earnestly recommended it to their brethren.

After briefly noticing the rise of Methodism, and the origin of the Methodist Episcopal Church, and inserting the articles of religion, they treat of the future Conferences; first asking what are the regulations and powers belonging to the General Conference, taking it for granted there was to be one, possessed of power, but subject to regulation. The three important topics are contained in the answer: first, the affirmative, or enabling clause, declaring that they should have full power to make rules and regulations for the Church, under certain restrictions. Secondly, the two first restrictions, prohibiting their changing or altering the articles or doctrines of the Church, or any part or rule of their government so as to do away Episcopacy, &c. And, thirdly, the proviso that, nevertheless, the two Conferences should *suffice* to *alter* any of a series of restrictions, including the first and second. The restriction and proviso do not say in terms that they might do away Episcopacy, nor does the enabling clause; it is said to be inferrable from the three construed together. But in the first place, did the power to dispense with Episcopacy exist *a priori* in the Conference which compiled the Discipline, or would it have resulted to the General Conference unless restrained, either, first, upon general principles, or secondly, from the enabling clause?

The Conferences are not elected bodies, representing their societies; they were set over them by the founder, or the order of events, they were submitted to, and without stopping to enquire to what degree the original founder might have remodeled a constitution which he had designed, after once setting it in motion, I am persuaded that no select body in the situation of these Conferences will be found entitled to a higher or more unrestrained discretion than a representative institution; and that whether regarded in a representative capacity, or as the original focus of power, they will be circumscribed by constitutional bounds, beyond which they cannot legally pass. I take it to be a rule of corporate governments, that whether vested in select bodies or in the members at large, or in delegated representatives of the latter, such bodies, while they enjoy an inherent or implied right to make by-laws, cannot transgress those limits which their constitutions, soundly expounded, expressly or constructively assign. The trust is supposed to be accepted on the one side, and yielded on the other upon this mutual understanding; and any such select body would be especially inadequate to subvert the constitution, or to introduce organic changes not consistent with the integrity of the structure, such as doing away a co-ordinate or component part, surrendering their own delegated power to strangers, or adopting any suicidal act destructive of themselves as integral portions of the establishment.

Viewing the Methodist Episcopal Church and the Conferences in this light, no vital change would be admissable, not compatible with the relative situation and duties of the latter towards the former, over which they were appointed to preside.

3rd. In the instance of mere voluntary associations acting under written articles, the rules of law would be found still more rigid and inflexible. I infer, therefore, from analogy to adjudged cases respecting corporations and voluntary societies, that the general undefined powers of internal management, allowed to administrative bodies over religious associations, should not be deemed more comprehensive than may be fairly considered incidental and necessary to the government and well-being of the same. And I do not think the General Conference can be sustained to the extent advocated on grounds of the last kind. Yet a more extensive discretion than ordinary might have been conferred by the members of the Church, through the tacit adoption of the Discipline, and in this document the right claimed is supposed to be embodied. If so, it must be contained in the enabling clause, for the restriction and proviso, however they may help to explain its meaning, do not, of themselves, superadd any thing affirmative. Then, does the clause itself give, or do the restriction and proviso lend to it that explanation which supports the rights asserted? I believe it is a rule of construction that restrictive provisions may be inserted from extreme caution without actual necessity, and without implying concession, or be introduced as essential limitations to abridge undoubted power; when questionable, judicial discrimination must determine the proper application.

The object here is to find out the true boundaries of the enabling clause—the restriction is referred to in aid of the solution; with the same view the proviso is taken into account, and for like reasons other portions of the Discipline and collateral circumstances demand attention.

In my humble opinion there was nothing in the affirmative clause calling for the first and second restrictions; to such extent, I think, the rules of law already restrained it, and had no others been imposed, it is not probable the proviso would have followed. It equally applies to several other restrictions, some of which might in progress of time be found to want modification or amendment; even those words in the second ("any part or rule of government") might afterwards be thought to require alteration, without weakening or affecting the prohibition respecting Episcopacy

At best it does not seem to contemplate the total recision of those restrictions; in terms it only speaks of their alteration, and distinguishes between doing away and altering. Most liberally taken it would not do more than sanction their repeal; and if revoked, the character of restraint would be entirely lost; they would not remain altered restrictions; and at all events, no new or affirmative law could result from their exclusion.

The power of the General Conference would consequently depend upon the enabling clause, explained by the restriction and proviso, but in connection with the rest of the Discipline and the tenets of the Church.

The members of the Yearly Conference in the United States which composed the first Discipline in the Methodist Episcopal Church, not being professional men, and doubting the legal effect of the empowering clause, may, to some necessary restraints, have added others that the law would have raised, and the proviso may have been extended to the whole inadvertently, or in the belief that no future Conference would be more disposed than themselves to disturb the settled order of the Church. The word "suffice," in this proviso, is a little remarkable, as importing a conceived previous authority in the whole to do whatever it contemplated.

Taking into view the whole Discipline, and not treating it as delusive in many grave particulars, but attributing to those who penned it, and to those who adopted it, religious sincerity in the premises, I cannot collect that the real spirit and intention of the general enabling clause sanctioned the relinquishment of Episcacy, as comprehended in the rules and regulations of the Church, thereby authorized to be made. It does not appear to me to constitute properly a rule or regulation for the Church, but a radical change in a constituent portion of the Church itself, and incompatible with the principles upon which the Society originally acquired the character of a Church, not only in the system of government, but in the appointments and functions of its ministry.

The admission of divers orders to be ordained by Bishops with imposition of hands in the language set forth in the eloquent and impressive prayers for the ordination services—the general superintendency of consecrated Bishops, and the scope of the disciplinary provisions throughout, appear to me to forbid the inference. I gather from thence that Episcopacy may be esteemed by many members of that Church upon two grounds:—First, as a judicious plan of mere Church government; and secondly, as of scriptural appointment, and peculiarly important in relation to the sacred ministrations; and I cannot say that those who adhere to such a system have not a legal right to be secured in the enjoyment of property obtained under it, and intended for its support.

It may be said that Episcopacy is not an essential ingredient in Methodism; but the term Methodism does not strictly imply a Church perfect in itself, and, if it did, it conveys no definite idea. An Episcopal, a Presbyterian, or a Methodist Church, designates no particular sect of Christians, for several classes range under each. In the Christian Church there are various separate bodies, some differing principally in doctrines and articles of faith, others principally in matters of government and orders of ministry. So in Methodism, there are several distinct societies—even the Wesleyans are subdivided, not only as between England and America, but in England alone—differing not in doctrine, but in church government and discipline. Wherefore, to point out any single society some adjective quality must be used to characterize it—as British Wesleyan, or Episcopal Methodists. It is evident these two branches have, since Mr. Wesley's death, grown and flourished under different circumstances; in America, Episcopacy being cherished; in England, disregarded, and at present a perfect analogy does not hold either between the two societies, or between the original founder and the succeeding Conferences. Of the former it may be said, that in England he formed and presided over a religious society; but that in America he formed and established a separate Christian Church. Of the latter, it may be predicated, that of both associations he was the prime mover and overseer, but that the Conferences followed under him in subordination to a system already matured and *sealed* by him—through his *Declaration* in England, and his *ordinations* for America.

Then it has been asserted of the Episcopal Methodists, that while they reject in terms the ministry of Presbyters, they do but conform to that of Bishops—that Mr. Wesley, being himself but a Presbyter in the Church of England, could not ordain at all, certainly not to any higher order than his own, even admitting his power to do so much, and that he could not by any act or ordination of his establish the Apostolic Church in the American Society. It may be so thought by Episcopalians of other churches Presbyterians may entertain contrary ideas; I shall not pretend to pronounce any opinion upon the subject. He may not have designed introducing Episcopacy, or he may have regarded Apostolic succession as a fable, or have looked upon Bishops as one order, though different offices. These are debateable points not calling for discussion here. Whatever he intended or thought, it is certain that Mr. Coke was already a Presbyter or Elder in the English Church, and yet that on his mission to America Mr. Wesley ordained him by imposition of hands to the office of *Superintendent*, and at the same time, with the like ceremonials, ordained two of the lay preachers (Messrs. Whatcoat and Vasey) to be Elders in the American Church—he being assisted by other Presbyters of the National Establishment, and no doubt he assumed and meant to exercise the prerogative of thus perfecting the Church in America in relation to the holy ordinances, the ministry, and form of government; in doing which we are assured that he preferred the episcopal mode to any other.

In the opposing sentiments of subsequent writers, touching the motives and effect of those ordinations, and their subsequent continuance in the American Connexion, it is not only safest, but on this occasion most proper, to adhere to the Discipline of 1829, because it must display most satisfactorily the sense and construction of those immediately interested, touching their true character and received meaning. The material consideration is, what are the sincere and conscientious sentiments of the Episcopal Methodists themselves; what are their notions of scriptural doctrine relative to the government, ministry, and ordinances of their Church?

Collecting them from the Discipline in evidence, we learn that they are "founded on the experience of a long series of years, and on the observations and remarks made on ancient and modern churches," that provision was deemed requisite for divers orders of ministers, as being of Divine appointment, and that the Conferences were fully satisfied of the validity of the Episcopal ordinations of Coke and Asbury, the two first Superintendents or Bishops placed over them.

It is not for me to gainsay this, or to investigate all the grounds on which the supposed validity of those ordinations were rested. Whether it was deemed competent to Mr. Wesley, as the father of Methodism and in holy orders, or as the head of an extensive religious society which Providence had raised up under his auspices, or as a case of emergency in which spiritual agency was believed to have hallowed the act, I know not. The members of the Conference, for themselves and in behalf of their people, were satisfied of their sufficiency, and a universal acquiescence confirmed the sentiment. How deeply the minds of Episcopal Methodists may be religiously imbued on these interesting subjects, I cannot tell. It is probable a unison of feeling does not prevail; indeed the recent change affords example that with many they form no matter of conscientious scruple; for numbers of learned, sincere, and pious members, both clerical and lay, have not hesitated to conform to the Discipline of their British Brethren. Yet they are dissentients, and it is their refusal to concur that has led to this suit; and from the whole tone and contents of the Discipline of 1829, I cannot refuse to them the right to entertain, sincerely, conscientious objections against a change which they may deem substantial, however congenial to others. Nor upon comparing the method pursued by the English Conferences in appointing to the ministry, with that adopted in America, do I discover that the present yearly President can be considered (in relation with Episcopacy) an effectual substitute for the former Bishops in the Canadian Church. I do not understand that the English Conference ordains by imposition of hands, in conformity to episcopal usage, or that their appointments to the ministry have been made and continued under persons sacredly invested by Mr. Wesley, as the American Church deems Mr. Coke and the two Elders who accompanied him to have been; or that upon being nominated to the office of President over the Canadian Society, any ordination is superadded as, in Coke's instance; although on reaching this province he is permitted to ordain candidates for the ministry here, by imposition of hands and a solemn service, assisted by brother preachers. It is true the Discipline of 1833, in the ordination service, (designedly or accidentally) acknowledges, in the same language as that of 1829, the appointment by the Holy Spirit of divers orders of ministers in the Church of Christ. Still I do not find that the British Wesleyan denomination contains more than one, likened unto Elders, but styled Ministers—contrary to the Episcopal Discipline, which provides for three (exclusive of lay preachers) called Bishops, Elders, and Deacons, without any designated by the general term Ministers. The dissentient members of the Methodist Episcopal Church may feel repugnant to such arrangements. They may not look upon the union as a mere change of name, but as indicating a serious deviation in church government and the calls to the ministry—and in my construction of their Discipline, I cannot deny them the right sincerely to do so on plausible grounds. The American Connexion is professedly episcopal—the British is practically presbyterian, and whatever distinguishes the one from the other, would equally distinguish "the Methodist Episcopal Church in *Canada* from the British Wesleyan Church in *Canada*," although the difference may not be so great as necessarily to destroy the identity of a Society, which, being the one, had been transformed to the other. The identity would be preserved if the change was legally accomplished.

Still it seems to me that the projected union would separate the Canada Connexion from the Methodist Episcopal Church altogether, and attach it to another body. It would take from it the character of episcopacy. It could not, at one and the same time, constitute a branch of the Methodist Episcopal Church, and of the British Wesleyan Society; but would be translated from the one to the other. So the members joining the one would leave the other, unless avowedly adherent to both. And when they become dissentient among themselves touching the preference, it cannot be urged that Mr. Wesley, by any thing he did, established a Presbyterian Church in England, any more than an Episcopal one in America.

If argued that since the American Conferences accepted Coke and Asbury as Bishops, they might have rejected them, and consequently may at any time dispense with their successors, it might be answered that until their arrival and recognition the Church was confessedly deficient. That Mr. Coke and the two Elders whom Mr. Wesley ordained (although there was anxiety on the subject) were not sent over as tendered by him for acceptance in the United States, but as appointed by him to supply the ministrations of the Church, under supposed competent ecclesiastical authority; for the language of his historians shews that up to this period he did not consider it a Church, but that in what he devised and did it was his design to make it one, as his letter to Mr. Asbury abundantly manifests. Mr. Coke's previous letter to him will help to explain how far the imposition of hands, and an episcopal order or office were thought to be important in the eyes of the American brethren; and Mr. Coke's conduct, subsequent to his arrival in America, exhibits his anxiety to persuade them all of the scriptural authority and efficacy of Mr. Wesley's ordinations, and with which the Discipline has ever since declared them to be satisfied.

Even could the American Conference have rejected Mr. Coke, (which, strictly speaking they could not, without rejecting Mr. Wesley also), it would not follow that the acceptance made was not a final step, not to be retraced; or that episcopacy would not have been eventually espoused from some other quarter.

If the Conferences could not lawfully enforce the late change in opposition to dissentient parties, it follows that as over the Church the attempt was a nullity, and that no alteration was in fact accompliished; also that their adherents left its pale and became component parts of another body, or else formed a new and separate society; the nonconformists would still continue in her communion, and might reorganize themselves and fill the Church with a qualified ministry, ordained by Bishops of the parent establishment. The property, too, would remain to their use.

I consider examples drawn from revolutions in National Churches inapplicable. They beg the question. On such occasions the change really takes place by adequate and permanent authority beyond the reach of higher control, and in the eyes of the municipal law a *change* is made. Here the gist of the controversy is whether any actual *change* has by sufficient authority been effected. If there has, all is well. If the power was wanting, the effort must prove abortive. Here the laws of the country predominate, and the right asserted being denied, is brought to a judicial test. If it existed, all are bound—if not, the Church and property remain *in statu quo*, and although many of the members may have departed, the use would be to those who refused to follow.

It may be objected that my views would exact perfect unanimity throughout the Society, to warrant the step taken, with security to the property. On the other hand, it might be replied that if the Conferences enjoyed the large powers claimed, a sufficient majority could not only reverse the whole system of government, but change the articles and doctrines—for the first restriction being removed would admit the latter as much as the removal of the second would allow the former—and *that*, notwithstanding the dissent of the minority of the ministers and all the laity; and the property would attend the change. Such extravagant suppositions do not, in my estimation, strengthen their pretensions, for a court of law cannot speculate upon the influence of moral checks. In deciding whether a power exists its possible exercises must be contemplated.

Further, upon a close attention to the terms of the Trust it would be difficult to point out how they could be fulfilled according to the recent change, consistently with the existence of independent Methodist Episcopal Churches in Canada, and in the United States. The estate is declared to be for the use of the members of the Methodist Episcopal Church in Canada, according to the rules and Discipline thereof, &c., with leave to *any* Methodist Episcopal ministers or preachers, being a member of such Church, and duly authorized by the Conference, to preach in the edifice mentioned in the Deed; which would allow the admission of any Methodist Episcopal minister duly ordained in the American Methodist Epicopal Church, or of any members belonging to that Connexion; all of whom would now be excluded, and those of the British Wesleyan Society substituted.

It is not a satisfactory reply that the assent of the Conferences being a condition precedent, might be withheld from Episcopalians; no arbitrary refusal on their part could have been anticipated when the Trust was declared. Other difficulties might arise, too, should all the trustees at any after time die or secede, from a want in the Wesleyan Methodist Church in Canada of a Quarterly Conference, as distinguished from a Quarterly Meeting, according to the Discipline of 1829, to which allusion is made in the conveyance.

After the best consideration, it is my humble opinion, as at present informed, restricting myself to the estate in question :—

1st. That the Deed of Trust does not in itself expand the powers of the Conferences over the property, beyond what the Discipline recognized or conferred.

2nd. That touching episcopacy, the Discipline conferred no new power, either in the enabling clause itself, or assisted and explained by the second restriction and the proviso.

3rd. That no power to do away episcopacy resulted or existed in the Conferences, either upon the original principles of the Church in its formation, or in their ultimate appointment over it, so as to bind the property, notwithstanding the disagreement of those members opposed to its relinquishment.

Consequently that the late arrangement was not within their authority.

1st. Upon original clerical rights under the law of England—or,

2nd. As a select body intrusted with the government of a religious association compared with corporate bodies—or,

3rd. In the light of a mere voluntary society under written articles.

Paying regard—

1st. To the inherent rights of the Conferences.

2nd. The original constitution of the Methodist Episcopal Church.

3rd. Subsequent usages; and,

4th. The Discipline and Deed of Trust; and looking particularly to,

1st. The empowering clause.

2nd. The restrictions; and,

3rd. The proviso—and construing the whole together as illustrating the meaning of those portions most material and mainly relied upon.

Consequently, that those of the Trustees who dissented are entitled to recover—the Church in whose bosom they remain having undergone no organic change—and that the others, as respects the legal title to the property in dispute, must be considered to have discontinued their membership and vacated the trust.

Such judicial authority as I have been enabled to consult seems to me to support the conclusion at which I have arrived.

When religious congregations like the present disagree among themselves upon leading points of government or doctrine, the original system attracts primary notice, and the rule I extract is, that when a religious congregation, society, or church, dissentient from the established church of England, is once completely organized with known doctrines, and a settled form of government, and property is afterwards given to or purchased for the use and support of such establishment, it is not *quoad* such property competent to one part (whether of a select body or of the whole Connexion) to change the doctrines or to remodel the government, or to adopt new doctrines, or a different economy, against the will of the residue; but that when they are dissentients, the original constitution of the association must be upheld, unless where it may, on the face of it, impart more ample powers in unequivocal language.

If this rule be sound, I have endeavored to apply it to the present case. The changes intended here appear to me equally substantial with some of those mentioned in the cases alluded to, and at least sufficiently so to bring this within the spirit of the rules by which they and other analagous decisions were governed.

I would refer to Attorney-General *vs.* Pearson; Per Lord Chancellor:—If it turns out that the institution was established for the express purpose of such *form of religious worship*, or the teaching of such particular doctrines as the founder has thought most conformable to the principles of the Christian religion, I do not apprehend that it is in the power of individuals having the management of that institution, at any time to alter the purpose for which it was founded, or to say to the remaining members:—"We have changed our opinions, and you who assemble in this place of worship for the purpose of hearing the doctrine, and joining in the worship prescribed by the founder, shall no longer enjoy the benefit he intended for you unless you conform to the alteration which has taken place in our opinions."

In such a case I apprehend (upon authority in the House of Lords upon an appeal from Scotland previously referred to) that where a congregation become dissentient among themselves, the nature of the original institution must alone be looked to as the guide for the decision of the Court; and that to refer to any other criterion, as to the sense of the *existing majority*, would be to make a new institution, which is altogether beyond the reach, and inconsistent with the duties and character of this Court.

I must here advert to the principle which was I think settled in the case to which I referred the other day as having come before the House of Lords on an appeal from Scotland, namely, that if persons seeking the benefit of a trust for charitable purposes should incline to the adoption of a different system from that which was intended by the original donors and founders; and if others of those who are interested think proper to adhere to the original system, the leaning of the Court must be to support those adhering to the original system, and not to sacrifice the original system to any change of sentiment in the persons seeking alteration, however commendable the proposed alteration may be. Upon these grounds I have nothing at all to do with the merits of the original system, as it is the right of those who founded this meeting-house, and who gave their money and land for its establishment, to have the trust continued as was at first *intended*.

2. Jac. & Walker 247, the Lord Chancellor said it was settled in the House of Lords that when the doctrines originally agreed to are not adhered to by all the Congregation, some having changed their religious opinions, the chapel must remain devoted to the doctrines originally agreed on.

The case alluded to in the House of Lords is reported in 1 Dow, P. C. p. 1-16, it is believed, or in 2 Bligh 529, Craigdallie *vs.* Aikman, *et al*; where it was said that if the members of the congregation who had left the Synod, (maintaining that they were the true church and that the Synod had departed,) adhered to the original doctrines of the church, for the support of which the Trust was originally created, they were entitled to the property, notwithstanding their secession. Inquiry was ordered on this head, but the court below reported that they could not find any material and intelligible distinction between them on the subject of doctrine, and that they differed only in some immaterial point in regard to the form of an oath, in consequence of which the decision of the court below against the seceders was affirmed.

I have not seen this report, and rely upon the statements I have met with elsewhere. Wood & Williamson's arguments, p. 55. See also ib. p. 162–3. Ewing's Op. 27–76.

AMERICAN CASES.

20 Johns R. 12—Trustees of the Reformed Calvinist Church of Canajoharrie *vs.* Diffendorf. 7 Halstead Den *vs.* Bolton *et. al.* 3 Dessausure 557, a case between two Masonic Lodges. 5 Mass. 554, 4. ib. 389, 2. ib. 435, 8. ib. 96. C. J. Ewing's opinion in Shotwell *vs.* Hendrickson & Decew, 27, the celebrated Quaker case involving a consideration of the dispute between the Orthodox Quakers and the Hicksites. He says we are not to interfere with their church government any more than with their modes of faith and worship. We are to respect their institutions and sustain them.

1 Dow, 16 Lord Eldon says, "The Court may take notice of religious opinions as facts, pointing out the ownership of property, Post (2.)

3 Mer. 412–13. Upon the clause respecting the desertion or removal of any of the Trustees which occurs in this Deed also, and contemplates the event that "the Trustees might change or become of any other religion (by providing [p. 362. 273] that when and as often as any of the Trustees should die, or desert, or forsake the said congregation, and should change or become of any other religion or persuasion whatsoever contrary to, and different from, the said congregation, then the surviving or other Trustees, &c., within days after such death, or *desertion*, &c., appoint others, &c.) I must observe, that if the question comes before the court in the execution of a Trust, whether a Trustee has been properly removed, and that point depends upon the question whether the Trustee has changed his religion and become of another different from the religion of the rest of the Society, it must be *ex necessitate* for the court to enquire, what was the religion and worship of the Society from which he is said to have seceded, not for the purpose of animadverting upon it, but in order to ascertain whether or not the charge is substantiated, &c.

3 M. & S. 488. Where several persons formed a company for brewing ale, and entered into a Deed by which it was agreed that the conduct of the business should be confined to two persons and the trade carried on in their names; should be Trustees and bring actions, &c.; that a *Committee should be appointed with power to make rules, orders and by-laws*, subject to confirmation by a majority of the proprietors at a general meeting, and that a general meeting of the members of the Company should be holden every quarter.

Also that the Directors, for the time being, should have power to direct and regulate the general affairs of the company. The Directors recommended the general quarterly meeting to appoint only one instead of two managers, who accordingly appointed the Plaintiff, who sued the Defendant (one of the Company) for beer sold. Lord Ellenborough said it did not appear the Defendant had notice of the appointment of one only—that a change had been made in the constitution of the company which could not be made without the consent of the whole body of subscribers. It was such a substituted alteration in its constitution as required the assent of all, and it was not shown that the Defendant *acquiesced* or even *knew* of the alteration. Bayley J. It is stated that the subscribers appointed the Plaintiff. If by that had been meant *all the subscribers, it might have made a* difference.

My opinion confined to the subject of Episcopacy, renders of secondary importance the power delegated to the British Conference touching the Presidency. Were it necessary to express an opinion on that head, I am disposed to think it was not in the discretion of the General Conference to subject the office to another jurisdiction, so as to place the right of electing the Head of the Church which belonged to themselves by the terms of the Discipline, in the hands of another body with which the Church had not enjoyed any previous inter-communion or immediate connection. And as little would it seem justifiable in the same Conference to merge its own existence in a new yearly Conference differently constituted.

JUDGE SHERWOOD'S DECISION IN THE WATERLOO CHAPEL CASE.

This action is brought to recover the possession of one acre of ground, in the township of Kingston, in the Midland District, which was conveyed by one Ferris, to the lessors of the plaintiff and others in fee, as "The Trustees of the Methodist Episcopal Church in the Township of Kingston, for the site of a church and burying-ground, for the use of the members of the Methodist Episcopal Church in Canada." The deed was executed on the 9th day of August, 1832, at Kingston, whereby the said Ferris, for the consideration of £3 of lawful money of Upper Canada, did give, grant, bargain, sell, assign, release, convey, and confirm to the said Trustees, the acre of land in question, to have and to hold to the said Trustees and their successors forever, for the use of the members of the Methodist Episcopal Church in Canada, *according to the rules and Discipline which now or hereafter may be adopted by the General or Annual Conference* of the said Church in Canada, in trust and confidence that they the said Trustees, for the time being, shall at all times thereafter permit any Methodist Episcopal minister or preacher, he being a member of the Methodist Episcopal Church in Canada, and duly authorized as such by the General or Annual Conference to preach and perform religious service in the said house and burying-ground, according to the rules and Discipline of the said Church." The deed then provides the manner in which the succession of each Trustee shall be appointed, and limits this election of each successor to the members of the Church exclusively; and expressly directs that when a Trustee *ceases to be a member of the Methodist Episcopal Church in Canada*, he shall then cease to be a Trustee. This deed was intended to be made conformable to the provisions of the Provincial Statute, 9 Geo. IV. ch. 2, entitled "An Act for the relief of the religious societies therein mentioned," the preamble of which is in the following terms: "Whereas religious societies of various denominations of Christians, find difficulty in securing the title of land requisite for the site of a church, meeting-house, or chapel, or burying-ground, for want of a corporate capacity to take and hold the same in perpetual succession; and whereas it is expedient to provide some adequate relief in such cases," the statute then enacts, "that whenever any religious congregation, or society of Presbyterians, Lutherans, Calvinists, Methodists, Congregationalists, Independents, and Baptists, Quakers, Menonists, Tunkers, or Moravians, shall have occasion to take conveyance of land for any of the uses aforesaid, it shall and may be lawful for them to appoint Trustees, to whom and their successors, to be appointed in such manner as specified in the deed, the land requisite for all or any of the purposes aforesaid may be conveyed; and such Trustees and their successors in perpetual succession, by the name expressed in such deed, shall be capable of taking, holding, and possessing such land, and of commencing and maintaining any action or actions in law or equity, for the protection thereof, and of their right thereto."

The execution and registry of the deed, according to law, were proved at the trial; and it was also shown that two or more of the lessors of the plaintiff were mentioned in the deed as the grantees of Ferris. The plaintiff, therefore, made out a *prima facie* case; sufficient to entitle him to recover in this action, unless there is something in the evidence on the part of defendant to do away the apparent legal right on the other side. Before I proceed to examine the objections of the defendant, I will state what I conceive to be the point on which this action must ultimately turn, which is this: In whom is the legal estate vested?

Another important inquiry may at some future period be instituted, namely, whether the legal owners have duly executed the trust reposed in them by the grantor for the proper use and benefit of those who were entitled to the beneficial interest of the estate; but that is a matter exclusively within the jurisdiction of an equitable forum, where the trust estate is recognized and protected to the full extent of the protection afforded to the legal estate in a court of law. The object of a trust may sometimes change by a change of circumstances, but the legal estate in my opinion, must exist in strict conformity with the principles of its original formation, if it exist at all; and the party clothed with the legal estate can recover at law even against the party himself, who is entitled to the equitable estate. 8. T. R. 118; 5 East 138; 11 East 334.

If the trustees are grantees by the deed, the terms of the instrument must determine what estate thay have, 8 East 248. When the grant is made to trustees and their successors, as a corporate body, and it becomes impossible to appoint successors according to the terms of the charter or of the instrument under the authority of which successors are to be appointed, then the body politic is necessarily dissolved, which dissolution is the civil death of the corporation itself; and in that case their lands and tenements would revert to the person who granted them, or to his heirs, because the law annexes an implied condition to every grant of this kind, that if the corporation be dissolved the grantor shall have the lands again. Cok. Lit. 13 B.; Gotbolt, 211; Moore, 283. The grant is only during the life of the corporate body, which, it is true, may last forever, and is put an end to by the actual dissolution of the corporation, the grantor takes it back by reversion, as in the case of every other grant for life. 1 Blk. Com. 484. If land be conveyed to an individual in his natural capacity as Trustee for another person, and the *cestui que trust* dies without heirs, the Trustee shall hold the land for the benefit of himself, and it shall not escheat to the king or lord paramount for want of an heir of the *cestui que trust*, as in Wheate *ats.* Burgess, 1 Blk., Rep. 123, where the whole question is elaborately discussed. It is very different in principle where the land is granted to a corporation, as I have already shown.

The Trustees in this case could not have been made a body corporate under the principles of the common law, for the purpose of holding the fee simple of any real estate for the use of others.—Plow 102–538. But the power of giving existence to this corporate body as it now is, originates entirely in our Provincial statute. All corporations are mere creatures of the law, established for specific and special purposes, and derive all their powers when formed by statute from the act which creates them; and consequently it is incumbent on them to show their authority for acting, and always to limit their acts to the exact rule, manner and subject matter prescribed to them by the law.—3 Bar. & Al., 12. 3 Bar. & Adol. 284.

The statute 9 Geo. IV., ch. 2. empowers the religious societies or congregations of Christians therein enumerated, to purchase and hold in fee a quantity of land not exceeding five acres, to be held for the chapel or church, and for a burying ground; and to enable them to secure to the society the benefits and advantages contemplated by the legislature, the Act gives them the following powers: first, to appoint Trustees to whom and to whose successors the lands are allowed to be conveyed in fee; secondly, to accept the delivery of a deed, in which the name of the corporate is to be expressed, and by which it is thereafter to be known and designated; thirdly, to settle with the grantors, who are to be the first Trustees, and the manner or mode of appointing their successors, and to cause the same to be set out at large in the deed of conveyance; fourthly, to institute and carry on suits at law and in equity, by the name expressed in the deed. The deed seems intended by the statute to be a *quasi* charter, and to serve as a land-mark to the body corporate for their guidance in the performance of all those acts which are necessary to perpetuate their existence. No successor can legally be appointed to the first Trustees in any other manner than that which is specified in the deed, and therefore, the legal estate can vest it in no other. The provisions of the deed on this head are very explicit, and clearly state who is to nominate the successors, and from what description of persons they are to be selected. And here I will observe that the whole scope and bearing of the instrument is exclusive in its nature and phraseology, and shows a fixed intention to place the legal estate in the hands of the Methodist Episcopal Church alone. I think no words in our language could have been chosen to express the intention of the parties with greater judgment.

It is a rule in law that the plaintiff must recover in ejectment upon the strength of his own title, and cannot found his claim on the weakness of the defendant's title; for mere possession gives the defendant a right against every man who cannot show a legal title. The party who seeks to turn another out of possession for the purpose of gaining it for himself, must first establish a legal right; and, therefore, when it is shown by the defendant that the legal estate is not in the plaintiff, but in some third person, then the plaintiff cannot recover. This is the general rule of law, to which, indeed, there are some exceptions, but they are inapplicable to this case.

The defendant professes to be a member of the Wesleyan Methodist Church, and belongs to a congregation in the town of Kingston, wholly composed of persons of that description. The minister of that congregation nominated a certain number of Trustees, who were appointed by some of the Trustees named in the deed, which latter *ceased* to be Episcopal Methodists, and became Wesleyan Methodists, after they were first appointed by the parties to the deed. The Trustees of the Wesleyan Methodist congregation put the defendant into the possession of the premises, to hold for the use of the Wesleyan Methodists, in exclusion of the Episcopal Methodists. A change from one religious denomination to that of another, by a greater part of the first congregation, is the origin of the present suit. It appears by the evidence on the part of the defence, that the General Conference of the Methodist Episcopal Church in Canada, met at Hallowell, in the district of Prince Edward, on the 13th of August, 1832, and that three-fourths of its members adopted a resolution to relinquish Episcopacy. The members of the General Conference are all ministers or teachers, and laymen are wholly exclu ed. After some time, the resolution to abolish Episcopacy was adopted. The ministers and preachers who adopted it, *formed another Church*, called, The Methodist Wesleyan Church in Canada, and the General Conference of the *newly* formed church entered into certain articles of union with the Wesleyan Methodist Church in England, by which it was stipulated that the

General Conference in England should annually appoint one of its own members to act as President of the General Conference of the Wesleyan Church in Canada. Both the Episcopal and Wesleyan Churches in Canada have written constitutions, which show the extent of the powers which are exercised by the General and Annual Conferences of each of them. At the trial of this cause a book was adduced in evidence, the authority of which was admitted by both parties, entitled, "The Doctrine and Discipline of the Methodist Episcopal Church in Canada," which contains the written constitution of the Church, showing the principles upon which its government is founded and conducted. In the seventeenth page of the book, under the head of the "General Conference," are the following rules or regulations, establishing the manner of forming the Conference, and defining its constitutional powers:

1st. The General Conference shall be composed of all the travelling Elders who have travelled for four full calendar years last past, and have been received into full connection. 2nd. At all times when the General Conference is met, it shall take two-thirds of its members to make a quorum for transacting business 3rd. One of the General Superintendents shall preside in the General Conference; but in case no General Superintendent be present, the General Conference shall choose a president *pro tempore*. 4th. The General Conference shall have full powers to make rules and regulations for our Church, under the following limitations and restrictions:—First. The General Conference shall not revoke, alter, or change our articles of religion, nor establish any new standard or rules of doctrine contrary to our present existing and established standards of doctrine. Secondly. They shall not change or alter any part or rule of our government, so as to do away with Episcopacy, or destroy the plan of our general itinerant superintendency. There are several other limitations and restrictions of the powers of the General Conference, but as they do not relate to the present subject in the least, I find it unnecessary to transcibe them. After ennumerating all the restrictions, the following general proviso is subjoined, "Provided nevertheless, that upon the joint recommendation of three-fourths of the Annual Conference, then the majority of three-fourths of the General Conference *shall suffice* to alter any of the *above restrictions*, except the 6th and 7th, which shall not be done away or altered without the recommendation or consent of two-thirds of the Quarterly Conferences throughout the Connexion." It seemed to be admitted throughout the course of the arguments of counsel, and also established by the nature of the testimony afforded by the constitution itself, that it had been virtually agreed to and adopted by the voluntary association of persons who styled themselves the "Methodist Episcopal Church in Canada."

On the part of the defendant the following grounds were taken, in support of the defence:—1st. That the written constitution gave three-fourths of the General Conference the power to relinquish Episcopacy, on the part and behalf of all the members of the Episcopal Church, both ecclesiastical and lay. 2nd. That the resolution of the General Conference did, in fact, relinquish Episcopacy, on the part and behalf of all the members of the Church, and that the legal estate in all lands belonging to the different congregations of the relinquished Church passed to, and became vested in, the Trustees of the congregations of the newly established Church, by such act of three-fourths of the General Conference. The plaintiffs deny both conclusions, and contend that the premises warrant neither of them, and that the General Conference had no authority to relinquish Episcopacy by the terms of the constitution; but if they had, still the relinquishment could not have had the effect of altering or modifying the deed or conveyance in any respect, but the legal estate in the lands remains where it was before the relinquishment occurred.

With respect to the first point—that the written constitution gave three-fourths of the General Conference the power to relinquish Episcopacy, on the part and behalf of all the members of the Episcopal Church, both ecclesiatical and lay:—

The General Conference of the Methodist Episcopal Church, by the fourth article of the written constitution, has full powers to make rules and regulations for the Church under certain special restrictions, the second of which declares that the General Conference shall not change or alter any part or rule of the established church government in such a manner as to do away with Episcopacy. Then follows the proviso, "that upon the joint recommendation of three-fourths of the Annual Conference or Conferences, then the majority of three-fourths of the General Conference shall suffice to alter any of the above restrictions."

Looking at the fourth article, the second restriction, and the general proviso, it plainly appears to be the intention of the whole instrument, that not less than three-fourths of the Annual Conferences should possess the powers of recommending any alteration of the written constitution, and not less than three-fourths of the General Conference should have the power of making any alteration upon such recommendation. Here a preliminary question naturally presents itself to the mind—namely, In what manner did the framers of the constitution intend that alterations might be made in it. Were they to be made orally or in writing? If oral alterations were made, they would soon be forgotten, and always liable to misstatement or misconstruction; but if the alterations were reduced to writing, like the constitution itself, they would become incorporated with the original instrument, forming a part of it, and being equally valid. I conclude, therefore, that the framers of the written constitution would always intend that all alterations of it should also be written, unless specially stated to the contrary in the constitution itself. In the present case it was not proved or even alleged, that the Annual Conferences ever recommended, or that the General Conference ever made any alteration, either oral or written, in the constitution. Three-fourths of them proceeded at once to relinquish Episcopacy, in the face of the written constitution, and against the conscientious scruples and wishes of the other fourth part of the members of the Church. The members of the Methodist Episcopal Church in this province are still numerous, consisting of many thousand souls; and it was therefore incumbent on the General Conference to proceed with caution and deliberation, as well as formal correctness, in all steps towards any alteration in the original compact by which the Church was governed. The fourth part, who still professes to form the Episcopal Church, have, in my opinion, just cause to complain of a violation of the constitution; because I consider it still unaltered, according to the spirit and intent of the instrument.

With respect to the second point, that the resolution of the General Conference did in fact relinquish Episcopacy on the part and behalf of all the members of the Church, and that the legal estate in all the lands belonging to the different congregations of the relinquished Church passed to, and became vested in, the Trustees of the congregations of the newly established Church by such act of three-fourths of the General Conference:

The equitable estate, beneficial interest or use of the land in question, belongs to a great body of people, whether it be the right of either one or the other of the contending parties, and cannot be the subject of a suit at law. If the construction put upon the deed of conveyance from Ferris to Trustees, by the defendant, be the correct one, then perhaps there would be an executory trust created by the deed, depending on such rules and regulations as the General Conference might from time to time make after the execution of the conveyance. If so, a court of equity might modify and direct such executory trust according to the intentions of the parties.

It would form a subject peculiarly within the cognizance of a court of equity, who might decree the use of the property to whichever party appeared entitled to the beneficial interest, according to the principles established in equity; but the legal estate executed by the Statute of Uses must be vested in such trustees as are appointed according to the manner or mode of appointment expressed in the deed and authorized by the statute.

It is contended by the defendant that the latter part of the habendum in the deed authorizes an alteration or modification in the manner of appointment of Trustees to be made by the General Conference as they may deem expedient, and that in effect they have made an alteration in the manner of relinquishing Episcopacy. The habendum is in the following words:—"To have and to hold to the said Trustees and their successors, in trust forever, for the use of the Methodist Episcopal Church in Canada, *according to the rules and Discipline which now are, or hereafter may be* adopted by the General or *Annual* Conference of the said Church in Canada, in trust and confidence that they, the said Trustees for the time being shall at all times thereafter permit any Methodist Episcopal minister or preacher, being a member of the Methodist Episcopal Church in Canada, and duly authorized as such by the General or

Annual Conference, *to preach and perform religious service in the said house and burying-ground, according to the rules and Discipline of the said Church.*"

The intentions of the parties to a deed should be carried into effect, so far as it can be done consistently with the rules of law. The intention should be drawn from the whole deed, taken together. The first Trustees were all members of the Methodist Episcopal Church; they bought the land for the exclusive use of the members of that Church; they took care that the deed should express that their successors be exclusively chosen from the members of that Church; they caused it to be stated in the deed that if any of the Trustees, or their successors, should cease to be members of the Church, they should cease to be Trustees, in the same manner as if they were dead. The members of both the Episcopal Church and the Wesleyan Church are all known by the name of Methodists, and both appear to have the same articles of religion and standards of doctrine in substance; but still they both disclaim being identical, and the distinguishing difference between them is found in the different forms of church government which they have adopted. The form of one is Episcopal, the other Presbyterian. It is not important to the decision of this case, I conceive, to attempt to trace the precise time of difference between them; it is enough to know that they publicly profess to form two different sects, or religious denominations of Christians. Now, it appears to me, the words in the latter part of the habendum, "according to the rules and Discipline which now or hereafter may be adopted by the General or Annual Conference," were intended to apply to the manner of using the church and burying-ground, and the performance of religious services in them, and not to the manner of appointing successors to the first Trustees. At all events, the words used could not be intended to relate to the act of relinquishing Episcopacy, because they expressly refer to that description of rules and Discipline which either the General or Annual Conference was competent to make by the terms of the constitution, and there is nothing in that instrument to authorize the Annual Conference under any circumstances to relinquish Epicopacy. Besides, the act of relinquishing Episcopacy cannot properly be called a *rule* or *Discipline;* it is a decided measure of abolition. The Annual Conference has the general superintendence of all ministers and preachers, and might make rules respecting the manner of performing religious services in the church and burying-ground, according to the written constitution; and therefore it appears more reasonable to suppose that the words before stated were inserted in the deed to direct in what manner the church and burying-ground should be allowed by the Trustees to be used, rather than to the mode or manner of appointing the successors of the first Trustees.

Supposing, however, that the intention of the parties to the deed was to the effect contended for by the defendant, namely, that they intended to give the General Conference the power, by virtue of the deed, of altering and modifying the manner of appointing the Trustees, according to existing circumstances, and as they might deem expedient; it is my opinion that such part of the habendum would be void for uncertainty, and for being unauthorized by the words of the statute 9 Geo. IV., chap. 2. The parties to the deed are permitted by the act to specify in the conveyance the manner in which the successors to the first trustees must be appointed. The word "manner," used by the legislature, must necessarily include both the act of selection, and the description of persons from whom the selection is to be made. The deed directs that a minister or preacher of the Methodist Episcopal Church shall nominate each successor from the members of that Church alone; and whenever a Trustee ceases to be a member, he shall cease to be a Trustee, and another Trustee shall be appointed in his place from the members of the Church. All the provisions of the deed appear to me to have this object steadily in view, namely, to vest the legal estate, and to continue it exclusively in the members of the Methodist Episcopal Church in Canada. One-fourth part of the original members of that Church throughout the province, and who form a large body of men, still profess to belong to the Church, and to adhere strictly to the written constitution, which forms the bond of their religious union; and it appears to me that there is as strong evidence of the existence of that Church now, as there was when the deed was executed. Both parties claim under the deed, and therefore, admit the existence of the Church at that time, because the deed expressly states the fact. The statute, in my opinion, does not empower the parties to the deed to delegate their authority to others, to fix the manner of appointing successors to the first Trustees; and I also think they themselves would not possess the power of altering the manner of such appointment, after it was once established, by executing the conveyance, and much less are they legally authorized to confer such a power on persons who would be strangers to the deed. It would be common justice, I think, to presume that the plaintiffs and their brethren refused to join the Wesleyan Church from conscientious motives, produced by sincere doubts whether its form of government could be sustained by the authority of the Scriptures or the practice of the apostles. In that case it would be altogether a matter of conscience, and the majority of the General Conference should be strictly held to shew their proceedings to be regular, according to a reasonable and proper construction of the written Discipline or constitution, adopted by all the members of the Episcopal Church before they are allowed to take from the latter the lands which were undoubtedly intended to be conveyed to the members of the Episcopal Church exclusively.

Upon as full a consideration as I have been able to give a case of the first impression, I am of opinion the lessors of the plaintiff have the legal estate in the premises, and are entitled to judgment on the following grounds, as well as others alluded to in the course of my remarks:—

First,—Being members of the Methodist Episcopal Church in Canada, they were eligible by the words of the deed to be Trustees, and were legally appointed.

Secondly,—The statute and deed do not authorize the appointment of Trustees from any other religious denomination.

Thirdly,—The members of the Wesleyan Church are incapable, under the statute and deed, of being appointed Trustees, or of holding the legal estate.

Fourthly,—If they are entitled to the equitable or beneficial interest and use of the premises, they must claim their right in a court of equity.

Fifthly,—The written constitution has not been altered according to the words, true meaning, and spirit of the instrument.

Sixthly,—The Methodist Episcopal Church exists, as it did when the deed was executed, although its numbers are diminished.

Seventhly—The legal estate must rest in the Trustees according to the terms of the statute and deed, without regard to any subsequent proceeding of the Conference.

Eighthly—The parties to the deed could not delegate a power to strangers to alter or modify the manner of appointing trustees as specified in the deed, and they had no authority to alter or modify it themselves.

Ninthly,—When a change of circumstance renders such an alteration equitable and just, application must be made, in my opinion, to the legislature, who are alone capable of making an alteration in the manner of appointing the successor of the first trustees.

CHAPTER XXVIII.

Political strife—The "rebellion"—Cause of the outbreak—State of party feeling—result on the Christian Church generally—Course pursued by the Methodists prior to 1833 concerning state grants—Course pursued by the organ of the Wesleyan Methodists subsequent to 1833—Who turned the elections of 1836 in favor of the Family Compact—Conference of 1838—Grief for the state of the country—Two of the M. E. ministers called home—Facts brought to light and admitted by leading Wesleyans during the controversy between the English and Canada Conferences—Reception of government money admitted and defended—Both parties claim the grant on the ground of the superior loyalty of each—Wesleyan opinion of the union after years of trial—Dr. Bunting declares it to have been a "mistake"—It was more—It retarded the settlement of the "Reserves"—What the union cost the country—Who received the money

THIS year of 1837 was one of strife, not only in the Church but out of it. The contest which had continued from year to year between the Executive, or Government, as it was called, and the parliament, now culminated in open rebellion. The shameful bribery countenanced by the Executive, in order to gain the elections of 1836—that the dominant faction might rule supreme—and the brutal violence of their followers at the polls, together, had aroused a storm of indignation throughout the country that could with difficulty be kept within bounds. But when, in defiance of what was known to be the wishes of a very large majority of the people, it was determined to establish the fifty-seven rectories, and, in spite of repeated remonstrance, to create an *Established Church*, this storm burst forth in all its might. The unhappy rising of December, 1837, was the consequence. The insurrection was put down almost before it became formidable enough to justify the name; but it left its mark upon the province, traces of which were felt for years.

During this sad time party feeling ran high, and the Christian Church suffered, as well as the state. Prior to the union the Canada Conference had been strongly opposed to Church and State connection, and its organ had taken strong ground against such connection and against the unconstitutional tyranny of the Family Compact. Almost immediately subsequent to that event both Conference and organ veered directly in the opposite direction, and threw the whole weight of their influence in favor of the Governor, Dr. Strachan, and his party, in the election just mentioned. It had transpired that the Wesleyan body were in receipt of a large sum from Government, through the English Missionary Society, and—not unnaturally—people attributed their change of political sentiments to their change of ecclesiastical relation. Had it not been for this political somersault of a large portion of Methodists, the majority of those embraced in the Wesleyan body having been induced to vote with their old enemies, the Family Compact, that party, notwithstanding the violence used at the polls, could not have gained the elections of 1836, and thus the rebellion might have been averted, and the country saved the misery and disgrace which followed.

The reception of the state grant, which amounted to £900 sterling, ($4,500), intensified this feeling of aversion to the union, as it was still called, and also increased the distrust of the leaders of that movement, which had been growing apace since the events of 1833. It also justified the action of those who had set themselves so resolutely in opposition to the union. The people of the Methodist Episcopal Church, while loyal to their young queen, were still consistent in their opposition to the connection of the church with the state. The entire freedom of the church from all entanglements with the state, as essential to the purity and efficiency of the former, was a principle for which they had contended since their first organization in the Province, and for which their church had suffered not a little contumely and reproach in days of yore. And now its leaders were obliged to bear much undeserved reproach poured upon them by those who had previously themselves suffered from the same calumny. Those who sought to crush the church by every means in their power hesitated not to assert that any who were unwilling to unite with the English Methodists were disloyal subjects; and this at a time when the country was in all the fearful excitement of an insurrection, when party feeling and passion were excited to their highest pitch. To some who would be likely to be influenced by such a representation they were called, "those Yankee Methodists, who if they dared would betray the country to the Americans." To others they were "those mal-contents whom the Americans would not countenance." Thus the church was misrepresented on every hand; but though deeply injured it was not destroyed, and truly loyal as the people were proved to be in those trying times, it continued to enjoy the confidence of the community at large.

Though deprived of their churches, and thus forced to use such places for worship as they could procure, the old societies continued to prosper, despite the political turmoil around them, and during the year several new churches were erected, some of them very much superior to those from which they had been so unjustly ejected.

The Conference of 1838 met at Trafalgar, June 20th, Bishop Reynolds presiding. George Turner was again appointed Secretary. During the year death had again been busy in their ranks. Two of their number had been released from the conflicts of earth to enjoy the triumphs of the redeemed in heaven. James Powley, who had, with Mr. Bailey, represented them at the Cincinnati General Conference, had died in great peace on the 23rd of February. Andrew P. Shorts, a young man of much promise, had only the year previous been taken into the travelling connexion, his health had failed almost immediately after he entered the itinerancy, and he had desisted from active labor, as there was no hope of his restoration. The fiat had gone forth, and he passed calmly to his eternal home on the 17th of September, 1837. Though saddened by the loss of their brethren, and deeply grieved at the unhappy state in which the country then was, they still found they had much cause for encouragement. They had peace within their own borders, and the work was prospering in their hands. Manifestly God was with them. The number of preachers this year was 32, besides the two who had died; two others had removed, one had been suspended from his ministerial functions, and one expelled. The membership this year numbered 4,177, making an increase over the previous year of 655. To many, the success of the Methodist Episcopal Church, notwithstanding all the disadvantages under which it labored, was a source of unbounded astonishment. Dependent, so far as human aid was concerned, wholly upon its own resources, assailed on every side, slandered at home, and looked coldly upon by the American Methodists, it is no wonder that its prospects had for a time looked dark, and it would have been no wonder if in the earlier years succeeding 1833, the preachers had given up in despair. But they were not the men to yield so vital a point as this, when they felt assured that they were right, and God was blessing their work in giving souls to their ministry. Still it was not an agreeable contest, competing with the other body. The church had suddenly sunk from comparative affluence to poverty; they were now in many places without churches, and a large portion of their membership was poor; while the other body had retained in their possession, not only the churches, but an institution erected by the M. E. Church, prior to 1833, in which they were educating their own young people, and exercising an influence over the young of other churches. They had, too, an organ, from which they could issue all that they might choose to advance in defence of their body and of its recent change of opinions, while the members of the M. E. Church were deprived of all these advantages. If they would defend themselves they were obliged to do so through the secular prints, and could not, therefore, go so thoroughly into the subject under discussion as if they had possessed a paper of their own.

But besides and in addition to all these, while the preachers ministering to the old societies were entirely dependent on them for their salaries, the Wesleyans had at command, through the agency of the Missionary Society, thousands of dollars, by means of which deficiencies on missions might be made up. This latter fact was strenuously denied by many of the leading men of the Wesleyan Connexion, in consequence of the openly expressed disapprobation of many of their own people to such a course of procedure. But their own after admissions, and assertions made by some of their leading men, together with the publication of the provincial accounts, and of Mr. Alder's letter in 1840, proved conclusively that they had not only been in receipt of the money, but had defended its reception on state principles. One or two extracts from these productions may not, in this connection, be inadmissable. In a pamphlet published in England, in 1840, the writer remarks:—*"In 1834," (the very next year after the union) "and 1835, Mr. Ryerson, as Editor of the official organ of the Wesleyan Conference in Canada, defended at large the right of the crown to apropriate, and the right of churches to receive aid from the casual and territorial revenue. In 1838, 1839, and 1840, Mr. Ryerson, in the same capacity, defended and supported measures for the division of the annual proceeds of the Clergy Reserves amongst various Christian denominations in Upper Canada. * * * * † It is admitted upon all hands that *the organ and members of the Wesleyan*

* See pamphlet by W. and E. Ryerson, page 36.
† Ibid, page 39.

Methodist Church turned the eventful elections of 1836 *in favor of the government and the established constitution.*" The secular history of Canada tells in whose favor that truly "eventful" general election turned and the result. In another place in this same pamphlet the writer asserted, "By official reports of the stations of missionaries in Upper Canada, it appears there were stationed in 1833, *at the time the grant of* £900 *was made*, eleven missionaries." Pretty strong admissions these, and yet the fact of receiving government money was denied even subsequent to the publication of this work and that of the reply by Messrs. Stinson and Ritchey.*

What was the opinion formed by some of the Wesleyans concerning the union, after a trial of several years, may be gleaned from the remarks of a late writer in one of the Methodist periodicals.† Discussing this matter he says:—

"The union happening at a time when the public mind was much agitated on the subject of state grants to religious bodies, and the Conference having taken such a prominent position in opposition to such grants, neither the country nor the Church were prepared for such a course as it had now entered upon. It was evident that other counsels were prevailing than those which guided the body in years previous to the union. The continued agitation growing out of the determined opposition of the Executive to the popular will, as expressed in parliament, the feeling of dissatisfaction, and growing discontent everywhere apparent, and which culminated in the rebellion, wrought injuriously upon the Church. With the government grant to the missions came loss of public confidence, loss of friends, loss of means, secession of members, strife and contention. After six years of toil, trouble and conflict, the returns

* The *Christian Guardian* of 7th January, 1863, denies most positively that the Canada Wesleyan Conference ever "received one penny from Government.

† Rev. J. A. Williams, Wesleyan Methodist minister, in the Methodist Quarterly Review, April 1867.

to the Conference of 1839 are five hundred and eighty-six members less than when the union was consummated, although during the six years previous there had been an accession of seven thousand. * * * * The intermeddling of the authorities of the British Conference with the local affairs of the province, was most unfortunate and disastrous to the Church. * * * * The union, as Dr. Bunting declared, had been a 'mistake;' more, it had been an injury—an injury to the Conference, to the Church, and to the country; and if the body of ministers had anything to answer for, it was the readiness with which they sought to conciliate the London Committee, at the expense sometimes of their own consistency."

Other public documents* prove that during the seven years that the first union lasted there was expended on the missions in Upper Canada the sum of £17,806 : 18s. : 11d., sterling, (equal to about $89,030) out of which the government paid £3,670 (equal to $18,350.) This estimate, of course, did not include self-sustaining circuits.

The British Missionary Committee claimed the exclusive right of managing this fund, which gave serious offence to the Canada Conference, and as a result both parties opened a correspondence with the Government, each claiming the grant as the price of their superior loyalty (?). A dissolution of the union was the consequence of the contention, and during the progress of the controversy between the English and Canadian Wesleyan Conferences, many facts were given to the public which had hitherto been carefully concealed, or, when asserted by others, positively denied.

One of the most plausible reasons given in favor of the union, both before its consummation and after, was the great benefit which the Indian missions would receive from their connection with the English Missionary Society. The question

* Dr. Alder's letter to Lord John Russell.

now began to be asked, "What had the union accomplished for the Indians?"

In 1833, just prior to the union, there were 1090 Indians in church membership, and there were 400 children attending the mission schools. The prospects were that, in the course of a few years, the majority of the tribes would be converted from paganism, and brought to at least a moderate degree of civilization. After the labor and increased expense of the seven years subsequent to this period—in 1840—there were in church fellowship but a little over 800 Indians, with 250 children in the schools, while they were, as a class, very far from having improved in habits of civilization or morality.

Nor had as much good as had been expected resulted from the union to the white membership. During the seven years preceding the union the increase in the Methodist Church was 9,164; during the seven years that succeeded it the increase in the Wesleyan Church was but 316, notwithstanding all the means which this Church had had at its command.* A decisive proof this that had the Canada Conference continued independent of the English Methodists, and maintained its own consistency concerning state grants, and the complete secularization of the Clergy Reserves, it would have had little to fear from the machinations of the "High Church party," or from their agents, either at home or abroad.

The consummation of the union, and the results attending it, had reduced the ranks of the Methodist Episcopal Church so that by the Conference of 1834 they numbered but little over 1,200. During the six years succeeding this, there was an increase of 4,225; and this in face of all the combined influences and opposition of the English and Wesleyan Conferences, and of those politicians who had schemed to bring the union about, that they might thus forever destroy Methodist

* See pamphlet of W. and E. Ryerson, page 34.

influence in the Province. For the year 1840 alone there was an increase in the Methodist Episcopal Church of 734.

The union was dissolved in 1840, but the cause of the trouble between the two Wesleyan bodies was not therefore removed. Both sides claimed the grant, and the share in the Clergy Reserves; but the Executive, not yet having accomplished all it desired, through the combined influence of these bodies, refused to comply with the demands of either, till they became reconciled. Thus the supplies from Government were stopped. Seven years afterward, the Canada Conference having, through their delegates, acceded to the terms demanded by the English Conference, the two bodies reunited, and then the accumulated fund was paid over to the accredited agent of the body by the Government. A Wesleyan authority* gives the following digest of the arrangements entered into between the two Conferences at the time of the reunion:

"The articles which form the basis of union do not differ materially in principle from those of 1833. Perhaps they are a little more exacting. The British Conference appoints the President and the co-delegate, on the nomination of the Canadian body, while the acts and doings of the latter body must be sent to the British Conference for their sanction before they are of force. The difficulty of the Government grant was settled by a joint application to the Imperial and Colonial authorities, that it might be paid to the Treasurers of the Wesleyan Missionary Society in England, a thousand pounds sterling having been secured to the Canadian Conference, as an annual grant for its mission work, and six hundred pounds sterling for its Contingent Fund. This arrangement has been faithfully adhered to for now nearly twenty years, although in a financial point of view it is considered that the English Mis-

*Rev. A. J. Williams, in the Methodist Quarterly Review, April, 1867.

sionary Society are great gainers by the contract. The large amount of commutation money received from the Canadian government upon the settlement of the "reserve" question, with the "arrearages" received in 1847, would at least be equal to the amount of outlay; and further it should be noted that it is considered by many as rather humiliating to a body of over five hundred ministers that their acts must be submitted to a Conference four thousand miles distant, which can know but little of the colony or its wants; and equally so, that the nommation of the chief officers must be confirmed by the same authority."

The writer might have added that the "model deed" places the Wesleyan church property as absolutely under the control of the English Conference as the transactions of the Canadian Conference are. Yet to such a humiliating position as this, some American preachers thought, and a few still think that the Methodist Episcopal Church ought to have submitted, by assenting to such a union! Does history exhibit another instance of one ecclesiastical body delivering itself thus bound hand and foot to the dictation and control of another body?

The union was something more than a mistake. It was, in one sense, a national calamity. The consequent change of the political sentiments of a large proportion of the Methodists in the province, turned the scale for a time in favor of the high church party, and thus enabled them to get, and for years to retain a hold upon the Clergy Reserves. It retarded their settlement, and by this means deprived the school and municipal funds of a large amount of money they would otherwise have received, and thus caused a proportionate increase in the taxation of the country. The amounts paid out of the government funds, to the various denominations, may therefore be measurably charged to the union. Grants paid to the Churches of England, Scotland, and Rome, prior to 1833, of course, cannot be charged to this account. What amount was paid these Churches before 1814 cannot now be ascertained, but what state grants to religious bodies have cost the country since 1814, may be gathered from the following statistics:—There was paid out of the reserve fund, territorial revenue, &c., to the Church of England in Upper Canada, between the years 1814 and 1850, $1,003,582.51; to the same Church in Lower Canada, $543,830.73; total to this body, up to 1850, was therefore, $1,547,413,23. During the same time the Roman Catholics received $148,-753.77; in Lower Canada the same Church received $46,-925; making a total to Catholics of *$195,678.77 ; Church of Scotland in Upper Canada received $291,065.77; in Lower Canada it received $50,695.33; making a total of $341,761.10. Presbyterian Synod of Upper Canada received $112,697.67. Wesleyan Methodist Church in Upper Canada received $109,275.50.† Making a grand total of amounts paid up to 1850 of $2,306,241.27. ‡ The approximate amounts granted to these churches from 1850 to 1855, inclusive, when the "reserve fund" was commuted, is as follows:—

Church of England, for the two Canadas,	$344,574 00
The Church of Scotland in Canada West	151,228 00
The United Synod Presbytery	11,313 00
The Roman Catholics	33,333 00
The Wesleyan Methodists in Canada West	11,155 00
Church of Scotland in Canada East	24,989 00
Total for the five years,	$576,592 00
Amount from 1814 to 1850, brought forward,	$2,306,241 27
Approximation of total paid up to 1855, inclusive,	$2,882,833 27

* This is independent of the regular revenues of that Church, derived from the valuable estate they hold, and from tithes, &c.

† Lindsay's History of the Clergy Reserves, page 58.

‡ The exact sum paid out between 1850 and 1855 is not known to the author, as he has not been able to possess himself of the "Public Accounts" for that period. The approximate amount has been obtained by taking an average of the preceding years.

The various churches commuted their claims upon the "reserve fund" as follows:—

Church of England, in both provinces,	$1,103,405 03½
Church of Scotland, for both the Canadas,	509,793 00
United Synod of the Presbyterian Church of Upper Canada,	8,962 20
Roman Catholics in Upper Canada	83,731 00
Wesleyan Methodists in Upper Canada,	39,074 17
Total commutation fund	$1,744,965 40½

The entire amount paid to the various religious bodies who would receive subsidies from the provincial government, from 1814 to the settlement of the vexed Clergy Reserve question in 1855, was, $4,627,798.67.

CHAPTER XXIX.

Conference of 1839—General state of the work—Encouraging prospects—Country drained by emigration—Creditable increase notwithstanding—Meeting of the General Conference of 1839—Its work—Preparation for the celebration of the first centenary of Methodism—A retrospect—Mighty results from a very small beginning—Contrasts—Exuberance of joy checked by recollection of contentions and strife where there should have been forbearance—Beneficial results of the centenary meetings—The *Religious Repository* commenced by G. D. Greenleaf—Extracts from it—Conference of 1840—What was done—State of the work—Gracious revivals—Great awakening in the west—Imminent danger of a young itinerant—He is providentially spared for future usefulness—Conference of 1841—General state of the Church continues prosperous—Reformation continues to spread—Preachers and people both work—No whining at Conference about bad circuits—Conference of 1842—Increased prosperity—Everything improving—Gratitude for past blessings—General and Annual Conferences of 1843—The work divided into two Conferences—Delegation to the General Conference in the United States—Closing session.

THE Conference of 1839 assembled at Sophiasburg, District of Prince Edward, commencing 4th of September, Bishop Reynolds presiding. James Richardson was appointed Secretary. The preachers met under more favorable circumstances this year than last. The country was becoming settled after the excitement consequent upon the rebellion, and excepting that many were removing from the province, matters generally were beginning to look more prosperous. Then, too, death had not thinned their ranks this year, they could meet for consultation without being saddened by the loss of friends. Nine candidates were received on trial; three were granted a supernumerary relation, and three were superannuated. The work was divided into 2 Districts and 23 circuits. There were 34 regular preachers and 6 supplies; and a membership reported of 4591, making an increase over the preceding year of 414. There had been many gracious revivals during the year; indeed nearly all the circuits had been visited with the outpourings of the Holy Spirit. But, on the other hand, the tide of emigration flowing toward the United States had robbed them of many of their best members, so that there was not so great an increase reported as would have been had the province not been thus drained of its population.

The General Conference was convened for the same time, but did little except making preparations for the celebration of the centenary of Methodism.

One hundred years had now passed since its founder—Mr. Wesley—had been visited by some eight or ten persons, who came to him earnestly enquiring the way of salvation. In striving to impart to them the instruction so necessary in their circumstances, he had been led on, step by step, as the anxious enquirers increased in numbers, to the formation of them into societies; and subsequently to the organization of them into a regular corporation. What changes had not these hundred years made! The ignorant masses of the English people Christianized and civilized through the instrumentality of the preaching of the Wesleys and their co-laborers; the established and dissenting churches of the United Kingdom, roused from their dead apathy to something like active exertion in the work of saving souls, by the example of these men, often through the direct agency of their preaching; and by the same agency, not a few of those even in the higher walks of life plucked as "brands from the burning.",

The seed sown with toil and in tears, in England and Ireland, had yielded an abundant harvest. From it one had blown across the broad Atlantic, and had taken root in the virgin soil of America, where, like the mustard seed, it had grown into a mighty tree. From the Atlantic, inland, other seeds had flown and tender shoots sprung up, till in process of years they had been wafted across the blue lakes and rivers that separated the young republic from the British provinces. Here, too, they had been planted in congenial soil, and taking root had brought forth fruit.

What a contrast between the meetings of Mr. Wesley and his lowly little flock in London, in 1739, and those held in grateful commemoration of that event, throughout almost every part of the Protestant world, in 1839. In 1739 the societies were only in embryo, now they were spread into bands. Then, they were thankful to be allowed to worship in peace in an old "foundry;" now, their churches and institutions of learning were dotting the surface of nearly every civilized land, and many uncivilized ones as well. It is true the rejoicings were marred by the knowledge that there had been bickerings and divisions in the societies since their venerable founder's death, but it was remembered that where there is liberty of conscience there will be difference of opinion, which will of necessity produce difference in action, or in government. Though divided into separate organizations, with different forms of church government, their doctrines and their aims were one; and in the celebration of these centenary meetings they all might, if they would, for once meet on one common platform, together taking up the thankful acclaim, "What hath God wrought!"

In Europe and the United States these meetings were attended with great success; and in Canada the occasion was improved, as far as circumstances permitted, very much to the advantage of Methodism itself, and to the spiritual benefit of other religious bodies in the country. It was to spiritual things that the minds of the people of the M. E. Church were more especially directed at this time, and numerous revivals resulted in consequence.

This year Rev. G. D. Greenleaf started the publication of a small magazine, entitled the *Religious Repository*. In one of the earlier numbers are several interesting items of religious information, from the pen of Rev. Benson Smith, at that time Presiding Elder of the Bay Quinte District. These give a very good idea of the then state of the Church in that part of the province.

"I have just completed," he remarks, "my second tour through the District. My first Quarterly Meeting for the year was held in the lower part of the province, on Augusta Circuit. When Bro. Lewis commenced his labors in this section of country, in 1835, there were but a few, comparatively speaking, who remained true to the interest of the Methodist Episcopal Church, and these few were derisively called the 'local band.' Bro. Lewis' circuit at that time embraced what is now called the Augusta and Elizabethtown Circuits. From these two circuits the following returns were made at the last Annual Conference:—Elizabethtown, 358; Augusta, 325; and several have been added to these numbers since Conference.

"The Lord is graciously visiting the people among whom Bros. Joseph H. Leonard and G. Shepard are laboring. I was much pleased to witness their animated zeal and success. Bro. J. W. Byam has recently formed two classes on the Elizabethtown Circuit, one in the township of Kitley, and another in Leeds. On Waterloo Circuit sinners are being converted under the labors of Bros. John Sills and D. Smith, although Bro. Sills has been so poorly he has had to stop travelling for a time.

"The Bay Circuit has suffered very severely by the apostasy of the preacher stationed there last year. As might have been expected, some of the members became disheartened, others lost a great degree of their spirituality, while some had doubts of the genuineness of the religion the preacher once so zealously advocated, but now declared to be imperfect. The most of them, however, are now recovering from the shock. The Mormon heresy is also doing the Church some injury on other charges.

"On the Belleville Circuit the Lord has poured out his Spirit in a copious manner. At the camp-meeting held in Sidney, in July last, signal good was wrought in the name of Christ. The cloud of mercy, however, seemed to move and settle over the rear of Thurlow and front of Huntingdon, where showers of grace have fallen upon the people. In the village of B—— the little few that remained—a number having removed—have many and great discouragements, but are not, I trust, disheartened.

"Hallowell Circuit is, in general, in a flourishing condition. Many, within the present Conference year, have been emancipated from the thraldom of sin and are now enjoying the liberty of the children of God. Bros. Norman and Johnson are laboring with a tolerable degree of success upon the Brighton Circuit, where accessions have also been made to the Church of not a few. The camp-meeting on this charge was an efficient means of bringing sons and daughters to God."

The work on the London and Niagara Districts was in an equally prosperous condition. In another number of the *Repository* Rev. L. D. Salisbury reports a gracious revival, which had commenced at a special Quarterly Meeting held on the Canboro' Circuit. "Two persons," he writes, "came forward and joined with us in prayer, and were soon followed by ten or twelve more, some of whom were deeply engaged, as much so as I ever saw, wrestling with God for pardoning mercy; a more affecting scene my eyes never beheld; sinners were weeping in every part of the house, mourning penitents crying aloud, Christians rejoicing, parents praying for their children, friends weeping over friends, and some, almost in despair, fearing that their day of grace was over; while others were enabled to testify that God has power on earth to forgive sins. I have received into society, since the last Conference, 160 members."

Similar reports of revivals were given from Nelson and other circuits in the west.

The Conference of 1840 commenced its session September 2nd, in Cummer's Church, Yonge St., Bishop Reynolds, presiding. Thomas Webster was appointed Secretary. Nine new candidates were admitted on trial, and five received into full connection. One located this year, four took a supernumerary relation, and two superannuated. The beneficial results of the centenary meetings, and of the other special efforts for the conversion of the people, were clearly indicated by the returns from the various circuits. There were now 49 preachers, including those who had superannuated; 3 Districts, and 24 circuits, with a membership of 5325, making an increase for this year of 734.

James Richardson was permitted by the Conference to receive the appointment of and act as agent of the Upper Canada Bible Society—an office which he filled with ability, and to the entire satisfaction of the Society, for many years afterwards. The session was a very agreeable and harmonious one. All things considered, there was every reason for encouragement, as will be seen by the following extracts from the "Pastoral address:"—

"It is with no ordinary degree of satisfaction and comfort that we, your ministering servants for Jesus' sake, in Annual Conference assembled, are enabled to address you in the accustomed epistle of congratulation and advice.

"The past year has been one of peculiar goodness and mercy from the good hand of our God toward our beloved country, our neighbors and ourselves. The toil of the husbandman being rewarded in the abundant productions of the soil, safely and timely secured in the garner; no pestilence or sickness to any extent being permitted to visit our clime; and the prevalence of peace within our borders, denote the gracious regard and kind dealings of Providence.

"The hand of death has been restrained, and in no instance among us, as a body of ministers, are we called to the painful duty of recording a case of decease among our brethren in the ministry, or of defection from our ranks.

"As a church we trust it may be truly said we have been kept in the unity of the spirit and bond of peace, the comfort of which is enjoyed only by those who possess singleness of heart, purity of intention, and oneness of design—who 'walk by the same rule and mind the same thing.' But what fills us with increased comfort is the powerful manifestations of the divine presence in our religious assemblies, and the seals to our ministry with which it has pleased the great Head of the Church to crown our humble labors the past year. The effusions of the Holy Spirit have indeed been copious and refreshing, so that in many of our meetings scores of believers, from blessed experience, could sing together,

"''Tis God with us, we feel Him ours,
His fulness in our souls He pours,'

while others were constrained to yield to the claims of dying love, and come forward to enrol themselves under the banner of the cross. * * * * * * *

"Several comfortable chapels have been erected, or are in progress of erection, through the exertions of our friends; and our finances, though far from being what they ought to be, are considerably enlarged and improved.

"We have the pleasure of saying that the proceedings of our present session of Conference have been characterized by harmony and love. Our multifarious conferential matters have been taken up, debated on, and disposed of, with calmness, forbearance and expedition."

The Conference year of 1840 was, like the preceding, one of great reviving throughout the entire work; but especially in the west. On the Thames Circuit, the old mission ground of Dr. Bangs, there were very extensive revivals, under the labors of W. Cartwright and W. D. Hughson. The awakening commenced on this circuit under the labors of Mr. Hughson, then quite a young man, one of the supplies of this year, who began a protracted meeting in a school-house, called the Widow Finley's school-house, about four miles below where the present village of Dresden is situated, on the river Sydenham: From this meeting the reformation spread through a large portion of the extreme west. Here the career of the zealous young itinerant had like to have been brought to an untimely end. After having held a special Quarterly Meeting he, in company with a brother minister, who had been assisting him in the services of the day, embarked with others in a boat, in order to cross the river. There being a number of people who were also anxious to cross, the boat was filled beyond its capacity, and when they were some distance across began to settle, the water also coming in; for some time the party were in imminent danger; but by considerable exertion the boat was at last brought safely to land, and the Church was thus spared the loss of one who afterward became one of her most able ministers. In the west Mr. Hughson's name is still as ointment poured forth.

On London Circuit there were times of unusual refreshing, particularly at the "Junction," now Lambeth, and in Manning's settlement, in Dorchester. East and west the work went on prosperously, and all good men rejoiced.

In 1841, the Conference commenced its session on the 1st September, in Trafalgar, Bishop Reynolds presiding, Thomas Webster, Secretary. Six new candidates were received on trial, and nine admitted into full connection. The Districts remained the same as the year previous, excepting that Rev. Benson Smith was removed to London District, and Rev. John Bailey to Bay Quinte. There were 26 circuits, and 52 preachers, with a membership of 6049, giving an increase of 724 over the year previous. The utmost harmony of feeling prevailed during the deliberations, and great forbearance was exercised during the debates.

The Conference was much pleased and highly edified during

its session by a visit from Rev. Hiram Shepard—a member of the Black River Conference of the M. E. Church in the United States. His counsels during the Conference were very serviceable, and were appreciated by the preachers as such.

The Conference missionary meeting was one of considerable interest, the principal speaker being Mr. Shepard, who dwelt at some length upon the various requirements of the mission cause, in order to render it an effective agency for good. The proceeds were in advance of the preceding years.

After having met and been mutually refreshed by each other's counsels and countenance, thankful that none of their number had been removed, either by death or expulsion, the preachers once more separated, to go to their respective fields of labor. The circuits were large and the work exceedingly laborious, in consequence of the newness of many parts of the country—especially in the extreme west, and upon the Ottawa and its tributaries; yet the cases were rare where there were fretful repinings at the appointments of the Stationing Committee. The men went cheerfully to their allotted work, and God blessed their labors accordingly. Quite a creditable number of churches were built this year, three very commodious ones having been presented to the church outright. With an active, working ministry, and a liberal-hearted, working people, as might have been expected, the work of God continued to abound more and more, the reformation flame spreading throughout the entire connexion.

The Conference for 1842 had been appointed for Yonge Street, and thither the preachers once more repaired, sure of a cordial welcome from those whose hospitality they had so frequently enjoyed before. The session commenced on the 7th of September, Bishop Reynolds presiding; Gideon Shepard, Secretary. Nine candidates were received on trial, and six admitted into full connection; five of the preachers took a supernumerary relation, and one was superannuated. None had died, and none had been expelled. One was left without an appointment at his own request. This year the work was divided into four Districts, viz., London, Niagara, Bay Quinte, and Augusta. The Presiding Elders were, James Mitchell, Henry Gilmore, John Bailey, and Gideon Shepard. There were 32 circuits, 60 preachers, not including the superannuated or supernumeraries, and a membership of 7,555 ; increase over 1841 of 1506.

Said the Pastoral Address this year :—" It is with no ordinary degree of pleasure that, after another year's vicissitudes, and toil, and danger, we are permitted to meet in our Annual Conference, and under most auspicious circumstances to greet you with our annual epistle.

" The hand of death has been stayed, so that during the year none of our fellow-laborers in the Conference have become its victims. Our lives and families have been graciously preserved in the hands of Him in whom we 'live, and move, and have our being.'

" We have also, dear brethren, to congratulate you on the healthy and peaceable state of our country ; the indications of the parental regard of our Heavenly Father, who 'giveth us rain and fruitful seasons, filling our hearts with food and gladness.'

" Our chief source of joy, however, is found in the enlargement of the borders of Zion, the peaceful and prosperous state of our societies, and the orderly walk and Christian conversation of our brethren ; and happy are we in knowing that this at present is an increasing joy ; yes, brethren, ye are our glory and joy.' * * * * * *

" The friends of our Zion have, in several places, given substantial proof of their attachment to and zeal for the cause, in the erection of substantial and commodious chapels, no fewer than ten such have been erected during the past year, or are in progress of erection and completion, and every year affords additional proof that, however despised and despoiled we may be by some, yet in the sympathy and esteem of others we happily have no inconsiderable share. * * *

"The deliberations of the present sessions of our Conference have been conducted with the utmost cordiality, mutual forbearance, and respect. The apostolic injunction,—'Let brotherly love continue,' we would ever bear in mind, more especially when conferring together to promote the 'great salvation' so dearly purchased by the sufferings of a dying Lord, and called for by the hapless and degraded condition of our fallen race."

It had been determined to re-establish a Book Room at the earliest possible period, in order to provide the Connexion with the books commonly published and read by Methodists. To further this object, then, an agent was this year appointed to travel at large throughout the entire work, and solicit donations for that purpose.

After a very harmonious session the preachers again sang the parting hymn, and separated to enter on the work assigned them.

Once fairly entered on the business of the new Conference year, both preachers and people set to work with fresh diligence and zeal, and their success was in proportion. The year was one of remarkable spiritual prosperity; revival followed revival on almost every circuit throughout the entire Connexion. In looking over the reports of this and the preceding years the success and prosperity of the so recently despoiled Church is a matter of astonishment. The labors of these self-sacrificing men were indeed owned and blessed of God, and in humble gratitude they acknowledged their dependence upon Him.

In 1843 the Conference met, agreeably to appointment, in the White Church, front of Sidney, Bishop Reynolds presiding. Mr. Shepard was again appointed Secretary, and the usual routine of business attended to. As one evidence of the almost unprecedented prosperity of the past year, twelve new candidates were admitted on trial, several of these men of very superior talents, and of fair literary attainments. There were, however, only four received into full connection; none had died, and none had withdrawn; one located; four took a supernumerary relation, and four superannuated. There were this year 70 preachers, not including those who were superannuated, or who had located, and an entire membership of 8,880, giving an increase over the previous year of 1,324.

After a session of several days, the Annual Conference adjourned for a time to allow the General Conference to hold its session, as it had been appointed for the same time. When the General Conference closed its session the Annual resumed business, and finished up the ordinary Conferential work.

At this General Conference it was, after much deliberation, deemed advisable to divide the work into two Annual Conferences, instead of having one, as heretofore. As yet, Canada was not in possession of those long lines of railroad which now traverse it from east to west, and in some more favored localities, jut off from these main lines to north and south; and travelling by stage or in private conveyance was, in the then state of the country, both difficult and inconvenient, especially to ministers with families to be transported hither and thither biennially at least. Besides, while there was but one Conference, it was necessary to hold the annual session, as nearly as circumstances would permit, at the extremes of the Province, alternately; and this obliged the preachers to be absent from their circuits a much greater length of time than was at all desirable or prudent. Then, it was thought that the general interest of the church would be benefitted much more by having two Conferences instead of one, and as the number of preachers increased from year to year, the hospitality of the people entertaining them would not be overtaxed. The work would be more compact; the preachers would not be subject to such long moves; and, in addition, each department of the Church could be more systematically arranged, and worked more efficiently. The proposed change caused some considerable debate, but the discussion was characterised by much forbearance, and a mutual good feeling prevailed throughout the session. The Annual Conferences were named respectively the Niagara and Bay Quinte Conferences. A deputation of three members of the General Conference, viz., Philander Smith, David Culp, and John Bailey, was appointed to attend the General Conference of the M. E. Church in the United States, which was to meet in New York, May 1st, 1844. Rev. Joseph H. Leonard was appointed Book Agent, subject to the Annual Conference in which he might reside, and a new edition of the Discipline was ordered to be issued. After the transaction of some other unimportant business, this session of the General Conference closed, having just before the rising of the last sitting appointed the next session to be held in Brighton, to commence on the second Wednesday in June, 1847, at 10 o'clock, A. M.

As soon as the General Conference closed its session the Annual Conference resumed business.

The Niagara Conference was divided into two Districts,—London, Benson Smith, Presiding Elder; Niagara, Henry Gilmore, Presiding Elder.

Bay Quinte Conference was divided in a similar manner,—Bay Quinte District, John Bailey, Presiding Elder; Augusta, Gideon Shepard, Presiding Elder.

Niagara Conference was appointed to be held at Southwold, on the 2nd Wednesday in June, 1844, and Bay Quinte Conference at Farmersville, to commence the first Wednesday in September, 1844.

The closing session of any Conference is an exceedingly solemn one to the ministers who have been engaged for the few days in such close association with each other, consulting together for the general good. They part not knowing that they shall see each others' faces again on earth, and they are, in a measure, saddened by the thought. But this closing session was more especially solemn and impressive from the fact that brethren who had toiled together for years, and had, in company, endured contumely and reproach, were now separating without the distant hope of meeting again next year. Of those who bade each other "farewell" at Sydney, many never met again till they met in that better land where past toils and conflicts, sufferings and labors, are all forgotten in the rest and enjoyment of a never ending blissful present.

CHAPTER XXX.

American General Conference of 1844—Mission of the delegates of the M. E. Church in Canada—Proposal of Dr. Bangs—Dr. Luckey's recommendation—The Wesleyan delegate allowed to influence the action of the Conference, while the other delegates were not allowed to defend themselves—Address referred to a committee, of whom Dr. Luckey was chairman—The "slavery" excitement—Its consequent effect on the Conference—Dr. Luckey again—The feeling in Canada consequent upon the treatment of the delegates—1844 a year of Methodistic strife throughout America, and in England to a degree—Dr. Bond's views with regard to the boundary question—Is reproved by a Canadian Solomon (?)—Dr. Bond asserts what the *rights* of the membership are—He denies the power of any Conference to *force* the laity into another communion, whether their doctrines are similar or not—Visit of an American preacher—He introduces himself to the Wesleyans and is cordially received—What reading a little book did—Visits an "Episcopal" meeting and preaches—Loses caste immediately—An invitation to preach recalled in a very gentlemanly (?) manner—The reverend gentleman reflects and acts—Special General Conference of 1845—Episcopacy strengthened by the election and ordination of Mr. Alley, formerly of the Black River Conference, U. S.—His short career—The establishment of the *Canada Christian Advocate*—Its purchase by the Church and removal to Hamilton.

ALTHOUGH the delegates of the Methodist Episcopal Church in Canada had not, in 1836, been received as legitimate representatives of Methodism in that country, by the General Conference in the United States, yet there were many members of that body who believed the Canadian M. E. Church to be a legitimate branch of the Methodist family, and were in consequence very much grieved at the course pursued by the Conference. Individual ministers in the United States, therefore, when from time to time they chanced to meet with ministers belonging to the M. E. Church in Canada, urged that a second deputation ought to be sent to the American General Conference, and the Church placed in its proper position before the Christian community. No further action was taken, however, by the Canadian General Conference till the General Conference of 1843, when the Revs. Messrs. Smith, Culp, and Bailey were appointed a delegation to represent their Church in the coming General Conference in the United States, to be held in May, 1844.

The delegates reached New York in good season, and on the 4th of May Dr. Bangs presented the address brought by them from the M. E. Church in Canada, having in a very appropriate manner introduced the subject. The paper was read to the Conference, and was, on motion of Rev. J. T. Peck, made the order of the day for the Monday following.

On Monday Dr. Bangs moved that the brethren appointed by the Canada Methodist Episcopal Church, whose address he had presented on Saturday, be recognized and invited to take seats in the Conference. Mr. Peck, seconded by Dr. Luckey, urged the reference of the address to a committee. Dr. Luckey's speech on this occasion was against the recognition of the delegates, or the Church they represented. He was, in fact, pledged to such a course before coming to the Conference. Being a warm personal friend of Mr. Ryerson, he had committed himself, in a letter to that gentleman, dated September 29th, 1837.

Mr. Ninde was opposed to referring the matter to a committee. "There could be," he said, "but two objects for so referring it. One was, that they might definitely arrange this plain question, and the other to prevent discussion, and give the weight of the committee to the question before it came into Conference. The subject, however, would be discussed. Men of strong minds and warm hearts were among them who would take up that question as strenuously as any other; and it would afford more satisfaction to the Conference and be more respectful to the delegates to have the subject directly before them."

Mr. Reed was for having it referred to a committee, and so was Mr. Covel.

Mr. Cartwright could not, "for the life of him, see the propriety of referring this to a committee. It was altogether vain for brethren to think they could give this question the go-by. It could not be done. And the report of a committee would elicit as much discussion as the question would now. It was not worth while to blink the question. They were prepared to meet it in open Conference and open discussion, without this reference. If light and information on the subject were to be had, let the Conference have them. They desired and wanted them, and did not expect to get them by referring to a committee. They wanted them in open Conference. If the brethren had a right to be recognized let them be, but if otherwise, say so."

Mr. Finley also objected to a reference. Mr. Ferguson thought "the reason assigned by Dr. Luckey for its going into a committee was reason against that course."

Mr. Mitchell supported Dr. Luckey, as did also Mr. Griffith. Mr. McFerren, too, was in favor of referring to a committee.

At this stage of the proceedings Rev. John Ryerson, one of the Wesleyan delegates, was permitted to address the Conference upon the question under discussion, and to represent the position taken by the body to which he belonged; while the delegates from the M. E. Church, from not having been received, were unable to reply or defend themselves from the misrepresentation to which they were subjected. Bishop Soule, who afterward went with the M. E. Church South, took sides with the Wesleyan delegation, and the question was referred to a special committee, of which Dr. Luckey was chairman.

The discussion of the slavery question came on the following day, by the bringing up the case of Rev. F. A. Harding. The debates on this case lasted five days, and with the appeal case of Mr. Frazei, of Michigan, the Pacification Resolutions, and the approaching case of Bishop Andrews, brought on such a storm of excitement and trouble in their own camp that the majority of the Conference forgot to take an interest in anything else. Not so, however, with Dr. Luckey. His pledge to his friends must not be overlooked; therefore, assisted by some of his brethren, who were like-minded with himself, he found time to make out a long, and a glaringly incorrect report, taking the representations of the Wesleyan delegation as the authority upon which to make it. This report afforded the Wesleyan delegates the greatest satisfaction, and of course caused the Messrs. Smith, Culp, and Bailey, with the Church to which they belonged, a corresponding amount of chagrin; for if they had not frequently been assured of a kind reception by many influential men in the United States, they would not have subjected themselves to a chance of the indignity of a second refusal to get a fair hearing.

The report presented the fact of the Methodist Episcopal Church in Canada occupying the same territory with the Wesleyan Methodists as the reason why it would be inconsistent for the General Conference to recognize the former body Yet delegates had been received by that same General Conference of 1844, from both the British Wesleyan Methodists and the Canada Wesleyan Methodists, though both bodies were occupying the same territory and disputing to their heart's content.

The Methodistical annals of this year present a sad sight of contention and strife, both in Canada and the United States. The two Wesleyan bodies existing within the province at that time were contending sharply with each other.

The subject of the report brought on a long paper controversy, which did not tend to make the feeling between the Methodist Episcopal Church and the Wesleyan body any the more cordial. But as fresh attacks continued to be made upon the M. E. Church, and its ministers found themselves maligned and misrepresented, both at home and abroad, it was absolutely necessary to defend themselves, no matter how painful such a controversy might be. And the question of slavery had rent the American Church in twain, bringing with it the bitterness and heart-burnings which strife engenders.

As was quite natural that it should—some of the circumstances of their separation being similar—the organ of the Wesleyan Church in Canada extended its sympathy in a marked manner to the South—the "*suffering south*," as it has recently been called by its ardent sympathisers. Among the disputes between the two Methodist Churches in the United States was one of boundaries. In an editorial on this question, in the *Advocate and Journal* of July 16th, 1845, Dr. Bond gave utterance to the following very pertinent remarks:—

"As members and ministers of the Church we claim our rights and privileges under the Discipline of the Church, containing the conditions and stipulations to which we consented when we voluntarily came within its pale. No General Conference nor Annual Conference, nor Quarterly Meeting Conference, can deprive us of our membership without a fair trial, upon accusation of misdemeanor, or violation of our engagement with the Church. Nor can the General Conference deprive us of our membership, even for gross immorality. The right to expel members or ministers is consigned to other tribunals whose procedings must be according to prescribed rules. * * With respect to churches or societies in the Conferences which have seceded, who do not concur in the separation, their rights as members of the M. E. Church cannot be impaired by the proceedings of Annual or General Conferences. They may receive preachers sent to them by the Church which they prefer, and should signify their wishes accordingly, and we hope all who are satisfied with the Discipline as it is will do so."

This, it will be remembered, was precisely the ground taken by the adherents to the M. E. Church in Canada in 1833. Here it was sustained by so eminent an authority in the

American M. E. Church as Dr. Bond, whose place when he was gone it was found so difficult a task to fill.

The *Christian Guardian* of August 13th of the same year took exception to Dr. Bond's remarks, claiming the right of the Louisville Convention to carry the societies with them without reference to the opinions of the membership, according to prescribed boundary lines. The following is an extract:—

"But the *N. Y. Advocate* has been contending that the General Conference had no *right* to bestow such powers. Strange that the primary organ of the General Conference should contend *against* rather than *for* the decisions of that body. What would be thought of the *Christian Guardian* arguing contrary to the formal decisions of the Canada Conference. The powers of an editor seem to be larger in the United States than Canada. * * In the controversy we have been struck, not only with seeing Methodist editors writing against the decisions of the General Conference which appointed them, but with their expressing opinions adverse to the acts of the Bishops of the Church. * * * *Bishops Andrews and Soule* are the Bishops we particularly refer to." These two men had led a secession from the Church, and done infinite harm to it and the nation by doing so, and yet their acts in so doing must not be even *questioned* by an editor loyal to the interest of the Church so injured.

On the action of the Louisville Convention Dr. Bond had written as follows:—"We exhort all who cannot heartily approve of the separation and unite with the new connexion formed by the Louisville Convention—no matter where they reside—to abide in the Methodist Episcopal Church, in humble dependence upon the God of our fathers, and assured of the sympathy of their brethren in that Church where they have heretofore found spiritual food. Our private advices already teach us to estimate what some of our brethren will be called to suffer by such a course. We know that persecutions and trials grievous to be borne await them."

Upon this the *Guardian* commented as follows:—"The above reminds us of the persecutions and trials grievous to be borne which a seceding body of Methodists in Canada talked and complained of a few years ago. Martyrs were they in their own belief, but no one else understood that they suffered at all. So it is, we expect, in the Southern States."

The cases *were* just about parallel, excepting that there being there little security from personal violence the loyal Methodists in the south suffered perhaps a little more severely, but the will of the opponents of the M. E. Church in Canada was quite as strong, had the law allowed it, as the above quoted paragraph clearly indicates. Oppressors never yet were found willing to acknowledge that those they wished to crush had anything of which to complain. Bonner would not admit that there was a martyr in Queen Mary's reign, though Protestants—in their ignorance, it is supposed—called her *bloody Mary.*

With regard to the similarity of doctrine between the two Churches, Dr. Bond, in a subsequent editorial, continued:—"We are aware of the argument founded on the alleged similarity of the two connexions. It is said that the brethren who complain are not required to go into a different Church. The new connexion is the same Church—the same in doctrine and Discipline. This is most transparent sophistry. Is not the M. E. Church South as independent of and distinct from the M. E. Church as that of the Protestant Methodist Church? * * Does similarity of doctrine and Discipline imply identity of jurisdiction or church membership? Certainly not. And if not, is there no injustice and violation of compact in driving them from our communion or transferring them to another without their consent? But it must not be forgotten that the laity have never agreed that their pastors should have power to transfer them to other communions, nor that they may withdraw from any portion of their flocks the services of God's sanctuary, by stipulation, treaty, or compact with any other Church or religious community."

The fundamental principles so clearly set forth in the above extracts, are precisely the same as those upon which the M. E. Church in Canada had based its claim for recognition by the American General Conference. The recognition would have given the Church a much better position in Canada than it had held since 1833. It had been refused, and their opponents allowed an unfair advantage over them; but the preachers and people were not therefore crushed. Disappointed they had been, but not overwhelmed. The recognition of Heaven had been given, in the souls given to their ministry, and secure in that, and in public confidence, they could and *did* stem all opposition and win their own way, without either aid or countenance from foreign sources.

Some time previous to the session of the General Conference in New York, Rev. J. Alley, a member of the Black River Conference, visited Canada on private business. He had taken quite an interest in Canadian Methodist affairs, and as some of the Wesleyan ministers, Rev. Cyrus R. Allison and others, had been at the pains to visit the session of that Conference held in 1841, and in setting forth the claims of their own Church made an unwarrantable attack upon the ministers of the M. E. Church, his (Mr. Alley's) interest in these matters was thereby considerably increased. Like many of his brethren, he had, without due consideration, accepted the Wesleyan view of the case as correct, and therefore on his arrival at Cobourg —the place where his business led him—he had introduced himself to the Weleyan minister stationed there, who received him with the utmost cordiality, and invited him to occupy his pulpit upon the Sabbath, which Mr. Alley did. During his sojourn in Cobourg Mr. Alley, at the house of W. Tourjee, Esq., saw and carefully examined a small pamphlet, entitled "The Union Considered," and after a perusal of its pages he expressed a desire to understand more fully the position and character of the body whose course was defended in the pamphlet just read. His investigation of the subject was, however, delayed for the time; but on his return to Cobourg some months later, he attended a Quarterly Meeting in connection with the M. E. Church, held not far from the town. Here Mr. Alley met with several of the preachers on their way to the Annual Conference, and thus made their acquaintance. The day was a beautiful one, the congregation large—as was usual on these occasions—the love-feast lively, and preachers and people apparently in the spirit on the Lord's day. Altogether the "Episcopals," as they were called, did not seem to be the very ignorant, despicable people he had been taught to believe them to be. At half-past eleven o'clock Mr. Alley preached to the very attentive audience, to the edification of all who heard.

During the week previous to this meeting Mr. Alley had been invited to preach in the Wesleyan chapel at Cobourg, but information having been given the minister in charge of that church that Mr. Alley had that morning attended a meeting of, and preached for, those "pseudo Episcopals,' he was politely informed that his services would be dispensed with that evening.

Bowing in his accustomed graceful manner to the gentlemanly messenger, Mr. Alley retired to reflect. Nor was he without a subject on which to meditate,—the action of the Black River Conference, the unchristian and intolerant spirit manifested by his formerly professed friends, and last, but by no means least, what he had learned and that day seen of the much traduced ministers and members of the M. E. Church in Canada. Upon his return home Mr. Alley published a series of letters in the *Northern Christian Advocate*, which in the end had a beneficial influence on the minds of many of the Methodists in the State of New York at least, as it gave them a more correct idea of the relative positions of the two bodies and of Methodism in the country.

Shortly after, when in consequence of the increasing years and infirm health of Bishop Reynolds, which rendered it inconvenient for him to travel long journeys, it was deemed advisable to elect another General Superintendent, Mr. Alley was requested to accept of the office, which he consented to do; and he was accordingly elected to it by a unanimous vote of the special General Conference held in the Grove Church, township of Hope, October, 1845. On the Sabbath of the General Conference Mr. Alley received ordination, by the imposition of hands of Bishop Reynolds, David Culp, and Philander Smith. But Mr. Alley's career of usefulness in Canada was short. While making preparations for removing from his former home, he contracted a severe cold, that brought on an attack of rheumatism, from which he never fully recovered, though for some months he continued to labor for the Church as he was able. While attending the Annual Conference at Belleville he had the misfortune to break his leg, when his illness took the form of bone disease, and after many months of very acute suffering, he was, in the early part of June, 1847, released from pain—not quite two years after his arrival in the country. His death was very deeply deplored by the entire Church, to which he had endeared himself during his short sojourn among them, by his fervent piety and genial manners.

During all the controversies consequent upon the events of 1833, the want of an official organ had been felt as a serious evil—a detriment to the Church in fact. Realizing this, and believing that the funds of the Church would not warrant the establishment of a paper just then, Revs. T. Webster and Joseph H. Leonard determined to start one on their own responsibility. If the enterprise succeeded, the Church would have the benefit; if it failed, the loss would be their own. The first number of the *Canada Christian Advocate* was therefore issued, at Cobourg, under the joint proprietorship of these gentleman, on the 2nd of January, 1845. During the two following years the success of the paper was quite equal to the expectations of those who originated it, but as many of the preachers and influential laymen in the Church thought that the accredited organ of the body ought to be under the control of the General Conference, considering themselves quite capable of sustaining it as a church enterprise, proposals to purchase it were made to the proprietors by the Book Committee, and the establishment was sold to them in July, 1847. In August of the same year the Book Room and Printing Establishment were removed from Cobourg to Hamilton, where they still remain.

CHAPTER XXXI.

The next great want of the Church—What became of promising young men—The Seminary a necessity—For whose instruction was it designed?—When incorporated—Affiliated to Toronto University, 1860—University powers conferred in 1866—Becomes Albert College—Ladies' school becomes Alexandra College—State of both Colleges in April, 1869—Contrast between 1843 and 1858—An act of the General Conference of 1858—Recognition by the American Conference again agitated—Delegates once more appointed—They are cordially received—Their address read and referred to Committee on Correspondence—The Committee report favorably and reply to the address—A delegation from the American M. E. Church appointed to visit the M. E. Church in Canada—They do so in 1862—Speeches of delegates—A delegation appointed by the General Conference at Cobourg to visit the American General Conference to meet at Philadelphia—They are cordially received and secure the object of their mission—The Church is placed on the same footing with the English and Irish Conferences—Extracts from American Discipline—The Church prosperous—Statistics—Conclusion.

THE Book Room and Printing Establishment fairly under way, with encouraging prospects of success, the next step of very material importance in the history of the Church, was the establishment of an institution of learning for the young people growing up in the Church and in the country generally. The want of such an institution had been felt ever since the loss of the Upper Canada Academy; but for many, many years the establishment of another was an utter impossibility. The consequence was, the young people who desired to enjoy the benefits of a thorough English or classical education, or whose parents desired it for them, were obliged either to attend the Wesleyan institution, subject to the inconveniences and annoyances consequent upon the controversies between the two bodies, or to go to the neighboring republic, where, in not a few instances, some of our most promising young men became lost to their native land forever. The founding of a seminary, then, under the patronage and control of the M. E. Church in Canada, became not only a matter of Church *convenience* but a necessity, on patriotic grounds. If young men were to be saved for the country and the Church they *must be educated in it.* Then, too, the education of young ladies in the higher departments of literature was shamefully neglected. Schools there were, it is true, here and there, in the province where a superficial knowledge of the sciences, and a few accomplishments were imparted to the favored few, but for the rest they were being left to the instruction afforded at the Common or Grammar Schools when they could gain admission thereto, or to that imparted in the nunneries, which were rapidly increasing in Canada West. Already the effects of education in convents was becoming apparent in the numerous perversions to Romanism of young Protestant girls belonging to the first families in the province. The evil was seen and deplored; and good men set themselves to work to remedy it, if possible, before it was too late. At last the establishment of the seminary became a fixed fact. But all this was the work of years—years of toil and earnest labor. It was not until 1857 that the scheme had progressed far enough to secure an act of incorporation, and after that the financial crisis of that year militated against its success very considerably for a length of time.

The seminary was intended, from the first, for the education of both ladies and gentlemen, in all the branches of polite and useful learning, and embraced in its facilities the whole compass of instruction, from elementary English to the advanced classics and mathematics; while at the same time it afforded the most ample opportunity of acquiring the modern accomplishments. It was and is, as an institution, free from all religious tests, and has always been as open to all denominations as any provincial school could be. In 1860 it was affiliated to Toronto University, and hence, as to the gentleman's section of the school, became "Belleville College." The ladies' school at the same time taking the name of "Belleville Ladies' College."

In 1866 the present charter, erecting the institution into a university, was procured of the old Canadian Parliament. In this charter it was called Albert College—its present name—and the ladies' college took the name of Alexandra College. The two institutions are perfectly distinct as to their powers and offices, and might be removed from each other and still maintain an independent existence. But the present arrangement affords to ladies the advantage of the lectures in Albert College, than which no better opportunities are given to ladies in the Dominion. Albert University has power, under act of Parliament, to confer degrees and diplomas in Arts. Albert College, the teaching body, had, in 1869, nine professors; four in natural science; three in languages, history, and literature; one in mathematics, and one in metaphysics, ethics, &c., together with tutors as required. There were attending it, during the academic year of 1868 and 1869, one hundred students. During the first two years that university powers were enjoyed eight young men had proceeded to the degree of Bachelor in Arts, four of whom also had taken, at that date, the degree of Master of Arts. There were also in that year eight undergraduates and fifteen candidates for matriculation, showing conclusively that the university classes were steadily growing. In the Alexandra College, under the authority of the Board of Managers, diplomas are also conferred upon ladies that have prosecuted and completed a three years course of study, after the novitiate or entrance examinations. Ladies graduating are required to take French, German, mathematics, ethics, metaphysics, natural sciences, &c. Latin, music and drawing are optional. When Latin is taken the degree is entitled Mistress of Liberal Arts, when music, Mistress of English Literature.

The buildings were erected in 1856, and the seminary formally opened July 16th, 1857. During its course of twelve years—up to April, 1869—it had had considerably over a thousand different students, attending from three to five or six years.

The building is of brick, with stone basement, in all, four stories. It has a front of one hundred and thirty feet, and a depth of ninety feet in the wings, and fifty feet in the main body. Besides its ample class and lecture rooms, its accomodations are such that it can lodge and board within itself about one hundred students. The original cost was $32,000, which was, however, much increased by accumulations of interest during a series of years, when, in consequence of many of the subscriptions not having been paid up during the financial crisis of 1857, money to meet payments had to be borrowed at a great disadvantage. The present President is Rev. Albert Carman, M. A., who is supported by an able staff of Professors. The Preceptress is also a very highly accomplished lady.

Since the general Conference of 1843 the great Head of the Church had signally owned and blessed the labors of the preachers in connection with the M. E. Church in Canada. Then, although in a prosperous condition, comparatively speaking, they were subject to much that was painfully annoying, from the lack of a paper in which to defend themselves; and the Church was without any institution in which their own young people could be properly educated. Now they were in possession of both these advantages, and both had proved to be not only a benefit to themselves, but to their country, for the real good of which so much labor had been given, and so much unjust reproach borne.

In point of position there was but one more thing to be desired, that of recognition by the parent body; and even this it had been proved was not necessary to the success of the Church. There were even those who were not particularly anxious for that which, though but a simple act of justice, had been so long delayed; but there were others who, from principle, were desirous that the Church should take its proper place as a legitimate branch of Methodism. The General and Annual Conferences had been visited—non-officially—from time to time, by leading ministers of the M. E. Church in the United States, and these brethren had declared that the matters in dispute between the two bodies in Canada had not been fully understood in either of the General Conferences of 1836 or 1844, and had again and again assured them that the scenes of those two Conferences would not again be repeated. Among those who were anxious to make reparation for past neglect were Revs. J. M. Fuller, J. B. Wentworth, J. Parsons, and several other eminent men in the Connexion.

After much deliberation the General Conference of 1858, held in St. Davids, not far from Niagara Falls, appointed three delegates to attend the ensuing American General Conference, to be held in Buffalo, in May, 1860. These delegates were, Thomas Webster, James Gardiner, and J. H. Johnson.

The Niagara Annual Conference held its session in Ingersoll, in April, 1860, and upon the last day of that month Bishop Richardson and Mr. Webster left that place, the Conference being still in session, in order to reach Buffalo for the commencement of the American General Conference. In consequence of the illness of Bishop Richardson, the travellers were delayed some hours on the road, but reached their destination on the afternoon of 1st May. They were kindly received and cared for by the preacher whose duty it was to provide homes for the delegates; but as Bishop Richardson had an old friend living in the city—Jesse Ketchum, formerly of Toronto—he and his companion found for the time a comfortable home with him. The other two delegates had not arrived, and Bishop Richardson still continued far from well, consequently the address of the M. E. Church in Canada to the American M. E. Church was not presented till the fourth day of the session of the General Conference, when Bishop Richardson and Mr. Webster were introduced to the Conference. The following account of the reception is extracted from the journals of that body:—

"J. M. Fuller presented the credentials of Rev. Thomas Webster, delegate from the Methodist E. Church of Canada to this Conference. Bishop Richardson of the M. E. Church of Canada, and Rev. Thomas Webster, one of the representatives of that Church, were then introduced by Bishop Morris to the Conference. The secretary read the address of the M. E. Church in Canada to this Conference, and the Bishop inquired if the delegation desired to address the Conference. Mr. Webster said he did not wish to detain the Conference now; he would defer it until some other convenient time, 'Perhaps Bishop Richardson may make some remarks.'

"The Bishop then addressed the Conference. His speech, which will be found in the *Daily Advocate* of the 5th May, was much more brief than it would have been had it not been for the infirm state of his health.

"Rev. H. Smith moved that a committee be appointed to prepare an address in reply to the one presented from the M. E. Church in Canada. Dr. Durbin suggested its reference to the Committee on Correspondence with sister Churches, and it was so referred."

Bishop Richardson continued so ill that he was obliged to return home. Mr. Johnson did not come to Buffalo at all, and the other delegate—Mr. Gardiner—having been detained by the session of the Bay Quinte Conference, did not reach Buffalo till very nearly the close of the session of the General Conference, when he arrived in company with Bishop Smith. They were as cordially received at almost the close of the Conference as Bishop Richardson and the other delegate had been at the commencement.

The General Conference continued over a month, during which Mr. Webster remained, most of the time, in the city, thus making the acquaintance of a very large number of the American preachers from different parts of the United States. He was therefore able to explain more fully the real position of the Church than he could have done in any other way.

The principal object of the delegation was to have the M. E. Church in Canada acknowledged as holding the same relation to the M. E. Church in the United States as the English, Irish and Canada Conferences do, and in this they were successful, the business of the Church which they represented having been brought before the three most important committees, viz., the Committee on Revision, on Itinerancy, and on Correspondence with sister Churches.

The report of the Committee on Itinerancy, as far as it concerned the M. E. Church in Canada, was as follows:—"That it would be satisfactory to the Church generally if the Discipline could be so altered as to admit ordained ministers from the M. E. Church in Canada into full connection, as all those coming from the Wesleyan bodies in Europe and Canada are."

The General Conference broke up without finishing its business, and this, with some other important items, was left over.

The Committee on Correspondence had, however, reported, had answered the address of the M. E. Church, and had recommended that a delegation should be appointed to convey to the General Conference of that body the salutations of the parent Church. Revs. G. Baker, F. A. Blades, and Peter Cartwright, D. D., were appointed, and in 1862 attended the General Conference of the M. E. Church in Canada, which was that year held in Cobourg. From their speeches in addressing the Conference the following are brief extracts:—

Dr. Peter Cartwright, of the Illinois Annual Conference, remarked:—"I am happy to meet with you under present circumstances, as one of the representatives of the American General Conference. I have a distinct remembrance of the ORIGINAL *relation of your body to the M. E. Church in the*

United States. I commenced to travel in 1804. This country was supplied with preachers by Bishop Asbury. The work here grew greatly until it became an Annual Conference in 1824. In 1828, on account of complaints of certain disabilities on the part of the preachers in Canada, the General Conference, held in Pittsburg, permitted the Canadians to organize a Church, under certain stipulations not necessary here to mention. I was acquainted with your ancestors, the old preachers. I was always in favor of your recognition, and of fraternal relations, years before it was carried out, and it afforded me the greatest pleasure when consummated."

Rev. F. A. Blades, of the Detroit Annual Conference, observed:—"I hardly feel at liberty to trespass upon your time at present, but I say amen to the remarks of Dr. Cartwright. However, it affords me much pleasure to meet with you. At much sacrifice, amid cares and public duties, I am here, and it gives me pleasure to bear to you the fraternal regards of the Church I represent, a duty, I regret to say, too long neglected. I have been recently very much interested in your Church. I knew not the fathers, and not many of the sons. But one of your ministers, (G. I. Betts), coming among us, found disabilities in connecting himself with us, which were very annoying to me and to many others. In connection with his case I commenced to examine your history, which I had before too much neglected. I felt then, and feel now, that you ought to have been recognized by us, as bone of our bone and flesh of our flesh: At the Buffalo Conference I acted in bringing this about, and for this reason, perhaps, I am one of the first representatives. I then felt an interest in your body, not now abated. I am glad to meet Bros. Webster and Richardson, whom I met at Buffalo. I rejoice in your prosperity, and to take part in these ceremonies which place you in our Methodist family."

Rev. G. Baker, of the Black River Annual Conference, remarked:—"I simply say, I am happy to be here as a representative of the M. E. Church in the U. S., and bear to you the salutations of the Church. I have no disposition to make a speech just now, but I concur in the remarks of my brethren. If I should make a speech, I would very likely slide off on the same topic, for we are all of a stripe. Permit me again to say, I am pleased to be here, and to bear a fraternal address from our Conference, which will be more than a substitute for a speech."

The visit of the American delegates was both pleasant to the members of the General Conference, and beneficial to the Church at large. At this Conference Revs. James Gardiner, S. Morrison, and S. W. LaDu were appointed as representatives to the American General Conference, to be held in Philadelphia, in May, 1864. Messrs. Gardiner and Morrison attended, and ably represented the interests of the Church, securing the completion of the unfinished business of 1860. The General Conference not only tendered them a cordial reception as *accredited representatives* of a legitimate Church; but also cordially received Bishop Richardson and Rev. T. Webster as visitors, and invited them to occupy seats upon the platform with the representatives of the other bodies of Methodism from Europe and from Canada.

At this General Conference the Committee on Revision recommended an amendment of Section twelfth of the Discipline, which the Conference adopted. The Section now reads as follows:—

"Section 12. *Question* 1.—In what manner shall we receive those ministers who may come to us from the Wesleyan Connexion in Europe and Canada, or from the Methodist Episcopal Church in Canada?

"*Answer.*—If they come to us properly accredited from either the British, Irish, or Canada Conferences, or from the Methodist Episcopal Church in Canada, they may be received according to such credentials, provided they give satisfaction to an Annual Conference of their willingness to conform to our church government and usages."*

Thus, after a delay of twenty-eight years, was this simple act of justice accorded to the M. E. Church. Many who had toiled on in sorrow, amid the discouragements consequent upon the former failures to get a hearing, had laid their burdens down and gone to receive the reward of their labors; but many others lived to rejoice over the success and prosperity of the Church. The decisions of the two Conferences of 1860 and 1864 gave to the Wesleyan delegates as much offence as those of 1836 and 1844 had afforded them pleasure. Indeed they left no means which they could command untried to prevent the delegates of the M. E. Church from being recognized even when they were, but without success.

During the past few years emigration has again taken many of our best members, and proportionately lessened the increase; but there is still great cause for thankfulness in the degree of prosperity enjoyed at this time.

The state of the work this year (1869) is as follows:—

Bishops, or General Superintendents, two, viz., Philander Smith, D. D., and James Richardson, D. D. There are three Annual Conferences, viz, Niagara, Bay Quinte and Ontario. Niagara Conference is divided into 4 Districts and 58 circuits, has 76 travelling preachers, with a membership of 7550; Bay Quinte Conference is divided into 4 Districts and 46 circuits, has 73 travelling preachers, and a membership of 6,700; Ontario Conference is divided into 3 Districts and 46 circuits, has 59 travelling preachers, and a membership of 5,441; making a total for the three Conferences of 11 Districts, 150 circuits, 208 travelling preachers, and a membership of 19,691.

The work of Christianity—and more especially of that section of it denominated Methodism—is the evangelization of the

* American Discipline, page 83.

world, and in Canada the M. E. Church bears not an insignificant part in this labor of love. But the country is fast filling up, and enlarging its borders, and with a larger breadth of territory and an increased population, increased zeal, devotedness of purpose, and *action* are demanded of the Church. It has been blessed, in the past, in proportion to the earnest labors of the servants of Christ. How will it be in the future?

FINIS.

CONTENTS.

HISTORY OF THE METHODIST EPISCOPAL CHURCH IN CANADA.

CHAPTER I.

THE ORIGIN OF METHODISM, 1729–1758.

	Page.
The Holy Club	1
Called Methodists	2
Birth, parentage, and incidents of the early life of John and Charles Wesley	5
The brothers sail for America, return in 1738	6
Their conversion—preach a present salvation	7
Having been shut out of the churches they preach in the fields	8
First meeting-house	9
The Foundry	10
Mr. Maxfield, John Nelson	11
Division of the societies into classes	12
First Conference	13
John Wesley visits Ireland	14
Charles Wesley mobbed in Dublin	15
John Wesley again in Ireland	15
He preaches to the Palatines at Court Mattress	16

CHAPTER II.

FROM THE EMIGRATION OF MR. EMBURY TO THE ORDINATION OF BISHOP ASBURY, 1760–1784.

	Page.
Methodism in Great Britain, Ireland, and the West India Islands	17
Philip Embury, Paul and Barbara Heck, and others reach New York	18
Mrs. Heck and the card players—at her entreaty Embury begins to preach	19
Robert Strawbridge and the old log meeting-house—Prioity?	20
Embury organizes a class in New York	20
Captain Webb—the rigging loft	21
John Street Church	22
Boardman and Pillmore sent to America	23
Asbury and Wright come to their aid	23
Mr. Wesley appoints Mr. Asbury General Assistant	24

	Page.
Rankin and Shadford arrive.	24
The first Conference, July 4th—its composition.....	25
Mr. Strawbridge and the ordinances	25
Second Conference........	25
Mr. Rankin and others return to Europe—Mr. Asbury remains	26
Dr. Coke, Messrs. Whatcoat and Vasey ordained by Mr. Wesley and sent to America	26
The Methodist Episcopal Church organized	27
Mr. Asbury ordained.......	27

CHAPTER III.

PIONEER METHODISTS IN CANADA. 1769–1788.

Embury removes to Ashgrove—followed by the Hecks and others........	29
Embury dies, re-interred half a century later.....	29
The Hecks and associates move into Lower Canada, but settle finally in Upper Canada..................	30
First society formed—its members	30
Mr. Tuffey preaches in Quebec	31
Geo. Neal arrives in Canada	32
He preaches, is forbidden by one in authority, but perseveres	33
Is ordered out of the country—the persecutor dies	34
Neal forms a society in Stamford	34
Mr. Lyons came to Apolphustown and held meetings	35
Mr. James McCarty settled in Ernestown and preached to the people...........	36
He is persecuted	37
Death of McCarty—prophecy of Mr. Robert Perry..	38
End of the persecutors.....	39

CHAPTER IV.

FROM 1789 TO 1792.

	Page.
William Losee in Canada...	41
Ordained Deacon and sent back, organizes the societies	42
An incident	43
Class of persons gathered into the Church.........	44

CHAPTER V.

FROM 1792 TO 1795.

Mr. Losee returns with Darius Dunham	46
First Quarterly Meeting in Canada	47
Mr. Losee repairs to his appointed field............	49
Forms the Oswegotchie Circuit	49
Cause of his retirement from the work	50
Canada a District, D. Dunham, P. E., Coleman and Woolsey preachers.......	51
The first Quarterly Meeting in the Niagara country...	51
Keeler added to the itinerate band in Canada..........	52

CHAPTER VI.

FROM 1795 TO 1799.

Woolsey and Keeler exchanged for Coate and Wooster	54
Powerful revival	54
Dunham, Wooster, and the "wild-fire"............	55
Revival continued—persecution	56
Wooster's labors, illness, death	57
Joseph Jewell, P. E........	58
Lorenzo Dow first travelling preacher in Lower Canada	59
He visited Canada twice afterward—incident of his last visit................	60

Page.

CHAPTER VII.

SECULAR AFFAIRS. PIONEER DIFFICULTIES AND DANGERS.

First permanent colony—trading points where Kingston now is, at Niagara and Detroit about 1673........ 61
Conquest of Canada........ 62
Upper part of province began to attract attention...... 62
Province divided 62
Extracts from Mr. Lymburner's speech in opposition thereto................. 62
Population of Upper Canada at this time............. 65
U. E. Loyalist—manner of travelling—means of sustenance................. 67
The route by water—sketch of pioneer times and perils by Bishop Richardson.... 68
Thomas Horner, first settler in the now County of Oxford 72
He brought machinery for the first saw mill from Albany 72
The father of Bishop Reynolds settles in Burford... 73
Style of architecture; preachers' welcome............ 74
Substitutes for mills....... 75
A novel bolt.............. 76
Primitive vehicles......... 77
"The hungry year;" a *Lentine* repast 78
Boy lost in the woods...... 79
The kind Indian 80

CHAPTER VIII.

FROM 1800 TO 1804.

Statistics; several new preachers 81
The Ottawa, or Grand River Circuit and its preacher, Mr. Pickett 82
The humble disciple and his maligner 83

Page.

The word applied to the sinner's heart, he confesses the truth............... 84
Camp-meetings commenced 85
Eleven preachers appointed to Canada.............. 86
Nathan Bangs begins to travel under the P.E..... 87
He goes to Bay Quinte..... 88
His journey from the Conference at New York to the Thames............. 89
Opened his mission where Thamesville now is...... 90
His own account of it...... 91
Ague and fever; he is obliged to leave............... 92
Passes a night in the woods, with snow on the ground. 92
Incidents of those days, the the work extended into Detroit................ 93
Mr. Bangs leaves Canada... 93
John Robinson and others; his labors and affliction.. 94
His old age............... 95

CHAPTER IX.

OF CAMP-MEETINGS.

Their origin.............. 99
Manner of conducting them 100
A camp-meeting at night, a picturesque sight........ 101
First camp-meeting held in Canada.................. 102
Good results.............. 103
Are camp-meetings still necessary or expedient?.... 104
The *pros* and *cons*.......... 105

CHAPTER X.

FROM 1804 TO THE COMMENCEMENT OF THE WAR OF 1812.

Extent of the work........ 106
Henry Ryan and William Case come to Canada..... 107
Ryan's character, illustrative anecdotes 108
William Case.............. 110

	Page.
Thomas Whitehead........	111
John Reynolds............	112
Genesee Conference formed, it embraces Upper Canada	113
Daniel Freeman, Joseph Gatchell, and S. Luckey..	115
The entire Canadian work placed under Genesee Conference.................	115

CHAPTER XI.

FROM THE COMMENCEMENT OF THE WAR TILL THE DEATH OF BISHOP ASBURY.

War declared..............	117
Order of Canadian Government that all American citizens should leave the country by 3rd July	117
Several of the preachers thereby prevented from coming to their work....	118
Of those appointed to Lower Canada only two came...	118
Those who labored in Upper Canada during the war...	119
Mr. Ryan calls a Conference in the emergency	120
Who compose it; death of Hibbard................	120
Mr. Ryan calls a second Conference.................	121
Another Conference........	122
Genesee Conference resumed control of Canadian work.	123
Great decrease during the war....................	123
Death of Dr. Coke announced	124
Notice of Bishop Asbury's visit to Canada in 1811...	125
His death; his remonstrance to the English Conference	126

CHAPTER XII.

DIFFICULTIES WITH THE ENGLISH MISSIONARIES.

	Page.
English missionaries sent to Quebec and Montreal....	127
Charge of disloyalty disproved by conduct of Canadian Methodists during the war	128
General Conference on the duty of obedience to the powers that be..........	129
Reasons of politicians for encouraging the intruders	130
Reply to Bishop Asbury's remonstrance	130
Action of the General Conference in the matter....	134
Memorials and petitions to General Conference from the societies in Upper Canada protesting against interference of the English missionaries	136
Letter to Bishop McKendree from English Missionary Secretaries.............	137
Resolution of the General Conference and address to the brethren in Canada ..	138
Rev. John Emory delegate from General Conference to English Conference...	140
Resolutions of English Conference relating to Canadian affairs...............	140
Letter of instructions from English Missionary Committee to Rev. R. Williams and others..............	142
Letter of instructions from Bishop McKendree to the preachers of the M. E. Church station'd in Canada	147
Bishop McKendree's letter "to the private and official members, trustees, &c., of the M. E. Church in Lower Canada"................	151
Remonstrance of General Conference to the English Conference respecting points in the agreement not fulfilled on the part of the missionaries	154

Page.

CHAPTER XIII.

FROM THE DEATH OF BISHOP ASBURY TILL 1819.

Session of Genesee Conference held at Elizabethtown 155
Prayers for the outpouring of the Holy Spirit; special subjects of prayer 156
Philander Smith 157
Great Revival 158
Dissension, strife, and civil disadvantages 158
Reason of the dislike of the high church party to the Canadian Methodists 159
False accusations 160
Inconsistency of opponents of the M. E. Church 161
Extension of the work 162

CHAPTER XIV.

INTRODUCTION OF METHODISM INTO THE VICINITY OF LONDON, &C.

Settlement of new townships in the west; Charles Pettis 163
Holds meetings in Jacobs' and Morden's settlement. 166
Difference in opinion as to time, Mr. Warner's statement 166
Mr. Pettis the first preacher who addresses a religious meeting in Lobo, and also at Kettle Creek 167
A Methodist exhorter settles in London 168
First sermon in that township, by Rev. S. Belton, in the house of Mr Webster. 169
His usefulness; his death .. 170
Sad catastrophe at Hay Bay 171

CHAPTER XV.

FROM 1819 TO 1823.

Genesee Conference 173
Contrast 174
First mission field proper in Canada 175
Mr. Peale in the Rideau country 176
Grand River mission and Alvin Torrey 176
Mr. Peale dies a martyr to his persevering zeal 177
Sabbath-schools. A Marriage Bill, its fate 178
The Family Compact 179
Some of the Methodist ministers solemnize matrimony 180
Rev. I. B. Smith sustained therein by a jury 180
London Circuit formed 181
Mission on Grand River; Alvin Torrey, E. Stoney, and Seth Crawford 182
Peter Jones 183

CHAPTER XVI.

FROM 1823 TO THE CONFERENCE OF 1826.

General Conference 186
Mr. Ryan annoyed—Cause and consequences 187
Canada Conference organized 188
James Richardson, Egerton Ryerson 190
David Culp, &c 191
Bishops Smith and Richardson still effective 194
Temperance movement 195
Misrepresentations by Dr. Strachan 196
Corrected by Egerton Ryerson 197
Christian Advocate 198
Work among the Indians ... 199

CHAPTER XVII.

EVENTS OF 1826–27.

Conference, Mr. Ryan withdraws 200
Aided by Dr. Strachan 201
Interference with Indian converts 202

Page.
Dr. Strachan's Chart........ 206
Report of the House of Assembly................. 207
Transmitted to the Home Government with address from the House to the King 208

CHAPTER XVIII.

Memorial to General Conference................. 212
Proceedings and reasoning thereon................. 215
Methodist Episcopal Church in Canada becomes independent................ 220
William Case General Superintendent *pro tem.*........ 221
The Marriage Bill.......... 222
Success among the Indians. 223
Address of Conference to Sir John Colborne.......... 225
Reply...................... 226
Statistics................. 227

CHAPTER XIX.

1829.

Conference. James Jackson. 228
William Slater............ 229
Christian Guardian......... 230
Extracts from "Claims of Churchmen and Dissenters," and early volumes of *Guardian*............... 232
Sunday-school Union formed 235
A mistake in the Minutes.. 236
Early advocates of temperance in Canada......... 238

CHAPTER XX.

1830.

Conference................ 240
Bishop Hedding, &c........ 241
He ordains the candidates.. 242
Erection of a Seminary resolved upon............. 243
Resolutions on temperance. 245
Religious prosperity....... 246
Seminary to be located at Cobourg................ 247

Page.
Called "Upper Canada Academy"................. 247

CHAPER XXI.

Donald Bethune's petition.. 248
Report of the House thereon 249
Clergy Reserves........... 250
Sending English missionaries again into Upper Canada contemplated.... 250
Pleas urged in justification.. 251
Peter Jones sent to England 253
How received............. 253
Result of his journey...... 254
Determination of English Conference to violate the contract of 1820 avowed.. 255
Canadian Mission Board protest.................... 255
A year of great spiritual prosperity.............. 256

CHAPTER XXII.

Schemes of Sir P. Maitland and Sir J. Colborne to counteract Methodist influence................. 257
Rev. R. Alder sent out...... 258
Conference; prosperous state of the Church........... 259
Rev. R. Alder present...... 259
Resolutions on the subject of union............... 259
Mr. Alder's letter to the Governor.................. 262
Contrast with Mr. Ryerson's remarks in *Guardian*..... 264
Rev. E. Ryerson delegate to negotiate the union...... 267
Resolution of a Local Preachers' Conference, July 6th, 1832.................. 267
Resolutions passed at a meeting of local preachers held at Smithville, Nov. 1832. 268
Extracts from an article prepared by Mr. Ryerson before his departure........ 270
Rev. James Richardson's editorial remarks........ 273

Page.

CHAPTER XXIII.

1833.

Conference. Statistics...... 278
Articles of union.......... 279
Union consummated....... 283
Grounds of objection....... 284
Dr. Bangs—Emory—restrictive rules 287
Mr. Ryerson's reasoning.... 289
Polity of Wesleyan body not in accordance with Mr. Wesley's opinions and designs 291
Ordinations by unordained men 293
Government grants 296

CHAPTER XXIV.

Mr. Ryerson's knowledge of opposition to the union before he sailed proved by his own letter in *Guardian* of March 6th, 1832....... 299
Saltfleet meeting in opposition thereto 299
Guardian's remarks thereon. 299
Similar meeting in Blenheim, Jan. 9th, 1834...... 300
Similar meeting in Belleville, Jan. 10th.......... 300
Guardian's remarks......... 300
Letter of Rev. John Reynolds 301
London Quarterly Conference protest, Jan. 25th ... 302
Mr. Ryerson's comments.... 304
Resolutions of Trafalgar Convention............. 304
Comments of *Guardian* on opposition to the measure 307
Mr. Ryerson in a new position 312

CHAPTER XXV.

1834.

Conference................ 314
Preachers present.......... 315
Objections; replied to; precedents 315

Page.

First Conference Mr. Wesley held 319
General Conference of 1835. 320
Bishop Reynolds elected and ordained 321
Conference which elected Bishop Asbury.......... 321
Methodistic authorities.... 321
Delegates to American General Conference 322
State of the work.......... 323

CHAPTER XXVI.

American General Conference, 1836.............. 324
It declines to interfere..... 326
Book Concern fund........ 327
Annual Conference........ 327
State of the work........... 328
Church property; suits; verdicts; appeal; decision... 328
New judges; reversal...... 330
Questions not fairly put; remarks 332
Conference, 1837. State of the work............... 335

CHAPTER XXVII.

Opinions of Hon. Judges Macauley and Sherwood on the Waterloo Chapel case 336

CHAPTER XXVIII.

Political strife; the fifty-seven rectories, and the rising of 1837........... 369
Other causes.............. 370
Conference of 1838 371
State of the work; disadvantages................ 372
Facts previously denied admitted during the controversy between the English and Canada Conferences.. 373
A Wesleyan opinion of the union after years of trial.. 374
Dr. Bunting declares it to have been "a mistake"... 375

Page.
It was more, an injury to the Church and the country.. 375
What it cost the country, and who received the money.. 378

CHAPTER XXIX.

1839.

Conference. Statistics..... 381
General Conference; centenary of Methodism........ 382
Religious Repository—extracts from 384
Conference of 1840. Statistics 386
Extract from Pastoral Addr's 386
Another year of revivals.... 387
Peril of a young itinerant—preserved for future usefulness................. 388
Conference of 1841. Statistics 388
Extensive circuits, hard labor, but no whining 389
Conference of 1842. Statistics 390
Book Room: spiritual prosperity.................. 391
Annual and General Conferences of 1843......... 392
Annual Conference divided; named respectively Niagara and Bay Quinte Conferences 393
Delegates to American General Conference.......... 393

CHAPTER XXX.

American General Conference, 1844............... 395
Address of M. E. Church in Canada presented........ 396
Discussion thereon........ 397
Report presented.......... 398
Separation of the South.... 399
Dr. Bond on the rights of the membership 399
Is rebuked by the *Guardian*. 400
Dr. Bond again............ 401
The principles for which he contended identical with those maintained by the M. E. Church in Canada.. 402
Mr. Alley, his election to the episcopate; death....... 402
C. C. Advocate commenced.. 404
It is purchased by the Book Committee.............. 405

CHAPTER XXXI.

Loss sustained by the Church for lack of an institution of learning 407
A Seminary open to both sexes erected 407
It becomes a college. Its history and present position. 408
Delegates appointed by the General Conference of 1858 to attend the American General Conference of 1860 410
Introduction of our delegates and Bishops to the American General Conference.. 411
The delegation successful in its object............... 412
Delegates appointed to attend the Canada General Conference 412
General Conference of 1862. 412
Delegates from the American General Conference...... 412
Extracts from their speeches 412
Delegates to the American General Conference of 1864 and their reception.. 414
Action of its Committee on Revision............... 414
State of the Church in 1869. 415

www.ingramcontent.com/pod-product-compliance
Lightning Source LLC
Chambersburg PA
CBHW032306280326
41932CB00009B/721
* 9 7 8 3 7 4 3 3 3 1 7 8 5 *